Marketing Management

Dawn Iacobucci
Vanderbilt University

CENGAGE
Learning·

Australia · Brazil · Japan · Korea · Mexico · Singapore · Spain · United Kingdom · United States

Marketing Management, First Edition
Dawn Iacobucci

Vice President, General Manager, Social Science & Qualitative Business: Erin Joyner

Product Director: Mike Schenk

Product Manager: Mick Roche

Sr. Content Developer: Elizabeth Lowry

Product Assistant: Meghan Fischer

Marketing Manager: Robin LeFevre

Content Project Manager: Darrell E. Frye

Media Developer: John Rich

Manufacturing Planner: Ron Montgomery

Production Service: MPS Limited

Sr. Art Director: Stacy Jenkins Shirley

Internal Designer: Patti Hudepohl

Cover Designer: Kathy Heming

Cover Image: © Hybrid Images/Getty Images

Rights Acquisitions Specialist: Deanna Ettinger

Credit Lines: © Aqwees/Shutterstock.com; © Bella D/Shutterstock.com; © alexwhite /Shutterstock.com; © Sergey Furtaev /Shutterstock.com; © Dr.OGA/Shutterstock .com; © marekuliasz/Shutterstock.com

For product information and technology assistance, contact us at **Cengage Learning Customer & Sales Support, 1-800-354-9706**

For permission to use material from this text or product, submit all requests online at **www.cengage.com/permissions** Further permissions questions can be emailed to **permissionrequest@cengage.com**

Library of Congress Control Number: 2013944273

ISBN-13: 978-1-285-42995-3

ISBN-10: 1-285-42995-8

Cengage Learning
200 First Stamford Place, 4th Floor
Stamford, CT 06902
USA

Cengage Learning is a leading provider of customized learning solutions with office locations around the globe, including Singapore, the United Kingdom, Australia, Mexico, Brazil, and Japan. Locate your local office at: **www.cengage.com/global**

Cengage Learning products are represented in Canada by Nelson Education, Ltd.

To learn more about Cengage Learning Solutions, visit **www.cengage.com**

Purchase any of our products at your local college store or at our preferred online store **www.cengagebrain.com**

Printed in Canada
1 2 3 4 5 6 7 17 16 15 14 13

There are several really good marketing management texts, yet this text was created because the Cengage sales force recognized an opportunity. Existing texts were seen as presenting numerous lists of factors to consider in a marketing decision but offering little guidance on how the factors and lists and multiple decisions all fit together.

In this book, an overarching Marketing Framework, used in every chapter, shows how all the pieces fit together. So, for example, when facing a decision about pricing, one must consider how it will impact a strategic element like positioning or a customer reaction like loyalty and word of mouth. This book is intended to be practical. The writing is very no-nonsense. This book is relatively short, also intentionally, to further heighten its utility. Everyone is busy these days, so it's refreshing when a writer gets to the point. After this relatively quick read, MBAs and EMBAs should be able to speak sensibly about marketing issues and contribute to their organizations.

Chapter Organization

The form of each chapter is very straightforward: The chapter's concept is introduced by describing what it is and why marketers do it, and the rest of the chapter shows how to do it well. This what-why-and-how structure is intended to be extremely useful to MBA and EMBA students, who will quickly understand the basic concepts, e.g., what is segmentation and why is it useful in marketing and business? The details are in the execution, so the how is the focus of the body of the chapter.

Key Features

Each chapter opens with a managerial checklist of questions that MBA and EMBA students will be able to answer after reading the chapter. Throughout each chapter, boxes present brief illustrations of concepts in action in the real world or elaborations on concepts raised in the text, also drawing examples from the real business world. Chapters close with a Managerial Recap that highlights the main points of the chapter and assists in addressing the opening checklist of questions. Chapters are also summarized in outline form, including the key terms introduced throughout the chapter. There are discussion questions to ponder, as well as video resources to serve as points for still further discussion. Each chapter has a mini-case that succinctly illustrates key concepts.

Instructor Resources

Web resources for the book at www.cengagebrain.com provide the latest information in marketing management. The Instructor's Manual, Test Bank authored in Cognero, and PowerPoint slides can be found there.

About the Author

Dawn Iacobucci is the Ingram Professor of Marketing at the Owen Graduate School of Management, Vanderbilt University (since 2007). She has been senior associate dean at Vanderbilt (2008–2010), professor of marketing at Kellogg (Northwestern University, 1987–2004), Arizona (2001–2002), and Wharton (Pennsylvania, 2004–2007). She received her MS in statistics and MA and PhD in quantitative psychology from the University of Illinois at Urbana-Champaign. Her research focuses on modeling social networks and geeky high-dimensional analyses. She has published in the *Journal of Marketing, Journal of Marketing Research, Harvard Business Review, Journal of Consumer Psychology, International Journal of Research in Marketing, Marketing Science, Journal of Service Research, Psychometrika, Psychological Bulletin,* and *Social Networks,* among others. Iacobucci teaches marketing management and marketing models to executives, MBA candidates, and undergraduate students and multivariate statistics and methodological topics to PhD students. She served as editor of both the *Journal of Consumer Research* and the *Journal of Consumer Psychology.* She edited *Kellogg on Marketing* and *Kellogg on Integrated Marketing.* She is author of *Marketing Management* (Thomson), *Mediation Analysis* (Sage), and coauthor on Gilbert Churchill's lead text on *Marketing Research* (Thomson).

Brief Contents

Contents

Chapter 11

Integrated Marketing Communications: The Advertising Message   196

Chapter 12

Integrated Marketing Communications: Media Choices   217

Chapter 13

Social Media   236

Chapter 17   Marketing Plans   305

Acknowledgments

Cengage's people are the best! I am a lucky author. I am grateful to Elizabeth Lowry (senior content developer) and Mike Roche (executive editor) for all their hard work and equally for their encouragement on this project. As always, a special thank-you goes to the Cengage sales force. This book is a result of your thoughtful feedback and trying to be responsive to the requests of our adopters.

Also thanks to all those who reviewed the text: specifically:

Sabah Alwan
The College of St. Scholastica

Donna Armelino
Red Rocks Community College

Tim Aurand
Northern Illinois University

Michael Barretti
Suffolk University

Sandy Becker
Rutgers Business School

Mike Behan
Western Technical College

John Besaw
University of Washington Tacoma

Susan Brudvig
Ball State University

Frederic Brunel
Boston University

Angeline Close
The University of Texas at Austin

Dr. Rick Corum
Campbellsville University

Gerard DiBartolo
Salisbury University

Timothy Donahue
Chadron State College

Anthony Dukes
University of Southern California

Kimberly Goudy
Central Ohio Technical College

John Grant
Ohio Dominican University

Albert N. Greco
Fordham University

John Hansen
University of Alabama at Birmingham

Gene Holand
Columbia Basin College

Chris Hopkins
Clemson University

Charles Jaeger
Southern Oregon University

Mark F. Johnson
Remington College

Jeri Lynn Jones
Oklahoma City University

Dale Kehr
University of Memphis

George Kelley
Erie Community College-City Campus

Susan King
Hillsdale College

Gil Logan
Bryant and Stratton College

Vaidotas Lukosius
Tennessee State University

Larry Maes
Davenport University

Melissa Martin
George Mason University

George E. McDonald
Laredo Community College

Mary K. McManamon
Lake Erie College

Joe Messer
Manchester College
Mark Mitchell
Coastal Carolina University
Sunder Narayanan
New York University
Beng Ong
California State University, Fresno
Dr. Karen Palumbo
Univ. of St. Francis
Mark Pritchard
Central Washington University
James Puetz
Rockhurst University
David Rylander
Texas Woman's University
Regina Schlee
Seattle Pacific University
David Schreiber
Greenville College
Deborah Sisson
University of the Ozarks
Kathy Skledar
Lake Erie College

Zachary Stahmer
Anthem Education Group
Carolyn Stephens
Vanguard University
Jeanine Stratton
Furman University
Lisa Toms
Southern Arkansas University
Hiep Van Dong
Madison Area Technical College
Doug Voss
University of Central Arkansas
Rebecca Wells
University of Dayton
Robert Wesoloskie
Elizabethtown College
Kevin Westbrook
Union University
Susan Williams
New Jersey City University
Ann Williams
University of Wisconsin–Milwaukee

PART 1 Marketing Management

Chapter 1

Why Is Marketing Management Important?

1-1 DEFINING MARKETING

Some people take marketing to be sales or advertising. Certainly these elements of marketing are important, yet in this book we'll see that marketing is so much more. We'll see how and why the customer orientation of marketing is so important in today's corporation. Companies that try to please their customers are usually those that are most innovative, most profitable, and most durable and robust amid economic and competitive perturbations.

In this chapter we'll begin with an overview of marketing concepts and terms. We'll use the "Marketing Framework" and define its terms: 5Cs, STP, and 4Ps. The framework offers a systematic way to think about marketing and a structure for the book.

1-2 MARKETING IS AN EXCHANGE RELATIONSHIP

Marketing is defined as an exchange between a firm and its customers. As Figure 1.1 indicates, the customer wants something from the firm, and the firm wants something from the customer. Marketers try to figure out what customers want, how to provide it, and how to do so profitably. The key to marketing is being customer oriented.

Ideally, this can be a nice, symbiotic relationship. Customers expect to pay for their purchases and often are willing to pay premiums if they really want what they're about to buy. Companies seek profits, naturally, but great companies really do care about their customers. If mutually satisfactory, the exchange depicted in Figure 1.1 continues iterating between the customer and the company, strengthening the tie between them.

As a lifelong customer, you are already somewhat familiar with marketing from the consumer side. Throughout this book, we will also see marketing from the firm's perspective.

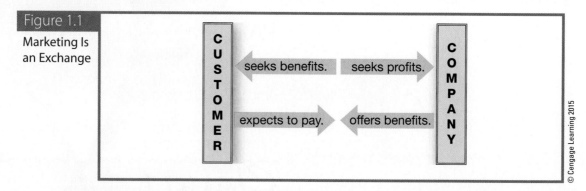

Figure 1.1

Marketing Is
an Exchange

© Cengage Learning 2015

In particular, we'll examine the issues that concern marketers in their efforts to deliver something of value to their customers, simultaneously trying to derive value from them.

Whether you're a brand manager, CMO, or CEO, don't forget to put yourself in the shoes of your customers every once in a while, to see the world and your brand from their perspective. When you do, you'll understand their wants and needs better. Doing so will give you an advantage over your competitors. Then return to your role as manager, and figure out what your company can do to make your customers happy!

1-2a **Marketing Is Everywhere**

Figure 1.2 illustrates that we can "market" just about anything. Marketing managers sell simple, tangible goods such as soap or shampoo and other consumer packaged goods (CPGs), as well as more expensive goods such as automobiles or jewelry. Some marketing managers work in services, such as haircuts, airlines, hotels, or department stores. Other marketers oversee experience purchases like theme parks or events like plays and concerts. Marketers help entertainers, athletes, politicians, and other celebrities with their images in their respective marketplaces, i.e., to fans, agents, intelligentsia, public opinion. Tourist bureaus have marketers who advertise the selling points of their city's or country's unique features. Information providers use marketing because they want customers to think they're the best, the most current, the most expansive, and so forth, so as to maximize their ad revenue. Marketers at nonprofits and government agencies work on causes, such as encouraging organ donation or driving without drinking or texting. Naturally, companies use marketing for their brands and themselves, and whole industries market themselves (think of the beef ads or the milk ads). Marketing can be used beneficially in all these situations.

1-3 WHY IS MARKETING MANAGEMENT IMPORTANT?

Marketing has evolved beyond being "product" or "production focused," where the company mind-set is "Let's just build a better mouse trap." We know that doesn't work; there's no point in producing unless customers want what we have to sell. There are still pockets of marketing naïveté in a number of industries. For example, some museum curators believe they don't need marketing. They think people should appreciate their exhibits, and if they don't, it's because the public is ignorant. Perhaps the general public is indeed relatively unsophisticated culturally, but marketing can be used to educate people.

Marketing is also more advanced than the old sales-oriented days when the action in the marketplace was "Let's make a deal." This mentality still exists in places like some drug

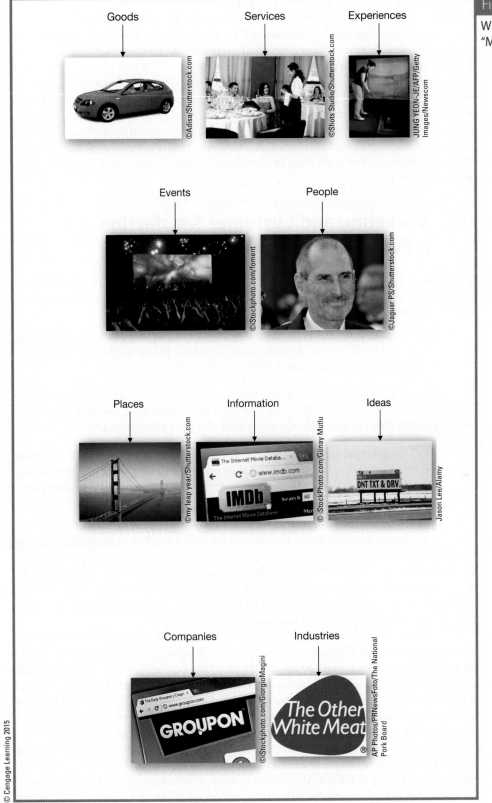

Figure 1.2

What Can We "Market"?

companies that push their sales forces to impress physicians. But usually sales dynamics exist where the product is perceived to be a commodity. In contrast, marketers should be good at communicating product distinctions. As much as direct-to-consumer pharma ads annoy physicians, they attest to the power of marketing. The ads result in patients asking their doctors for particular brand names.

Marketing is evidence of evolved markets; it signals that an industry or country has moved beyond production and sales and seeks true relationships with its customers. Today's marketing world is truly customer oriented and customer empowered. Marketers seek to identify their customers' needs and wants and try to formulate attractive solutions. Marketing can make customers happier, thereby making companies more profitable. Great companies do great marketing. And embracing marketing will enhance your career. Throughout this book, you'll see how.

1-3a Marketing and Customer Satisfaction Is Everyone's Responsibility

Management gurus say that marketing has succeeded so well that it isn't just an organizational function anymore. Marketing is a philosophy—a way to approach thinking about business. The marketing orientation should permeate the organization:

- Those in accounting and finance need to acknowledge the importance of marketing because their CEOs do. Thinking about customers is unimportant only if you're a monopoly, and even then you won't be one for long.

- Salespeople understand marketing immediately because they're the frontline interface with the customer. They want to push their firm's stuff, but their jobs would easier if their company actually made stuff that the customers want.

- R&D people tend to understand the marketing spirit too. They're hired because they're technically sophisticated, but they enjoy watching their inventions sell and become popular. It doesn't take much marketing research to test concepts or prototypes and veer an R&D path one way or another.

Today's marketers are under pressure to show results. It's fair to hold any part of the corporation accountable, and results may be measured for a number of marketing activities. The CFO who wants to see that a recent coupon promotion lifted sales can get reasonably good estimates from the CMO about effectiveness, e.g., percentage sales increase attributable to the coupon introduction. The COO who wishes to know whether a recent direct mail campaign to target customers has been effective in encouraging frequent buyers to go directly to the Web for purchasing can also get good estimates.

However, it is important not to go overboard in these efforts to quantify. For example, how does one assess the value of a good segmentation study? If segments are poorly defined, any subsequent marketing efforts would be completely off, so a good segmentation scheme is invaluable. Advertising is also a little tricky. Nonmarketers have the misconception that advertising is supposed to bump up sales. It can, and that bump is easily measured. But really great advertising isn't intended for a short-term effect on sales. Great advertising is intended to enhance brand image, which is a goal that is relatively longer term and thus more difficult to measure.

In addition to quantifying the effectiveness of marketing programs, marketers are motivated to translate their efforts into dollars for another reason—to have a "seat at the table"—to make sure that the CMO carries as much weight in the firm as any of the other C-people. The other Cs speak finance, so the marketer is frequently motivated to translate progress into financial terms. Fortunately, technology and data are increasingly enabling many more opportunities for the marketer to make such assessments; e.g., a good customer relationship management (CRM) program allows marketers to run a field study to assess the impact of a new promotion, and tracking Web data allows marketers to determine the product combinations that are most attractive to customers.

1-4 THE MARKETING FRAMEWORK: THE 5CS, STP, AND 4PS

Figure 1.3 provides the marketing management framework. Marketing is captured by the 5Cs, STP, and the 4Ps. The 5Cs are customer, company, context, collaborators, and competitors. These Cs force a businessperson to systematically frame the general analysis of the entire business situation. Figure 1.1 showed that the *customer* and *company* are the central players in the marketing exchange. The *context* includes the backdrop of macroenvironment factors: How is our economy and that of our suppliers? What legal constraints do we face, and are these changing? What cultural differences do our global segments manifest? The *collaborators* and *competitors* are the companies and people we work with vs. those we compete against (though drawing the line is sometimes difficult in today's interconnected world).

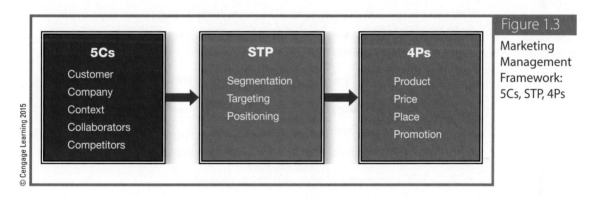

© Cengage Learning 2015

Figure 1.3

Marketing Management Framework: 5Cs, STP, 4Ps

STP stands for segmentation, targeting, and positioning. A company or a brand may want to be all things to all people, but it just doesn't happen. It's best to identify *segments*, or groups of customers who share similar needs and wants. Once we understand the different segments' preferences, we're in a position to identify the segment we should *target* with our marketing efforts. We then begin to develop a relationship with that target segment by *positioning* our product to them in the marketplace, via the 4Ps.

The 4Ps are product, price, promotion, and place. A marketer is responsible for creating a *product* (a good or service) that customers need or want, setting the *price* for the product appropriately, *promoting* the product via advertising and sales promotions to help customers understand the product's benefits and value, and finally making the product available for purchase via appropriate distribution channels, or *places*.

Marketing management oversees these 5Cs, STP, and 4Ps components with the goal of enhancing the marketing exchange (of goods, services, payment, ideas and information, etc.) between a customer base and a firm. It sounds simple: Group your customers, figure out which group to target, create a position in the marketplace via features of the product, its price, your communications and promotions, and your distribution choices. Yet obviously marketing is not that easy (after all, consider how few companies do it well), so we will see how to excel at it.

If marketing is an exchange, then just like an interaction between two people, a company has its best chance at keeping its customers happy if it is in close communication with them. The company that does its marketing research and really listens to its customers will be able to deliver goods and services that will delight those customers. The best marketers try to understand the perspective of its customers: What are they like? What do they want? How can we play a role in their lives? In this book, we'll elaborate on these themes. Throughout the book, if you ever get overloaded, you can always step back and remember that you'll always be a step ahead of your competition if you simply think about your customers. All marketing strategy derives from that.

Start with a situation analysis, and sketch answers to the following questions:

- *Customers:* Who are they? What are they like? Do we want to draw different customers?

- *Company:* What are our strengths and weaknesses? What customer benefits can we provide?

- *Context:* What is happening in our industry that might reshape our future business?

- *Collaborators:* Can we address our customers' needs while strengthening our B2B partnerships?

- *Competitors:* Who are the competitors we must consider? What are their likely actions and reactions?

With that background analysis, proceed to strategic marketing planning via STP:

- *Segmentation:* Customers aren't all the same; find out how they vary in their preferences, needs, and resources.

- *Targeting:* Pursue the group of customers that makes the most sense for our company.

- *Positioning:* Communicate our product's benefits clearly to the intended target customers.

Marketing tactics to execute the intended positioning similarly derive from a customer focus:

- *Product:* Will customers want what our company is prepared to produce?

- *Price:* Will customers pay what we'd like to charge?

- *Place:* Where and how will customers purchase our market offering?

- *Promotion:* What can we tell our customers or do for them to entice them to purchase?

If that isn't enough of a challenge, consider that customers' preferences change and that the competition is also dynamic. Who they are and what they offer your customers change. And factors that are out of your control change as well. For example, as marketing manager or CMO, you won't have a say in whether your company is merged with another whose image seems inconsistent with your brand's, but you'll have to reconcile that difference. Further, the legal environmental in this country may be different from that in another country, and each may be always in flux. So the inputs keep changing, and these are contingencies that modify marketing plans.

As Figure 1.3 indicates, if we keep an ongoing read on the 5Cs, it will make us better informed as we approach the STP task. These background indicators will apprise us as to which qualities of a customer base are likely to be relevant as we identify segments, and the "P" of positioning in STP is done via all 4Ps. Thus, the 5Cs, STP, and 4Ps operate interdependently. Optimal business solutions (in real life or in classroom case discussions) should reflect a working knowledge of all of these elements and their connections; e.g., as a contextual factor changes, what would the predicted impact be on distribution channels? As a collaborator shifts their demands, what will that do to our pricing structure? As our company sells off a nonperforming function, what impact might that have on our positioning and customer satisfaction?

1-4a Book Layout

Marketing is involved in designing products that customers will enjoy, pricing them appropriately, making them available for purchase at easy points of access in the marketplace, and advertising the products' benefits to the customers. Throughout this book, we'll assume that we're talking about a global touch of customers. This internationalism is already true for most big firms, and it will be true even for small entrepreneurs via the Internet or once they're successful and grow. We'll also assume the omnipresence of the Internet and always consider it a factor in data intake or customer channels of interactions with the company. In addition to aiming for global citizenship and recognizing the Internet as essential as air, we sought fresh, fun examples throughout the book, such as Vegas and Ferrari, instead of laundry detergent (not to dis suds).

This book will train you to think like a marketer. You'll see that great marketing is not soft; it's not an art, nor is it intuitive. Great marketing is based on sound, logical—economic and psychological—laws of human and organization behavior. You will learn the scientific and rigorous way to think about marketing issues, so that in the future, when your situation looks nothing like the ones you've talked about in school, you'll know how to proceed in finding your optimal solution.

1-4b Learning from the Marketing Framework

There are two key features to how the material is organized in this book. First, MBA and executive students learning marketing management typically want to see a framework depicting how all the marketing pieces come together to form the whole picture. To give you the big picture as well as provide you with the in-depth details, we use Figure 1.3 to begin every chapter with a Managerial Checklist of questions and issues that the reader can expect to understand better at the close of the chapter. Those questions are revisited at the end of the chapter in a list format called "Managerial Recap." The chapters are mapped onto the framework, as depicted in Figure 1.4.

You'll become very familiar with this marketing management framework. You will see the 5Cs, STP, and 4Ps repeatedly, such that great marketing will come naturally to you.

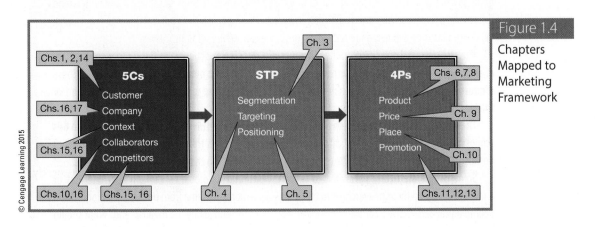

Figure 1.4

Chapters Mapped to Marketing Framework

© Cengage Learning 2015

You'll know that any marketing strategy and planning must begin with the 5Cs assessment, then a strategic look at STP, before turning to the strategies and tactics of the 4Ps.

When you're

…working on a case for class, or
…trying to answer an interviewer intelligently, or
…trying to impress your boss at work, or
…trying to launch your own business,

and you need to remember everything that needs to be addressed and how all the pieces fit together, you'll see this framework in your head, and it will facilitate your processing these marketing questions very thoughtfully and very systematically.

1-4c The Flow in Each Chapter: What? Why? How?

The presentation scheme we've adopted in this text is that each chapter covers the What, Why, and How. Specifically,

* *What* is the topic in this chapter?

* *Why* does it matter?

* *How* do I do this? Show me what to do so I can be successful.

Between the marketing framework and the practical flow of the chapters, you'll gain a strong, clear knowledge of marketing both at the strategic, conceptual level and at the tactical, hands-on level. Both levels of insight will help ensure success throughout your career, whether you're a marketer, brand manager, advertising exec, CMO, or well-informed financial analyst, CEO, or world guru.

Have a Heart

Every business function has management ethics issues. We'll discuss the marketing concerns in their broader contexts, so, for example, we'll discuss the problem of price discrimination in the pricing chapter.

We can prepare for the discussions of the specific issues by understanding ethics debates more generally. In particular, when any ethical or moral dilemma arises, it helps to analyze it and understand it from the perspective of a philosophical framework. These perspectives fall roughly into two camps: (1) We can focus on achieving fair outcomes, or (2) we can strive for fair processes.

The first perspective, a focus on the outcomes of a decision or action, is called *consequentialism*, or *teleological ethics*. The motto in this camp is "The end justifies the means." A manager applying these utilitarian norms would ask, "Which decision choice should we take to produce the most good (and/or the least harm)?"

The second perspective, a concern about fair processes, is called *deontological ethics*. The idea in this school of thought is that there are categorical imperatives, things that should be done (or not done) because it is proper, regardless of the results. The motto here is "Do the right thing (just because)."

Some people are nearly hardwired to see the world and its problems through only one lens or another. But a good thought exercise is to try to consider a moral dilemma from both the teleological and deontological perspectives. For the teleological, ask, "Does the end justify the means?" and "What should we do to produce the most good?" Then switch gears, and from the deontological vantage ask, "Is there an action that is proper according to some value or principle without concern of subsequent outcomes?"

Yet, let's face it, either extreme position can have somewhat disturbing implications. If we focus on good outcomes, do we really not care how the goals are achieved? If we focus on fair processes and on following value-laden directions, do we really not care what happens?

Furthermore, either position can seem defensible when factoring in the points of view of multiple constituencies. For example, deontologically, we might say, "We never price-discriminate," whereas teleologically, we might say, "To maximize value to our shareholders, we should charge different prices to different customers segments."

Here are two more examples:

- Consider the long-standing debates between forest preservation and the lumber industry. The first is an environmental right and a value that should be supported unequivocally from a deontological point of view. The second provides local jobs, an excellent outcome from a teleological or consequentialist point of view.
- Similarly, we may wish to the support the prohibition of cheap labor from a human rights, deontological perspective. Yet, in contrast, we might also characterize minimizing costs, so as to allow for the provision of competitive prices, a good from a teleological perspective. Presumably better prices for customers, likely enhanced margins, and shareholder value are all desirable outcomes.

That second example highlights a frequent source of tension—that of some ethical goal and the simple economic goal on which business is founded: profitability. Most industries struggling with going green or developing sustainable systems believe that what they're doing is right and hope that the modifications pay off in the long term because they're rather expensive in the short term. Analogously, many financial institutions offer mutual funds that customers can buy into that support social causes or that avoid investing in controversial industries or regions in the world. Yet these social funds do not tend to perform well financially and are therefore less popular than might be expected for people who surely embrace the social efforts.

These differences all begin to show us why perfectly rational, sane, intelligent people can differ radically in their perspectives in taking certain actions. We see that differing opinions may arise from natural tendencies to be process or outcome oriented, or from being a stakeholder in a different part of the organization, or from considering immediate vs. future impacts. Thus, if someone in your company were to propose, "Let's go green," one question is, "What exactly does that mean?" Another is, "Who does this benefit or hurt, and when and how?"

Many young business leaders are surprised to find how quickly they are confronted with ethical issues on the job. We will confront several issues throughout the book to prepare your thinking as best as possible.

Some words of wisdom come from the American Marketing Association. The preamble to its ethics statement says that the organization

commits itself to promoting the highest standard of professional ethical norms and values for its members (practitioners, academics and students). Norms are established standards of conduct that are expected and maintained by society and/or professional organizations. Values represent the collective conception of what communities find desirable, important and morally proper. Values also serve as the criteria for evaluating our own personal actions and the actions of others. As marketers, we recognize that we not only serve our organizations but also act as stewards of society in creating, facilitating and executing the transactions that are part of the greater economy. In this role, marketers are expected to embrace the highest professional ethical norms and the ethical values implied by our responsibility toward multiple stakeholders (e.g., customers, employees, investors, peers, channel members, regulators and the host community).

Time Management

Time management is a big concern for MBA students and young professionals. MBA students must manage class schedules, group meetings, corporate presentations, and extracurricular leadership activities. Time management is about becoming more productive and more efficient at achieving goals within limited time frames.

Goals. All the time management gurus advise making one list of long-term goals and another of short-term goals. The difference in the time horizons depends on what you're comfortable with and can change over different periods of your life, e.g., one week vs. one school term or one year vs. five.

Tasks in each goal. Next, start with the shorter-term goals, and break each into a sublist of tasks that must be achieved to make progress toward completing the larger goal. It helps to make these lists of tasks as specific as possible because goals that are too big and abstract can be daunting and discouraging. Thus, for example, if a goal is "do well in Fin 250," then delineate subtasks: (1) "Read course text at least 5 hours a week." (2) "Keep running list of questions from book and lecture." (3) "Pose questions to the TA each week." (4) "Pose harder questions to the professor at office hours once every other week." (5) "Assess confidence prior to, and performance after, the midterm to consider whether to advertise for a tutor," etc.

Prioritize goals and tasks. The next step is to go back to the level of the goals and prioritize them. Use whatever system makes sense to you, e.g., labeling the goals A, B, etc. Priorities arise from a combination of your personal values or deadlines that create time urgency.

Time management gurus will tell you that you should always be working on something with relatively high priority. If you're not, you're "wasting time" and should stop and pick up a project of higher priority. Priorities can obviously change with time, as in a deadline that looms larger as it approaches.

Tips for managing your time well:

1. Groups:
   a. The biggest surprise to MBA students is how much time they spend in group meetings (preparing analyses, cases, projects, etc.). Some face-to-face time is required for functioning groups, but there should be a limit. A meeting should begin promptly, and it should end promptly, even if the ending is a realization that another meeting needs to be set and new tasks divvied up and assigned before the next meeting.
   b. Related to group meetings, don't come late, and don't miss deadlines. Your group members may begin with a lenient attitude, but with time they will resent the unprofessional behavior.
2. Balance:
   a. For some students, it's tempting to focus on classes while in B-school, but don't forget to get involved in some extracurricular activities and clubs. They're fun, and they're good opportunities to demonstrate leadership.
   b. For other students, it's tempting to blow off classes in favor of the many practical opportunities, but don't forget that this is your chance to gain a breadth and depth of knowledge that you'll need to draw on over the varied circumstances that will be your career.
3. Life:
   a. Do schedule time for meals, transportation to and from classes, getting to the gym, etc. It's unrealistic not to, and you don't want to set yourself up for failure.
   b. Before you go to bed, double-check your to-do list and set up what your tomorrow should look like. Doing so gives you clarity the next morning, and it will help you sleep better.
   c. Don't multitask when you're working on a high-priority project. Studies have shown that people think they're better at concentrating then they really are, and their performance (e.g., in writing a paper) suffers accordingly.

Managerial Recap

Marketing can make customers happier and therefore companies more profitable. Marketing will enhance your career, and marketing can also make the world a better place.

- Marketing is about trying to find out what customers would like, providing it to them, and doing so profitably.

- Ideally, marketing facilitates a relationship between customers and a company.

- Just about anything can be marketed.

- The overarching marketing management framework—5Cs, STP, 4Ps—will structure the book and help you think methodically about the big picture of marketing.

- Stay focused on your customer; if you can remain customer-centric, you'll be five steps ahead of the competition.

Chapter Outline in Key Terms and Concepts

1. Defining marketing
2. Marketing is an exchange relationship
   a. Marketing is everywhere
3. Why is marketing management important?
   a. Marketing and customer satisfaction are everyone's responsibility
4. The marketing framework: 5Cs, STP, and the 4Ps
   a. Book layout
   b. Learning from the marketing framework
   c. The flow in each chapter: What? Why? How?

Chapter Discussion Question

1. Before reading this chapter or beginning class, what did you expect marketing to be? Ask family members, classmates, or coworkers what they think marketing is. See whether you can persuade them that marketing enhances a mutually beneficial exchange between a customer and a company.

2. What are examples of brands and companies you like? Why do you think you like them? What is a brand you can't stand? Why not?

3. Think about a recent time when you bought something or tried to do so and you were treated poorly as a customer. What was the essential problem? If you ran the company, what would you do to ensure happier and more loyal customers?

4. List three brands you're loyal to. List three things you tend to buy on sale. How are the product categories represented on these two lists different for you?

5. What social problem do you think is the world's biggest? Wars? Global warming? Resource imbalances? How could you start to solve a big social problem through marketing?

Mini-Case

How to Issue an Attractive Credit Card

A large national retail bank wishes to issue a new credit card. The bank wants its customers to use the card so the bank can make money, of course. In addition, the bank would like to obtain data about the customers' profiles, in terms of spending, debt, risk, etc., in at least this one part of their financial consumption.

Credit cards vary in many ways, and initially the bank managers proposed to issue a card with a fairly high APR (annual percentage rate) and a $50 annual fee, and, to get the supplementary data, they thought they'd issue periodic surveys, about once a quarter, via e-mail. The sole, young marketer at the table asked, "Well, that's good for us, but how is it attractive to our customers? Why would they want this card when there are plenty of other cards out there?" One old manager shot a withering look. But the senior-most manager spoke up and said, "Well, you're right, we're only looking at it from our point of view. What would a card look like that our customers would want—and that can be profitable for us?"

Well, that'll teach the young person to speak up in the meeting. What would help this marketer? What steps could the bank take to design a card that would be both optimally appealing to its customers (and perhaps attract new customers), as well as optimally profitable to the bank?

A card can vary on many parameters, such as APR, annual fee, brand (e.g., Visa or Mastercard), benefits (e.g., affiliation with an airline, or a professional sports team, or one's college alma mater). Which features would should be recommended to the bank as it designs the credit card?

This bank has little experience in marketing research as well, so the older managers were uncertain as to how to proceed. One mentioned a focus group, another suggested an ethnography, and a third mentioned surveys. The information that is sought, as well as the method by which the information would be obtained are both to be determined. Naturally, the bank wants to roll out the new card as soon as possible, and the research project will be underfunded.

Mini-Case Discussion Questions

1. Are the old managers right? All the other banks focus on APR and annual fees. Isn't that what this card should do to be seen as a legitimate competitor and not confuse customers?

2. Are the finance people in the room a good proxy for their customers? Are they marketers? Are the young managers a better proxy than the older ones?

3. What additional information would be helpful to strengthen a recommendation?

4. How would that information best be obtained?

Video Exercise: *Southwest Airlines* (13:55)

The Southwest Airlines brand is that of a low-fare carrier with the highest level of customer service—and with fun added into the flying experience. Southwest Airlines strives to provide its customers with a total product experience that includes check-in, boarding, flying, and baggage claim experiences. In providing this total product experience, the airline desires to fully meet the needs, wants, and desires of its customers. Southwest regularly surveys its customers regarding all components of the product experience in order to foster continuous improvement. Southwest also conducts extensive quantitative and qualitative research to better understand customers' needs, as well as to explore possible product experiences that the company might offer in the future. Southwest operates on the premise that having new products is what makes a company successful over time. Thus, while maintaining its commitment to low fares, excellent customer service, and fun, the airline seeks to identify product experiences that different market segments would like to have. The company then builds those experiences into the ticket price structure rather than charging customers with numerous add-ons. Taking this approach enables Southwest Airlines to better tailor its total product experience to the wants, needs, and desires of its different market segments.

Video Discussion Questions

1. Describe the marketing exchange relationship between Southwest Airlines and its customers.

2. Describe the 5Cs of the marketing framework as they pertain to Southwest Airlines.

3. How does Southwest Airlines' approach to providing a total product experience capture the marketing framework elements of STP (segmentation, targeting, and positioning) and the 4Ps (product, price, place, and promotion)?

Chapter 2
Customer Behavior

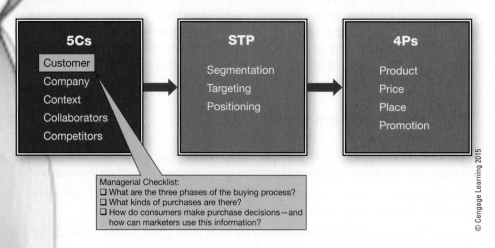

Managerial Checklist:
- ❑ What are the three phases of the buying process?
- ❑ What kinds of purchases are there?
- ❑ How do consumers make purchase decisions—and how can marketers use this information?

© Cengage Learning 2015

Marketing Management Framework

Many known, reliable patterns govern the science of consumer behavior, and this chapter shows how managers can use this knowledge wisely. The chapter begins by showing the three major phases that consumers go through when making any purchase. Consumers also make different kinds of purchases, which are important to understand because they modify the consumer thought processes. Finally, the consumer decision-making process is described in detail.

2-1 THE THREE PHASES OF THE PURCHASE PROCESS

Customers go through predictable stages in making a purchase. In the prepurchase phase, the customer identifies that something is lacking—a need or a desire has to be satisfied. Critics sometimes say that marketers create desires in people that they didn't already have. There is some truth in that (e.g., "Is your breath fresh?" "Do you own the coolest running shoes?"), but even without marketers, people really do need and want all kinds of things. Then the hunt begins. Buyers search for information about products and brands that may be suitable.

For example, a newly minted MBA student has multiple wants—new clothes, a car, a condo and furnishings, restaurants in a new city to take clients or visiting friends, a new dentist, a drycleaner, etc. Such consumers might search for alternative solutions by going online or asking friends. They might evaluate alternatives by reading comparative shoppers, such as *Consumer Reports*. By comparison, a newly promoted business executive might want a corporate jet. Possible vendors would need investigating, and alternatives could be evaluated by soliciting and entertaining bids. While the objects of purchase or the details of these two purchases may look different, they both entail a variety of prepurchase activities.

During the purchase phase itself, the consumer is creating a consideration set that includes all the brands that are deemed potential candidates for purchase and that excludes brands that have been rejected. The MBA student may limit the car search to include only hybrids. The condos considered would be only those within a certain price range. The restaurants selected might be only those with menus that may be previewed online. Analogous considerations factor into the executive's jet quandary: Which attributes are important? Which are essential? Which are to be avoided? Which attributes are inconsequential and therefore will not justify high prices?

The final stage is the customer evaluation postpurchase. Buyers assess their purchase and the purchase process, posing questions about customer satisfaction, repurchase intentions, the likelihood of generating word of mouth, etc. Figure 2.1 shows an example of a complete process: A woman realizes she needs new shoes, she selects a pair of shoes, and she decides that the shoes achieved their mission.

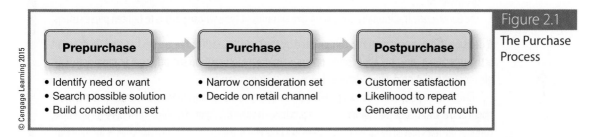

© Cengage Learning 2015

Figure 2.1

The Purchase Process

Prepurchase	Purchase	Postpurchase
• Identify need or want • Search possible solution • Build consideration set	• Narrow consideration set • Decide on retail channel	• Customer satisfaction • Likelihood to repeat • Generate word of mouth

The buying process is consistent whether the buyer is a consumer or a business. Consumer buying is easy to relate to; it involves people buying something for themselves or their households. A business customer is an agent buying something on behalf of an organization. The agent can be an administrative assistant deciding to use UPS or FedEx, or the agent can be a group of people, representing different aspects of the organization (accounting, ops, etc.) comprising a collective buying center. All purchases, B2C or B2B, go through the three stages, but the amount of time spent in any stage depends in part on what is being bought. For example, sometimes the prepurchase phase is extensive, and sometimes it is very quick.

B2B Customers

B2B customers are often classified according to what they sell:

- Installations (e.g., equipment for new factories)
- Accessories (e.g., computers to help run the office)
- Raw materials (lumber, plastics)
- Components (processed items that are components in a later finished product)
- Business services (e.g., insurance, legal, consulting)

However, just like end-user consumers, the most important classification ultimately is how much the customer (consumer or business) cares about the purchase. Then we'll know whether they care primarily about quality or price.

While consumer and business customers are analogous with regard to understanding their level of involvement and therefore their likely predilection for quality or price, they are different at least in degree. Certainly B2B purchases are often more complicated than consumer purchases, in part because they tend to be big and expensive. In addition, B2B purchases are complex because the business customer is an entity—an organization or a group of people, a so-called buying center. Rarely does a single person at a company have unilateral purchase rights. As a result, the B2B purchase involves group decision making.

Several kinds of colleagues have input in business purchases. These different perspectives need to integrated and reconciled before the decision process is complete and an order submitted. Imagine a small company deciding to purchase a new printer. The typical roles in a buying center are these:

- *The Initiator:* Such as an administrative assistant who notices that one of the printers in the office is frequently breaking down
- *The User:* Every staff member who tries to use that printer
- *The Influencer:* The IT guy who says, "Well, Brand X is cheaper, but I like Brand Y"
- *The Buyer:* The head administrative person whose responsibilities are to facilitate supplies but also to answer to . . .
- *The Gatekeeper:* Traditionally, a conservative accountant type whose job it is to tighten purse strings.

A decision to buy a new printer is complicated by the fact that each of these roles has slightly different attributes: Some care only about price, others want great features, and still others may appreciate wiggle room negotiating delivery dates or follow-up customer service.

To return to a perspective that emphasizes the similarity between consumers and business customers, we might also acknowledge that some consumer purchases involve the input of multiple members. For example, consider the roles played by different members in a household, e.g., parents, who make choices for their kids, or women, who are select restaurants more often, and men, who make the next automobile purchase.

2-2 DIFFERENT KINDS OF PURCHASES

Marketers distinguish among types of purchases. For consumers, a convenience item is a purchase that doesn't require a lot of thought, such as staples or standard, frequently consumed goods like bread or gas, or impulse purchases such as candy or magazines that are available near grocery checkouts. There are also shopping purchases, which require some thought or planning, as when using citysearch or OpenTable to find a restaurant before heading out of town. Third, there are specialty purchases such as a car or new laptop. These purchases are occasional, they are often more expensive, and as a result they require more thought.

For B2B customers, the terms are different, but the ideas are analogous. A purchase can be a straight rebuy, such as when the office copier needs toner and the office administrator buys the usual brand. Another purchase may be a modified rebuy, such as when the copier lease comes up and the boss wants to try a different vendor. Third, there is the new buy; for example, perhaps the office is considering buying teleconferencing equipment for the first time, and some investigation is required to even identify the relevant attributes to consider.

As Figure 2.2 indicates, what differentiates these purchases is not the product itself. The distinction is more in the minds of the customers and their involvement with the brand and product category. For example, the purchase of the same product—an energy drink—can be convenience when shoppers mindlessly put their usual brand in their grocery cart, it can be a shopping purchase when customers see a new offering that they consider trying, and it can be a specialty purchase when customers see an expensive brand that promises antioxidants, which they chose to read up on before making the purchase.

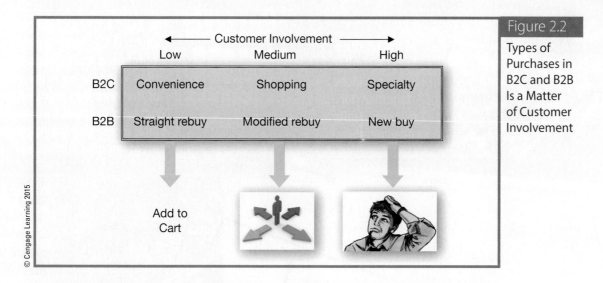

© Cengage Learning 2015

Figure 2.2

Types of Purchases in B2C and B2B Is a Matter of Customer Involvement

Consumers purchase convenience items, or business customers a straight rebuy, fairly mindlessly. It's the proverbial no-brainer. They won't spend much time thinking about brands or attributes because they just don't care enough to do so. The challenge for marketers is to break that rote behavior and shake up the consumer with news of their brand.

For items that customers care more about, they'll expend some time and effort prior to the purchase, seeking out more information to be a smart shopper and obtain good value. For even higher customer involvement, as in specialty purchases or new buys, the customers are definitely engaged. There is a great deal of effort put into researching the best brands, quality, and price. The marketer's challenge is to convince the buyer that their brand is the best choice.

The category a brand and target segment is in will suggest the appropriate marketing activities we'll implement, as we shall see in the chapters that follow. For example, for lower involvement purchases, we can expect customers to be somewhat more price sensitive. They'll pay more when they buy things that they really like or want (e.g., a cutting-edge laptop) or that they expect to be of high quality (e.g., a great restaurant) or that is important to them (e.g., schools for their children).

Consider the implications for loyalty programs. The marketer can create such programs regardless of the level of customer engagement, but they'd take different forms, e.g., price discounts for low-involvement purchases vs. brand communities and events for high-involvement products and brands. Customer satisfaction can be fine for low-involvement purchases, but customers won't generate word of mouth—they don't care enough. In contrast, for high-involvement purchases, strong followers and satisfied customers can be zealots and brand ambassadors.

Consider next the implications for channels of distribution. Low-involvement products need to be widely available so the customer can pick them up without thinking. High-involvement products will be sought out by more customer activity.

Finally, consider the implications for promotions. For low-involvement products, the marketer just hopes to cut through the noise and clutter, getting the customers' attention only long enough to register the brand name in the mind of the customer for sheer familiarity. With high-involvement purchases, customers are hungry for information, and marketers can provide much more.

So how do customers learn about brands and make choices? In the rest of the chapter, we'll look at how customers think and how marketing can have an impact on their decisions and choices.

Anatomy of a Grocery Store

In the produce section similar items are close together (for example, fruits and vegetables).

Ron Buskirk/Alamy

The dairy section contains milk, which is the most commonly purchased item. Because of this, it is located in an area of the store that requires the customer to travel through the store, increasing the likelihood of impulse purchases.

© Richard B. Levine/Newscom

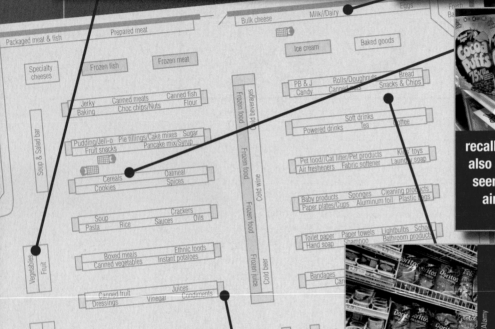

© Cengage Learning

In grocery sto consumers fo consideration (and then cho brands) as function of br recognition (b recall helps when searching online). Retai also place specific brands where they can seen by specific customers, such as bran aimed at children shelved at eye level t toddlers seated in shopping carts.

© Richard B. Levine/Newscom

Complementary items are close (chips and dip).

Jeff Greenberg/Alamy

Checkout counters provide the store the opportunity to capture customer information through the use of loyalty cards, and bar codes can provide a wealth of data that can be mined to provide insights into customer purchasing decisions.

© Karlheinz Schindler/dpa/Landov Media

Layout is designed to facilitate the shopper. Upon entering, the shopper has a choice of selecting a traditional shopping cart, a smaller basket, or shopping carts designed for shoppers with children. For physically challenged shoppers, motorized shopping carts are often provided.

© David R. Frazier/DanitaDelimont.com "Danita Delimont Photography"/Newscom

The end of each aisle and the area at the checkout lar are likely to hold high-profit items or grouped items (s as marshmallows, chocolate bars, and graham cracke for s'mores) designed to inspire impulse buys. Sometin those aisle-ends are used to promote sale items. "Peo are 30% more likely to buy items on the end of the ais versus in the middle of the aisle—often because we th what's at the end is a better deal," says Brian Wansin Cornell University and author of *Mindless Eating*.

2-3 THE MARKETING SCIENCE OF CUSTOMER BEHAVIOR

Marketers seek to understand what consumers need and to deliver suitable products. Consumers are human beings and, as such, are sometimes simple and predictable but often rather complex. Indeed, marketers are frequently surprised at how complicated consumers are and how challenging it is to predict their behavior.

It may be useful to compare the attempts to model and predict consumer behavior to trying to predict the weather. Weather is relatively simple compared to human decision making and purchasing. It's comprised of very few components: wind, water, dirt particles, gravity, temperature. Yet a typical forecast is "Tomorrow's weather will look something like today's."

By comparison, consider the relatively greater number of factors that enter into a simple purchase of toothpaste: The consumer balances what brand is on sale, what flavor is appealing, whether a whitener is desirable, whether there is a coupon to be redeemed, etc. It is helpful to know that, much like the weather predictions, for low-involvement products, marketing forecasts are often optimized by simply saying, "The next brand purchased will likely be the same as the one the time before."

The complexities of consumer psychology involve sensation and perception, learning and memory and emotions, motivation, attitudes, and decision making. These topics follow.

2-3a Sensation and Perception

When marketers formulate positioning statements or produce perceptual maps, they presuppose a complicated system through which consumers sense and perceive their environment. An enormous wave of sensory stimulation washes over and through us every day. We are selective in our attention, choosing to consider certain stimuli and effectively screening out others. For example, a consumer who is in the market for a car will tend to watch TV ads for cars. Consumers who are not in the market for a car barely "see" the TV ads for cars. Consumer involvement creates a state of heightened motivation to learn more about a purchase or pay attention to advertisement. The human organism is very efficient at adapting to the multitude of stimuli, helping us focus and block out what is deemed to be irrelevant.

Marketers can use information through each of the senses. Visual stimuli are obviously important to marketers. Ads show products, product design, print information, imagery visualization to facilitate desirable lifestyles, etc. Even simple colors imbue brand associations and can be integral to some brand identities:

- Toothpaste packaging is dominated by whites and blues, implying freshness, cleanliness, water, etc.

- Red often denotes bold action, befitting of news providers CNN, BBC, and ESPN.

- The breadth of Google's information searches is signaled by the diversity of its multicolored logo.

If consumers understand colors, marketers can use that information. For example, when the iPod was launched, all headphones in the market were big and bulky but, more to the point, black or silver. Recall the splash that Apple's ads made by showing people in black silhouette with the product and ear pods brightly contrasted in white. A choice of a unique color adds to the buzz of the brand's distinctiveness.

Colors also come to convey cultural meaning. In the U.S., brides wear white because it symbolizes purity. In India, it's red that conveys purity. In the U.S., red conveys danger and passion; a bride in red would be . . . unusual. Even within Western civilizations, there are differences: Blue represents femininity in Belgium and the Netherlands and masculinity in Sweden and the U.S. (So, how shall we package razors and deodorant?) There are a zillion colors and many cultures. Imagine the challenge for a brand manager to select packaging or logo designs for global multinational brands.

Hearing is also important to marketers. Research shows that when retailers play background music that is energetic, with a quick tempo, customers spend more. There are other aural brand associations:

- The sounds of the T-Mobile vs. AT&T ringtones

- Fancy Feast's television commercials featuring a high-pitched "ding, ding" (a fork clinking against fine crystal) to imply that the food is special (and worth its higher price)

Car and bike enthusiasts know that manufacturers are meticulous in delivering distinctive sounds, and, as a result, consumers have come to learn the sounds, expect them, and pay for them. A high-end Honda motorcycle runs about mid-$20k, whereas a Harley is in the high-$30k range. Obviously, the sound is not the only difference between the two bikes, but if the Harley didn't sound like a Harley, a biker won't fork over the extra $15k. Similarly, a Porsche 911 turbo at $150k is no clunker, but Ferrari's engineers create a symphony of car sounds and charge $250k. Again, even acknowledging their other differences, sound is nevertheless a part of it.

Even the sound of a brand name can have an effect on consumers' perceptions of that brand. Marketing linguists tells us that the sound of a long e, reminiscent of the sound that small animals make such as a mouse (squeak) or a little bird (cheep), are fitting for products that are positioned as small and quick: Beetle, Miata, Neon. In contrast, vowel sounds like short o sound slow, large, heavy (e.g., ox, cow) and should be used for naming larger, more powerful products to convey their heft: Durango, Bronco, etc.

A third sense is smell. Shopping malls excel at wafting out scents, from the Cinnabon in the food court to the coffee store in the corner. Samples of new perfumes are inserted into magazines, and women work cosmetic counters in department stores to spray shoppers. Scent is featured in ads for cleaning products—things that make our houses smell fresh or lemony. Given the biology of scent, it's not surprising that there are gender differences, e.g., Hummer's fragrance for men says it's the smell of testosterone, whereas Elizabeth Arden's perfume Splendor, for women, is called "a sparkling love story" and "wonderfully romantic."

A fourth sense is taste. A classic marketing exercise is to run blind taste tests in order to declare that one's own product is superior to the market leader. These tests can be dramatic and compelling. They are also interesting to marketers because they clearly distinguish the power of the brand from the product itself.

A fifth sense is touch. The predominant means of conveying brand imagery through touch is when marketers create well designed products, compared to products intended to be positioned for value. Design can mean good ergonomics, as in OXO's Good Grips kitchen utensils, wrist-friendly mice or keyboards, or the iPhone compared with other mobiles. Design can also mean clean lines, simplicity, and beauty, and it can certainly mean a sensual experience, like leather interior options in cars, compared to less expensive, less touchable alternative materials.

Finally, a discussion about sensation and perception wouldn't be complete without a mention of so-called subliminal advertising. The idea is that an ad can be shown very quickly, on TV or in the movies, so that it doesn't quite meet the threshold of liminal recognition and consciousness, and therefore it is said to be subliminal. Yet somehow the vision is captured subconsciously, and marketers hope the message will compel action (e.g., buy more popcorn). Print ads depend not on brief time exposure but on ambiguity. For example, does the logo for the Chicago White Sox baseball team in Figure 2.3, at whitesox.com) spell Sox or sex? The research seems to indicate that subliminal advertising DOESn't work.

Staff/MCT/Newscom

Figure 2.3

Subliminal Ad

Although marketers have debunked the notion that subliminal advertising works, they nevertheless conduct a great deal of research in areas called mere exposure and perceptual fluency. Neither of these effects is subliminal, per se, but they share a certain subtlety. For example, mere exposure, as its name suggests, says that, while consumers might not think that the billboards they drive past every day are having a persuasive effect, nevertheless they do. Marketers know that repeated exposures to a brand name or an ad bring familiarity, and with familiarity comes a comfortable, positive feeling. Thus, brands advertised on billboards are familiar and would probably rate fairly positively.

Perceptual fluency is also a subtle phenomenon. When consumers thumb through a magazine or click through websites, they are probably paying most of their attention to the content of the message. However, other information is being expressed. Colors and fonts can make a message seem more professional, more emotional, more contemporary, more gothic. Those cues make an impression as well. The cues are liminal but subtle and are part of the brand.

2-3b Learning and Memory and Emotions

All those sensory and perceptual impressions can become brand associations. To say that consumers have brand associations means that, in their memory, they have stored certain attributes attached to the brand. When the brand is mentioned, those associations are brought to mind. Learning is the process by which associations get past the sensory and perception stages into short-term memory and then, with repetition and elaboration, into long-term memory. Of the several theories about learning, two are so fundamental and pervasive that every marketer should know them.

The first way that people learn is through *classical conditioning*. This type of learning is so well known and integrated into our culture that most people have heard of the experiments by Ivan Pavlov on his salivating dogs. The learning goes through stages:

1. A food bowl, placed in front of a dog, naturally elicits its drool.
2. A bell rung in front of the dog initially elicits no response.
3. A bell rung while a food bowl is placed in front of the dog elicits drool.
4. With time, a bell rung in front of the dog elicits drool. The dog has come to learn that the bell is associated with food.

A consumer might be more sophisticated than a dog. However, consider Figure 2.4. It's common to hear that sex sells, but why, or how does it work? The process is this:

1. An attractive person elicits drool.
2. A car or other product initially elicits no response.
3. A car with an attractive person draped over it elicits drool.
4. With time, a car elicits drool.

Figure 2.4

Sex Sells Due to Classical Conditioning

That might sound a little far-fetched, but that's the learning process. Consider more neutral stimuli, such as the logos in Figure 2.5 for Adidas, Nike, and New Balance. At their introduction, these abstract symbols convey no information and function much like the bell in Pavlov's lab. With time, even though logos might not elicit drool, consumers come to learn and associate these fairly similar looking symbols with their unique brands and brand images.

It's also worth noting, in this ever changing world, that sometimes companies want to shed negative associations, and they change their names and logos to do so. For example, in recent years, Blackwater became Xe, Philip Morris became Altria, ValuJet became AirTran, and Andersen Consulting became Accenture. The hope is that the slate has been wiped clean, so that fresh associations might become attached to the new company names and logos.

A fun use of classical conditioning is jingles. It takes only a few exposures before people learn the catchy lyrics. Consider these jingles. It's hard to resist finishing them, and it's hard to stop thinking about them:

- Wouldn't you like to be a Pepper too?

- Like a good neighbor, State Farm is there!

- Snap, crackle, pop: Rice Krispies!

- The U.S. Army's "Be all that you can be!"

Figure 2.5

Logos Gain Meaning Through Classical Conditioning

STAN HONDA/Staff/AFP/Getty Images

Bloomberg/Getty Images

michael anhaeuser/Art of Focus/Alamy

And the master of all jingles:

- Two all-beef patties . . .

The second way that people learn is through *operant conditioning*. This type of learning is also so well known that most people have heard of Skinner boxes. B. F. Skinner studied pigeons pecking at a target or rats pressing a bar to receive food pellets. The pigeon learns the desired behavior by being rewarded. The behavior is said to be positively reinforced.

Skinner boxes are programmed to reward the pigeon every time it pecks or only after every 4th peck or only at 20 after the hour, etc. When the bird is rewarded every time or every 4th time, the reinforcement schedule is said to be on a fixed-ratio reinforcement schedule. When the bird is rewarded on average every 4th time (so perhaps after 2 pecks, then after 6 pecks, then after 4, etc.), the reinforcement schedule is said to be variable ratio. This difference matters because the unpredictability drives the birds (and humans) a little nuts. In the same amount of time, say 30 minutes, the bird will peck a lot more if it is rewarded on the variable, rather than on a fixed-ratio schedule.

So how might a marketer make use of this knowledge? Consider loyalty programs. Marketers reward consumers who carry their loyalty cards by giving them every 10th coffee free, for example. If marketers want their consumers to purchase even more frequently and ring up more sales, they would design a variable ratio reinforcement program. Each coffee card could have a scratch-off number that indicated the customer would receive a free coffee after, say, 7 coffees. The next card might say 5 or 15, etc.

With current programs, the customer's behavior is very predictable. With a variable program, the customer would be excited about the 7 because it means a free coffee is coming much faster than after 10. Even when they scratch off and get a higher number like 15, they'll still recall that they have had smaller numbers in the past, so the sooner they get to 15 and redeem this card, the sooner they'll get another card, perhaps with a smaller number.

Reinforcement schedules are also based on duration lapses. For example, Southwest Airlines allows passengers to obtain their boarding pass classification 24 hours prior to the flight but no sooner. Passengers who wait too long get less desirable status, so many fliers find themselves poised over their keyboard to press the right letters at just the right time. Keyboard pressing is not that different from pigeons pecking.

As any student knows, a big factor in learning and memory is motivation, and that topic is considered shortly. However, before doing so, it's important to understand that learning and brand associations aren't limited to rational cognitions. Emotions are also extremely important in understanding consumers and their connections with brands (topics examined in Chapter 7).

Consumers' emotions help explain phenomena like brand communities and brand zealots—people whose admiration for their favorite brand goes beyond a cognitive comparison of utilities. Consumer emotions also help marketers understand more moderate consumer behaviors, such as customer satisfaction or dissatisfaction. Furthermore, different scenarios can trigger different emotional responses in customers, which in turn would require different corporate responses. For example, if a staff member at the Apple Genius bar spoke rudely to a customer, the customer would likely become upset and conclude that the salesperson is unpleasant. Alternatively, if that salesperson (politely) pointed out that the customer was using an app incorrectly, the customer may simply be a bit embarrassed. In both circumstances, the customer would have experienced a negative emotion, but the emotions themselves are different, the thought processes contributing to the emotions are different, and all of those differences have implications for Apple. In the first scenario, steps toward service recovery would be appropriate, beginning with an apology. In the second scenario, the salesperson can offer guidance to the customer and very likely turn the situation into one of customer satisfaction. These scenarios also illustrate how consumers' cognitive and affective processing are inextricably linked.

2-3c **Motivation**

Figure 2.6 depicts psychologist Abraham Maslow's hierarchy of needs. Consumers have to meet basic needs—put food on the table and a roof overhead—before considering buying nice clothes. Once basic needs have been met, consumers are driven by more abstract motivations, such as love and esteem, qualities that begin to define humanity. At the peak of this pyramid is self-actualization, an achievement of one's ideal self, with no needs, no excessive wants, no jealousies, etc.

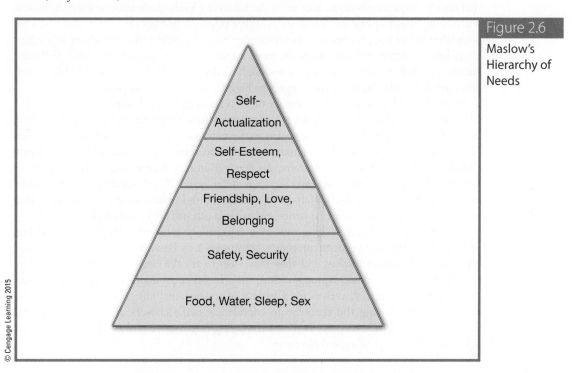

Figure 2.6

Maslow's Hierarchy of Needs

© Cengage Learning 2015

One way that marketers use this hierarchy is by identifying their product with a certain level of needs. They use imagery to appeal to those motivations. For example, the VW crash ads appeal to consumers' needs for safety. Similarly, the entire Volvo brand is positioned for safety. Beyond cars are examples that involve different kinds of security. For example, in B2B, they used to say, "You won't get fired for buying IBM." Even though IBM was often the most expensive choice, buyers knew that the quality would be good, so any risk-averse buyer would feel secure in having chosen a good brand.

Many consumers are fortunate enough to have their simpler needs met, so a great number of brands are positioned to heighten a consumer's sense of belonging or, in the next level, social acceptance and respect. Belonging can be signaled by explicitly affiliative products, such as team logos, or conspicuously branded products, as in certain men's athletic shoes or women's handbags. Belonging can also be more subtle; many ads appeal to a person's concern with fitting in with the norm—wearing the right clothes, driving the right kind of car, etc.

On the higher level, the acceptance by self (esteem) and others (respect) is often signaled by marketers by pointing a consumer toward an aspiration group. MBA students may find ads appealing that display the clothes, restaurants, and cars that successful CEOs wear, dine in, and drive. The aspirations begin to shape consumer preferences accordingly, so that, when they achieve that desired executive status, the purchases will be appropriate and exhibit good taste.

Another way that marketers have used this hierarchy is to offer an extended brand line that encourages a customer to reach ever higher in the pyramid. For example, Mercedes makes their entry-level C-model for the driver who wants the brand but cannot afford much. Mercedes hopes that the driver will like the C-model and, when they're ready, trade it in for an E-, then S-, then CL-model. This product range is a simple manifestation of customer relationship management.

Yet another way that the hierarchy is used is when brand managers think about positioning their brands as high in the pyramid as possible. Walmart may make basic sneakers that satisfy simple needs at the bottom of the hierarchy. Well-made athletic shoes, affiliated with strong brand equity, can command a higher price not just because the product may be somewhat better but also because the consumer wants to believe that the shoes will make them better—better athletes, more fit, more attractive, better people. The basic Walmart sneakers probably can't be positioned too high in the pyramid, but it would behoove any other sneaker maker to strive for imagery as high in the hierarchy as possible.

Beyond the Maslow pyramid, there are other ways to distinguish needs and motivations. Many consumer psychologists speak of utilitarian vs. hedonic products, fulfilling needs and wants. Consumer psychologists also point to the motives that coexist in all of us for either conformity or individuality. Throughout a person's life, sometimes one need is more salient than another, or, in different situations, one motivation may flare stronger than another. If conformity is winning, the consumer buys a popular brand; if individuality is more important, then the consumer finds an atypical, quirky brand. Luckily, most product categories come in large brand assortments; hence, either need can usually be satisfied.

A final means of distinguishing consumer motivations is whether they are risk seeking or risk averse. In some product categories, consumers may be avid customers, very knowledgeable, and opinion leaders, and they may wish to try the newest that the market has to offer (the newest music, laptop, fashion, etc.). In other product categories, those same people may be more risk averse for a variety of reasons, including caring less about the category or not having the expertise to confidently make choices. For these purchases, these consumers would be more conservative, trying to prevent a bad purchase, rather than promoting the hopes of a good purchase.

2-3d Attitudes and Decision Making

Marketers want to understand how consumers think and what motivates them so that they might persuade consumers to have a positive regard for a brand and see it as superior to all others, at least for their needs. Attitudes and decision making affect the extent to which consumers will buy a particular brand, repeatedly purchase it, become loyal, recommend it to others, and be so loyal as to be insensitive to price increases. Thus, marketers need to understand how to enhance attitudes about brands and encourage particular brand choices, raising at least two questions: What are attitudes, and what does the decision-making process look like?

Attitudes are conceptualized as a mix of beliefs and importance weights. Beliefs are opinions, such as BMWs are fast, they're nice to look at, they're expensive, etc. Importance weights reflect how much consumers care about whether their cars are fast, attractive, or expensive. People can differ on both their beliefs and importance weights. Some people might say that BMWs aren't that attractive or expensive relative to other cars. Some people might not care how much a car costs but care very much about speed.

Importance weights are like the concept of customer involvement discussed previously. It is an important truism in marketing, with its natural implications, that in any purchase category, customers can be classified according to how much they care about the given purchase. For the things consumers care about, they spend more timing learning about the options and brands, and they're usually willing to pay more for excellence. For the things consumers care less about, they spend less time investigating, and it's likely that they won't want to pay much.

The job of marketers is to play with both components of attitudes—beliefs and importance weights. Marketers seek to make the beliefs in an attribute or benefit more positive and to make the attributes on which the brand is dominant seem even more important. The beliefs and importance weights are modified or strengthened through learning and memory and by appealing to consumer motivations that the brand purportedly satisfies.

Attitudes contribute to decision making and brand choice. In some product categories, there aren't that many choices, so brands can be compared fairly readily. In categories with a lot of choices, consumers usually proceed through two stages. In the first, quick stage, they decide which brands should be considered in more detail vs. those that shouldn't make the cut to be in the consideration set. The second stage is more prolonged, during which consumers compare the brands in the set to make a purchase choice.

The first stage is thought to be conducted quickly by noncompensatory mechanisms. Noncompensatory means that some attributes are very important, and if the brand has them (or doesn't), then it may be considered further, and if not, the brand is precluded. Even if the brand excels at something else, that other excellent attribute does not compensate for the lack of the first, important quality. An example of this approach is called lexicographic; the idea is that a customer would compare all the possible brands along the attribute or dimension that is most important (e.g., quality, price, size, color, etc.). Whichever brands make the cut on this first dimension continue to be considered. That subset of brands is compared on the next most important attribute, and so on until the set is reduced to only a few brands.

Once the consideration set has been reduced to a manageable number, consumers switch gears and use a compensatory model. This model uses a costs and benefits logic, whereby excellence on one attribute can make up for the fact that the brand is not so great in some other ways. One such model is that of averages; e.g., if a brand is strong on attribute A and only so-so on B, it may dominate a brand that was average on both attributes A and B.

A lot of online sites allow consumers to select from a number of brands or models to enable a side-by-side comparison. This information sorting helps consumers see which brands are best on the attributes they care most about. The algorithms request that consumers first select the brands to be compared, thus mimicking the noncompensatory stage in reducing the number of possible brands to a more manageable number for further consideration. The online comparators facilitate the second, compensatory stage in that the attributes are lined up for easy viewing. A brand choice is made, and the decision process is completed. It is also possible, of course, that a customer can choose to delay a purchase; that is an action of a sort also. Delaying a purchase decision allows buyers time to gather more information, form clearer opinions about brand choices, etc.

2-3e How Do Cultural Differences Affect Consumers' Behavior?

In addition to individual differences in how consumers respond to ads and brands, there are also predictable sociocultural effects. Consider two simple examples: social class and age.

Some societies have clear class distinctions, but gradations in socioeconomic standing are discernible even in relatively classless societies. Even in the U.S., social class matters, at least for the marketer. Social class is a construct that is more complicated than just economic access to resources. Income is important, but so is family background (cf., old money vs. nouveau riche) and career paths (i.e., there is some allowance for social mobility). Old-monied people seek exclusivity in their brands to affirm their special standing in society. They are alarmed

Cross-Cultural Consumer Differences

When multinational companies launch brands internationally, they face the global–local decision. Should the brand be a unitary, global entity, the same in every market, or should it be tailored for the tastes and preferences of local customers? Those who argue for a single global brand say that there needs to be brand consistency across markets to keep a brand strong and its image clear and to allow some financial and operational efficiencies. Those who argue for tailored offerings say that customers will be more favorably inclined to build a connection to a product that is more meaningful to them. The essence of this strategic decision will be revisited throughout the book, but in this chapter the main concern is an understanding of consumers.

There may be ways to leverage some similarities across some countries and cultures so that a company can enjoy some efficiencies and not have to reinvent a truly unique brand for every marketplace. Many researchers have studied the similarities and differences among many countries, but perhaps the best-known framework is that of Geert Hofstede. He uses four primary dimensions to differentiate countries:

1. *Power distance* is the extent to which a culture is delineated between those who have power and those who do not. High-power-distance cultures are typically very hierarchical, such as Brazil, England, Japan, Portugal, and many Latin, Asian, and African countries. Low-power-distance cultures are more egalitarian, such as Israel, New Zealand, Norway, and the U.S.

2. Cultures also vary along the continuum from *individualism*, in which people mostly look out for themselves, to *collectivism*, in which people's identities and esteem are rooted in the groups to which they belong—their families, their companies, their country, etc. Does a person tend to think in terms of I or we? Individualistic countries include the U.S. and Canada, Australia and New Zealand, England, France, and Germany. Collectivistic cultures dominate Asia, Latin America, and Africa.

3. Countries and cultures differ on whether they are characterized as *masculine*, focused on achievement, success, and assertiveness, or *feminine*, and more focused on modesty, caring for others, and enhancing the quality of life. Masculine countries include China, Hungary, Italy, Mexico, the U.K., and the U.S. Feminine countries include Chile, Denmark, Finland, the Netherlands, Portugal, and Sweden.

4. *Uncertainty avoidance* is the extent to which people are uncomfortable by ambiguity and therefore try to resolve such situations, usually by imposing rules and structure. Countries with high uncertainty avoidance are Belgium, France, Germany, Greece, Italy, Portugal, and Spain. Countries with relatively more tolerance for ambiguity are Denmark, Ireland, Poland, Sweden, the U.K., and the U.S.

These differences and observations would merely be interesting if they did not have clear marketing implications. But they do. For example,

- The marketer can expect more conspicuous consumption in masculine countries, in which achievement is celebrated, thus helping Cartier, Rolex, and Philippe Patek be judicious in the marketing dollars they allocate across countries.
- Similarly, in high-power-distance countries, such as Brazil or Japan, people tend to dress up a bit formally to show respect and to reflect their own position. By comparison, people in low-power-distance countries dress more casually. It's no accident that casual Friday was invented in the U.S.

by the mass-class movement, in which designers of high-end luxury goods produce far less expensive lines (albeit not of the same quality) that allows brand access to relative peasants.

In contrast, nouveaus are trying to make purchases to attain their status, the purchases being the so-called status symbols. They indulge in conspicuous consumption, e.g., buying goods with garish, loud branding that shows the world they've made it. Obviously designing products, brands, and marketing communications for these two different groups involves different approaches.

Alternatively, consider age. Age cohorts also produce reliable, predictable shopping patterns. Some patterns are obvious, following the household composition and income availability. Young people first buy furniture and kitchenware, then entertainment and travel and large-screen TVs. They proceed to the stage of buying diapers and toys and minivans. Soon there is college to pay for, and then maybe travel, and so on.

Age groups are particularly important when they are large. The baby boomer group is graying and beginning to retire. Older people are traditionally ignored by advertisers who like to feature youth, but the deep wallets of baby boomers will soon force companies to pay attention. Cruises will sell, whereas sophomoric movie comedies might decline.

The baby boomer generation was always societally minded, so we might expect to see large-scale altruism and record levels of infusions of resources into nonprofits. Oddly, coincidentally, this generation was the same that was dubbed the me generation, and indeed sales of Viagra and cosmetic surgeries have also begun inching upward.

Social class and age cohort are among the various sociocultural factors that impinge upon how buyers form impressions and preferences, collect information, form opinions, and make brand choices. Gender matters—men and women are socialized differently, they think about products differently, and they shop differently.

Finally, ethnicity and country culture provide different perspectives, and they can be very interesting (and complicated). Note that it is difficult to provide generalizations without devolving into stereotypes, so it is important to acknowledge that there are always exceptions. To foreshadow a few observations:

- China's rising economy is creating a large demand for luxury goods from successful businessmen, from newly empowered businesswomen, from pairs of grandparents doting on their sole grandson, etc.

- Danes are fond of luxury goods, and their society is so egalitarian that they believe luxury goods should be accessible to all.

- European brands tend to dominate the high end due not just to a perception or cultural heritage, but also to structural industry differences, such as
  - Fine craftsmanship in watches built in Switzerland.
  - Fashion or exotic cars designed in Italy.
  - Supply chains such as extensive fields of flowers or vineyards for perfumeries or vintners in France.

- In South Korea, the big buyers of luxury brands are young women, and it seems that their goals are both to be recognized and to fit in with their friends.

- Online retail continues to grow strongly:
  - U.S. online retail is about $250b, almost 10% of which is through smartphones, and another 10% through social media networks.
  - Euro e-sales are at $210b, Brazil is at $16b, India is at $60b, and China is at $710b.
  - From the beginning, reasons for buying online are primarily convenience, access to a broader assortment, and an easier ability to make price comparisons. In addition, many consumers enjoy reading product reviews and ratings, and searching for coupons.

Managerial Recap

Keep the buyer in mind, whether you deal with consumers or business customers. Marketing managers can be nimble and adaptive to industry changes if they have a basic understanding of consumer behavior:

- The three major phases of consumption are prepurchase, purchase, and postpurchase.

- There are three major classes of purchases: For B2C, these are called convenience, shopping, specialty; for B2B, these are called straight rebuy, modified rebuy, and new buy. The differences among the three have to do with customer involvement.

- How do consumers think?
  - They begin with sensing and perceiving information, which may be learned and stored in memory.
  - Motivations help marketers understand what consumers are seeking so that they can make customers satisfied with their purchases.
  - Attitudes and decision making are subject to influence by good information as well as biases.
  - Finally, social norms, such as generational preferences or choices based on wealth, also define us.

How to Prep a Case: Effective Case Analysis for Class or for an Interview

Cases are used frequently in business school classes and consulting interviews. A case begins by describing the company and industry, and then a dilemma or set of dilemmas are posed to be addressed. Cases simulate putting the student into the role of the decision maker, in a scenario based on a real-life management situation.

A good case analysis proceeds by first reading the opening and closing paragraph or two and then skimming the case, paying attention to the section headings and the exhibits to see the basics. During this initial pass, some rough questions will begin to form.

Next, in a more careful read of the case, the soon-to-be familiar marketing framework—5Cs, STP, 4Ps—will provide a systematic way of thinking and structuring the case questions and concerns, along with the issues involved in any possible solutions.

Step 1 is a *situation analysis*, which achieved primarily through the 5Cs. The company is described, as are the current customer base, the actions of the competition, the collaborators, and the industry context as the setting in which this business action occurs. Not all the Cs (or Ps) will play a primary role in every case. However, among the Cs, the context is often a driving force, e.g., the business or economic environment is changing toward more e-commerce, more global initiatives, more legal entanglements, more green requests of consumers, etc.

Step 2 involves *identifying the focal dilemma* in the case from among the several that are stated or implied. A SWOT analysis is a really useful tool for problem identification. Keep in mind that the relatively peripheral issues may bear on the central issue, or they may help shape the ultimate managerial recommendations.

For marketing cases, STP follows the 5Cs. The key goal for marketers is to keep their customers coming back—repeat purchases and/or upgraded purchases and/or word of mouth. So the next phase of the case analysis is to understand who the customers are, what they want, and whether the company is delivering better quality (or value or service) than its competitors. Frequently a company is in the marketplace with no good idea as to which segment(s) would be ideal to serve given the company's strengths.

Step 3 is to *propose solutions* to the central problem. It is most informative and persuasive if the suggestion about what the company should do is supported with an explanation of the why, that is, show that solutions are being generated and evaluated according to certain criteria. It is most important that the criteria are tied to the identified problems. For example, if there is a concern about losing market share, one criterion should be whether the proposed solution will enhance market share.

The ideal solution and supportive logic are next fleshed out in positioning. The proposed forms of the 4Ps need to be consistent with each other and with the goals. A final nice touch is a suggestion regarding how to measure the success of the plan, if implemented.

Chapter Outline in Key Terms and Concepts

1. The three phases of the purchase process
2. The different kinds of purchases
3. The marketing science of customer behavior
   a. Sensation and perception
   b. Learning and memory and emotions
   c. Motivation
   d. Attitudes and decision making
   e. How do cultural differences affect consumers' behavior?

Chapter Discussion Questions

1. If consumers are being deluged by sensory over-stimulation, what can a marketer do to cut through the clutter?

2. Using the principles of classical conditioning or operant conditioning, design a marketing program for a nonprofit or for a political candidate.

3. What should ads say to help brands make the first (noncompensatory) cut in decision making to be included in a consumer's consideration set? What should ads say to help a brand be chosen, once it is in the set?

4. Run a blind taste test. Compare Pepsi vs. Coke, or bottled water vs. tap, or an expensive bottle of wine vs. the boxed stuff. Note participants' level of knowledge and surprise.

5. In teams, observe each other making choices in product categories with large assortments (soft drinks, cereals, cell phone plans, car models). As one person proceeds to include or discard products or brands, have them think aloud so the observers can note the information-processing schemata.

Mini-Case

Insight into Consumer Decision Making for 3-D TV

Various media equip consumers to make side-by-side comparisons of brands' relative strengths (e.g., *Consumer Reports*, bizrate.com, etc.). These comparisons are not acclaimed from the manufacturer but by a third party, so they're perceived as objective and neutral. The following table (based on reviews at cnet.com) compares 3D televisions on a number of criteria. The attribute of cross talk (in the table) is not a good thing; it's the ghost-like double images that shadow some 3D objects depending on the technology; hence, less is better. All the TVs are about 65 inches currently. The 3D glasses must be purchased with each TV (the technology is proprietary within the firm and the TV, so the Panasonic glasses won't work with the LG TV, for example). The glasses run about $150 a pair.

Sometimes customers know just what they want: a particular brand or a particular feature. Sometimes their thought processes meander a little more. Some consumers are rather systematic decision makers, such as when they follow a procedure that will eliminate alternatives by certain criteria. Use the table to simulate the thought processes of a consumer.

Brand	Panasonic	LG	Sony	Samsung
Model	TC-PVT25	PX950	XBR-HX909	UNC8000
Technology	Plasma	Plasma	LCD	LCD
Price	$2,479	$1,850	$2,497	$2,999
Least crosstalk	☺☺☺☺	☺☺☺☺	☺☺	😐
Clear color	☺☺	☺☺☺	😐	😐
Clear, deep black	☺☺☺	☺☺	😐	😐
3-D from angle	😐	😐	☹☹	😐
Flicker	😐	😐	☹☹	😐
3-D glasses	Ugly and uncomfortable	Rechargeable via USB	Comfortable, good peripheral	Light to wear

Mini-Case Discussion Questions

Imagine you were a consumer thinking about buying a 3D TV.

1. Quickly, at a glance, which TV do you think you would buy?

2. On what criteria do you think you based that decision?

Each of the following questions is a thought exercise employing different decision-making processes. Try each, see what brand results for each, and see how confident you feel about the resulting brand suggested from each approach.

3. Which attribute do you find least informative? Eliminate that row. Continue to do so until a clear brand winner emerges.

4. Which brand of TV would seem to be the riskiest to buy? Eliminate it. Continue until an obvious choice results.

5. If you made a price-based decision, would you be happy?

6. How would your final brand choice define you?

Which of these criteria wouldn't have concerned you? How similar was this thought process to your natural analysis? How can you find out if your consumers think along these lines?

Video Exercise: *Scholfield Honda* (5:48)

The video features Roger Scholfield, owner and general manager of Scholfield Honda, located in Wichita, Kansas, and several of his employees describing the characteristics and profiles of the dealership's customers. With respect to purchases of both new and used vehicles, customers tend to be very interested in ones that are fuel efficient and environmentally friendly. The video focuses on describing the key characteristics of customers who are interested in and knowledgeable about hybrid or alternative fuel vehicles. Factors such as the customer's age, level of education, attitudes, and needs are explored. Roger Scholfield acknowledges that prospective customers often comparison-shop at other dealerships, and he says that he welcomes such buyer behavior. He believes that his dealership has a competitive advantage over other dealerships because of the friendly atmosphere and exceptional experience that people get at Scholfield Honda. Appealing to customer's needs, desires, attitudes, and beliefs enables Scholfield Honda to attract and retain customers.

Video Discussion Questions

1. Using the purchase process (i.e., prepurchase, purchase, and postpurchase), analyze the customer information provided by the owner and employees of Scholfield Honda.

2. Chapter 2 identifies three types of purchase decisions for consumers. Describe the type of purchase decision that characterizes the buying behavior of the customers of Scholfield Honda.

3. What attitudes and needs seem to be influential in people deciding to patronize Scholfield Honda?

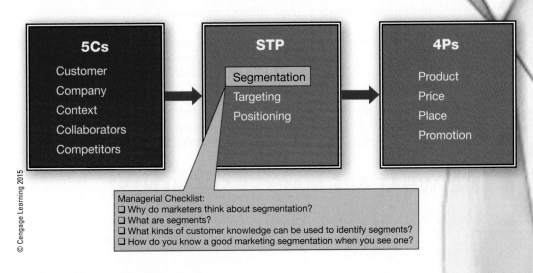

Managerial Checklist:
❑ Why do marketers think about segmentation?
❑ What are segments?
❑ What kinds of customer knowledge can be used to identify segments?
❑ How do you know a good marketing segmentation when you see one?

Marketing Management Framework

3-1 WHY SEGMENT?

Think about the last time you went to a movie with a couple of your friends. Afterward, when you talked about the movie, how did people respond? Was everyone in complete agreement about whether they liked the movie? Did everyone agree on the acting or special effects or music? Probably not. Even among friends, who tend to be similar to us, people's tastes and opinions vary. No one is right or wrong. (Well, okay, you were right, and your friends were wrong.) It's just a matter of differences in preferences and attitudes.

Psychologists would say that people have different motivations. Recall, from Chapter 2, Maslow's hierarchy from biological needs to more abstract ones. Consumers purchase products to fulfill their needs. For example, consumers who are price conscious make purchase decisions using value as a primary attribute, whereas consumers with high needs for social approval purchase brands with much less of a concern for price.

Economists talk about this as *imperfect competition*; that is, consumers have unique needs and desires, so collectively a marketplace of consumers is heterogeneous. Differences in perceptions and preferences require that different products be provided to satisfy the different segments' needs. When a large, heterogeneous market is segmented into smaller, homogeneous markets, a company can focus on meeting the demands of one or two of these groups and create something that is closer to what their customers want.

Marketers deal with these customer differences through segmentation. An entrepreneur might create a new gadget, or a brand manager a new line extension, or a consultant a new piece of software, and each might hope that the whole world will like and buy his or her market offerings. But it won't happen. And going after the whole market is not smart marketing:

- How could you provide a product that is high enough in quality to satisfy premium customers and yet priced low enough for price-sensitive customers?

- How could you afford to place your advertisement in the disparate media that different customers enjoy, e.g., online, in teen or car or cooking magazines, on network television, etc.? And how many versions of the ad could you afford to create so as to communicate effectively to those different audiences?

- How could you develop a brand image that appeals to the masses who seek comfort in conformity and simultaneously appeal to fashion setters or mavericks or other customers who seek to express their individualism? The goals are incompatible.

Instead of trying to appeal to the entire marketplace, the smart marketer and the smart company will try to find out what different kinds of customers might like and decide which groups they can serve best. That strategy begins with market segmentation.

3-2 WHAT ARE MARKET SEGMENTS?

A *market segment* is a group of customers who share similar inclinations toward a brand. On a continuum from mass marketing to one-to-one marketing, market segmentation is in the middle (Figure 3.1).

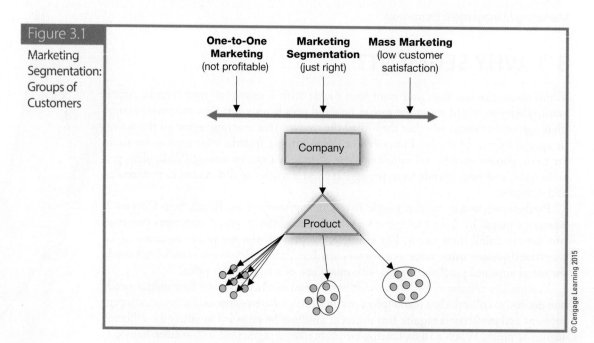

Figure 3.1

Marketing Segmentation: Groups of Customers

One-to-One Marketing (not profitable)   Marketing Segmentation (just right)   Mass Marketing (low customer satisfaction)

Company

Product

© Cengage Learning 2015

Mass marketing means that all customers would be treated the same. This approach might sound attractive because it simplifies the business (i.e., only one product needs to be offered), but it is usually unrealistic (because customers differ). Think of a simple, commodity product like flour. We should be able to mass-market flour; flour's flour, right? Well, there is flour, unbleached flour, wheat flour, brown rice flour, buckwheat flour, organic soy flour, whole grain oat flour, self-rising flour, flower power, etc. Different types of flour are available to meet the distinct needs of the flour-using segments.

At the other extreme, *one-to-one marketing* means that each customer serves as his or her own segment. This approach sounds appealing from the customer's point of view because the product would be tailored specially for each person's idiosyncratic desires. Some manufacturers of computers and cars are experimenting with letting customers design their own models. Are these companies truly offering one-to-one tailored products? Not really. Dell's website may seem to do so, but users are allowed to choose only from short lists of features. Nevertheless, even those variations result in a large number of combinations, such that one person's computer seems rather different from another's. The result approaches one-to-one marketing.

Some companies tried mass customization but scaled back because it was not cost-effective or made quality control difficult. Yet increasingly technology offers the benefits of scales of economy. Financial services don't need to have set rates; instead, they can vary depending on a customer's portfolio. Coupons that are printed at grocery checkouts are a function of items that the customer just purchased. Ads that pop up on many websites are eerily responsive to what the surfer has been typing.

Between these two extremes is the typical concept of *segmentation*. The marketplace is thought of as composed of several segments, each of which is more (or less) favorable to your brand. The segments that like your brand might not be the customers you want, but that is a marketing issue of targeting and (re)positioning, topics to be addressed in subsequent chapters.

As the contrasts of mass and one-to-one illustrate, segments become more heterogeneous as they increase in size. As a result, they are more difficult to satisfy with the same product (the problem with mass). The goal of homogeneity in customers' likes or dislikes is more likely to be achieved as the segment size gets smaller, but if the segment is too small, it might not be profitable (the problem with one-to-one). So we need to understand how to find optimal, serviceable segmentation schemes.

Niche marketing is a type of segmentation in which the company strategically focuses, targeting a smaller market, with particular needs that the company can serve well. In Figure 3.1, niches would fall between the one-to-one and segment strategies. Niches might be small segments, but they can be very profitable.

Positioning identical products differently to different segments

© 2xSamara.com/Shutterstock.com

For example, the same baby diaper can appeal to parents:

- thinking about their baby's comfort,
- who want to avoid messes, and
- who desire to be green.

Yet it's the same pooper scooper.

3-3 WHAT INFORMATION SERVES AS BASES FOR SEGMENTATION?

3-3a **Demographic**

All kinds of information about customers have been used in segmenting markets (Figure 3.2). Some customer attributes are easily identified. For example, in many product categories, a company produces two varieties, one for men and one for women, such as razors, vitamins, running shoes, and television channels. Sometimes the products are constructed differently, e.g., four blades on razors for men, vs. a razor shaped to fit in the palm of a woman's hand to facilitate shaving sensitive areas. Sometimes the product formulations are identical, but the perceptual factors differ in the marketing appeals. Alternatively, a company might focus on serving only the men's or the women's market.

Figure 3.2

Bases for Segmenting in B2C and B2B

Segmenting Consumers	Segmenting Businesses
• **Demographic** (e.g., age, gender, income and education, household life cycle, number of kids, marital status) • **Geographic Bases** (e.g., country, area [e.g., Northeast, vs. Southern CA] climate, market size) • **Behavior** (e.g., media [magazines, cable, online, movies], loyalty programs, purchase frequency, copurchase patterns, affiliations [e.g., political party, alma mater]) • **Attitudes** (e.g., awareness, involvement, price sensitivity, risk tolerance, convenience, prestige, traits [e.g., extraversion], brand attributes sought [e.g., quality or value])	• **Demographic** (e.g., company size, NAICS industry, account size) • **Geographic Bases** (e.g., country, sales force coverage) • **Type of Firm** (e.g., architects bidding for government [conservative projects, slow to pay but big], retailer [aesthetics important], manufacturers [efficiency is important], etc.) • **Attitudes** (e.g., price sensitivity, risk tolerance, corporate culture, profitability, high- vs. low-maintenance accounts)

© Cengage Learning 2015

Other easily identified demographic qualities of customers include their *age, household composition*, and *stage in the life cycle*. Spending is quite predictable:

* Young adults are more likely to be interested in music technologies than in purchasing diapers for their as yet nonexistent children.

* Young couples buy furniture and vacations together.

* Families start financial planning to support their kids' college educations.

* Older couples who are empty nesters start dreaming of spending their greater discretionary income on travel and hobbies.

* Still older people investigate health care options and charitable giving.

The reason that we constantly hear so much about the baby boomers (in the U.S. and worldwide) is because this group of customers is so huge that it affects the sales of nearly every product category. A note to the budding entrepreneur: Make something that older people like or need because boomers are heading in that direction.

Two additional demographic characteristics frequently used in segmentation studies are *education*, which helps shape consumer preferences (e.g., opera vs. opry), and *income*, which facilitates certain consumer choices (e.g., Four Seasons vs. Motel 6). You've heard it said, "Time is money," but in fact, time seems to be negatively correlated with money. Families with higher household incomes hire more service workers (e.g., lawn care, nannies) to help with their daily needs because of their time draught.

Ethnicity is clearly important. In the U.S., the African American and Hispanic American populations each number about 40 million, and Asian Americans are at about 12 million. Any one of these groups is sizeable enough to influence a market.

Many more demographic variables have been used in segmenting consumer markets, and any variable has potential depending on its relevance to the product category. While demographics have an advantage of being clear and easy to recognize, they sometimes border on being simplistic stereotypes, e.g., your male (or female) friends are not all alike in the clothes they wear, the cars they drive, or the foods they eat. Analogously, some older people are uncomfortable with the Internet, but, counter to the stereotype, others are online and very savvy. So what sense would it make to segment the market into men and women or into older and younger people, if there are at least as many differences within the groups as between the groups? Marketers seeks the men . . . who like their product and the women . . . who like their product. So some quality other than gender is driving whether men or women like the product, and that's the quality that we need to find and use as the segmenting variable.

3-3b Geographic

Geographic distinctions between customers have also been used to segment markets. For example, given societal differences, international tourist destinations can wreak havoc with logistics, e.g., while Brits and Germans tend to be orderly in queuing, customers from many other *countries and cultures* are less so. There can be cultural differences within a country, e.g., a spicy salsa in the U.S. Southwest is very hot, whereas it is formulated to be milder for customer palates in the Northeast. *Urban* living affords certain elements of entertainment, and smaller town living is different. *Climate* offers still another consideration; snowblowers tend to sell better in the North than in the South, whereas the reverse is true for chlorine.

When geographic and demographic information is combined, the segmentation schemes can be even smarter. A service called Prizm posits that MBAs who live in New York have more in common with MBAs in London and São Paulo, for example, than they do with their neighbors in New York, who are relatively less educated or wealthy, for example (Figure 3.3).

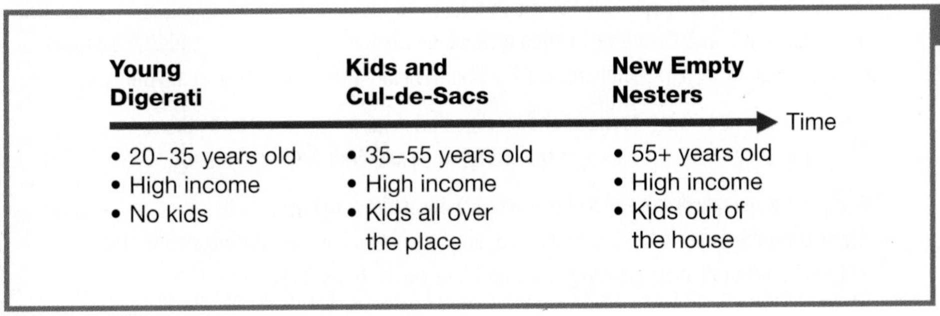

Ethnicity Numbers

African Americans:

- Large minority group: 34mm, 12.1% of U.S. population

- Buying power: Almost $1T

Asian Americans:

- Size: Over 10mm, 3.6% of U.S. population

- Buying power: Over $600B

- 90% come from India, China, the Philippines, Vietnam, Korea, and Japan.

Hispanic Americans:

- Large and fastest growing minority group: Over 35mm, 12.5% of U.S. population

- Buying power: $1T

- Quickly growing online and social media hugely popular

Young Digerati	Kids and Cul-de-Sacs	New Empty Nesters
• 20–35 years old • High income • No kids	• 35–55 years old • High income • Kids all over the place	• 55+ years old • High income • Kids out of the house

→ Time

Figure 3.3

Meet Your Future!
(Brought to you by Prizm Segments)

© Cengage Learning 2015

3-3c **Psychological**

It would be ideal to get inside the heads and hearts of our customers: What do they want (do they know)? Could they be persuaded to like our brand? Could we change our brand to match their interests better?

Psychological traits vary in terms of how much insight they lend to issues of marketing and brands:

- For example, Democrats and Republicans might make some different consumption choices, but the political identifications are less likely to affect other categories, e.g., cereal consumption, cell phone plans, theme park attendance.

- Or, for example, extraverts and introverts might differ in purchases of vibrant colors of clothing or in their tendencies to throw dinner parties vs. attend book club readings. But they might not differ in the pets they own, the restaurants they frequent, or the investments they make.

It would be more useful to the marketer to understand the psychological and lifestyle choices that are relevant to the brands the marketer is pitching. For example, if we know that a consumer is an avid reader, a sports nut, or a wine aficionado, we know something more about what the consumer enjoys and the categories of purchases that would seem enticing. We can cross-sell Kindles or iPads to the reader, season ticket packages and large-screen TVs to the sports fan, and expensive refrigerators and trips to Argentina to the wine connoisseur.

A popular tool for segmenting using psychographic data is Vals. The idea is that people's attitudes and value systems determine their orientations toward certain product categories and brands. For example, *strivers* are people who are trendy and fashionable in order to impress others, and they are often impulsive buyers. Marketing managers would study their customers to understand what they value and then would be able to communicate more persuasively to those customers. For example, Vals has been used to identify potential customers for cosmetic surgery—who would be interested, who could afford it, why they want it?—all of which shapes the advertising.

Naturally, customers vary in their marketing-oriented attitudes. Hobbies are examples of purchase categories in which customers vary in their level of expertise (some novices and others more experienced). Customers vary in their levels of involvement with the purchase category (how much they care about it). If customers are known for their expertise and involvement in a category, and if they've demonstrated a willingness to share information

Lifestyle Values Segments
Vals segments people based on three motivations: ideals, achievement, and self-expression (http://www.strategicbusinessinsights.com/vals):

- *Ideals* people are guided by knowledge and principles.
  - These consumers buy the newest laptop technology, are the first to adopt e-readers, do extensive information searches comparing all the brands before they buy just about anything.
- *Achievement* consumers buy products and services that demonstrate success to others.
  - They drive sexy, expensive cars, and they carry, wear, and drink high-end brands.
- *Self-expression* people desire social or physical activity, variety, and risk.
  - These consumers are the first to go bungee jumping, heli-skiing, kite surfing, or any other extreme sport (and accompanying gear), and they can be brand fickle.

and give advice, they will be perceived by others as opinion leaders or innovators, and they would be ideal persons for the marketer to identify as people likely to generate word of mouth. Some customers are *early adopters*, caring about new developments in their category, seeking out new products. Other customers either care less about that category or are more risk averse, and they wait for someone else to try the new gadget before they purchase the item for themselves.

All of the qualities that marketers care about may be mapped onto segments in any product category. For any purchase, there will be a segment of customers who seek premium purchases, another that is brand conscious, and another that is price sensitive. And, of course, just to provide us with a challenge, a customer who seeks quality benefits in one category (e.g., clothing) might be price sensitive in another (e.g., travel).

In addition to understanding who customers are and what kinds of activities they enjoy, it is also important to gauge whom customers wish to become. These aspirations help us predict the new categories they will enter and the copurchasing that will result. For example, when a person picks up a how-to book (e.g., remodeling), he or she will likely buy more such books before moving on to learn a new skill. Someone enrolling in beginner's tennis lessons will begin to notice brands and attributes of tennis equipment and start gearing up. One reason a celebrity spokesperson is thought to be effective is that ordinary people aspire to be like the celebrity, in whatever manner that is achievable—if not the celebrity's full lifestyle, then perhaps the hairstyle, or brand of sunglasses.

3-3d Behavioral

Beyond attitudes, psychographics, and lifestyles, marketers would like to know what customers purchase not just what they report they intend to purchase. Grocery scanner data are an example of compiled behaviors; customers might report to be eating healthy foods, but evidence of their M&M purchases would belie their good intentions.

Behaviors are important in and of themselves (e.g., to help us make predictions regarding future purchasing). In addition, watching what consumers do tells us something about who they are. Attitudes are not directly observable, but we can use behaviors to infer attitudes and psychological states. For example, people have preferences for movie genres, and marketers know it. Thus, when we go to an action movie, we'll see previews for other action movies, and when we go to a romantic comedy, the previews are a different batch.

One behavioral segment of great importance to the marketer is the *current user* of the focal brand. It is relatively easy to communicate to this group (e.g., from messages on soup packaging to direct marketing on a favorite website, depending on the level of relationship the company has with its customers), and they've already shown an affinity for the brand. Some current users may be high maintenance, but most will be worth trying to keep satisfied.

In contrast, it is more challenging to identify, obtain information on, and woo customers who are currently using a competitor's brand, or who aren't even purchasers in the category altogether. The first group asks, "Why should I switch? Why is your brand better than what I'm familiar with and relatively happy with?" The second groups asks, "Why do I want to buy this?" In addition, when given the choice, customers vary in their preferred means of contact and access—shopping online or through catalogs or at the mall.

Also within the current or competitor's user groups are variations on the extent of loyalty, or ease with which customers may be lost and gained, as well as their frequency of usage, which can have impact not only on revenues but also on logistics costs. You've heard of 80:20, meaning 80% (or so) of your sales come from 20% (or so) of your customers. You've also heard the rules of thumb: "It costs 6 times more to acquire a new

Segmentation in Action

Some people mistakenly refer to segments of products; for example, in the hospitality industry, managers sometimes refer to the number of hotel rooms in the luxury chain segment or in the long-term stay segment. But segments are groups of customers. The confusion is understandable because companies doing good marketing try to offer different products to serve different segments. Each segment has different needs, and rather than trying to force-fit one product on the whole market, and rather than forgoing the business of many customers in the market, the company offers different products or brands or brand extensions so as to optimize the satisfaction of its customer segments. And, indeed, the hospitality industry excels at this differentiation. For example, Marriott Hotels are upscale and cater to businesspeople or pleasure travelers willing to pay its room fees. In addition, Marriott offers complementary product and service lines including the Ritz-Carlton hotels ("the finest in accommodations and service"), Gaylord Hotels ("breathtaking vacation and convention options"), Residence Inns (for extended stays), Fairfield Inns (for "exceptional value"; Marriott.com/Marriott-brands).

If it is lucky, a company can find that a single product appeals to multiple segments. For example, Porsche owners vary in their motivations to own their cars: Some drivers are hotshots and want to be noticed in a cool car, whereas others purchase the car to celebrate some career achievement. Harley-Davidson also finds different personality types drawn to its vehicles: Some are practical and others are more adventurous, and some are more introverted and like riding alone whereas others are more extraverted and like riding with friends.

However, typically, different segments have different needs. In a white paper, "All Visitors Aare Not Created Equal," McKinsey reported on varieties of online behavior. Some people went online to just a few websites to buy things rather than having to run out to make the purchases. Other people are online entertaining themselves, watching videos, and surfing amusing sites. Others are serious shoppers doing price comparisons, etc.

The different behaviors and desires of various segments have many business implications. For example, a retail banking chain with an investment arm found that some banking customers are interested in investing if they don't have to pay commissions, whereas other customers are less knowledgeable and want the availability of a broker's advice. The chain pursued these motivations in a pricing study to see what the price sensitivities would be accompanying varying levels of service.

This particular trade-off (of cost and quality) is seen time and time again, particularly in B2B markets. For example, Hewlett-Packard sees differences among its buyers of high-end network servers: Some want a good, reliable, affordable machine, whereas others seek compatibility with complicated intact systems and access to service personnel who can facilitate all the machines communicating with each other. In reading between the lines in these scenarios, we can assume that access to additional services implies the companies can charge those segments of customers more.

Even in B2C consumer goods, there can be price implications. For example, people buying aspirin are usually seeking one or two attributes: How strong is the pain reliever, and is it safe or upsetting to the stomach? Customers who value safety might reach for Bayer (and pay $8.49), whereas the segment seeking strength might choose Excedrin ($12.99). Some customers might want both safety and strength and select Extra Strength Tylenol ($16.99). And some customers might simply want a basic pain reliever and may be happy with the store brand ($3.79).

Even nonprofits have found segmentation analyses useful. In Prince and File's book *Seven Faces of Philanthropy*, they report on the motivations of donors, identifying such profiles as the "Communitarian"—men with high school educations who got rich as entrepreneurs and who like to give to their local community. There are "Devouts"—college-educated men who donate for stewardship, to share God's bounty. There are "Socialites"—college-educated women who attend the celebratory social events and who enjoy the prestige of doing so. And there are "Dynasts"—college-educated men and women with inherited wealth who share to carry on family traditions.

In many, many arenas, segmentation is useful. It helps you see your customers and their particular desires more clearly, and it can provide efficiencies, e.g., in ad spending, when brands and communications are targeted accordingly.

customer, compared with retaining a loyal customer." Thus, these behavioral tendencies—frequency, loyalty, etc.—are worth knowing, so we'd like to be able to identify frequent users.

Marketers also study patterns of copurchasing—that skis are purchased or rented with boots, snowsuits, lift tickets, hotel rooms, and spiked cocoa. An increasingly popular means of using copurchasing patterns to generate cross-selling suggestions are Internet recommendation agents. Providers like Amazon examine what you've bought (and clicked on to view), and they make suggestions by comparing your data with what other customers have bought.

3-3e **B2B**

Although we have been focusing on categories of segmentation data that are particularly useful for consumers, marketers segmenting their business clients most frequently use size. *Size* can be defined in a number of ways: company sales, market share, number of employees, client's share of provider's business, etc. Businesses plan for and interact differently with their larger clients than they do with their smaller ones. They assign more client service personnel and extend more relationship management efforts because these customers are worth it: Larger clients tend to be profitable ones.

However, size does not always correlate with future growth potential or with costs associated with high-maintenance clients, who might not be worth retaining regardless of the size of their orders. So, per Figure 3.2, there are other bases for segmenting business customers. Note the close analogies with the consumer concepts.

The primary distinction between segmenting businesses and consumers is that the data sources tend to be different. There aren't scanner data prevalent for businesses, for example. On the other hand, the number of businesses who comprise one's customer base will be far fewer than the potentially millions of consumers. In addition, there tends to be good corporate knowledge about business customers, in part because such transactions typically rely on a sales force, so a knowledgeable front line is interacting with the business customer. Of course, companies could do a better job of systematizing the sales force knowledge, which would provide a clearer database for segmentation studies and other purposes.

3-3f **Concept in Action: Segmentation Variables**

Chapter 15 describes cluster analysis, the technique used to form segments once the marketer has these demographic, geographic, psychographic, or behavioral variables. Here is an example from the automobile insurance industry, which is huge and competitive. So it's not surprising that companies turn to segmentation to get an edge.

This particular company began with survey data on its customers. The first analytical question is to find survey questions allowing for variability in how respondents think about an issue. No variablity says that the customers are homogeneous in their perceptions, which in turn indicates that that variable is not useful in the segmentation. Remember, splitting customers into segments requires some differences across groups.

For example, Figure 3.4 shows simple results on two survey items. The question at the left indicates that most customers like the convenience of consolidating their home and car insurance with a single company. While that information is interesting, it is not useful for segmenting because most of the customers are in agreement.

Figure 3.4

Insurance: Looking for Segmentation Variables

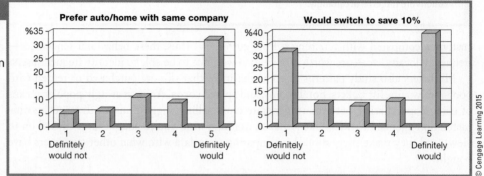

© Cengage Learning 2015

In contrast, the survey question about the discount (on the right) shows much greater promise as a variable that would help distinguish segments. These data indicate two groups: one who would switch to save a mere 10% (the price sensitive customers) and one who would not (the brand loyal customers, or those yielding to inertia). This variable would be included in the company's segmentation analysis.

3-4 HOW DO MARKETERS SEGMENT THE MARKET?

Marketers identify segments best when iterating between two approaches: a managerial, top-down ideation and a customer-based, bottom-up customer needs assessment. Marketers begin with some knowledge base about the marketplace—the customers, competitors, and the company's own strengths—and they gather information to understand the customer perspective.

Knowledge of the marketplace also clearly enters into the decision of which of the segments the company should eventually target. A market segment may look desirable in terms of its size and even future growth potential, but it may already be saturated with offerings by other competitors. The potential opportunities may be richer in other segments. The managerial perspective is also clearly important in terms of assessing the extent to which the servicing of a particular segment is consistent with corporate goals.

As an example of the required integration between the managerial and customer perspectives in formulating segments, consider the service industry of personal investment advisors. These professionals know that their client base may be divided according to certain demographic variables, such as income level, and psychological traits, such as risk aversion. They can obtain geographic data as a proxy for income, which would help them conduct a cost-effective direct mailing to zip codes that are known to be proportionally wealthier. Upon identifying sales prospects, the financial advisor can send the potential clients surveys to measure their comfort level with risk. The advisor is using extant knowledge and data (e.g., about income and zip codes) so as to prime more favorable responses and complements this knowledge with personal evaluations (e.g., comfort with risk) to know which financial products might seem most appealing to the client.

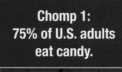

Chomp 1:
75% of U.S. adults eat candy.

Chomp 2:
Snickers is number one market share candy (8%).

Chomp 3:
Half of Snickers eaten by 2.5mm target customers (young men).

Mars might want to advertise to all U.S. consumers, but you've been to Chewniversity (hey, Mars's word!), so you know it would be wiser (and result in better ROI) to take advantage of the fact that 8.3% of its customers buy and consume 50% of its Snickers bars. That segmentation information is useful. We shouldn't just Nougetaboutit (also Mars's)!

The iteration between the managerial and customer perspectives is also important because sometimes a marketing manager might hold beliefs that are not consistent with the customer data. For example, say a marketer for a London theater production company believes that some customer behavior such as income is predictive of the behavior of interest, i.e., the purchase of theater subscriptions. That belief might be based on years of anecdotal data (listening to friends, overhearing transit conversations, etc.). But those anecdotes were not systematically gathered data and probably do not represent an unbiased selection of customers. Thus, the marketer's beliefs would need to be reconsidered when confronted with real, better data indicating that, in fact, the correlation between income and theatergoing isn't that strong. Empirically, arts-related behaviors (such as the frequency of museum attendance) are better predictors of who belongs to the theatergoer segment.

3-4a How to Evaluate the Segmentation Scheme

The iteration between marketing managers' good sense and the customer-based data continues when evaluating potential segmentation scenarios. A set of segments may be very clear from a statistical perspective, but they need to be useful from the managerial point of view. So the question is, "How do you know a good marketing segmentation when you see one?"

Data to identify segments. If one element of an iterative segmentation is a smart marketer, the other element is good customer data. Are data available of the sort you'd like to use to identify customer segments? For example, census data are always available, but they might not be stored in refined categories, and so they prove too rough to be useful. Commercial data, such as Prizm or Vals data, are available at a cost. If you have a large budget, you're fine, but if you're an entrepreneur, you might need to approximate their results on your shoestring budget. If you're seeking surveys of very specific topics, such as consumer reactions to electronics, the data may be trickier to locate.

Databases to access segments. A related question is whether databases are available that identify potential customers because, after you identify segments, you want to access the customers in the target segments. For example, if you want to communicate to people who own homes in Manhattan and Palm Beach, how will you do so? Are there listings of such people, and will you have access? Could you find indirect access by advertising in the in-flight magazines for airliners carrying passengers between those cities or by sponsoring promotions with the two cities' rental car, limo, and taxi agencies?

Profitability matters. Most marketers are curious about the relative sizes of the identified segments, but it's not size that matters so much as how profitable the segment is or is likely to be. Segment size is just numbers of customers, but profitability is smarter information: How frequently do the customers purchase, how deep ($) is their purchase, how price (in)sensitive are they, how stable is the segment, what is its growth potential, etc.? Together, the numbers and profits information can be used to project the value of approaching any of the segments. Sometimes small segments can be highly profitable if the marketer pays attention and satisfies those customers' needs—the essence of niche marketing.

Sometimes segments appear small only because the clustering was done too finely. If you're working with too many segments, you'll know it because, when you try to describe each segment, their descriptions are blurred. For example, if segment A is a fashionista who is young, female, cares about shoes and hair but not cars, and segment B is all that but she cares about her car marginally more, are you working with distinct segments or with minor variants on a theme? If you're Saks, you'll assume the former and combine the segments; if you're Jiffy Lube, you would take advantage of the latter and keep the groups distinct.

Fit with corporate goals. Clusters and segments can be clear but unattractive with respect to providing solutions to the existing marketing objectives. For example, an upscale segment is always a tempting one for marketers to target because they assume that those customers can afford to purchase their goods or services with a little less price sensitivity than that of other customers. However, if your marketplace image is one of being a store with EDLP (every day low prices), you'd confuse the extant customer base if you tried to appeal to a high-end customer with some new SKUs. Further, new high-end customers might not pay attention to your ads because to date your offerings hadn't been relevant.

Another strategic question regarding segment selection has to do with the strength of competition devoted to that same segment. The ideal goal for the marketer is to find an untapped (or underserved) group of customers whose needs can be met easily and profitably. But if others have beaten you to that group, or if they could easily redirect their efforts after watching your success, the segment gets divided, effectively reducing its size and profitability.

Actionable. Lots of segmentation schemes fail because marketers focus on the wrong criteria. Specifically, the statistics and clusters might be crystal clear (e.g., four clear clusters of customers), and even the interpretation and managerial meaning might be clear (e.g., one segment in particular seems to be a great fit), but the segmentation is useless if the marketer is at a loss as to how to put that information into action.

For example, customers' psychological profiles—their basic needs, wants, motives—are extremely important to understand so as to shape an appealing market offering. But, although attitudes help the marketer understand the why of the customer, the marketer needs demographic information also in order to understand the who and where of the customer. The who information helps advertising creatives depict the target in ads (e.g., matching gender, age, income level), and the where helps inform the design of the channel structure (e.g., where do the customers live and shop and where to advertise). A good segmentation scheme should come alive. You should be able to imagine your customer segments, know what they look like, and know what they'd like to talk about.

It's not unusual to see a segmentation study composed of some usage variable (e.g., heavy vs. light users) or some attitudinal variable (e.g., positively inclined toward our brand vs. loyal to a competitor) in a cross-tab with some demographic variable (e.g., gender or age in some breakdowns like the census: 18–25, 26–45, 46–65, etc.). While the behavior usage or attitude information is the most relevant information, the demographics help take action (e.g., selecting media for ads). The hope is to find relationships among these variables—that the men end to like our brand, or the middle-agers tend to be loyal to a competitor, etc. Then, the variables of gender or age become our workable proxies for the attitudinal variables that we really want.

We'll close with a preview of what marketers do with segments. Figure 3.5 depicts several segments identified in a marketplace. Figure 3.6 illustrates a company that is trying to reach more than one segment with its product. Figure 3.7 illustrates a strategy whereby a company has decided they want to be everything to a particular segment, serving those customers very well. Figure 3.8 depicts a strategy of customizing the market offerings—different products for different segments. Any of these strategies can be smart and sustainable, depending on the company's strengths and the marketplace environment (e.g., competitors).

Finally, consider the topic of business expansion (see Figure 3.9). If you currently market primarily to women between roughly 25 and 55 years of age, by placing ads in women's magazines, but sales are flat, in which direction would you expand your business? Would you advertise via multiple media to the same segment of women? Would you try to shape the product and imagery to be compatible with men's goals? Would you

Figure 3.5

Segments in
the Market-
place

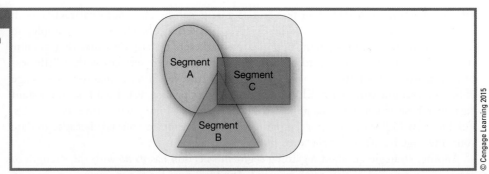

Figure 3.6

Breadth
Strategy:
Reaching
Multiple
Segments

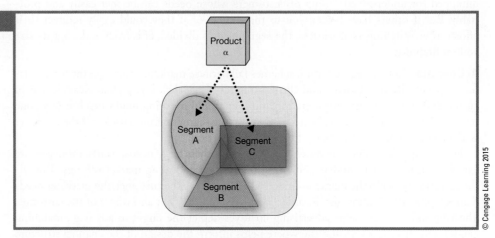

Figure 3.7

Depth
Strategy:
Serving One
Segment
Well

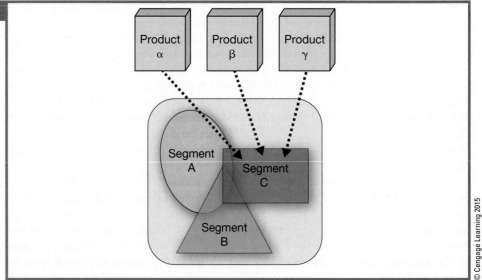

try to extend your market base by age, appealing to younger or older consumers than your
current purchasers? Clearly, profitability analyses and questions of corporate fit must be
addressed, and these issues are clarified by a sound understanding of the segmentation
structure of the marketplace.

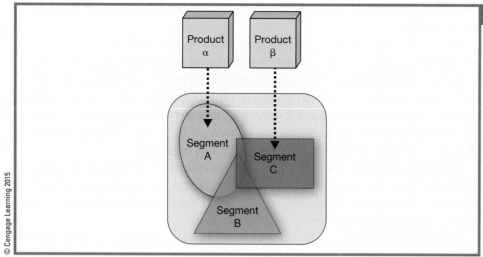

Figure 3.8

Tailored
Strategy:
Customizing
for Segments

© Cengage Learning 2015

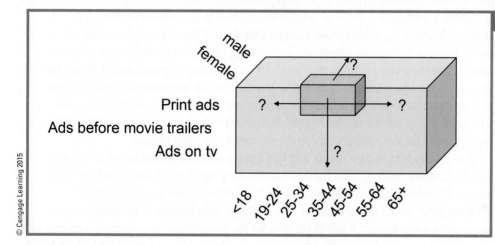

Figure 3.9

Serving a
Segment and
Branching
Out

© Cengage Learning 2015

Working in Teams

A lot of deliverables in b-school require working in groups. This can be fun and productive, and you can learn a lot. At times, it will also make you bonkers. Here's how to survive.

First, for every project, pick a team leader. If your accounting class is graded mostly on individual things (participation, exams, etc.) but has one case presentation at the end of the term, then you'll need only one team leader. In marketing, you might have 2 case write-ups and a final project, and then you'd need to select 3 leaders.

The leader for a project might be the one who cares the most about the course or project content or the person the group believes has the greatest expertise required of the project. If there is no clear leader, or if the leader you would like is reluctant to serve (e.g., perhaps he or she is already serving in that role in several other classes), then you should "flip" for it. Most groups are bigger than just 2 people, so it's not really a coin toss. Here's how to choose a person randomly. Say you have 5 people in your group. Count off, 1, 2, to 5. Then go into Excel, click on a cell, type: =randbetween(1,5), and the computer will generate one of the integers 1, 2, 3, 4, or 5 with equal probability, and then you have your designated leader.

The team leader does not carry the burden of doing all the work. But this person coordinates meetings, holds people to task, and generally keeps the project moving forward. Ideally, the group decides among themselves on how to apportion the work of a project, but when there are ambiguities, the team leader clarifies a member's role to be sure the work gets done. Unfortunately, the team leader might also have to step in to resolve conflicts. Doing so requires some pretty basic therapy skills—staying calm and not getting sucked into the emotions, paraphrasing back to the complaining party what the concerns are, try to offer a path or two of resolution, and diffusing the situation.

Meetings shouldn't exceed 2 hours. They should begin and end on time, with a summary before the group breaks. The project manager keeps the group on point during the meeting. The project manager doesn't have to be a babysitter; if issues arise, say, with the work of one member being suboptimal, the project manager can ask the other teammates for their assessments.

The role of project manager is made easier when the team members play their parts. Interpersonal interactions are enhanced by the simple rule of "Listen!" Try not to dominate the discussion; rather, try to learn from your classmates, especially those who by personality or culture are shy or hesitant to speak up.

Conflict is a difference in points of view that has escalated to the point of discomfort. It helps to resolve such conflict, and simply to make progress on the project if there is a shared expectation of the group's processes. For example, procedurally, decisions, large or small, are probably most likely to be democratic, with one vote per person. But if another process is desired, the process needs to be decided on as early as possible in the development of the project. If the vote is motivated by a conflict in how to proceed with the project, it is probably best to go forward with the (new?) project manager being a person who voted with the winning majority. That person's enthusiasm for doing a good job will be greater than the possible resentment of a person who voted for the losing proposal.

Most MBA students are hard workers, with Type A personalities that are hard to turn off. But every class has its shirkers, and they might find their way into your group. The group can confront the shirker, with specific examples of work not being completed in a timely manner or of lesser quality than desired, etc. If the shirker doesn't change his or her ways, you might bring the issue to the attention of your professor or teaching assistant. It feels icky to do so, but this feedback is actually important. In the long run, shirkers are busted in the sense that they earn a bad rep among classmates such that no one wants to work with them.

Finally, if you're uncertain of what good group behavior looks like, think of Girl Scouts and Boy Scouts: (1) Be prompt. (2) Come prepared. (3) Share your materials. (4) Don't criticize (too harshly). (5) Don't brag (too much). For all the course work and extracurricular activities that b-schools offer regarding leadership, it really comes down to behaving well and setting a good example (whether you're the project manager or just a member).

Managerial Recap

Rather than trying to capture the entire market, the smart marketer—the smart company—segments the market and is selective in which groups it targets. Segments don't have to be huge, but they must be profitable; otherwise, we would just fold the group in with another segment and offer the same product to both groups. The marketer must be able to identify the segment; hence, the reliance on demographic and behavioral data in addition to data on attitudes and purchase intentions. Segments must also be accessible; that is, some media must be able to reach them, hopefully in cost-efficiently. And last but not least, the segments selected for targeting must match the soul of the company: its position in the marketplace and its marketing and production capabilities.

- Marketers create segments because customers vary in their preferences, and pleasing all customers with one product is usually impossible.

- Market segments are groups of customers with similar reactions to the company's brand.

- Segments can be formed on nearly any kind of differentiating information, e.g., demographics, geographics, psychological attitudes, and marketplace behaviors.

- Segments are best created iterating between the managerial understanding of the marketplace and good data that may be processed (e.g., via cluster analysis) to identify similarities in purchasing propensities.

- The resulting segmentation scheme should be based on data, sustained by a database to help access the customers, be profitable enough to serve, be sensible with respect to the larger corporate goals and planning, and, finally, be implementable.

Chapter Outline in Key Terms and Concepts

1. Why segment?
2. What are market segments?
3. What information serves as bases for segmentation?
   a. Demographic
   b. Geographic
   c. Psychological
   d. Behavioral
   e. B2B
   f. Concept in action: segmentation variables
4. How do marketers segment the market?
   a. How to evaluate the segmentation scheme

Chapter Discussion Questions

1. You've got a friend who is an entrepreneur. She's making the best software—wine, whatever—that the world has ever seen. She is certain that everyone will like her new product, so she thinks your idea about segmentation is not necessary. How can you convince her and help her with her business?

2. What variables would be useful to segment visitors to your city's public aquarium?

3. How might you obtain data to segment visitors to your city's public parks, by day of week and by time of day? What would you expect to find?

4. Who do you suppose is the ideal customer segment to target for donations to
   a. American Cancer Society?
   b. Your university?
   c. World Relief Funds?

Mini-Case

Health Care Tourism

In the face of ever rising health care costs, more people than ever are looking for the best medical treatment at the best price, and they're willing to go anywhere in the world. Most of the businesses in this space are the health care providers themselves—hospitals, globally connected networks of specialty centers, etc. However, increasingly the hospitality industry is waking up to the opportunities that this type of travel may afford them. Several large hotel chains that already have international presence are seeking medical business and airline partners to create packages of seamless service for health care tourists. The airline partnerships are nearly in place; these classes of entities have been cooperating together for decades. The medical alliances are trickier because ultimately the medical service providers still care most about health care provision, and concerns regarding business are still relatively novel; e.g., they find it somewhat distasteful to be approached by a hotel chain to talk business.

Secondary data shed a clear light on the segments of customer-patients in this burgeoning world. There are essentially three groups of customers (not necessarily exclusive or exhaustive):

1. First, some people seek primarily relaxation and stress reduction. They travel to health spas to enjoy aromatherapy massages, herbal and homeopathic treatments. They engage in yoga classes, and they expect the resort's menu to be detoxifying.

2. A second group of health care travelers are getting elective surgery done, and they want to recover away from their friends and family. These people are having faces lifted, liposuction, breasts increased in size, etc.

3. The final class of traveler has relatively serious medical conditions that are fairly essential to their health. The procedures these folks are looking for range from joint replacements to cancer treatments to heart surgeries. The operations require more extended hospitalization, and the primary motive of this segment of traveler is price reduction compared to home, even for patient-customers with insurance.

Most of the hotel chains have access to this segmentation information. Some have not sought it out. Others have seen it but are not considering it because they figure that their service, beginning with the hotel room itself, would be welcome by any of these travelers.

There's a hotelier based out of London that is considering using this segmentation information. Its competitors think its nuts and will be depriving itself by definition, of access to the other segments' business. The London firm, however, thinks the segmentation-based approach may be a good way to begin. The information would allow the firm to be more selective in its appeals, both to the end users (the patient-customers) and in these still early stages of finding medical partners. The firm reasons that, as it gains access, experience, and credibility, the doors to other medical partners may open later.

Mini-Case Discussion Questions

1. Which kind of hotel manager do you agree with: the ones who do not wish to limit themselves, given that their business is good for all three segments of travelers, or the London firm and its approach? Why?

2. If you wish to follow the first strategy (all customers could benefit), what would your marketing communications be to the end-user patient-customer? If you followed the second strategy, what would your marketing communications look like?

3. If you were based in London, which countries would be the first you would approach to develop such relationships? If you were based in Paris, which countries would you approach for your network inclusion? If you were in Houston? Rio? Why?

Video Exercise: *Raleigh Wheels* (5:14)

Founded in 1887 in Nottingham, England, Raleigh Wheels became known as the original all-steel bicycle manufacturer. Eventually, ownership of a Raleigh bike became a status symbol. Raleigh's product development has been significantly influenced by trends in the European market, where biking had long been a lifestyle choice. Then, in the past 10 to 15 years, technological advances have fueled bikers' desires for equipment that is lighter, faster, and better. All companies in the industry, including Raleigh, began incorporating these technological advances into their products. Sensing that it was getting lost as a company, Raleigh returned to what customers really expected. It returned to its roots as a steel bike producer for customers who have committed to bikes and biking as a lifestyle choice. Part of this impetus for returning to the all-steel bike came from the desire for messenger-style bikes by customers of Raleigh America. Customers who pursue biking as a lifestyle choice want durable equipment and a quality ride, both of which are provided by the all-steel bike. To ensure that Raleigh continues to satisfy its customers' wants and needs, Raleigh America's marketing manager constantly uses various venues to gather input from bike enthusiasts.

Video Discussion Questions

1. How can market segmentation be useful for producers of bicycles?

2. On what factors does Raleigh Wheels base its market segmentation?

3. How can Raleigh Wheels benefit from the market segment that it pursues?

Chapter 4
Targeting

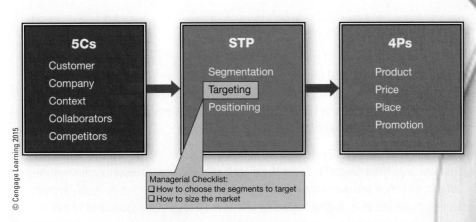

5Cs	STP	4Ps
Customer	Segmentation	Product
Company	Targeting	Price
Context	Positioning	Place
Collaborators		Promotion
Competitors		

Managerial Checklist:
❑ How to choose the segments to target
❑ How to size the market

© Cengage Learning 2015

Marketing Management Framework

4-1 WHAT IS TARGETING, AND WHY DO MARKETERS DO IT?

At this point, there is a segmentation scheme based on customer variables that are both important (e.g., they're tied to psychological profiles of attitudes and brand preferences) and useful (e.g., demographics or media choices). We now proceed to targeting.

The idea of targeting is selection. We have analyzed the marketplace, our competitors, and our internal strengths, and we can see that they align better with some segments than with others. So we will try to serve the segments whose needs match our abilities to deliver, and, in doing so, we hope to make very happy, very loyal customers, who will be very profitable to us.

Recall that the reasons we segment and target is that it's foolhardy to try to be all things to all people. Most markets are not comprised of customers with identical tastes, thereby facilitating the identification of segments. The targeting question is this: Which of those segments do we want to be our customers?

4-2 HOW DO WE CHOOSE A SEGMENT TO TARGET?

There are two perspectives in assessing the attractiveness of each segment in terms of its potential for our targeting, and it is extremely important to consider both. We will iterate between our top-down vision of corporate strategy and a bottom-up data-informed approach to segment size and profitability.

55

4-2a **Profitability and Strategic Fit**

The first perspective in assessing segments to target is a view of the segments themselves, and the primary question is how likely is it that the segment will be profitable (and just how profitable)? Potential profitability is a function of the current market size, its anticipated growth, current and anticipated levels of competition, and customer behavior and expectations (e.g., some customer segments are high maintenance and not worth serving).

Tourism

Targeting, or selecting an optimal segment(s) to serve, requires that we have a clear understanding of customer segments as well as our corporate strengths. In the global tourism industry, it's the strengths of the destinations that we must try to match with the customer segments. Many savvy marketers have done just that. Consider these examples.

1. Even when global economies are strong, there will always be a value-seeking segment. Germany offers Motel 1, the Netherlands offer Citizen M, and Spain offers Sidorme, all budget accommodations, but each with more personality than just being cheap. Attractive color schemes, quality bedding, technology like free wi-fi, docking stations for phones and iPods, etc. are appreciated by travelers. While we typically think of business travelers on lush expense accounts, nearly as many of them take advantage of these inexpensive hotels as leisure travelers spending their own money.

2. Marketers know that awareness precedes attitudes and purchasing, so South Tyrol has a challenge. South Tyrol is an Italian province in northeastern Italy, bordering the Alps yet not far from the eastern Mediterranean inlet, with a population of just over 500,000. Its citizens want more visitors and believe the region has many attractions—Italy's best white wines, apples grown there and distributed throughout Europe, and an especially tasty bacon. Instead of selling all those items separately, the town marketers were smart enough to suggest an umbrella brand, so that the enhanced awareness of South Tyrol's wines would have an ancillary effect in helping the awareness of South Tyrol's apples. The province wishes to position itself with an emphasis on nature and culture, and so its target customers are not young spring-break-partying travelers.

3. In contrast, Africa cannot advertise as a single, homogeneous brand destination because its commerce and tradition for supporting tourism are mature in the north but still developing in the sub-Saharan countries. To build up awareness and try to promote a sense of stability, these countries try to promote local crafts, traditional arts and music, and touring with professional guides. Regions seeking more tourism must support infrastructures (e.g., highways) and services (e.g., retail shops), all of which benefits the area directly in job creation. Targeting tourism is also currently being enhanced with the popular wave of volunteer tourism, in which travelers can assist locals in building wells or schools, for example.

4. At the opposite end of the pyramid, luxury travel is such a mature industry that effective targeting requires a refined view of subsegments within the larger segment of luxury travelers. Luxury travelers may be further classified according to whether they seek concierge service (e.g., delegating all daily responsibilities), personalized services (e.g., being guided to off-the-beaten-path places), pleasure services (e.g., indulgences such as fun or peacefulness), and so on.

5. Some traveling is reminiscent of pilgrimages; the industry loosely known as spiritual tourism can involve church group bus tours or yoga retreats. The travelers usually share certain motivations, such

as a religious or cultural desire to seek meaning. Location is important to signal the out-of-the-ordinary as holy or different. And the travelers are aided in their quests by attractions such as churches or museums or festivals or traveling routes of historical note. Programs designed for the church groups involve certain attractions, and programs for the yogis involve others; in addition, these built-in groups function as efficient sources of targeted communications.

There are many good books on tourism, such as Conrady and Buck's *Trends and Issues in Global Tourism* series.

The second perspective requires that we understand our own business capabilities: Does this market segment fit with who we are? Are we going to be able to satisfy this segment? Can we pull it off? What are our strengths? What resources do we have? What is our experience? What is our corporate culture? What are our current brand personalities? According to all these indicators, which segment(s) could we serve best?

Figure 4.1 captures the possibilities. In the upper left, if a market segment looks attractive and serving that segment fits our corporate abilities, the pronouncement is simple: "Go for it!" For example, if we manufacture athletic clothing and we learn that corporate volleyball teams are growing in popularity, and that they need team shirts with their logos, we can do that and likely be successful.

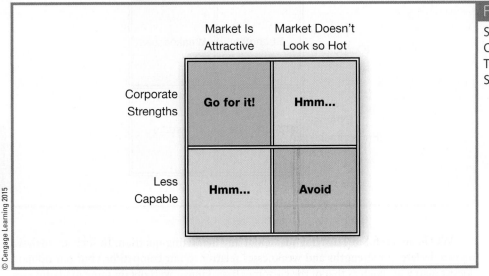

Figure 4.1

Strategic Criteria for Targeting Segments

At the lower right, if a segment doesn't look promising and it doesn't fit naturally with us anyway, we let the "opportunity" go. For example, e-books are taking off, but with varied platforms; there are still uncertainties ahead. Furthermore, just because our company manufactures PCs, it doesn't mean we'd have any particular advantage at the e-book technology or distribution. So let's not bother.

Those two cells in the matrix were the no-brainer choices (go and no-go). Now things get more complicated.

In the lower-left quadrant, the scenario is that the market looks good but we're not particularly capable (e.g., video games are profitable and growing, but we produce thumb drives). A key question would be whether we can develop sufficient capabilities. Depending on how far the newly required capabilities are from our current in-house expertise, taking this path could mean a huge investment (in time and money). Maybe that's an investment we wish to make.

If we're private or have patient shareholders, we may have the time to develop new skills (e.g., hire new people, create new channels, whatever it takes). Or maybe it's an investment we'll simply have to make, if some trend suggests that the segment is growing.

Finally, the upper-right quadrant, there is another dilemma scenario: What if the market doesn't look so great but we are expert at creating products of this sort? The key question in this case is whether we can develop a market. Can we get a segment to understand the benefits of what we provide? This strategy would also require investing but in different things: in marketing research to understand the customer's level of knowledge and points of resistance, in possible product modifications to make it more appealing, and in advertising to educate the customer about these stupendous products.

We will have more to say about corporate fit in Chapter 16 on strategy, but at the moment, a simple, popular framework for trying to objectively assess one's own corporate strengths is the SWOT analysis (Figure 4.2). SWOT stands for strengths, weaknesses, opportunities, and threats. In the S & W, we're characterizing the company: What are our strengths and weaknesses? And in the O & T, we're characterizing the broader environment (e.g., industry, suppliers, government, etc.): What are the opportunities and threats S & W are said to be considerations internal to the organization, and O & T, external.

Figure 4.2	
SWOT: Strengths, Weaknesses, Opportunities, and Threats	

	Favorable	Unfavorable
Internal (Corporate)	**S**trengths	**W**eaknesses
External (Environment)	**O**pportunities	**T**hreats

© Cengage Learning 2015

SWOTs are useful in clarifying just about any marketing question. In such an analysis, we can declare our strengths and weaknesses relative to our competitors, but our opinion doesn't matter as much as that of the customer base. Hence, we'd obtain some marketing research data, such as the perceptual maps described in the section that follows. If our brands, product lines, and company have perceived weaknesses in areas that customers care about, we should be motivated to make changes to address those shortcomings. If our brands and products have perceived strengths, we will consider what we can do to assure that these will be sustainable competitive advantages, and we'll advertise them like crazy.

Opportunities and threats are usually driven by changes in one of the 5Cs: The economic or environmental context might be changing, a supplier might be morphing into a competitor, a competitor might be offering extended services that are desired by our customers, etc. Whether any of these shifts is perceived as a threat or opportunity depends a bit on corporate philosophy: Is the glass half empty or half full? Are we nimble enough to respond and react, thus seeing the changes on the horizon as opportunities? Or are we bureaucratic or not very creative and react pessimistically to the changes as threats?

SWOT Analysis

Companies constantly face the decision of how to grow by serving their current or new customers with current or new products. The decision requires two kinds of information: first, a SWOT analysis and, second, estimates on the sizing and profitability of the potential growth paths.

SWOT stands for strengths, weaknesses, opportunities, and threats.

- The S & W characterize our own company and are said to be internal to the organization.
- The O & T characterize the broader environment (e.g., industry, suppliers, government, etc.) and are factors external to the company.

Regarding our strengths and weaknesses, ideally we'd conduct or commission marketing research to obtain the perceptions of our customers. It is most meaningful to assess our S & W relative to our competitors. If our brands, product lines, and company have perceived weaknesses in areas that customers care about, we should make changes to address those shortcomings. If our brands and products have perceived strengths, we will do what we can to assure that these remain sustainable competitive advantages, and we'll advertise them like crazy.

Opportunities and threats are usually driven by changes in the 5Cs. If the context is changing, are our competitors being affected in the same way? Are our collaborators changing, say, through an acquisition, a supplier is morphing into a competitor, etc. Which opportunities should we pursue? Which threats pose the biggest risks? How shall we respond, and how is the competition likely to counteract?

The second element to the company's choice of growth patterns is the estimation of market potential. We wish to size the likely current market and forecast, or predict, growth in the future.

We will return to SWOTs, particularly when considering marketing strategy. In the section that follows, we begin to see how the relative strengths and weaknesses may be determined, as seen through the customer lens.

4-2b Competitive Comparisons

A company can try to assess its corporate strengths in terms of absolute measures. However, relative comparisons to its competitors may be more relevant. After all, customers make purchase choices based by comparing brands. Thus, companies typically assess their corporate strengths relative to their competitors.

Figure 4.3 is an example of such a comparative analysis, called a perceptual map. This map shows customers' perceptions of our strengths (and weaknesses) vis-à-vis our competitors. The two dimensions of quality and price might look generic or abstract, but, indeed, most attributes and benefits in many product categories can be whittled down to these two. Price is self-explanatory. The important thing to remember about quality is that the defining dimensions vary with industry: For sporting goods stores, quality might mean huge variety at stores like Sports Authority or depth of category at stores that specialize in, say, camping equipment. For campus restaurants and bars, quality might be the food and drink, the ambience, etc. For a suit for interviewing, quality might be whether one feels like a million bucks wearing it, and so forth.

In the market depicted in Figure 4.3, there is good news and bad news. Our firm isn't seen as the worst provider or the most expensive. But neither are we seen as terrific on

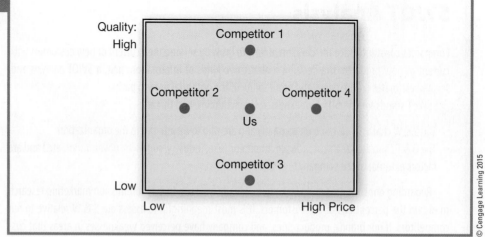

Figure 4.3

Competitive Analysis

© Cengage Learning 2015

either aspect. Indeed, we are seen as relatively average on quality and on price. We dominate competitor 3 on quality and 4 on price. However, we too are dominated by competitor 1 on quality and by competitor 2 on price.

What does this information gain us with respect to targeting? If a segment we are considering as a target is price sensitive, we have to be especially wary that competitor 2 will react. They will be attuned to such a move in the marketplace because they own that price point identity. Given that price is their strength, they could and probably would react swiftly, and in all likelihood they would win. Similarly, if we are considering targeting a segment that values quality, we would be more concerned with competitor 1 than with any other.

Figure 4.4 offers a comparison of the segment profiles along various business parameters. These simple profiles enable us to assess the likely attractiveness of each segment. Regarding segment 1, it's not the largest existing market—2 and 4 are bigger. But it's growing the fastest, which makes the market exciting. Of course, growth can be a double-edged sword; although competitors are few in number at the moment, should the market grow big enough, more will be attracted. Yet the fit is the best with whom we are. So even if more competitors enter the marketplace, we should be able to take them on because we know we can serve this segment well.

Figure 4.4

Strategic Segment Comparison

Characteristics:

	Size	Growth	Competitors	Fit	Priority?
Segment 1	$1 mm	5%	Few	yes	★
Segment 2	$2 mm	3%	1 big	ok	?
Segment 3	$1 mm	3%	Few, weak	ok	?
Segment 4	$2 mm	1%	Few, weak	no	🚫

© Cengage Learning 2015

Segment 2 has possibilities. It looks attractive because it is a big market and it's growing reasonably quickly. Yet two issues give us pause: One dominant competitor may be daunting, and it's not our best corporate fit.

Segment 3 has its strengths (e.g., few competitors), and we could likely dominate those that exist. But it has its weaknesses too: It's not a huge market, it's not growing the fastest, and ultimately it's also not a great fit with our corporate abilities.

Segment 4 is one we can pass on with few regrets. It's the smallest, slowest growing, and, regardless of any level of competition, we wouldn't know what to do in that market anyway.

In sum, segment 1 should be our priority. If segment 1 is sufficient in size for our goals, we're good. But if segment 1 is too small, we might consider expanding our targeting of segment 1 to include either or both of segments 2 and 3 down the road. We could roll out and target the segments sequentially after we've spent the resources to reach and penetrate segment 1, and if we can produce a consistent market offering and communication to additional segments without putting off customers in segment 1.

We began this section by saying that the choice of a target segment involves information about both the size of the market and the fit with corporate goals. In many ways, the second is the more challenging; e.g., it's easy to get swept away by a big segment, making us think we should serve it, when in fact we may have no particular strengths to guarantee we can serve it well, and we need to say no. Ultimately, that assessment is conceptual—who are we as a firm and who do we want to be. The other piece of information, however, the size of a market segment, is something we can estimate, and so we see how to do so next.

Have a Heart

Ethical marketers are supposed to consider whether any harm is likely to come to a particular at-risk or vulnerable segment and, if so, whether the segment should not be targeted. Unfortunately, there have been some poor practices, such as targeting

- Sugary cereals and junk food to kids.
- Cigarettes and alcohol to minorities.
- Confusing and exploitative financial instruments to the elderly.
- Marked-up goods and services to socioeconomically disadvantaged groups.
- Not marketing certain services (e.g., in health care) to segments that would not likely be profitable (e.g., the elderly, people with certain chronic conditions).

The good news is that, while some people and companies are indeed awful, most are pretty amazing.

4-3 SIZING MARKETS

In Figure 4.4, segments were described in terms of market size and likely growth rate. The inquiring marketer is no doubt wondering how to derive such characterizations. We turn now to sizing markets and then will discuss projecting growth rates.

We'll walk through a couple of scenarios of creating estimates so you get the logic. You'll see that some of the inputs into these estimates will be numbers you're confident about. The numbers you're less confident about, you'd want to have a rough "interval" around, and probably do some what-if scenarios, varying those numbers, seeing how sensitive the ultimate

Anatomy of a Target Segment

American male

~60% married

Growing and peak earning years (35–55 years old)

U.S. population is 309,000,000, men 35–55 is approximately 43,000,000 (~13.9% pop.)

Subscriptions to *Sports Illustrated;* picks up *Esquire, GQ, Men's Health* at the airport or online

DVRs and relaxes with *Mythbusters, Handyman, Dexter, The Simpsons, Deadliest Catch,* and *Stuff MY Dad Says*

Watch by TAG Heuer, Citizen, or Omega

Infiniti sedan (parked in lot), has a Chevy Silverado or Ford F-350 at home, wants a Corvette

Shoes (below) by Hugo Boss, Kenneth Cole, or Nike

Suit by Ralph Lauren, Diesel, Calvin Klein, or Gucci

We know our target customer:
- What he's like
- What he likes
- And media we can use to reach him

projections are, and what are the likely upper and lower bounds on your predictions. A lot of estimates go into the final calculation, so each component needs to be as precise as possible; otherwise the errors in the estimation just get compounded. One helpful factor to consider is that the more precisely defined the target market is, the easier the numbers are to estimate.

We'll look at an example of estimating the size of a market in the context of selling recreational vehicles to retiring baby boomers who want to tool around and see the country (you might not be a boomer, but your business will benefit greatly if you figure out how to serve them). We'll then consider more generally the kinds of factors that you'd include for estimating your particular product-segment market size.

4-3a Concept in Action: How Many Can I Sell?

Imagine that a friend comes to you for advice. He is considering entering the business of selling or renting recreational vehicles (RVs) to baby boomers as they begin to retire. He wonders how much money he can make. You're going to help him "size this market" by estimating potential demand.

A terrific online source of U.S. demographic data is census.gov; there we can find the raw numbers of retirees or soon-to-be retirees (see factfinder.census.gov). Figure 4.5 captures the basic statistics. The U.S. census is currently estimated at about 301 million. The segment 65 years old or older is 12.6%. The census data contain a number of further descriptors—some information we might use and some we might not. The gender breakdown of the 65+ crowd is 42% men, 58% women. Their marital status is mostly either married (53%) or widowed (31%). Finally, the census data inform us that 67% own their homes and 33% rent.

Figure 4.5
Market Sizing: Baby Boomer Recreational Vehicle

U.S. population = 301,000,000
65 years or older = 12.6%

- 42% male, 58% female
- 53% married, 31% widowed
- 67% own home, 33% rent

So market potential is

301,000,000 people
× 12.6% retired
× 67% own homes
= 25,410,420
~25mm potential boomer RV buyers

At the moment, let's say that we can't see why gender would matter. So a basic cut on the data is to construe a chain of probabilities: 301 million citizens, 12.6% of whom interest us. That gets us to 37,926,000 respected elders. Your friend wants to target the homeowners, figuring they probably have more money. With such an asset, maybe an RV wouldn't be a temptation the buyer couldn't really afford, which makes the enterprise feel more ethical. But another consideration is to go after the renters because those people might want to own some kind of home, even if it's on wheels. Beginning with the home owners scenario, we take the 37.9mm figure, condition it on 67% home ownership, and tentatively say that the potential RV buyer market is just over 25 million.

Sports and CRM

Sports marketers have embraced customer relationship management (CRM) systems wholeheartedly. They know that if they have good databases, they'll be able to profile their current customers. Knowledge of serious and even casual fans helps them target fairly precisely who will be good prospects for the sales of postseason tickets, upgrades on next season's tickets, or even simple T-shirts and memorabilia.

Any given team will have solid contact information on serious fans: names, addresses, e-mail addresses, phone numbers, and so forth that is based on sales data and that may be used for marketing communications and direct mailings. Websites—the team sites, but also fan clubs and sponsors—can obviously also capture some basic demographic and transaction information. Phone sales may have declined in many retail industries as online shopping outstrips catalogs, but phone sales are still very popular in sports arenas ticket sales, and they too offer a means for gathering basic fan data.

Data on more casual fans or data on fan media consumption is usually created by supplemental marketing research. For example, short surveys may be taken of box office walk-ups to get a sense of which TV channels, websites, and magazines are favorites, so as to plan advertising media expenditures wisely. Surveys usually also query the fan's frequency of game attendance, TV or streaming viewership, attendance occasions (e.g., with a few friends, or bringing the kids).

The 80:20 rule, that 80% of most businesses come from 20% of the customers, holds true in sports too—across the board. For example, golfers have been segmented according to their avidity: serious golfers who play more than 50 rounds a year and spend $5k or so, all the way to very occasional golfers who play maybe once a week and only during the summer and who spend very little. Similarly, fans who follow thoroughbred horse racing range from those who really know the sport and place many bets throughout the season, to fans who might attend occasionally but bet less frequently, to fans who watch the races on TV and don't ever bet. In both these sports examples, the teams or hosts may wish to focus on the hardcore fan because they do generate a lot of profit. However, no sports can neglect the more casual fan, simply because there are so many of them.

Most game attendance and even most fandom are regional, and marketers will frequently offer promotions through partners, like local restaurants, in part for the fan promotion itself, as well as the public relations that result with the partner businesses. Obviously the promotion sourcing is easily tracked, which, of course, contributes to efficient planning for the next preseason.

Maybe one of the best marketing gigs out there is to be a mystery shopper for a sports team. Mystery shoppers have been used traditionally on flights, in hotels and department stores, etc. People are recruited to simply fly or shop and act like a regular customer while making note of the quality of customer service and to report back to the marketing research firm. In sports marketing, similarly, a mystery shopper fan would get complimentary tickets to attend games and watch the team, the fans, wander about the facility, and experience the ambience, food, merchandise, service, and then inform the research firm afterward. The sports marketer can then identify the strengths and weaknesses in the typical fans' experience and modify the elements as need be.

A nice overview of these issues is *Sport Marketing* by Mullin, Hardy, and Sutton.

Though that seems like a huge opportunity, you explain that the 25mm figure is obviously a ceiling estimate. In addition, nothing yet has been factored in regarding prices, costs, or margins of the RVs, and presumably multiple RV models would be offered that varied along quality and price dimensions to the customers, which would also affect profitability.

Another concern is that no secondary data exist regarding boomers' interests in RV travel. So the next task is to spend a couple of weeks interviewing customers and managers at RV rental shops. Doing so reveals two segments.

In turns out that people who are married vastly prefer to buy (rather than rent) an RV. By comparison, the widowed segment demonstrates a completely different customer behavior. The men tend to travel with 2–3 of their buddies (e.g., they pull up to fishing destinations and such on their so-called mancations), and the women tend to travel with 2–3 of their female friends (e.g., going to Vegas, seasonal botanical events, and bridge tournaments). These same-sex groups tend to go on 3–4 trips a year together, so most of them rent, rather than own an RV. The actual proportions are provided in Figure 4.6.

Potential Users	Segment Size	Number of Occupants	Number of RVs for Transport	Number Who Buy	Number Who Rent
Total Market	25,410,420				
Married (53%)	13,467,523	~2	6,733,762	95% = 6,397,073	5% = 336,688
Widowed (31%)	7,877,230	~4	1,969,308	20% = 393,862	80% = 1,575,446

© Cengage Learning 2015

Figure 4.6
Market Sizing: RV for Couples vs. Buddies Usage Segments

In the married segment, the 13.5mm people really represents half of that number in terms of the RV unit of analysis (presuming the marrieds are traveling with their spouses), which is 6,733,762. The marrieds will mostly own (95%), thus representing buying 6,397,073 RVs.

The 8mm widowed people traveling in groups of about 4 people implies about 2mm RVs. These RVs would be used approximately 3.5 times a year, and only 20% of them (393,862) would be owned. Hence, if a group of men or women were looking for an RV, they'd mostly be looking to rent.

Outright ownership, then, is estimated to be 6,397,073 plus 393,862, which sums to 6,790,935. Also note that the rental potential is substantial, and renting an RV (by a boomer) presupposes that someone (a manager) owns it, implying even more sales (to the RV rental manager constituency).

Is the RV market potential big enough to be attractive? That's a subjective call, but the estimation process demonstrated the basic steps: Get all the data you can, make your assumptions clear, and think hard about segment differences. Some of the data inputs will seem like pretty good estimates (e.g., population size from census.gov). For other data inputs, we may have less confidence in the numbers. If that's the case, it is worth doing some sensitivity analyses: Take each numeric input, drive it up, and redo the analysis, and drive it down and do the same. Doing these thought experiments provides two great results: First, it helps to identify the elements in the estimation that are important (because the outcomes change a lot when they are changed). As a result, these pieces should be estimated the most precisely. It may be worth paying for additional data to obtain greater accuracy on these values. Second, it illuminates upper and lower bounds on the overall market sizing, which helps with planning.

Additional Factors. We began this chapter by discussing a number of criteria that together make a market more or less attractive. This analysis is so far only about market size. We should also consider growth, and we could easily lift more data from census.gov regarding the size of the next age cohort, such as the 55- to 65-year-old crowd.

It's always a little risky to extrapolate and predict growth, but a smart technique would be to obtain sales data in this industry for the past 3 or 4 or 10 years and extrapolate through a moving average. A 3-year moving average would take the data from years 1, 2, 3 and compute a mean for years 2, 3, 4 and compute a mean for years 3, 4, 5 and compute a mean, etc., and then you'd fit a curve to these data (e.g., via regression). The idea is that including data on the surrounding years helps stabilize the estimates. If there's an atypical year somewhere in the series, it doesn't unduly influence the prediction of the future.

A second issue is that we don't yet know the likely profitability of these markets. We haven't addressed issues of pricing (we'll do so in Chapter 9), so we can put this discussion off for now. We can probably assume that the profitability, per customer, depends on their segment membership, but we don't know yet how to translate the numbers into dollars.

A factor that will enter into those profitability estimates derives from the difference between selling and renting RVs; the former is more of a good, and the latter is more of a service. Services are usually associated with more variable costs than goods. Fixed costs for selling goods as varied as cereals and laptops include a plant, some machines, a few employees, and so forth, and the variable costs would include things like our suppliers' raw materials. In services such as retail, a fixed cost would be the shop, some equipment, and so forth, but many materials and the employees themselves would be variable costs because as the retail service takes off, it would need a bigger staff.

A third issue that we'd be naïve not to consider is that as yet we have no information regarding competitors. One quick "analysis" would be to take a look at yellowpages.com for whatever cities the guys are considering. A search for "recreational vehicles" at the yellowpages.com site for, say, Iowa City (population 67,830) shows 20 RV dealers listed; at the yellowpages.com site for, say, St. Louis (population 356,587), 98 providers pop up. Obviously, others are profiting in RVs; the question is whether a new business could break into the market.

B2B marketers sometimes have it a little easier at market sizing. The census.gov site cross-classifies businesses by sector (e.g., NAICS codes) and size (e.g., by sales or number of employees). If you produce the RVs, the industries to which you could sell would be limited only by your imagination: not just retirees or rental agencies, but mobile blood collections, mobile pet services, mobile haircuts, dentistry, piano lessons, whatever.

Regardless of whether you're working B2B or B2C, the logic in market sizing estimation is always the same. We start with the total population, and break it down into the relevant proportions.

A very general way marketers have approached this analysis is by estimating the purchase decision-making process: the elements of awareness, trial, repeat, etc. For example, the first cut would be to take the total population, multiple it by the percentage of customers who are aware of our brand, and compute population × %aware. Next, ask what proportion of customers have tried our brand? Next, ask how are we doing with regard to repeat purchasers? So far, this logic looks like the following string of proportions:

$$\text{population x} \times \text{\%aware} \times \text{\%trial} \times \text{\%repeat}.$$

We could drill down further by asking how much does each customer tend to buy when buying? Then our analysis resembles the equation that follows:

$$(\text{population} \times \text{\%aware} \times \text{\%trial} \times \text{\%repeat}) \times \text{per annum purchase}.$$

Translating this per customer annual consumption into dollars is easy; just multiply the number by the average retail price paid.

Market sizing isn't difficult. Good demographic data exist for consumers and businesses, for the U.S. and international markets. The final probability estimates in these examples indeed requires additional information, e.g., industry knowledge or data that may be obtained from surveying customers for their opinions.

Determining which segments to target depends on an interplay of two factors: (1) quantitative issues such as size of segment, profitability, and growth and (2) strategic issues, primarily that of the fit of the segment needs to corporate philosophy and intended positioning. We have focused on target sizing in this chapter. Profitability is a topic covered in Chapter 14 (on customer satisfaction and loyalty).

Managerial Recap

Targeting is important but not difficult.

- Choosing the market segment(s) to serve involves iterating between understanding corporate fit and having information about segment size and likely profitability.
  - To help clarify corporate fit, marketers find SWOT analyses helpful. Ask of your company, "What are our strengths and weaknesses?" And of the industry in general, ask, "What are the opportunities and threats?"
  - Segment sizing is relatively straightforward. Many secondary data help get the probabilities started (e.g., demographics at the B2B or B2C levels), and customer survey data on attitudes and preferences and behavioral data (past purchasing) can smooth out the remainder of the estimation.

Chapter Outline in Key Terms and Concepts:

1. What is targeting, and why do marketers do it?
2. How do we choose a segment to target?
   a. Profitability and strategic fit
   b. Competitive comparisons
3. Sizing markets
   a. Concept in action: How many can I sell?

Chapter Discussion Questions

1. These questions give you more market sizing practice (it's a skill you'll need). Using the logic from the chapter, try to estimate the possible market for the number of pairs of football pants a manufacturer could sell in your city. *Hints:*

   a. Go online and find the number of high schools in your city's school districts. If you live in a large city, focus on only the largest school district.

   b. Assume that 90% of those high schools have both a varsity football team (with 40 players) and a junior varsity team (35).

   c. Assume also that each player gets 2 pairs of game pants (one in the dark school colors and one in the light) and, on average, 1.5 pairs of white pants for practice.

2. Go to your b-school's home page. In the general information somewhere will be basic descriptive statistics on your student body demographics. Use that data to size the market for vending machines that dispense thumb drives, flavored coffees, and packets of NoDoze. What other data would be helpful to increase the accuracy of your estimate?

Mini-Case

GoodBite

GoodBite is interested in selling a new form of teeth-whitening strips. They dissolve in your mouth and leave less of a gunky residue feeling than current competitors.

White strips seem to appeal to people 20 to 29 years old. Competitors' data on existing strips suggest that they appeal to women slightly more than men, but, for the moment, GoodBite is not planning on differentiating on gender in the advertising. So let's ignore gender and just consider that 20- to 29-year-old age category.

Say the U.S. population is 301,000,000, with 41.1 million in the target age bracket. About 7.5 million people have tried competitors' white strips (GoodBite's aren't on the market yet), and roughly 3 million of them are semiserious, frequent users.

GoodBite is trying to guesstimate the size of its target market, and its likely profitability. The GoodBite product is sold in packages of 14 sets of strips (each set is an upper and lower set).

GoodBite isn't yet sure of the frequency with which a typical purchaser will buy a set because the product category is still relatively new. However, it reasons that an upper bound would be about 26 boxes bought by a consumer a year (52 weeks in the year, divided by the 2 weeks' supply sold in each box). A more conservative estimate would half that (13 boxes; roughly 1 bought each month). A still more conservative estimate would be that a customer buys "a few" (2 or 3) boxes a year.

GoodBite expects to charge $25 per box.

Mini-Case Discussion Questions

1. Should Goodbite launch its product?
2. What assumptions were made that might be revisited?

Video Exercise: *ReadyMade* (6:46)

ReadyMade is a magazine targeted toward consumers who are DIYs (do-it-yourselfers). The primary readership of the magazine is the Gen Nest market segment, a segment with clearly identifiable characteristics. The median age of Gen Nesters is 28 years, and 90% are college educated. Gen Nesters include both men and women who are advancing in their careers, buying first homes, upgrading to second homes, getting married, and having children. Gen Nest is a market segment that spans 25-plus years of people's lives. Interestingly, Gen Nesters are more involved with do-it-yourself projects than are baby boomers, another market segment with an inclination toward do-it-yourself projects but consisting of the parents of Gen Nesters. *ReadyMade* contains articles on do-it-yourself projects and products that appeal to Gen Nesters, as well as advertising for such products. The magazine is changing, becoming more polished and little more grown-up; the readership is changing along with it, losing some of its younger readers and gaining some older ones. Even with the upward shift in the readership's median age, *ReadyMade* continues to target "readers who are interested in creativity, design, and creating a personalized space."

Video Discussion Questions

1. Describe the market segment toward which the *ReadyMade* magazine is primarily targeted.
2. What key attributes of *ReadyMade* magazine appeal to this market segment?
3. How is the target market of *ReadyMade* magazine changing, and why is it changing?

Chapter 5
Positioning

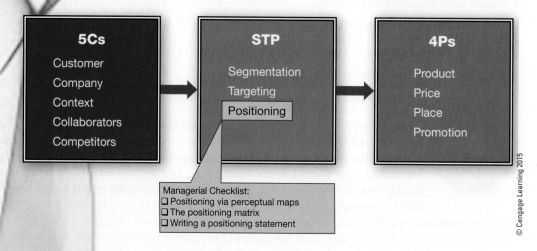

Marketing Management Framework

5-1 WHAT IS POSITIONING, AND WHY IS IT PROBABLY THE MOST IMPORTANT ASPECT OF MARKETING?

After segmenting and targeting, we proceed to positioning in STP. Positioning has many physical elements, but even more perceptual ones. It's about identity: who your brand or company is in the marketplace vis-à-vis the competition and in the eyes of the customer. Once you see who you are, you can also determine who you want to be.

Positioning comprises much of a marketer's responsibilities. It requires designing a product with benefits that the target segment will value (how do you want your customers to think about your brand?), pricing it so that it's profitable yet seen as valuable (how high a price can you command for your brand?), building distributor relationships to make the market offering available (where do customers go to find your brand?), and communicating all of this to the customer through an array of promotional activities (what do you say about your brand?). In other words, positioning involves all the marketing mix variables. This chapter kicks off the rest of the book. We'll discuss the concept of positioning in this chapter, and we'll see the details of the marketing mix activities in the chapters that follow.

We begin with discussing the concept of positioning via perceptual maps. We then see the positioning matrix, which will help structure how to think about the marketing mix 4Ps variables in subsequent chapters. We close with guidelines for writing a positioning statement.

5-1a **Positioning via Perceptual Maps**

They say a picture is worth a megabyte of words. Marketers and senior managers like to see graphical depictions of where their brands are, and where their competitors are, in the minds of their customers. These pictures help us envision how customers think about our brand and give us initial answers to many questions: What are our strengths and weaknesses? What are those of our competitors? Even though we think of certain companies and brands as our competitors, do customers view it the same way? What is our position in the market space? Who do they think are our closest substitutes for the benefits they seek when they're buying in this product category? Perceptual maps provide these pictures (see Chapter 15 for details regarding their construction).

Figure 5.1 depicts a perceptual map of hybrid car models. Brands depicted as points in the map close together are those perceived as similar (e.g., Lexus and Lincoln), whereas brands farther apart are seen as more different (e.g., Prius and Telsa). The north-south, east-west directions are perceptual, and in this map may be interpreted as the quality of the car and the relative expense.

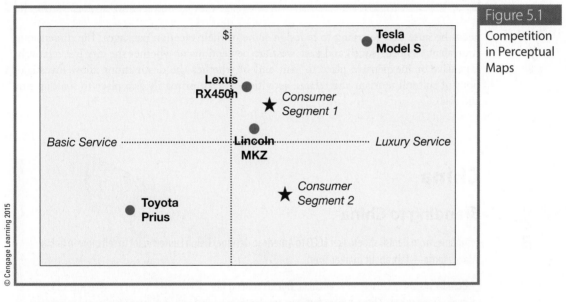

© Cengage Learning 2015

Figure 5.1

Competition in Perceptual Maps

The brand managers and corporate headquarters of all of these firms would probably not be surprised by these results, in that they indicate customers view Lexus and Lincoln as most interchangeable, at least among this set of brands. In comparison, the Tesla and Prius are not competing with each other. We also see information on customer segments. Customer segment 1 is situated near Lexus and Lincoln, and these models would predict that one of these two cars would be the segment's first choice. The segment might not be loyal to Lexus over Lincoln, or vice versa, but either is preferred over the Telsa or Prius.

Customer segment 2 is at the lower right, where there are few brands. Holes in perceptual maps offer intriguing possibilities for new market opportunities. In this particular case, we might not wish to pursue the opportunity; these customers seek luxury at inexpensive prices. A car company might not find this position profitable or the image desirable (it's hard to be convincing that one provides luxury at base prices).

Figure 5.2 is a perceptual map of cities in which a large, global hotel company has resorts. This map conveys perceptions, not geography, so the cities are not aligned north-south and east-west, as they are IRL. The company wants to know more about its customers' travel

Figure 5.2

Positioning via Percep-tual Maps

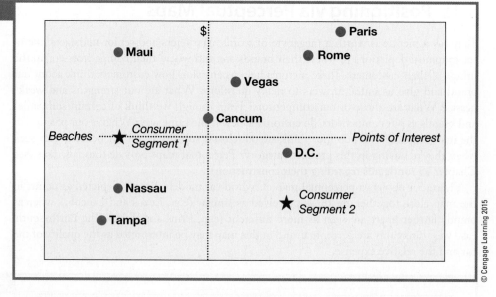

needs because they're trying to redesign some of their vacation packages. The dimensions equivalent to north-south and east-west are perceptions of whether the city is a relatively expensive or inexpensive place to visit and of whether the destinations allow investigations of cultural tourism and related activities or serve primarily as a place to soak up sun and relax.

China

Branding *to* China

Companies from Danish shoemaker ECCO to American designer Ralph Lauren want to sell more in China. (Makes sense—talk about market size!)

- Branding is still relatively new to China. Brands coming from China tend to carry the stigma of low quality (and cheap). Chinese manufacturers are also learning that they can charge higher prices if their brands were viewed as higher quality. Hence, many companies are trying to reposition their brands.
- Brands that have been sold primarily through Hong Kong are reaching out in branding (to compete with Prada and Armani) and distribution (more retail in Shanghai and Beijing).
- Coors nearly doubled their sales volume when they looked at a positioning map and found two markets without existing competitors in premium beers: Kunming and Lhasa.
- Ikea tried to enter China as a high-end brand, but sales took off when they modified their positioning to emphasize their contemporary and popular designs and their affordability.
- With a growing middle-class, aspiration brands are thriving in China. GM's Buicks are selling like crazy. The cars symbolize the drivers as having achieved a better, richer life, co-opting the American dream and happiness. GM succeeded in part by changing their model names, from Regal to the Chinese for A King's Might and from LaCross to A King's Advancement.
- KFC noted the popularity of chicken as a cuisine among Chinese and embraced a new tagline: "The U.S. Fried Chicken Expert."

Consumed in China

You've heard of "Made in China," but how about this: China is the #1 consumer of bikes and motorcycles, shoes, cars, cell phones, and luxury goods and the #2 consumer o home appliances, consumer electronics, jewelry, and Web time.

Branding *from* China

China's self-pride is growing with its global importance, so they are beginning to build brands:

- They want to export their Chery cars and their Haier refrigerators.
- They're creating Chinese-centric social media: Youku.com is their YouTube, Dangdang is like Amazon, RenRen is like Facebook, Jyayuan.com is a dating site.
- They're reaching out globally and branding their country as the "World's Safest Tourist Destination."
- And, finally, to enhance brand equity and positive brand associations, they're trying to be socially responsible in bringing telecom to rural villages, cutting energy use in vehicles, building foundations for orphans, etc.

This perceptual map tells us about the positioning of these cities vis-à-vis the dimensions of expense and activity. Paris and Rome are seen as places with lots to see and do, but they're relatively expensive. Nassau and Tampa are perceived as beach trips that are relatively affordable.

Given that these maps capture perceptions, one question in the mind of a marketer is always, "Is my brand optimally positioned?" or even, "Is my intended position the one that customers perceive?" For example, this hotel company had spent a lot of money on an advertising campaign trying to make potential travelers aware of the many cultural offerings of Nassau. That is, the company was trying to move the Nassau position farther to the right. It doesn't look like they were very persuasive.

The map also identifies two customer segments. This survey was conducted on the company's typical traveler, and the sample was obtained from visitors to all of its hotels. That is, the perceptions are those of their current customers, not of their potential customers, who might belong to a different segment. The hotel is known for being reasonable in its rates, and so it tends to attract younger crowds who don't have quite the deep pockets of older travelers. As you might imagine, the hotel likes that it has a youthful appeal (or position) but realizes that it's somewhat unfortunate that it's also drawing people with less money. Probably older, wealthier travelers would agree that Paris is more expensive than Tampa, but they could afford it and would travel there nevertheless. Their repositioning might also consider an ad campaign that emphasized the hotel's reasonable rates even in destinations known to be more expensive.

The customer segments on the perceptual map offer another diagnostic to the company about what's going on in the marketplace. The first customer segment is very well served; they are looking for beaches and cheap trips, and the company has hotels in both Nassau and Tampa to cater to those tourists. The second customer segment, however, is seeking more to do on their holiday, yet still hoping for reasonable rates. The company has less to offer them, although perhaps they can play up Washington, D.C.

Figure 5.3 offers a different kind of perceptual map. It contains descriptors for a single-service provider, a health club. Patrons have rated the gym on a number of qualities: the

Figure 5.3

Perceptual
Map:
Strengths and
Weaknesses
of Gym 1

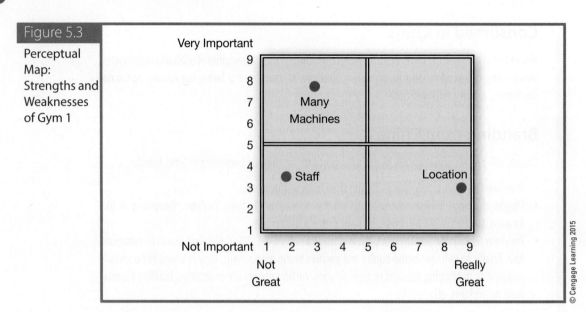

convenience of the location, the variety of the machines it offers and particularly whether there are enough new machines so that there's never a long wait, and finally whether the staff is helpful, friendly, and trained to give good workout instructions. Customers have also given their judgments on the importance of each of the qualities when choosing a gym.

The figure tells us that the gym is conveniently located, but people don't seem to care about that attribute. The staff isn't great, but luckily that doesn't matter much. More problematic is that the number of machines isn't huge, and that's an important quality.

This type of perceptual map may be modified for a competitive analysis, as in Figure 5.4. This figure allows us to determine the perceived strengths and weaknesses of our gym (gym 1), compared with our competition (gyms 2 and 3). This map is not great news. Gym 1 is relatively expensive or at least no better than gym 3, whereas gym 2 provides better value. Then, on the attribute of machines, we're dominated by both of our competitors. Something's got to give, unless customers value some other attribute in which we excel and that's not represented in this plot.

Part of the problem with the plot in Figure 5.4 is that we can look at only two attributes at a time, so we'd have to look at many plots. Figure 5.5 doesn't look like a map per se, but it's definitely still expressing the competitors' profiles of perceptual data. Here, more attributes may be presented with these three (or more) gyms for comparative purposes.

5-1b The Positioning Matrix

Just as consumers are quite demanding, wanting the very best of everything (fast car, good mileage, great looks, and, oh by the way, also low prices), companies can be equally irrational. Most companies offer mission statements on their websites or in their annual reports that say they are the very best at everything, their customers are their sole reason for existence, they care about their employees who are the very best in the workforce, and all that. Well, customers can't have it all, and companies can't be great at everything.

So the question is what do you want your position in the marketplace to be? The coolest brand? The brand that offers the best value? Either of these goals is achievable. But both at the same time are probably not. Let's look at the marketing 4Ps and see what makes sense.

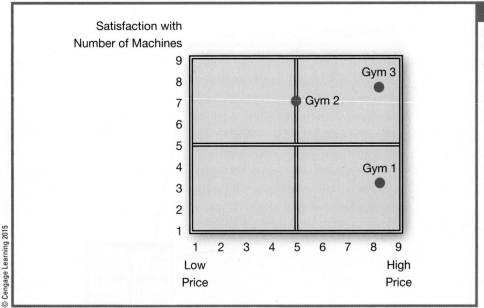

Figure 5.4

Perceptual
Map:
Competition

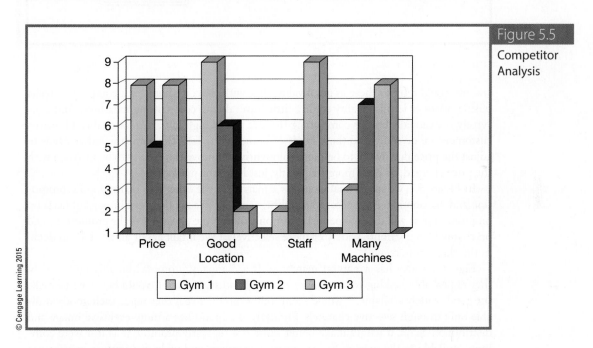

Figure 5.5

Competitor
Analysis

© Cengage Learning 2015

© Cengage Learning 2015

In Figure 5.6, we see the juxtaposition of two marketing Ps, product and price. As a warning, we're going to make some simplifying assumptions for a while. First, let's say that we could choose a low vs. a high pricing strategy. That's already a simplification, allowing no shades of gradation in between. Let's also say that the product may be characterized as low vs. high quality, again with no compromise intermediate brand and no specific attributes of the product represented, just general quality levels.

In the basic 2×2 matrix in Figure 5.6, we can see already that a match of low-low and high-high—that is, low- or modest-quality stuff but cheap vs. high-quality stuff at a higher price—makes sense. Occasionally brands come along that offer high quality at low prices,

Figure 5.6

Marketing
Management
Framework
Product
Quality by
Price

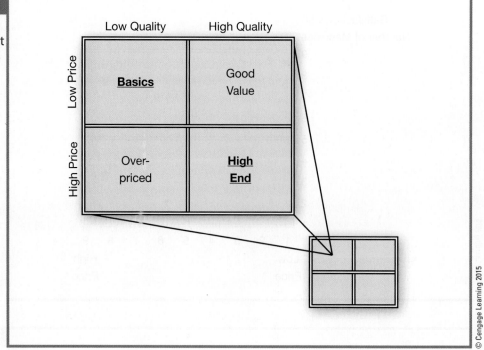

and we would refer to these as good values, but with time, it's hard for a company to resist raising prices or letting quality settle a little lower due to cost-cutting measures. And conversely, occasionally brands come along that are priced high but are poor quality. However, customers are no fools, and these kinds of brands don't last. The company either needs to adjust the price downward to be more competitive, improve the quality to be in synch with the price charged, or, even more frequently, just leave the marketplace.

In Figure 5.7, we see an analogous 2 × 2 matrix for the other two marketing Ps, promotion and distribution. Here too, to keep things simple, let's say the most important decision on promotion is whether to spend a lot or only a little (i.e., heavy vs. light promotion) and on channels to distribute widely or more selectively. (We'll talk about all these Ps in detail in the chapters to come.)

Figure 5.7 also has a natural matching. If a company promotes broadly and heavily, they're probably looking to move a lot of merchandise, and so it would be smart to make the goods widely available. It would seem counterproductive if they made their goods available only through selective channels. Similarly, if a brand has a more exclusive image and distribution chain, it would make better sense not to overly promote it as if it were common, available to the masses. So the heavy promotions and wide distribution pairing and the lighter promotions and exclusive distribution pairing make more sense than the other options.

In Figure 5.8, we have all 16 combinations of our 4 Ps. At this point, we can acknowledge that, sure, theoretically any combination is possible. You could provide high quality in exclusive channels and promote lightly and still charge cheap rates, but why would you? S, let's see if some other combinations are more or less sensible.

Figure 5.9 suggests eliminating the low-price and exclusive-distribution combinations. Presumably, if a brand is priced low, the company needs to sell a lot of volume to make money. This characterization is an assumption, of course, because the company really needs

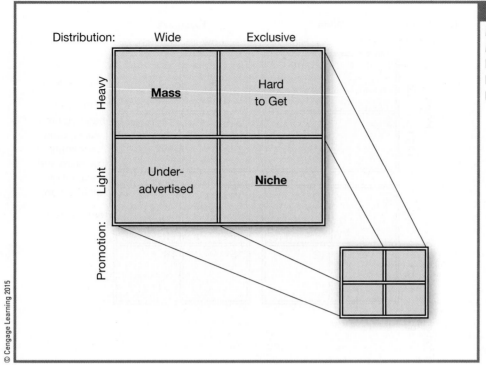

© Cengage Learning 2015

Figure 5.7

Marketing Management Framework Promotion by Distribution

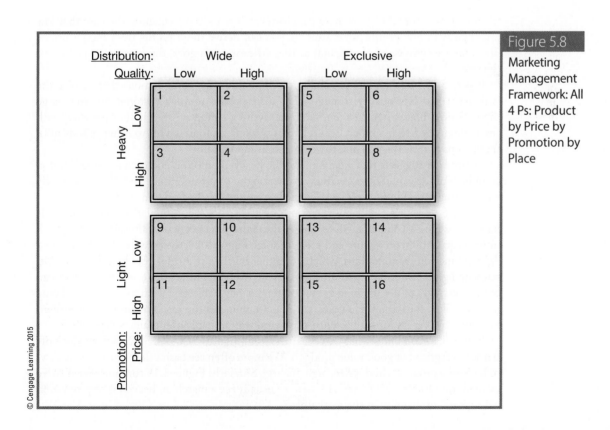

© Cengage Learning 2015

Figure 5.8

Marketing Management Framework: All 4 Ps: Product by Price by Promotion by Place

Figure 5.9

Some Strategies Don't Make Sense

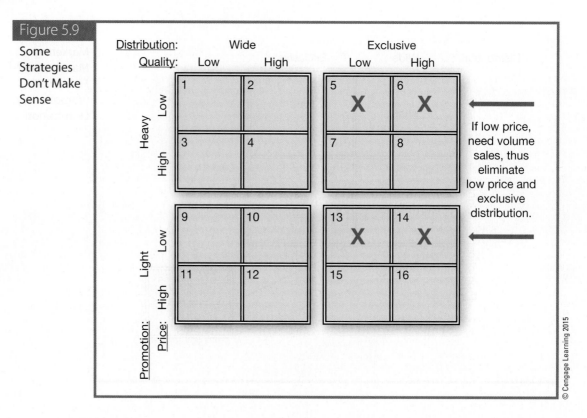

If low price, need volume sales, thus eliminate low price and exclusive distribution.

© Cengage Learning 2015

to look at the profitability, or margins. However, it is indeed frequently the case that low prices go with low profitability; after all, you can derive more profits from higher prices. There are exceptions, of course, but, as the old expression goes, the exceptions just prove the rule.

Figure 5.10 indicates the possibility of eliminating the combinations that involve the high-price and low-quality strategies. It's disrespectful to your customer to overcharge them. For example, when *Consumer Reports* says of a laptop as "stylish but expensive" with "undistinguished tech support and reliability," won't customers veer to other brands until that company feels the pressure to get its prices more in line?

Figure 5.11 suggests that we eliminate the heavy-promotion and exclusive-distribution combinations. It would be exceedingly frustrating to a customer to be tantalized constantly with messages to "Go buy our stuff!" and then not be able to find that stuff.

Figure 5.12 shows the good value purchases—high quality at relatively low prices—is hard to sustain. A company will be tempted to raise prices or let quality slip, settling back into an equilibrium on quality and price. Similar, Figure 5.13, shows wide-distribution and light-promotion combinations, which are rather inactive strategies. The brand is available, but with light promotion, the company is paying the brand little attention. This strategy can be characteristic of mature brands that customers buy habitually, such as a cash cow being merely milked for money. However, with no attention by the marketer and no investment to assure the brand's future existence, the brand will probably eventually collapse.

Figure 5.14 combines what we've learned from Figures 5.10 and 5.12: that we don't often see overpriced or good value products. We more often see basics (low price, low quality) or high-end products (high price, high quality). Similarly, Figure 5.15 combines what we've learned from Figures 5.11 and 5.13: that we usually see a match on heaviness of promotion with greater availability in the marketplace.

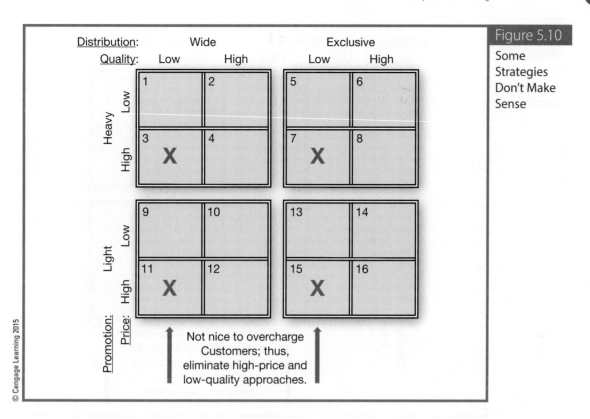

Figure 5.10

Some
Strategies
Don't Make
Sense

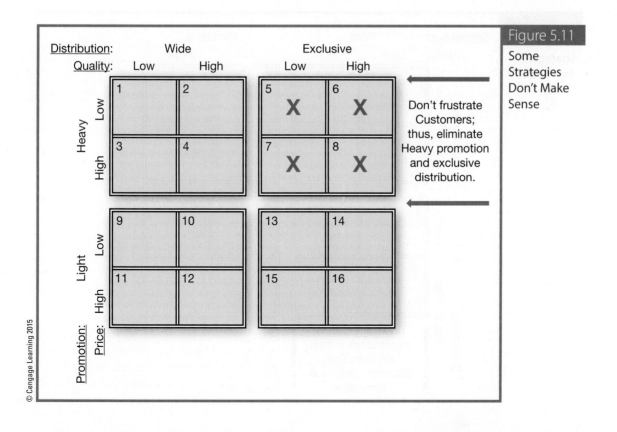

Figure 5.11

Some
Strategies
Don't Make
Sense

Figure 5.12

Some
Strategies
Are Hard to
Sustain

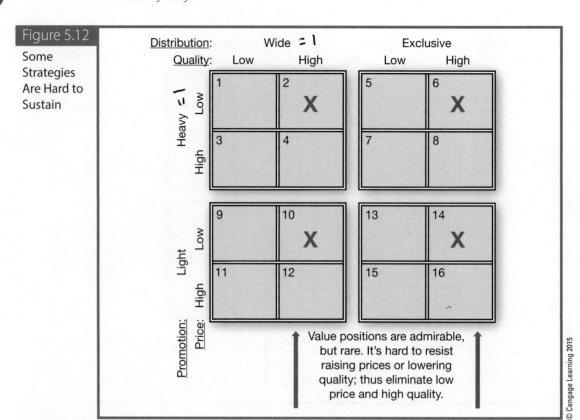

Value positions are admirable,
but rare. It's hard to resist
raising prices or lowering
quality; thus eliminate low
price and high quality.

© Cengage Learning 2015

Figure 5.13

Some
Strategies
Are Hard to
Sustain

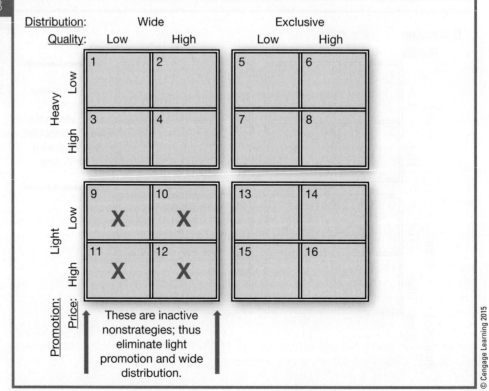

These are inactive
nonstrategies; thus
eliminate light
promotion and wide
distribution.

© Cengage Learning 2015

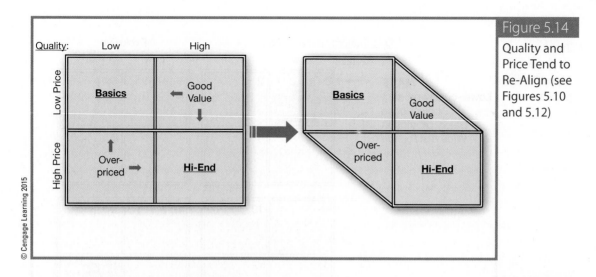

Figure 5.14

Quality and Price Tend to Re-Align (see Figures 5.10 and 5.12)

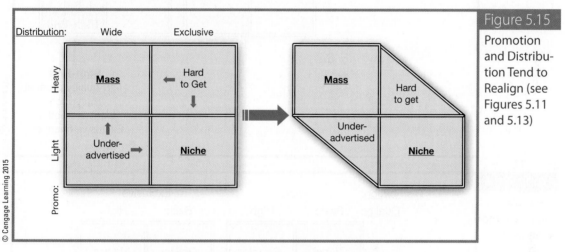

Figure 5.15

Promotion and Distribution Tend to Realign (see Figures 5.11 and 5.13)

At this point, even though we began with 16 combinations, we've simplified this positioning matrix to essentially the two strategies depicted in Figure 5.16:

1. Low price, low quality, widely available, heavy promotions.
2. High price, high quality, exclusive availability, light promotions.

The advantage of these simplifying assumptions is that the two extremes give us very clear goals to work toward. We can either position our brand as low price, low quality, etc., or we want to achieve high quality and charge high prices, etc. If we have reason to modify one of the Ps, say, go with low price, low quality, widely available, but we want to lighten up on promotions, then that is our strategic and tactical choice. It might not be wise, but we can try it. But these two extremes clarify the goals of a brand's position in the marketplace and can help us align the many decisions that need to be made, all the way from product design to channel choice for deliver to the marketplace.

In Figure 5.17, we see Target and Mayo displayed in the extreme upper-left and lower-right cells; these combinations are optimal and the most common (many brands may be classified here). Nevertheless, let's back up and briefly acknowledge that, while we've been making simplifying generalizations (ones that hold up frequently in the

Figure 5.16

Two
Strategies
Make Perfect
Sense

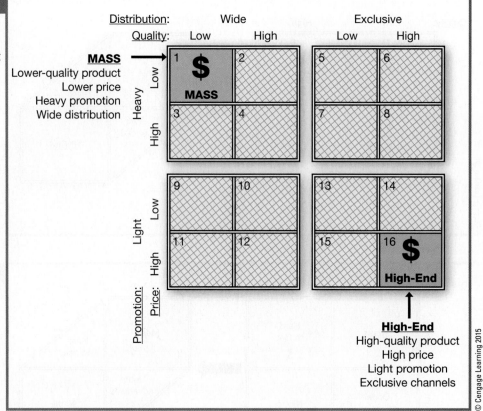

MASS
Lower-quality product
Lower price
Heavy promotion
Wide distribution

High-End
High-quality product
High price
Light promotion
Exclusive channels

© Cengage Learning 2015

Figure 5.17

Example
Brands in the
Framework

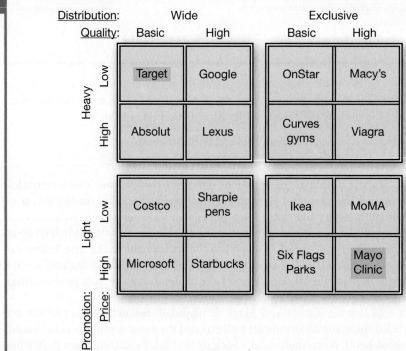

© Cengage Learning 2015

real world), there can be exceptions. That is, some brands appear in all the other subop-timal combinations. We might question how long a company or brand can sustain in a suboptimal position, but at any given point in time, market offerings could be spanning the matrix.

Note that the positioning matrix is consistent with many management strategy gurus who observe common themes underlying market leaders. For example, Michael Treacy and Fred Wiersema, in *The Discipline of Market Leaders*, describe three basic corporate strate-gies to creating value and achieving market stature: (1) operational excellence (i.e., these companies are good at production and delivery and at price and convenience, such as Dell, Southwest Airlines, Walmart and Costco);, (2) product leadership (i.e., these companies pride themselves on quality and innovation, such as Johnson & Johnson and Son;, and (3) customer intimacy (i.e., companies willing to tailor their products to their particular customer needs, which can be expensive but is expected to pay off in long-term loyalty and enhanced customer life time value, such as Nordstrom, Home Depot, or Amazon). In the matrix, operations and products would map roughly onto the low-cost and high-quality cells, respectively. Customer intimacy is simply good service, so we could classify that in the high-quality cell as well.

Similarly, Michael Porter, in his book on *Competitive Strategy*, discusses generic strate-gies driven by keeping costs down and prices competitive, leading by differentiation (e.g., excellence in quality or innovation), or, when appropriate, by niche positioning. The latter is merely a matter of exclusivity and size, and the first two again can be mapped onto our low-price vs. high-quality basic combinations.

Thus, the assumptions we made in the positioning matrix are not unduly restrictive, and the matrix provides a useful focus when making decisions in many marketing scenarios: Very simply, do we go basic (low price, low quality, wide availability, and heavy promotion), or do we go upscale (higher price, high quality, exclusive availability, and lighter promo-tion)? You can move off these two extreme positions in the matrix, but you better have a reason. Is that what your customers want? Can you make money there?

5-1c Writing a Positioning Statement

Once a company has decided on its positioning, either for the corporation as a whole or for one of its brands, it must be able to communicate succinctly the parameters of that position to a number of different audiences (to customers, employees, shareholders, general public, etc.). A positioning statement is that communication, and it takes a pretty standard form.

Just as marketing itself begins with the segmentation part of STP, a positioning state-ment also includes the specification of the target segment(s). As we have tried to illustrate in the chapter on segmentation, you don't want to strive to be all things to all people. So your positioning statement should address your target segment. Anything else you say in the positioning statement will have no meaning to customers who are not in that segment. As an example, in consider the positioning statement, "We at Alphatronics are the gym for the serious body builder." The target segment is the serious body builder, presumably implying that the weekend weightlifter or the soccer mom need not apply. Indeed, the customers not in the target will probably be intimidated because the positioning statement implies a collection of steroid-pumped dudes. You wouldn't want to compete with or hang out with them.

The next element of a positioning statement is what has been called the unique sell-ing proposition (USP). The idea is to express your brand's competitive advantage clearly and succinctly. The USP concept captures two things: First, what is the product category (the SP), and second, how does your market offering dominate these other providers (the U). Why should a customer buy from you and not one of your competitors? How are you better?

If you cannot answer this question, much less put it into a positioning statement, either your position is not clear, or your product has little differentiation. There is no excuse for this situation, given that your position can be based on real attribute differences or perceived differences driven by images you've built. If you don't have real differences and cannot see a way to create them, then create an image-based difference.

It's also important that these statements should be succinct. A simple statement facilitates communication and an understanding in the marketplace. Thus, while you might think your brand excels on many attributes, try to think of a word that captures all their essence and use that word. Or make a list of your brand's benefits and prioritize them. Then take the most important, most compelling difference and make that the difference you insert into the positioning statement. You can cycle through the other qualities in some of your communications, but they should all be consistent with the basic message in the positioning statement itself. This goal is more easily achieved if we can abstract from the level of the brand's attributes to the more general intangible benefits to the customer. All we have to do is ask why would a customer care?

The Alphatronics positioning statement compares itself directly to other gyms, so gyms comprise the product category or the competitive frame. However, its point of differentiation is implied more than stated explicitly. For example, the "-tronics" part of the gym's name suggests the presence of high-tech gym equipment.

So a positioning statement captures the qualities of how you wish to be perceived. To compose a positioning statement, answer the following questions:

1. Who are you trying to persuade? (Who is your target segment?)
2. Who are you competing with? (Who are your competitors? What is your major product category? What frame of reference will customers use in making choices?)
3. How are you better? (What is your uniqueness, your competitive advantage, your point of difference? Do you have any attribute or benefit that dominates competitors?)

Put these elements together, and the result is your positioning statement:

For customers who want … [segment], *our brand* is the best at … [unique selling proposition—competitors and competitive advantage].

Some positioning statements are a bit surprising. For example, Volvo is known for safety, yet at Volvo.com you'll see: "We offer transport solutions to demanding customers around the world." Perhaps Volvo's dominance on safety is so well-known that the benefit doesn't need stating.

Some positioning statements are straightforward, such as FedEx's "Dependable Solutions for Your Shipping Needs," YouTube's "Broadcast Yourself," and Club Med's "Where Happiness Means the World." Others are abstract and inspiring, such as Honda's, "The Power of Dreams," Apple's "Think Different(ly)." Other elements may be only implied, e.g., Volkswagen's, long running advertising tag line, "Drivers Wanted," states the target segment clearly and reflects their position by implying the competitive frame and its superior position within the category.

Finally, brand positions can also evolve. For example, consider the positioning statement, "Zipcar car-sharing is for urban-dwelling, techie consumers, who want to save money instead of owning a car." The target customers are urban techies, the competition is car ownership, and the superior advantage is saving money. Zipcar could modify that positioning. Instead of emphasizing saving money, it might try to appeal to the green-sensitive consumer, e.g., "Zipcar car-sharing is for urban-dwelling, techie consumers, who wish to demonstrate their commitment to protecting the environment for future generations."

The positioning statement serves as an internal memorandum keeping all managers aligned as a basic guiding principle in all their collective decisions, so as to enhance the likelihood of consistencies in the results of those decisions. Positioning statements also serve as the foundation of the communications offered to external audiences, including customers, shareholders, and the like as advertising tag lines or more extensive messages. Given these audiences, positioning statements should be succinct, to communicate efficiently, and positive and passionate, to be noteworthy and to spur attention and affection.

Green

An important manifestation of corporate responsibility is today's heightened environmental sensibilities. Companies are seeking to recreate and reposition their brands so as to be greener and to communicate to consumers about their greenness, hoping to win over customers for their efforts. For example, Clorox's Green Works line is positioned as "clean cleaning products," products that are effective at cleaning and are also environmentally safe. Similarly, Nike's Considered brand is a line that continues the company's usual emphasis on athletics but adds the attributes that the shoes are created with components and in a manner that are environmentally friendly. As a result, the shoes have two major benefits, and Nike can highlight the athletic aspect to one segment and the green aspect to another.

One of the benefits frequently copromoted with a green brand is some kind of price savings to the consumer. For example, compact fluorescent light (CFL) bulbs are energy efficient, and they last longer, so they can be promoted as saving the consumer money. Multiple benefits allow a brand to appeal to more than one customer segment. Similarly, hybrid cars are good for the environment because they require fewer fillups at the gas station, which, of course, in turn also implies that they will save the consumer money. Hybrid cars can reach still more segments by highlighting other resulting features, such as a quieter ride or the social status of a caring driver.

Yet if the green product is going to save the consumer money or result in less purchase turnover, the question arises as to how the company will make the product profitable. As the wise philosopher Kermit warned us, "It isn't easy being green." Companies may well know that a green path is a way to win the hearts and minds of many customers, and they may well desire to create sustainable products and business practices for their own sakes. But they are struggling to find solutions that provide quality and value to the consumer, environmental friendliness, and all that with strong economic performance. For example, Timberland incorporates recycled rubber into its shoes' soles. Yet the product life cycle of a shoe is relatively short, so it is a challenge to the company to create products that are less harmful to the environment and low cost so that they may produce revenue.

That tension is not uncommon. Many companies and marketers have sought to please customers with green products and efforts toward environmental friendliness. They develop new product concepts that sound appealing to customers in the early stages of concept testing. Given such encouragement, products are developed, and they often fare well in product testing with customers as well. Unfortunately, in later phases of new product development, the company must turn to practical questions of feasibility, and the determination of price points that will enable the sales of the new product to be profitable. At this point, the pragmatics may prove overwhelmingly challenging or the profitability goals may necessitate a price point so high as to be problematic.

If marketers can position green brands as having attributes that are important, there is no reason for not actually charging a premium for their very green-ness. For example, organic produce is said to be comprised of crops raised in environmentally friendly ways that also imply safety for the consumer, with the ingestion of less unnatural elements, and the ultimate result of better taste. Not coincidentally, organic produce usually commands higher prices. The question is then how does the laundry detergent manufacturer, tire manufacturer, etc. express such a premium quality so as to exact a higher price as well.

Consumer tolerance of price points is likely tied to age cohorts. The 1970s broke a lot of green ground, with the founding of the EPA, the passing of various clean air and water acts, endangered species movements, and so forth. Just as people born since, say, 1990 take the Internet for granted, so do those born just thereafter fully insist that corporations behave in socially responsible manners and expect products to be environmentally friendly and sustainable. In other words, it will be more challenging to impress younger people with efforts to go green.

Finally, two sets of green fun facts: (1) A Natural Marketing Institute survey showed that more than 50% of consumers say they regularly turn off lights when they leave a room, turn off electronics when they're not in use, conserve water, recycle plastic bottles and jars, and recycle paper. Car pooling and public transportation did not fare as well (approximately 20% of consumers engage in these activities). (2) Green management gurus point out that there are many ways to achieve green-ness, including sustainable harvesting and mining, recycled components, source reduction, organic growers, fair trade, reducing toxicity, using local growers, energy and fuel efficiencies, water efficiencies, reusability, and safe disposal.

For more information on green marketing, and management, see Dahlstrom's *Green Marketing Management* or Ottman's *The New Rules of Green Marketing*.

Managerial Recap

Positioning is central to the marketing manager's activities:

- Seen through the eyes of the customer, perceptual maps facilitate an understanding of a company's or brand's position in the marketplace.
- Positioning is achieved via a manipulation of the marketing mix 4Ps, and the positioning matrix demonstrates that certain combinations make more sense than others.
- Positioning statements help guide marketing strategies and tactical actions. They include an indication of the target segment, a competitive frame of reference, and a competitive advantage or the brand's unique selling proposition.

Chapter Outline in Key Terms and Concepts

1. What is positioning, and why is it probably the most important aspect of marketing?

    a. Positioning via perceptual maps

    b. The positioning matrix

2. Writing a positioning statement

Chapter Discussion Questions

1. If you were to create a perceptual map for the product category of watches, what attributes should you include to illustrate both the similarities and differences among the brands?

2. Find a company that is struggling. Where is it in the positioning matrix? Could the company be more successful if it changed any of its Ps (e.g., to head to the low-low-low-low or high-high-high-high cells)?

3. Write a position statement for yourself to convince your favorite company to hire you.

Mini-Case

Positioning Health Care

Hospital Well-Health is located in a Northeastern city in the U.S. It has an excellent reputation. It rarely advertises, even locally. Its outcomes are thought to be superior to others in the area, but it is privately owned and highly selective in the statistics it releases.

The hospital is very particular about which insurance plans it will accept, having been burned by payment-related lawsuits once or twice in the past. A result of this policy is that many of its patients pay cash. At the same time, given the hospital's reputation, most of their departments, procedures, and docs have long backlogs of patients waiting to be served.

Across the river is the health care group MarksHealth. They try to appeal to the people, treating their patients as customers, a label the health care sector has been reluctant to use. They are known for vigorously using the retail-pharmacy sector. They reasoned that 80% of the cases they see are for rather simple conditions that can be treated by people with basic medical training and certification. In their early experimentation, they were blown away with the positive responses of the patients they treated due to the convenience of being attended to in the patient's own community at a local drugstore. These patient-customers also loved to be able to pop in as walk-ins without worrying about making appointments. Insurance covered none of the visit or service, but it did cover the usual amount on prescriptions (which were filled while the patient-customers paid to leave).

These health care providers come to their patients with very different philosophies. On the surface, they appear to have little in common, other than their sector. Yet their competitiveness is intense, with the MarksHealth group calling referring to Well-Health as Wealth for short. Well-Health is not above the fray; they respond that MarksHealth is really MarxistHealth.

Mini-Case Discussion Questions

1. Characterize these companies' positions in the marketplace based on your best estimates as to the customers' perceptions. In which cell does each exist in the positioning matrix?

2. Why do the hospital and health care group see each other as such threats?

3. What could Well-Health change to make its business (profitability) even stronger? What could it change to differentiate itself more from MarksHealth? Now take the opposite point of view: What could MarksHealth do to enhance its business and to further distinguish itself from the hospital?

Video Exercise: *Numi Organic Tea* (6:50)

Consumers frequently become acquainted with Numi's organic teas through sampling promotions in upscale venues or in partnership with other companies that are promoting organic and fair-trade products. Numi's product line is positioned in the marketplace as a premium-tasting, premium-quality tea that uses premium ingredients. Because Numi's raw ingredients are more expensive than those used by many of its competitors, the Numi product line is not positioned as loss leader or as a commodity tea. Rather, Numi is positioned as an upscale product appealing to customers of natural and health food stores, fine dining restaurants and hotels, universities, and coffee shops. There has been surprising growth in the mass marketing of the Numi products in the United States at grocery stores and club stores and on websites. Customers in the mass market are attracted by the high-quality, organic, sustainable product line that Numi provides. This mass market distribution can create conflicts in positioning the brand as an upscale product. According to Numi's managers, the key to dealing with this conflict lies in knowing who the company's customers are and where they are shopping.

Video Discussion Questions

1. Describe Numi's product line in terms of the four Ps of marketing: product, price, place, and promotion.

2. Incorporating product, price, place, and promotion into the strategic marketing management framework, describe the strategic positioning of Numi's product line.

3. Does this strategic positioning make good marketing management sense? Explain your answer.

Chapter 6
Products: Goods and Services

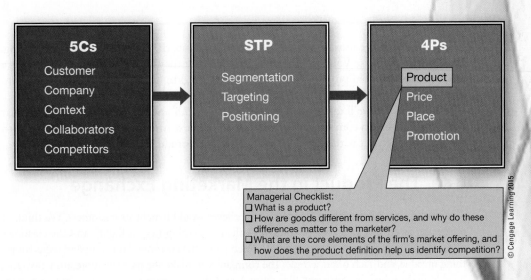

5Cs	STP	4Ps
Customer	Segmentation	Product
Company	Targeting	Price
Context	Positioning	Place
Collaborators		Promotion
Competitors		

Managerial Checklist:
❏ What is a product?
❏ How are goods different from services, and why do these differences matter to the marketer?
❏ What are the core elements of the firm's market offering, and how does the product definition help us identify competition?

© Cengage Learning 2015

Marketing Management Framework

6-1 WHAT DO WE MEAN BY PRODUCT?

A "*product*" is the general term we'll use for both goods (e.g., skis) and services (e.g., ski lessons). We'll talk about how these classes of purchases differ and build on the differences when necessary, but remember that, in either case, the fundamental objectives of marketing are the same. Marketing managers want to understand and please their customers whether they're the brand manager for NordicTrack machines or for the clubs they're in, like LA-Fitness.

Sometimes the term "*product*" is also used more generally to refer to the full product profile, that is, the entire market offering, including the product along with its price, the image of the brand, etc. We discuss product, price, place, promotion separately because each element has so many details to consider. But the execution of the 4Ps is integral; each piece needs to send a consistent message for the overall product to be attractive to the customer.

What Does *"Product"* Mean?

The word *"product"* is:

- A broad term that refers to goods (e.g., "C'mon down to meet us at Jack's dealership, where we sell only the best product!").
- A general term that includes services (e.g., "Here at Phalanges Crossed, we sell only safe financial investment products!").
- Captured by one of the 4Ps (product, price, place, promo).
- Sometimes a reference to multiple entities (e.g., a product line).
- A term that can be used to refer to the entire a portfolio of 4Ps (e.g., the product that BMW sells is the car, but "product" also implies price, dealership service, and promotion and image—all wrapped up shorthand by saying the "BMW product.").
- Part of the customer-company exchange.
- A mathematical term for multiplication.
- Yes, all of the above!

The product is the most central of the 4Ps, the ultimate thing the customer is purchasing. Drivers who purchase Volvos are buying safety, yes, but they're buying a safe car. Safety is a modifier; the essential product is the car. Volvo worked to create good product features to distinguish the product into a brand that's become *sine qua non* for safety.

In this chapter, we'll distinguish the qualities of goods and services, acknowledging that most purchases are a combination of the two. In the next two chapters, we'll continue with the P of product, but with a focus on brands and new products.

6-1a The Product in the Marketing Exchange

The product is something that the company believes would benefit its customers. We think of marketing as an exchange, so the company offers something (e.g., a flight), and the customer offers something in return (e.g., payment). Each party, the customer and company, seeks something of value, and each offers a trade. The company can make the package more attractive (e.g., reliable flight schedules, frequent flier points), and the customer can too (e.g., by being more loyal, purchasing more often, generating positive buzz to coworkers). Of course, the company can also make the package less attractive, intentionally or not (e.g., downsizing employees so that customer service suffers), and so can customers (e.g., by being high maintenance and demanding customized attention from a system designed for high-volume, quick, and standardized service).

Several questions arise in the marketing exchange. First, what do customers want? Some segments of customers will seek value and low prices, whereas others will seek premium quality. But what do "value" and "quality" mean for a particular product and industry? Still other customers seek specific attributes, sometimes quite idiosyncratic features and benefits. These questions about insights into customers' needs and wants are addressed through techniques of marketing research (Chapter 15).

The question from the other side of the exchange is what is the company well suited to offer to its customers? What will the company's value proposition be? Given the company's position in the marketplace (who they are) and the vision of what the company would like to evolve toward (who they'd like to be), is there an optimal, profitable intersection of what the company can do for the customer and what certain segments of customers would like?

It would be most desirable if the market provision had a clear point of differentiation because commodities cannot sustain as competitively advantageous. These issues are questions of corporate and marketing strategy (see Chapter 16).

Marketers have long realized the benefits of morphing short-term-oriented purchase-transaction exchanges into longer-term relationship marketing. This notion is reflected in such sayings as "It costs 6 times more to get a new customer compared to retaining a current customer." The repeated nature of a relational exchange begins with customer satisfaction and loyalty, and such interactions strengthen and come to fruition in customer relationship management (CRM) and in database marketing systems (discussed in Chapter 14). Marketers put together combinations of goods and services to try to strengthen those customer relationships.

6-2 HOW ARE GOODS DIFFERENT FROM SERVICES?

Some marketers make a big deal of the differences between goods and services, and others say, "Marketing is marketing"—that it's the same whether you're marketing pretzels or medical checkups. We're going to play it both ways; we'll emphasize the similarities to facilitate your learning However there are many tactical differences in the marketing of goods and services, and also some conceptual and strategic differences too. So throughout the book, wherever there are marketing implications, we'll consider how goods differ from services and why those differences matter to marketers.

6-2a Intangibility

Marketers have always talked about goods and services being on a continuum. As depicted in Figure 6.1, some products seem like so-called pure goods (e.g., socks, pet food), and some services seem like pure services (e.g., financial investing, opera). Other purchases seem like a mix of obtaining both a good and a service (e.g., car rentals). The key seems to be the extent to which the purchase is *tangible*. When you purchase clothing, you have

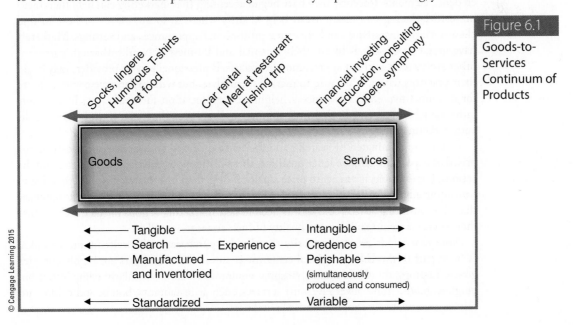

Figure 6.1

Goods-to-Services Continuum of Products

© Cengage Learning 2015

something concrete to take home from the store. When you go to a symphony, it's a fun time, and you might come home a changed person, but the changes aren't necessarily visible to someone else. Or with consulting, you're getting advice; consulting is largely intangible.

The symphony is an example of *experience marketing*, where the experience is the main part of the service. For example, themed retail outlets, such as Build-a-Bear, ESPN Zone, and Crayola Café, are as much about providing a shopping and playing experience as they are about moving merchandise. Cirque du Soleil promises not so much a circus and acrobatic performance as a one-of-a-kind-experience. MotorTrend.com offers car enthusiasts an opportunity to try out their favorite cars through virtual road tests and simulations. The user gets to see the performance of the car in action.

6-2b Search, Experience, Credence

The goods-to-services continuum is related to the concepts of search, experience, and credence. *Search* qualities are those attributes that may be evaluated prior to purchase, as the customer learns about the competitive offerings. For example, when you go to a department store to purchase socks, you can just look at a pair and know before buying them whether you'll like them. You can see the color, the price, the material they're made of, and you can imagine immediately what they'll feel like on your toes.

Experience attributes are those that need some trial or consumption before evaluation. So, if friends recommend a new restaurant, you might trust your friends and expect to like the restaurant, but it's not until you personally go there, experience the ambience and service, try the food, pay the bill, etc. that you can judge the purchase as satisfactory or not for yourself.

Finally, *credence* qualities are those that are difficult to judge even postconsumption, hence the term "*credence*." You just have to trust or believe that the quality is good. When you leave your psychotherapist's office, did the therapy improve you? Did that vasectomy work? Sometimes credence means we go beyond trust to sheer hope, e.g., we hope the mechanic fixed our car and didn't cause any new problems. This sentiment is captured perfectly when Charles Revlon says of his company, "In the factory we make cosmetics; in the store we sell hope."

Professional service providers (e.g., doctors, accountants, architects) are dominated by credence elements. Recently they have begun accepting that marketing can help their businesses. Marketing consultation can help identify where to locate offices or how to find clients. Marketing advice can help create professional appearances and settings. Marketers have urged professionals to tap their personal and business networks, through parties or other events such as client appreciation breakfasts. Professional service providers may begin their practices with a reluctance to market themselves, but with experience comes a desire for a competitive edge and hence a heightened appreciation for marketing. Increasingly professional schools (medical, dental, architectural) are providing courses in business skills and marketing.

Goods are dominated by search and experience qualities, and services are mostly comprised of experience and credence qualities. These distinctions drive some marketing implications. For example, it's easier to price a pair of socks than it is to attach a numeric value to consulting advice. And given that customers can more confidently assess the socks purchase than the consulting advice, consultants need to take marketing actions to cue the client that their advice is sound and that the quality of their service is excellent.

Note that goods aren't necessarily the simpler purchases and services more complex. A huge part of the U.S. and global economy is automobiles, and cars are highly complex goods. Laptops, durables, aircraft, hospital equipment—all are similarly complicated but tangible goods. And conversely, some services, such as restaurants, hotels, and credit card services, are relatively simple, standard purchases.

Sports

What's being sold and purchased in sports? What's the core? What're the value-addeds? Sports marketers identify that the game itself—the particular sport, the rules, the techniques, and the athletes and their equipment and apparel—are all part of the core. Some would say the venue is core, and perhaps it is indeed central or important. But the specifics of the core can change the fan experience; e.g., compare the fans at the ballpark or at a sports bar or watching on television at home or watching surreptitiously online at work.

The value-added elements in the sports industry are many: the tickets and programs obtained at the on-site venue, the luxury of a box if applicable, the music played on the field or floor, the mascot and cheerleaders dancing, and much more. The food is important if the customer is at the on-site venue, and the merchandise and memorabilia are important regardless of where the fan is consuming the sports event.

Fans usually hope that the core sports event is high quality, but not always, cf., the long-suffering Chicago Cubs fans. Indeed, sports marketers rue that even teams with deep enough pockets to hire the best athletes and coaches still cannot control the particulars of the events. They say that sports are the ultimate reality TV.

A further extension from the core is the licensing: clothing or other products that bear the brand name and logo of a collegiate or professional sports team. With such merchandise, the fans may continue to profess their beloved teams beyond the duration of the relatively brief sporting contest and, of course, even beyond the season. These products are not limited to the T-shirts and jerseys and caps of young fans; they include neckties in fan colors, e.g., Army's black and gold or Notre Dame's navy, green, and gold, allowing a subtle and sophisticated support of one's team even while acting professionally.

Just as the team names and colors are controlled, so are the athletes. Players' likenesses are more controlled than those of other public figures, perhaps because companies can make money on athletes, such as with trading cards, that could not be done as well for actors, singers, or politicians.

Sponsorship is a different kind of commercial agreement, with two companies or brands coming together, sometimes for only a brief partnership. The form of the sponsorship is highly varied, from an expensive television advertising spot during the Super Bowl, to a sticker affixed a car in Daytona or NASCAR, to a banner posted at a tennis game, to a soft drink being the exclusive sponsor of an NBA all-star game, to an entertainment channel offering sole coverage of Olympic games, etc.

All of these elements are value-addeds beyond the core of the game. As technology allows or as fans demand, more product and opportunities will be created wherever a team or a partner finds it profitable.

6-2c Perishability

Services differ from goods in other ways: Services are *simultaneously produced and consumed*. Whereas goods can be manufactured and then inventoried in distribution warehouses, most services have to be created on the spot in the presence of the customer. For example, you have to be present to have your haircut. This inseparability of production and consumption leads to the inevitable result that services tend to be more perishable. When an airplane leaves the ground with some seats vacant, the airliner cannot recoup those empty seats during rush traffic. Your time is inelastic in this manner too; if you're a tax consultant, the hours you spent twiddling your thumbs in August cannot be applied toward crunch time in early April. Perishability has consequences for the marketer to even out demand, a topic we'll consider in Chapter 9.

The inseparability of production and consumption also has consequences in the interaction between the service provider and the customer. For example, a cast rehearsing a Broadway play is offering roughly the same service during the rehearsal as when they performing during showtimes, but when the audience is present and able to respond with laughter or applause, the cast is more energized, and the adrenaline and pheromones in the theater make for a different experience. The nature of interactions varies with setting and societal norms, of course. An orchestra playing in the same auditorium would generally expect no laughter and applause only at appropriate breaks in the music; premature applause would be censured by frowns of other patrons at the offending novice. (The real world is more gray, of course. For example, while services tend to be more perishable than goods, certainly some goods are more perishable than others [e.g., bananas vs. Jet Skis]. Further, marketers can make goods more perishable when striving for other desired ends; e.g., just-in-time delivery systems comprise very little [if any] inventory, toward the goal of being responsive to customers' needs.)

6-2d Variability

The final major difference between goods and services is that services are said to be more *variable*. Manufacturers of goods can set quality standards like Motorola's 6σ (i.e., only 3 or 4 errors per million pieces produced) because a machine is producing their products. For a service provider, say a hairstylist, experiences vary across customers or even within a customer across time. Your friend might swear by this stylist, but you prefer classic styles and your friend's hair is always a little … edgy. Even with your own stylist, someone you typically like, some days you're in one mood or the other, or the stylist is. The heterogeneity across experiences is due in large part to the people component of services. The service marketing exchange happens between a customer and a service provider representing the company. The frontline rep and you have different and changing needs, abilities, etc., and the customer service interaction can be either fruitful or frustrating.

Self-service is advancing in many industries, such as banking, airport check-in, prescription renewals, and so forth. When customers interact with technology and machines, the

Goods and Services Are Mostly Different, and Yet …

Remember, goods and services lie along a continuum, and the distinction can be a little fuzzy. Some simpler services may resemble goods. For example, we call a variety of things financial services, and yet …

- A service is intangible, but you can hold your credit card.
- A service is inseparable production and consumption, but you don't need to be at your bank to access your checking account.
- A service is perishable, but you can use your credit card whenever you want.
- A service is variable, but there is standard, mass production of insurance policies, savings accounts, data systems for bond traders, etc. (fsmhandbook.com).

variability of the service encounter is reduced by the standardization of the equipment. It should be noted that, like cholesterol, there is good and bad variability. Bad variability involves errors in the system (e.g., poor customer service), and people in logistics and human resources and in marketing are concerned with its reduction. In contrast, good variability involves the customization and tailoring of the service delivery for the customer's unique needs, and, not surprisingly, it often enhances customer satisfaction. Automated services are usually introduced to reduce the errorful (bad) variability, and with time, as menus become more sophisticated and offer more options, it is conceivable that good variability may also be enhanced (at least for customers who can deal with the technology).

Perhaps the most pervasive and successful example of self-service is online shopping. Shopping at home when one cannot sleep at 3 a.m. is the ultimate in convenience. In addition, comparing information on prices and product attributes is easier online than IRL and made even easier with the AI of shopping bots. Furthermore, the advantages of the technology and standardization are clear: A website may occasionally crash, but it's seldom cranky. The online purchase is a mix of goods and services and of tangible and intangible.

6-2e To Infinity and Beyond Goods and Services

Intangibility, the search/experience/credence qualities, inseparability, and variability comprise the fundamental differences between goods and services. Throughout the book, we'll bring in each concept as appropriate when discussing marketing issues. There will be issues regarding advertising (e.g., portraying a realistic service encounter to set clear expectations), branding (e.g., communicating a consistent image in the face of the variability of the service encounter), pricing (e.g., for yield management), logistics (e.g., creating a clear flow process for the customer service), human resources (e.g., empowering the frontline employees to facilitate service recovery), etc.

It is helpful to think of goods and services along a continuum because many purchases have both elements, and the distinctions can be blurry. For example, Xerox sells copiers as well as customer service packages. Customers buy toothpaste and also hope it will make them more attractive.

6-3 WHAT IS THE FIRM'S CORE MARKET OFFERING?

Some marketers say that everything we buy has some element of a good and some element of a service—that perhaps only raw materials such as coal or wheat are examples of pure goods. Everything else, they say, has been processed, and that processing is value-added service. Thus, we can examine any business and consider what is the core vs. the value-added services. Distinguishing these elements also helps us identify our competition. For example, Figure 6.2 depicts a hotel for which the provision of sleeping quarters, cleanliness, and safety might be considered the core purchase. Those are the corporate fundamentals, the reason the hotel is in business, and they're the qualities that the company better get right. They're the basics of what customers expect. The value-added supplemental services are those on which the hotel might distinguish itself from other hotels. They might claim that their check-in processes are quicker and smoother, that their beds are fluffier, that they offer designer spa potions, and so forth.

When we discuss customer satisfaction (in Chapter 14), we'll see another distinction between the core and value-addeds. The core elements have come to be expected; they're a given. So if they're good, a company doesn't earn points in the eyes of the customer, and the customer won't rave to friends about how great the brand is. But if the core elements are

Figure 6.2

Core and
Value-Added
Offerings

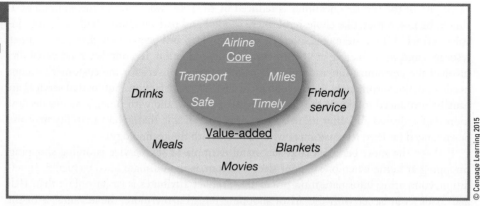

bad (e.g., the hotel room isn't clean), they can definitely trigger dissatisfaction. In contrast, a marketer can affect a customer's level of satisfaction (or dissatisfaction) through good (or bad) value-addeds (e.g., more luxurious amenities in the hotel room). Companies can compete on the value-addeds. For example, Starbucks is known for its service and combinatorial menu selection. Want just a regular coffee? Yeah, they do that too.

While the concepts of core and value-added seem straightforward, it's not as easy as it looks. Companies can make the mistake of being myopic when they define their core business, focusing on their product offerings (e.g., "We sell laptops"), instead of recognizing that their true goal is offering benefits and value to their customers (e.g., "We sell IT solutions"). When business is good, this myopia is not a problem. But as Internet sites increasingly offer software and storage, the particular configuration of the end user's machine becomes less important. If the company fixates on their laptops, instead of recognizing that the laptops are morphing into dumb terminals, they may be out of business soon. Had the company defined its business more broadly, it might have been on the frontier of developing software platforms for their customers.

6-3a Dynamic Strategies

Core businesses change as industries change or as a firm's competencies change. For example, the business of the Victoria's Secret megabrand used to be driven 70% by apparel, but it is now 70% beauty and fragrance lines. As the production and sales proportions evolve, the questions relate to adaptation: What business are we in? What benefits do we want to provide to the consumer? Who is our competition? If Victoria's Secret sees itself as primarily a lingerie provider, it would compete with department store lingerie departments. If it has come to see itself as a provider of beauty and fragrance goods, it would compete with the department stores' cosmetic counters.

In the huge and hugely profitable business of sports, we may identify the core service as the ball game and the value-addeds as the experience at the park or even on TV or online. The performing teams might be great (or not), and a family or friends can have a great consumer experience. It is smart to define competition broadly here also: While the team competes with others in its league, the marketer competes for families' weekend amusement dollars with other sports (e.g., for corporate skybox dollars) and other forms of entertainment, such as movies.

The definition of a company's core business is somewhat like asking for its mission statement. When a company says, "We're an advertising agency," is that it? What precisely are you good at? What distinguishes you from the next ad guy? A more informative (albeit a little clumsy) statement is "We're the ad agency who can help integrate your customer Web interactions and targeted direct mailing efforts."

Figure 6.3 shows just how broadly competition can be defined in the minds of customers. It's important for brand managers not to focus on defining competition too narrowly when we compute market shares. Fandango is fighting not just imdb.com but also anything that provides information about the entertainment industry. Toyota's Prius competes with other hybrids, as well as other cars, as well as bus routes.

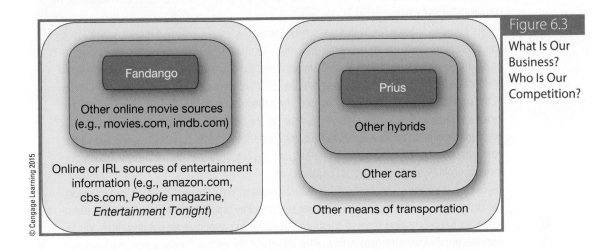

Figure 6.3

What Is Our Business? Who Is Our Competition?

6-3b Product Lines: Breadth and Depth

All product-related issues become more complicated when we broaden our scope to include not just one particular brand of focus but also the company's larger portfolio. Managers speak of a product mix, composed of several product lines, which can vary in both width and depth. In Figure 6.4, we see a Salon offering only hair care products but providing many options within that category. They have no width but plenty of depth. By comparison, a grocery store offers a broader product line, and a large discounter, like Costco or Walmart, offers far more product lines but with even less depth of options within any product category.

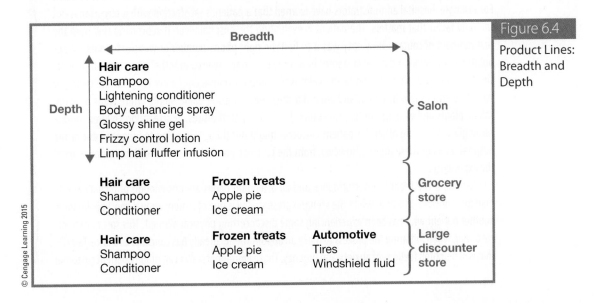

Figure 6.4

Product Lines: Breadth and Depth

Services

"All the world's a stage," claimed renown services marketer William Shakespeare. Contemporary services marketers continue the tradition in recognizing that a customer and service provider play specific roles in a business setting, or stage. Many service providers wear costumes and have been trained with certain dialog and actions.

For example, imagine the health care service drama in which a customer notices it is time for an annual checkup. The customer phones or goes online to make an appointment or reservation with a physician. The customer provides personal information, but payment has been ongoing through his or her place of employment for this year as if the customer were a season ticket holder. On the day of the appointment or theatrical performance, the patient drives to the medical center theater and increasingly frequently is met by a valet to park the car. The customer checks in at the receptionist's box office and signs in to receive a seat in the queuing. The customer looks around the venue and notices other attendees and other administrative ushers, settling in to read over the performance program in the form of old *Highlights or Woman's Day* magazines.

In Act 2, the preliminaries have concluded, and the customer is ushered into the performance room. The customer is asked to don a paper costume and is met by supporting actors and actresses whose scripts are heavy on asking series of questions. The customer's responses are not prewritten, but the customer usually knows the general flow of the dialog and the tenor of the discussion. If the customer veers from that form, as in attempting humor, the interaction is startled out of synch until either party resumes the script. At some point, the maestro or lead actor or actress appears, and a variation of the script is repeated and expanded.

In Act 3, the customer has redressed and follows an actor to another group with whom he or she concludes the details of the business show—perhaps payment, perhaps the receipt of prescriptions, etc. The customer retrieves his or her car and drives home, perhaps to call or e-mail friends that the performance was a good one and that the show is highly recommended.

With the performance concluded, let us examine three lessons. First, this characterization of a service encounter as a drama is not at all intended to belittle either; rather, metaphors are useful when they prompt us to think of possible similarities and differences and of the implications we may draw. For example, hospital administrators have learned that a patient's satisfaction with a physician is not the only factor that matters. The patient is evaluating the hospital, even if subconsciously, from the first moment of contact: How easy was it to find the right phone number or website to make an appointment? How long did the customer have to wait—days, weeks, months? Was there sufficiently clear signage such that parking or the valet was a smooth transaction? How long did the customer have to wait in the office area, and what did they see—peeling paint, sterile white walls or warm colors, plants and evidence of life, separation from messy staff offices, or screaming children, or disturbingly sick-looking others? A patient customer might not think, "I'm going to judge my doc or the hospital on all of these things." However, from the patient's point of view, all the elements are part of the experience.

Second, if the theatrical performance and all attending issues are not enough of a challenge to manage, consider also that, while the scenario presented was one of a mere annual checkup, imagine another patient who has been experiencing some disconcerting physical ailment. This sort of patient-customer, when initiating the process to make an appointment, already has concerns and uncertainties that will heighten feelings of anxiety and urgency. Those emotional states can modify patient customer expectations, such as turning a typically reasonable person into one who at least temporarily may exhibit less tolerance with frontline staff.

Third, one of the ways that services marketers try to understand, manage, and control the service encounter experience is to borrow from operations the notion of flowcharts. In services flowcharts (or blueprints), there is a delineation between what a customer sees (e.g., the valet) and what the company produces to make that part of the encounter as flawless as possible (e.g., sufficiently numbers of valets who are well trained to be polite and good drivers, plentiful nearby parking, etc.). Next, within each section—what is visible to the customer, or on stage, and what is behind the scenes—the service encounter is described in steps that flow over time to simulate the process of the encounter, This process begins with paying for *Yellow Pages* entries, billboards, or website search engines to make the company hospital as easy to find as possible and continues setting the scene of the reception area, and so forth. Finally, in the spirit of quality measurement, many flowcharts feature several key performance indicators to be measured at each step so that a constant read may be taken as to what is working well and what needs to be streamlined in the process.

While a brand manager's responsibilities are to focus, supervising product line managers must oversee these entire portfolios. Product lines can be pruned (e.g., if customers see no distinctions between brands or lines) or supplemented (e.g., if the company recognizes an opportunity for producing something that customers will value, especially if the company can make the new brands or lines easily and better than competitors; we'll see in Chapter 16).

When economic times are good and one's current market offerings and brands are financially healthy, it is tempting to leverage one's strengths and successes into more products (in either the breadth or the depth direction). Doing so can absolutely be a good thing. Indeed, in many ways, it's a smart thing to diversify products in the same way that you're taught to diversify investments. After all, a brand is an investment.

Figure 6.5 shows a different way to think about expansion. The left two scenarios depict a company serving its customer base very well by offering one or more products that suit their tastes.

At the right, a company is trying to offer different products to different customers. This strategy is rather inefficient, given that it doesn't leverage the company's knowledge of its customers or its products. Extensions into breadth or depth business ventures have to be done for smart, strategic reasons. Are the new launches consistent with the current positioning of the brand or company? If not, can the brands be directed to different target segments without diluting the existing position? We'll continue with questions like these in Chapter 7 on brand building and in Chapter 8 on new products.

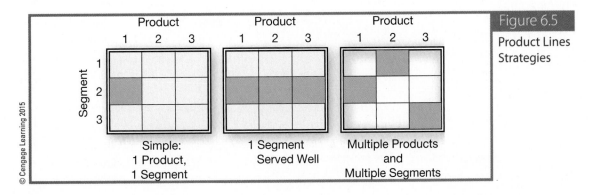

Figure 6.5

Product Lines Strategies

Managerial Recap

Products are goods and services, a central offering in the marketing exchange between a customer and a company.

- Goods and services, along with their marketing and management, share many similarities, but there are differences too. Services are relatively more intangible, inseparable and perishable, and variable.

- A firm's market offering is comprised of the core (the central element of what is purchased and the value-addeds. The core helps define company's target segments, and the value-addeds enhance their customer satisfaction.

- Competition should be considered broadly, and a company's competitors can evolve over time, as product lines are further developed in length and breadth.

Chapter Outline in Key Terms and Concepts

1. What do we mean by product?
   a. The product in the marketing exchange
2. How do goods different from services?
   a. Intangibility
   b. Search, experience, credence
   c. Perishability
   d. Variability
   e. To infinity and beyond goods and services
3. What is the firm's core market offering?
   a. Dynamic strategies
   b. Product lines: breadth and depth

Chapter Discussion Questions

1. When you get your hair cut, what's the core of what you buy vs. what are the value-addeds in the purchase? What's a consultant's core vs. value-addeds? What are the core vs. value-addeds for music?

2. Consider one of these purchases: health care, a car, a time-share condo. What elements are tangible vs. intangible? How do the tangible vs. intangible components contribute to your satisfaction or dissatisfaction with the consumption?

3. Some companies had traditionally been known for their excellence in tangibles—e.g., Xerox in copiers, IBM in computers—who now describe themselves as primarily service companies. Do you agree? What does it take for a company to declare itself a service organization (e.g., a percentage of business, a certain strategy or mission)? What would it take for you to believe such a claim?

Mini-Case

Volta Financial

The core of Volta's business is the financial investment instruments it wants to sell. Its value-addeds include financial advisors who provide nearly free counsel.

Like most financial advisors, Volta's people sell products that seem simple to them but that are complicated to most of their customers. Financial investments are a classic credence purchase, implying that the customer won't know for a long time whether the advice to invest in certain ways was indeed optimal. Volta's clients come for advice because they figure that the advisors have knowledge and abilities that they don't.

Volta is a business and, as such, has a business manager. Some 18 months ago, the manager asked the advisors to have their clients fill out periodic customer satisfaction surveys. The survey captures customers' perceptions regarding whether a receptionist was polite when taking a call to make an appointment to see an advisor, how quickly the appointment could be made, how professional was the advisor, whether the advisor's work area appear to be organized and professional, and so on.

Mini-Case Discussion Questions

1. What do you think about the survey? What measures do you believe would be good indicators of an advisor's performance?

2. How could the brand be positioned to be more tangible and experiential so that consumers could be more confident in Volta's quality and Volta would have more obvious bragging rights about its brand?

3. What elements of financial investment assistance would you classify as core, and what would you list under value added? How could Volta distinguish itself from other financial advisor firms by modifying their core or value-added services?

Video Exercise: *Kodak* (9:21)

Kodak's Graphics Communication Group (GCG) is one of the company's largest growing businesses. On one hand, Kodak's GCG serves customers using offset or analog printing that requires long production runs to be cost-efficient. On the other hand, the company also serves customers who use digital printing to provide quick, on-demand, short production runs. The company markets four types of products—digital printing, consumables, workflow, and services—to commercial printing, corporate, and government customers. Most of the customers are commercial printers, which is one of four market segments targeted by the GCG. The other three market segments are the packaging industry, publishers, and customers engaged in transactional printing (i.e., printing of checks and documents). To more precisely target customer subsets within these different market segments, the company relies on a customer relationship management (CRM) system that contains a variety of detailed information about the needs, location, and characteristics of the customers. The company also seeks lots of feedback from its customers to better understand their needs and their perceptions of the company's operations vis-à-vis the customers. This feedback is used to foster continuous improvement.

Video Discussion Questions

1. What are the main products offered by Kodak to its customers, and how would you position these products on the goods-to-services continuum of products?

2. Describe the core elements and the value-added elements of Kodak's product line(s).

3. Describe the breadth and depth of Kodak's product line(s).

Chapter 7

Brands

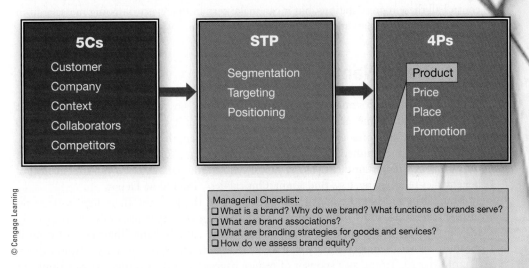

5Cs

Customer
Company
Context
Collaborators
Competitors

STP

Segmentation
Targeting
Positioning

4Ps

Product
Price
Place
Promotion

Managerial Checklist:
❑ What is a brand? Why do we brand? What functions do brands serve?
❑ What are brand associations?
❑ What are branding strategies for goods and services?
❑ How do we assess brand equity?

© Cengage Learning

Marketing Management Framework

7-1 WHAT IS A BRAND?

What do you think of when you hear these names Apple and Microsoft, McDonald's and Burger King, Rolex and Cartier? How can brand strategies at The Gap and Versace both be strong and yet so different? Branding is important, so we need to understand how to do it well.

Marketers care about brands because brands have value above and beyond the benefits of the product itself. It's not just that Coca-Cola is a well-known name; it's that the name immediately invokes certain images—the shape of the Coke bottle, the logo, the red color, some of their ads. So while a brand begins with the name that a company uses to label a specific product, a good brand goes well beyond that; it's a portfolio of qualities associated with that name.

The brand associations begin with qualities under the company's control. The product shape and its packaging can be distinctive; e.g., from that Coke bottle to a Corvette or the iPad. Brand logos are shapes and symbols that may begin with little inherent meaning, but they come to be associated with the brand and become shorthand for the brand itself; e.g., KFC's colonel is internationally known. Some brands are closely associated with particular colors, e.g., Target's red-and-white target logo.

Beyond the name and other tangible qualities, other associative elements may also enhance the imagery and market perceptions of brands. Companies build associations via classical conditioning in consumer learning, e.g., a jingle, a slogan, a spokesperson. The hope is that the catchy tune is in your head when you're at the grocer (e.g., "Ask any mermaid you happen to see…"), or that the slogan suggests the company has a worthy mission (e.g., "Like a good neighbor, State Farm is there"), or that the spokesperson is admired and the customer emulates the person through the purchase (e.g., Halle Berry for Revlon).

Other brand associations are not under the company's control but are every bit as real; e.g., maybe when you were a kid, your mom substituted 7Up for root beer to make you ice cream floats, or your soccer coach had cold 7Ups waiting for the team after every game, or in college you felt awkward asking for a 7Up instead of a beer at a party. The company can't control all these representations, but it can make certain that every outgoing message from the company to the marketplace is excellent and positive.

7-1a Brand Name

A brand is first and foremost a name. Some marketers say that a brand is a symbol, but it first has to be a name, or else how would you dot-com it, register it, or search for it. To the extent that all words are symbols in communication, then, fine, brands are symbols. Some brand names immediately convey information, e.g., YouTube capturing the essence of user-created entertainment. Other brand names originate as not a far stretch from a benefit they're implying, e.g., Bud Light, Optical4less, The Home Depot.

Many firm and brand names are merely those of the founder. These tend to have no inherent meaning, show little creativity in marketing, and serve primarily as an ego trip for the founder. Yet, as brands, family names aren't entirely lame. Their lack of explicit meaning allows them to translate well to other brands across the firm, e.g., Trump Plaza, Trump Marina, Trump as a sponsor of beauty pageants. And with time, no one thinks of the people, e.g., Henry Ford (1903) or Walter Chrysler (1925); rather, a person thinks of their companies' subsequent cars. (Still, entrepreneurs are best cautioned to choose a brand name that conveys customer benefits.)

7-1b Logos and Color

Brand name meaning continues to build over time through the firm's communications to customers. The marketer educates customers about the meaning of the brand as well as its logos and symbols. Just as the brand name engages the customers verbally, the logos and packaging colors engage the customers visually, sensually. Think of how distinct the fonts of *The New York Times* and Google look: The first is an elegant, old-fashioned cursive, in black and white; the latter is san serif, bold, simple, colorful. These simple cues are sufficient to identify the brands.

Figure 7.1 shows logos that combine a brand name with a symbol meant to suggest the brand's value proposition. The NBA figure captures a basketball player; Subway's arrows imply the speed of its service; Red Bull helps us by spelling out "Energy drink."

Figure 7.1			
Brand Names and Symbols as Logos			

TP/Alamy   © iStockphoto.com/Willowpix   Glen Argov/Landov   © Cengage Learning

Companies lucky enough to survive for decades need to adapt, and so do their logos. Figure 7.2 shows the Xerox logo over time. It began as a torch, morphed into playing up the "X," and subsequently got simplified and stylized. Do you like the changes over the years? (Does it matter? Would you avoid a company because of a logo change? Probably not.) Companies use brand names and logos as a shorthand way to communicate to the customer: "This is who we are. This is what we look like."

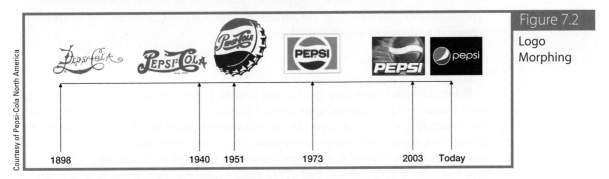

1898   1940 1951   1973   2003 Today

Figure 7.2

Logo Morphing

7-2 WHY BRAND?

The U.S. Patent office issues more than 100,000 new brands every year. Some say that Americans are becoming less brand loyal, but, let's face it, with such continued brand explosion, companies are splitting their money pies more and more finely. Together, the sheer numbers of brands, and the heightened competition over them, indicate that branding is more important than ever.

So why all these brands? Brands first *convey information* to customers. Brand names identify company production and ownership; e.g., when Sony puts its name on a DVR player, a television set, or a portable music device or computer, it's saying, "We're proud to offer these products. These are ours." And, with time, the brand name has gained status among consumers as having high quality "Sony is a good *brand*"; that is, anything that comes from the house of Sony is good.

Brand building is based fundamentally on the predictability of the item being purchased. It would be difficult for a customer to say that they value Apple's Macs if some Macs worked well and others didn't. Brands can gain reputations for being bad, but the goal of a marketer is to create a product that is *reliable*, or *predictable in quality*. And, indeed, Macs have avid fans because they work not just predictably but fabulously.

Why Brand?

For the customer:	For the company:
• Brands convey information.	• Brands enhance loyalty.
• Brands signal consistent quality.	• Brands allow charging premium prices.
• Brands confer status.	• Brands inoculate the company from some competitive action.
• Brands reduce customer risk.	• Brands assist in segmentation, targeting, and positioning.
• Brands makes many purchase decisions easier.	• Brands encourage channel partners' support.

The Brand Building Challenge

It's worth noting that brand building can be a challenge for services marketing. A brand implies consistency, and some services are rather standardized, so creating a service brand for a hotel chain, an airline, or even a restaurant is much like doing so for tangible products. But many services are more heterogeneous due to the interpersonal exchange between the customer and the frontline service provider. Thus, to enhance reliability and branding, service providers should be highly selective in hiring and spend more resources on training employees who interact with customers.

When the brand name is an assurance of reliable quality, the customer's *decision making is made easier. Less perceived risk* is associated with the choice among the products offered in the marketplace when the customer knows which are the good brands. Risk, as in financial transactions, is essentially a measure of variability. Reliability is the opposite; it implies a consistency or a predictability in the performance of the product. Reliability is a signal that time and again the product will perform to quality standards; thus, across time or customers, the product performs with little variability but high quality. The brand is a known entity. Customers can count on it to perform as they've come to expect it to.

It is also clear that many brands serve as *status symbols*. The reason for knockoff designer handbags or watches is that it's thought to be cool to own one, yet the prices of the genuine articles are out of reach for many consumers. The reason Mercedes and BMW have entry-level cars is for young successful people who want to show the world they've made it (yet who need to pay as little as possible to own a piece of the brand). The prestige of such brands bolsters the consumer's self-image.

If those are the benefits of branding for customers, let's consider the rewards of brands for their companies. Good brands can *induce loyalty*. Repeat purchasing might be unthinking due to inertia, whereby the customer just reaches for the familiar (brand name, package, logo, color). If the brand is known to be high quality and reliable (i.e., not risky), the brand choice is easy to justify, and customers don't have to think about the purchase or brand choice anymore. Repeat purchasing and true brand loyalty can also be a more mindful process, whereby customers return to the brand because, quite simply, they like it. With that brand, customers obtain the particular attributes and features they seek, which in turn further supports their perceptions of high quality.

To a company's delight, most customers are willing to *pay premium prices* for brands they value. Customer so appreciate the reliability, high quality, and status of their favorite brands that they're less price sensitive, knowing that they're getting something good even if they're paying somewhat more.

Companies can also use brands or variants of their brands to provide different offerings to satisfy different *market segments*. For example, Porsche's 911 sells predominately to men (92%), who are 52ish with a household income over $300k. Their Boxster profiles slightly younger (47ish) and more to women (30%). These different car lines allow the macho 911 driver to not be offended by the infiltrating women buying the sister model.

How does a brand name come to convey meaning, imply quality and consistency, reduce the riskiness and ease decision making, induce loyalty, achieve prestigious status, and command higher prices? The mechanism that gives brands meaning is the set of associations linked to the brand in the customer's mind. These associations are created through a number of sources: They're built from the company's advertisements and communications in the marketplace, the customer's own experiences with the brand and company and competitors' brands, and the stories related about the brand by other customers. So let's look at brand associations.

7-3 WHAT ARE BRAND ASSOCIATIONS?

If branding begins with simple physical qualities (a name, logo, color, packaging, etc.), the far more interesting and flexible aspects of a brand are the intangible cognitive and emotional associations that the company helps the customer connect to its brand. Marketers talk about a hierarchy of brand associations. At the bottom of a brand value hierarchy are the concrete product attributes, such as color, size, shape, flavor. As we travel up the hierarchy, these brand attributes extend to product benefits; e.g., this blue sweater will be flattering; this sized jar of salsa should be enough for the recipe; the shape of the new Ray-Bans is too boxy; the flavor of the beef at Fogo de Chão is just spicy enough. Benefits are more intangible than attributes. Emotional benefits are the next level, and they're more intangible yet; e.g., a flattering sweater is a means to be attractive; a good meal is a means to please family or friends, etc.

Strategically, the concrete features are easiest to deliver and explain to customers, but they're also relatively easily matched by competitors. The more abstract benefits are values that are more meaningful to customers and easier for a company to claim as a competitive advantage, but they're also more difficult to create.

The key brand association is the extent to which the customer feels a personal connection to the brand. For example, think of the middle-aged man who rides a Harley, telling himself, "I'm so cool!" Brands aren't just extensions of the customer, they are expressions of the customer's *ideal* self or the self to which they aspire. A brand carries a promise that it can help customers achieve their desired persona. This aspiration function of brands begins in childhood, when kids believe that their popularity and acceptance are partly a function of wearing the right sneakers or listening to the right music on the right MP3 player. Adults may deny that they use brands in the same manner, but watch their behaviors: They attend "certain" schools, drive "certain" cars, and wear "certain" designers' clothing and shoes.

Brands can also serve other social functions. Brands can become the focal point of bonding, as in so-called brand communities, exemplified by the well-known Harley treks, Mac user groups, Lego clubs (club.lego.com), or even traditional fan sites (e.g., hundreds for Beiber), etc. To nonmarketers, rabid fan dedication can be surprising; people talk about loving (some) brands.

All of these connections can be depicted, as in Figure 7.3, in a brand association network. The nodes in the network include elements such as the brand name (and perhaps competitors), along with attributes and abstract benefits about the brand. The links between the nodes indicate some connection (unlinked nodes have either no or weak connections), and strong links are depicted with bold lines.

This mapping is not meant to be a literal representation of what customers have in their heads, and yet it's not a bad metaphor. This idea is that we have stored quite a lot of information about a brand in memory, and, when the brand name is activated (e.g., through advertising), the brand associations are subsequently (even instantaneously) triggered (like brand information jumping across neurons). Links that are further from the brand may take milliseconds longer to retrieve and activate than those most closely and directly associated with the brand. Thus, while the brand associations in the figure indicate that Bose is perceived to be expensive, that attribute is not likely to be one of the very first qualities that comes to mind when the brand name is stimulated. In addition to memory implications, there are attitudinal ones as well. For example, measures of customer satisfaction with the brand are most heavily affected by the positivity or negativity of the nearest links.

When company advertising emphasizes one benefit, the cognitive maps may be simple: e.g., Volvo's link with safety dominates everything else, and ditto Nordstrom's link to good

Figure 7.3

Brand
Association
Network

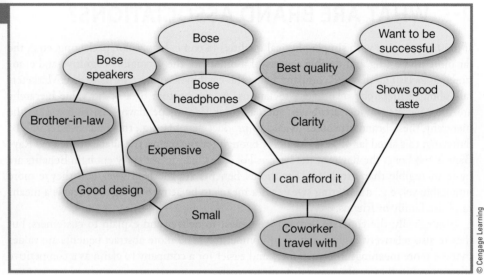

© Cengage Learning

customer service. If those solitary links are strong and positive, the focused message has been delivered, and the position of the brand in the marketplace is clear and positive. Networks can be more complex, due either to a long heritage in the marketplace (e.g., McDonald's may be linked to fries, quickness, inexpensiveness, the two-all-beef-patties jingle, road trips, fat food concerns, etc.) or to inconsistent advertising messages or customer experiences.

In addition to classic studies of brand associations to understand customers' memory and attitudes, recent research has examined two special classes of brand associations: brand personalities and brand communities. We'll look at each.

7-3a Brand Personalities

One way that marketers get customers to relate to their brands is by creating a brand *personality*. A brand doesn't have to be personified or anthropomorphized, as with Keebler's elves. Any brand can be said to have a distinct personality.

In Figure 7.4, we see a conceptualization of five different kinds of brands: sincere, competent, exciting, sophisticated, and rugged. The personalities capture information specific to the brand, as well as holistic perceptions about the brand and company position in the marketplace. For example, when customers say Ben & Jerry's is sincere, they mean partly the ice cream (e.g., they use only quality ingredients) and partly the company (e.g., those ingredients come from fair trade sources).

None of the personality profiles is better than the others; they're just all different. If the brand strategy had been to attain a certain personality and customer perceptions concur that the brand achieved that characterization, then the branding and marketing efforts succeeded. If the brand manager doesn't like the brand's current profile, then new marketing initiatives may be undertaken to reposition the brand. For example, a marketing manager of a competent brand might be envious of an exciting brand, but competent is good, just different. There's a lot of space and reward in the marketplace for competent. A brand would begin to lose its identity and its own personality (not to mention its current customers) if it aimed to be exciting.

Consistent with their personalities, different brand experiences highlight different elements. Figure 7.5 depicts that Disney appeals more to customers' hearts, building blocks to customers' heads, and iPods to how people navigate their worlds.

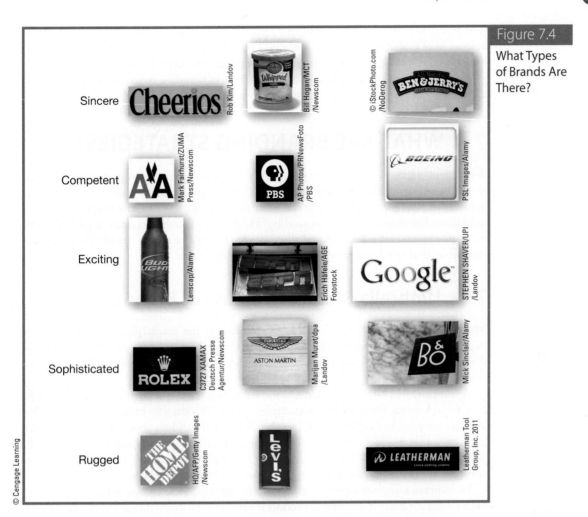

© Cengage Learning

Figure 7.4

What Types of Brands Are There?

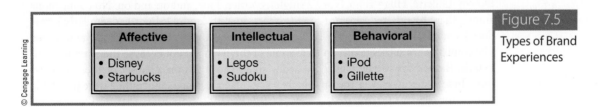

© Cengage Learning

Figure 7.5

Types of Brand Experiences

7-3b Brand Communities

While many brands speak of engaging their customers' hearts and minds, increasingly marketers are seeing (and encouraging) even more extreme attachments. There are brand communities around iPhone, Lego, Jonessoda.com, and Dell's ideastorm.com. Some customers are so passionate about their love for certain brands that they like to connect with other like-minded customers. Whether these brand communities take the form of social media interactions or interactions IRL (like a Harley posse who rides together), customers are coming together over brands. Currently, marketers don't quite know what to do with these communities (other than trying to engage them to spark viral campaigns). Will brand communities enhance the bottom line? Probably. How could it not be a good thing if people gather to rave about your brand, but how will that be monetized? Companies are still figuring that out.

Next, we turn to the more macro, corporate topic of branding strategies: What might we do with all our knowledge of our customers' brand associations?

7-4 WHAT ARE BRANDING STRATEGIES?

A company needs to answer several important branding questions as part of their overall marketing strategy. First, will the company offer multiple products under the same brand name or roll them out with distinct brand names? Second, what are the purposes of brand extensions, line extensions, and cobranding? How is brand equity determined and valuated? How are brands best rolled out globally? What is the role of a store brand? We'll examine the factors that affect the answers to each of these questions.

7-4a Umbrella Brands vs. House of Brands

Most companies start by offering a single product in the marketplace. The brand name might be the company name. As the company adds products, it has to decide: Should it put the corporate name on every new product, or should new brand names be chosen for the subsequent products?

A company that attaches the same brand name to all of its products is using an *umbrella branding* approach. There are lots of examples, such as Honda, who makes cars, motorcycles, and lawnmowers, and calls them all Hondas. Nike makes athletic shoes, sports jerseys, gym bags, and other products, all of which bear the same company brand name and swish logo. All of HP's products say "HP." Canon's cameras and photocopiers say "Canon." GE puts its corporate brand on its diverse lines of appliances, lighting, financial services, and engines.

In contrast, a *house of brands* approach is one for which the company introduces a new brand name for every major line of product it brings to the marketplace. Procter & Gamble is a famous house of brands. It produces some 80 major brands, including Charmin, Crest, Downy, Gillette, Hugo Boss, Ivory, Pringles, Swiffer, Tide, and on and on. No connections among these brands are apparent to customers. In B2B land, DuPont had similarly introduced a portfolio of great brands: Kevlar, Kalrez, Lycra, Teflon, Thinsulate, and Stainmaster. The company has subsequently sold off some of these brands not because they weren't good brands. Rather, for strategic purposes, they sought to focus on a subset of their business lines. Indeed, because even the brands they sold off had strong equity, they were profitable transactions.

Each approach has strengths and liabilities. With an umbrella branding approach, once the company has established the key brand name in the marketplace, subsequent product introductions sharing the same brand name are easier for the customer to understand and accept. The new product line begins with higher-than-usual levels of awareness. In addition, given that the two products share a brand name, there is some overlap between two the products' associations. Thus, it is critical that the majority of the existing brand's associations be positive, or the new product will be introduced to the market with a perceived handicap.

In contrast, given the nature of the multiple brands' autonomy in the house of brands approach, the independence between brands assures that any problems with one brand shouldn't negatively affect any of the other brands. Even if a brand isn't in the spotlight for being a problem (e.g., tires that blow out, beverage bottling problems, weight control OTCs that cause heart problems), a company with multiple brands almost surely is watching those brands from different points in their life cycles. A brand whose image is waning is less a liability in a house of brands where the names aren't shared across the product lines. A more positive way to interpret this brand independence is that the brand images need not be consistent, allowing the company to reach multiple segments. For example, Marriott's portfolio has Courtyard and Fairfield to serve one part of the market, with Ritz (without the Marriott name) at the high end, and none of the segments is confused or would expect an experience that the other hotels offer.

Evidence suggests that the umbrella branding strategy provides stronger financial outcomes to the company than the house of brands. One reason is that certain costs are cut; e.g., the house of brands approach requires more advertising to build the multiple brands' equity, whereas advertising for the umbrella brands builds the shared brand name synergistically across the products. In addition, psychologically, customers seem to build stronger connections to the specific, concrete product; thus, customers think positively about Ivory without necessarily considering anything about its manufacturer, P&G. For umbrella branders (e.g., Sony), the product-level associations replicate the same name across multiple products (Sony memory sticks, Sony theater systems), and thus the attitude is reinforced (Sony, Sony, Sony), in turn, enhancing brand loyalty.

7-4b Brand Extensions and Cobranding

Brand extensions are a strategic use of a brand's equity, in which the marketer leverages the brand's good name to get customers to buy something new. Recall the breadth and depth dimensions of product lines from Chapter 6; here, too, the brand name may be applied within a product line to go for depth; these are called *line extensions*. Or the brand name may be applied across different kinds of products; these are called *product category extensions*.

Figure 7.6 illustrates brand extensions in the direction of breadth (product category) and depth (line) in a familiar context. The vertical, or line, extensions provide varieties of the core product, and the horizontal, or product category, extensions are the company's ventures into other product categories. Sometimes a company seems to prefer one direction of expansion to another:

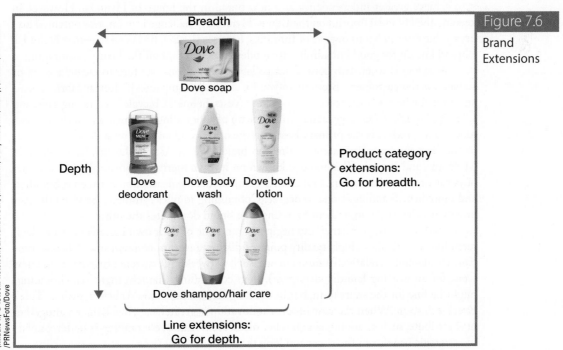

Figure 7.6

Brand Extensions

Some companies focus on deepening brand extensions:

- QuickBooks has versions of its software for PCs, Macs, small business needs, and a premier packet for professionals, nonprofits, retailers, etc. They're all called "Quick-Books."

- Quaker Oats rolls out different flavors (oatmeal, toasted oatmeal in brown sugar or honey nut, oatmeal squares in brown sugar or cinnamon).

- So does Ben & Jerry's (Jamaican Me Crazy, Neapolitan Dynamite, Turtle Soup, Black and Tan).

Other companies focus on brand extensions intended for breadth:

- Arm & Hammer began with baking soda, then took its freshness value proposition and brand name to offer toothpaste, deodorant, carpet deodorizer, kitty litter, and laundry detergent.

- Amazon.com has famously extended from books and CDs to drugstore goods, computers, furniture, jewelry, services (e.g., registries), just about everything—all of which have the Amazon imprint.

Sometimes the distinction between a brand and a line extension isn't crystal clear. For example, Hyundai has long been positioned as the provider of relatively inexpensive, small cars (e.g., Elantra, Accent), and these might be considered brand extensions that extend the line (depth). But with the introduction of the Equus model, Hyundai is dipping its corporate toe into the luxury car pool, an altogether different business venture, targeting a segment with different needs, and so this venture would probably be better considered a brand extension that crosses product categories (breadth).

The difference is a matter of degree: A slight new model twist may be going for depth; a vastly different model/product extends the breadth. Per the logic described, Hyundai might have launched the Equus without reference to the umbrella Hyundai brand name, allowing it to achieve greater independence as a new brand in the house of Hyundai. However, in keeping the Hyundai imprint on the Equus, Hyundai's challenge is to impress potential luxury car buyers—previous owners of Infinities, Lexuses (Lexi?), BMWs, etc.—that Hyundai, a brand known for good but admittedly modest cars, can pull off the luxury positioning.

Cobranding is when two companies collaborate in a joint venture to create a good or service for the customer: "Brought to you by … [both companies]." Kevlar fabric is used and touted when selling protective body gear (vests, helmets), bicycle tires, racing sails, and so forth. *Ingredient branding* is the primary form of cobranding in which one of the companies and its product is the primary host, and the other company and its add-valued product to the host product. For example, Brembo brakes are in Aston Martins, Lamborghinis, Maseratis, and Paganis. The brand is known on its own merit, but obviously the customer buys the car, of which the fine brakes are a component. The distinction between cobranding and ingredient branding is one of degree: Cobranding implies symmetry between the two providers, whereas, in ingredient branding, one brand dominates the other.

Marketers might go further and begin to brand one of their own ingredients to make it seem like a particularly high-quality point of distinction from competitors. When a company is launching a relatively minor change, such as tweaking a current attribute (e.g., a new scent for an existing laundry detergent), then cobranding (namely, ingredient branding) might be fine for the short term, but in the long term, a self-brand is better, such as Tide's EverFresh scent. When the new product innovation is greater, e.g., involving an altogether new attribute, such as adding cough relief medicine to candy, cobranding is better, providing strategic benefits in the short and long term.

Anatomy of a Brand Extension

First movie, *Cars*

Success begets success . . .

and excess . . . ?

Second movie, *Cars 2*

 **and** 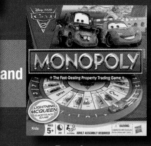 **and**

Video games

Board games

Die-cast car toys

. . . but wait, there's more!

Disney/*Cars 2* Partners

. . . and still more!

Disney forges partnership with many manufacturers— temporary cobranding arrangements, where synergistic sales are boosted by both brands. *Cars 2* pictures are found on packaging for GoGurt, Juicy Juice, Band-Aids, and Kellogg's snack packages.

"Friends to the Finish" T-shirts

Kids' shoes: hook 'em young

Disney also forms partnerships with retailers. For example, Target is the exclusive supplier for retail sales of *Cars 2* products. Disney gets a premium on sales, and Target gets an advantage over other retailers such as Sears and Walmart.

7-4c How Are Brands Best Rolled Out Globally?

First, what is a global brand? To be defined as global, at least 30% of the brand's revenues should come from other countries (no more than 70% from the brand's home country).

Second, how do we roll out global brands? Analogous to the house of brands vs. umbrella branding decision, some companies go global with different brand names in different countries, with the motto "manufacturer globally, brand locally," the philosophy of so-called glocalization. Other companies maintain the same brand name in every country they enter.

Just as it was said to be typically more advantageous to choose the umbrella path vs. the house of brand path, here, too, there appear to be greater advantages to maintaining a single brand name worldwide, if possible.

A true global brand (and perhaps not surprisingly nor coincidentally, the biggest brands), carries one brand name and logo anywhere it is offered, and it is available in most markets in the world. Amazon.com looks just like amazon.co.uk, for example, or google.com looks like google.fr. There are corporate efficiencies to using the same brand information, communications, and strategies everywhere. Strictly speaking, true global brands are those that seek, achieve, and maintain similar positioning in all their markets.

If a company wishes to serve different kinds of customer segments in different markets, they would opt to use different brand names in those different markets. For example, one of the functions of a brand name is quality assurance, but quality per se might be of varying importance, depending on the culture, segment, or product. And, of course, we've all heard

Legal Stuff

- A *trademark* is the legal ownership of identity that can include just the brand name, or just the logo, or, more inclusively, the name, logo, phrases, symbols, design, colors, sounds, etc.
- Claims of trademark infringement occur when a me-too competitor makes part of their brand identity too similar to an extant trademark, which could lead to confusion by customers and purchases of the me-too rather than original brand.
- The symbol *TM* essentially means, "Hands off, these are our ideas" (trademark rights are claimed). When TM graduates, it becomes a registered trademark (®), a more serious designation that means, "Hands off, or our lawyers will get you" (the trademark has been registered).
- If you want to use a word as a brand name that, prior to your use had no particular inherent meaning, such as Geico (before the insurance company), you'd get a *fanciful* trademark. If you want to appropriate a word with common meaning, such as Amazon, you'd file for an *arbitrary* trademark. Finally, *suggestive* trademarks are those for which the brand name suggests the customer benefit (e.g., Jiffy-Lube).
- With time, what had been company property can change, especially, perversely, if the brand becomes too successful. For example, "Aspirin" had been a trademark of Bayer, but the name is now deemed generic so other pain relievers can also call themselves aspirin.
- Trademark issues arise online in the form of domain names and ownership. Generic names cannot be defended as registered.
- Laws in different countries are wildly different, but services are available that search for prior brand elements (brand names, slogans, etc.) to see if they're free of ™ or ® (e.g., in the states, via the U.S. Patent and Trademark Office: uspto.gov).

the examples of brand names that simply do not translate well. Finally, legal restrictions may curtail certain marketing activities and even brand names (e.g., Diet Coke vs. Coke Lite) that vary with country. Still, these (admittedly big) caveats aside, the best marketing guru thinking seems to be, if you can, use the same name globally.

7-4d Store Brands

What's the role of store brands? While it sounds like an oxymoron, store brands are big business. The traditional idea behind private labels is that they're less expensive and more of a me-too product offering than an innovative brand. Most of us are price sensitive in some product categories that are usually (by definition) those we don't care much about. In product categories we care more about, we're less price sensitive. Some customers seem to be price sensitive across the board; these are customers with sort of a cheap gene—a broader trait or propensity to go for store brands—across numerous categories (perhaps due to limited resources).

Cost savings for customers isn't the only motive for store brands. Retailers are also offering premium private labels. Although traditionally generic (non)brands were packaged unattractively and thought to be of lesser quality, these days the packaging and quality are usually on par with the big national brands, and many customers don't know that the store brand is a store brand. Walmart's brand of Sam's Choice might be an obvious name, but consider Safeway's Eating Right, Target's Archer Farms, Kroger's Private Selection, and Costco's Kirkland Signature. These are high-end or specialty products made available at value prices.

The retailer can offer decent quality for lower prices because certain costs are reduced; e.g., they can advertise very inexpensively in fliers in the local weekend newspaper and radio spots, and they can easily promote the brands in-store. Thus, to the customer, it looks like a brand, and it smells like a brand, so it must be a brand. And if it's a brand, it might be high quality. As is always the case, the advertising helps ensure trial, and the quality of the product determines satisfaction and repeat purchasing.

A lot of private label and pricing games go on in retailing. Retailers naturally want their shoppers to buy their brands, and, given their tremendous growth in power, they have been demanding better package deals from other source manufacturers. Between the added competition (including the store brands) and the aggressive deal demands, the manufacturers aren't going to sit still, of course. Premium ("real") brands are launching their own second label, priced near the store label to provide an alternative to price-sensitive customers, rather than losing them to the store brand (or other competitors). What do the premium brand manufacturers do next? They raise the price of their original premium brand.

It's also important to note that, if brands represent culture, then nonbranded goods are embraced by various countercultures. Free spirits from skateboarders to yogi to Burning Man attendees eschew big national brands due to the commercialism they represent.

7-5 HOW IS BRAND EQUITY DETERMINED?

In recent years, the popularity of branding, coupled with factors that have required marketers to be more accountable for their marketing expenditures and programs (e.g., slow economy, intense competition), have resulted in efforts to measure the worth of a brand. Figure 7.7 lists the top 20 U.S. and non-U.S. brands as reported annually by *BusinessWeek*. Do any of the brands on the list surprise you? Are there any parameters on which these aren't great companies or brands? If Coca-Cola were to slip to #10 or #11 in next year's poll, would you really consider it a lesser brand?

Figure 7.7	U.S.	Non-U.S.
Top Brands	• Coca-Cola	• Samsung
	• Apple	• Toyota
	• IBM	• Mercedes-Benz
	• Google	• BMW
	• Microsoft	• Louis Vuitton
	• GE	• Nokia
	• McDonald's	• Honda
	• Intel	• H&M
	• Disney	• SAP
	• Cisco	• Ikea

© Cengage Learning

The rankings use Interbrand's method (at interbrand.com). How are those ranks determined? When Rolls-Royce sold its brand to BMW for $60 million, where did that number come from? Let's see what goes into the consideration of a brand's value.

The basic idea in brand valuation is to derive measures that translate as best as possible into a financial vocabulary. The reasoning seems fair and sound: If marketers argue that their brands are assets, then they should be able to attach a monetary-like figure to that worth.

Some of the numbers that enter into these calculations are available in annual reports for public firms. Other numbers are obtained from customer survey data. Still other numbers are proprietary to the firms, such as Interbrand, doing the calculations.

One approach is to find out just what sort of price premium the brand can demand. A conjoint study can be run in which one attribute is brand (e.g., Shell Oil vs. unbranded fuel). Price can be one of the other attributes, or it can be what is measured (e.g., "How much are you willing to pay for gas at a Shell station?" vs. "How much are you willing to pay for gas at a local gas station?"). (We'll say more about conjoint in Chapter 8 on new products and in Chapter 15 on marketing research.)

A related approach focuses less on the price *per se* but compares the brand to an unbranded form of the product that is otherwise matched, feature by feature. Preferences and customer choices are measured (e.g., "How much do you like this Sony flat screen, costing $799, with screen-within-a-screen, and holograph projection?" vs. "How much do you like this unknown brand flat screen, costing $799, same features, etc.?").

The Interbrand method is essentially to assess the value of a firm, subtract its physical and financial assets, and call the rest the value of the brand. That's a little simplistic because, although this calculation exposes a firm's intangibles, there are other intangible assets beyond the firm's brand (e.g., real investments in human resources or R&D, such as patents), and so they still have to tease out the effect of the brand. These days, some 50% of a typical firm's value is estimated to be determined by intangible assets, including its brand names. It may be challenging to estimate the value of those intangibles, but it is certainly done, and therefore it is important to do it well.

So, how to actually do it. Figure 7.8 tracks the following computations. First, open up this year's annual report for your favorite brand and pick off the number representing the operating earnings generated by that brand (e.g., a corporate earnings number for either an umbrella brand or a brand number for a brand in a house of brands). Say you find that the net sales figure is $25,000,000 and that the operating earnings figure for that brand is $7,000,000. Those earnings are taxed (at, say, 25%), so subtract off the taxes (–$1.750,000).

Figure 7.8

Brand
Valuation

	Worksheet	Numbers Needed	
a. Net sales (revenue for the brand)	$25,000,000		
b. Operating earnings		$7,000,000	
c. Tax on earnings	25% × b	→	−1,750,000
d. Tangible capital	$12,500,000		
e. Rate of return	6% × d	→	− 750,000
f. Intangible earnings		$4,500,000	
g. Brand contribution index (bci)	40%*		
h. Brand earnings	g × f	$1,800,000	

*Depends on product category

Say the tangible capital figure is $12,500,000, and multiply it by a rate of return of, say, 6% (a little conservative) and subtract this $750,000. The result is the figure for the earnings based on intangibles.

The next step is the magic of teasing out the brand effect. Interbrand estimates that brands are very important for perfumes, e.g., 90% of a firm's intangibles may be attributable to its brand, less important for cars (40%), and still less for retailers (20%). When this brand contribution index is used as a multiplier against the intangibles, we derive the proportion of those intangible earnings that we may claim are due to the brand. We have an estimate of the brand value.

The method's not perfect, and the proprietary nature of the indices is annoying, but work in the area of brand valuation is new, so look for better developments soon. Regardless of any of the methods' shortcomings, when customer judgments of numerous brands are gathered, and the data are correlated with their companies' financials, marketers find clear evidence of strong positive relationships linking brands to shareholder value.

Strong brands deliver greater returns, and with less risk (the classic desired state: higher means, lower variance) than comparable benchmarks. Marketing matters. Brands make companies financially healthier. Marketing adds great value!

Brand Equity

Here is a quick reference on how brand equity is determined and valuated:

1. Start with the firm's net operating earnings (for the entire company, e.g., a corporate brand, or for a specific brand in a company's portfolio).

2. Subtract taxes on these earnings.

3. Determine the amount of tangible capital associated with the brand and by some expected rate of return (e.g., a conservative rate might be 6%). This rate of return is also subtracted from the firm's net operating earnings. The resulting figure after we subtract taxes and the rate of return expected is the earnings based on intangibles.

4. Use a brand contribution index (which varies based on the type of brand) to identify a multiplier against the earnings based on intangibles.

5. The result reflects the intangible earnings related to the brand (i.e., estimated brand value).

The Four Dimensions of Brand Experience

In their recent article in the *Journal of Marketing*, Brakus, Schmitt, and Zarantonello studied and tried to characterize consumers' brand experiences. These marketers interviewed many people about many products and collected their thoughts about their brands. For example, of Starbucks, people said, "Smells nice and is visually warm" and "It's comfortable and puts me in a better mood." Apple's iPod was described as "A product that goes with my way of life" and "I love the touch and feel of the products."

Next, the researchers identified themes running through these consumers' descriptions of brands. Ultimately, their research distinguished four distinct elements of brand experiences:

1. Consumers experience emotions, such as when they pick out a Hallmark greeting card.
2. They experience a taste sensation, such as when they drink their Starbucks Frappuccino.
3. They face an intellectual challenge, such as when they try to solve crosswords and Sudoku puzzles.
4. They encounter behavioral challenges, such as when they play various sports.

In the following figure, several brands are noted that exemplify one of the four dimensions, such as Ferrari being an unashamedly sensory experience, or some combination, such as iPods being both a source of sensory stimulation and a factor impacting consumers' lives and how they may choose to be entertained. These dimensions offer additional insights into how consumers perceive brands and whether those perceptions are aligned with the brand manager's intended positioning, as well as whether they suggest alternative positioning that may seem more desirable with slight modifications of the brand imagery.

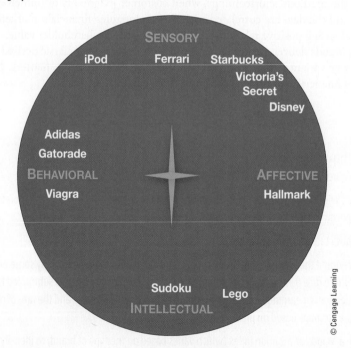

© Cengage Learning

Managerial Recap

Brands are promises to customers. Brands are names and logos and colors and fonts. In addition,

- Brands signal information to customers about predictability in their purchases, about anticipated reliability and expected quality.

- Brands can command higher prices, because the brand offsets any uncertainties or risks associated with the purchase in the mind of the customer.

- Brand associations are the cognitive and emotional elements that combine to create the larger brand story.

- Companies can employ any of a number of strategies with their brands. They can put their corporate name on everything (i.e., an umbrella brand), or they can create a portfolio of different brands (i.e., the house of brands).

- Brand valuation, e.g., per the method of Interbrand reported in the *BusinessWeek* annual polls, are all the rage, and are likely to continue to be important to branders for the future.

Chapter Outline in Key Terms and Concepts

1. What is a brand?
   a. Brand name
   b. Logos and color

2. Why brand?

3. What are brand associations?
   a. Brand personalities
   b. Brand communities

4. What are branding strategies?
   a. Umbrella brands vs. house of brands
   b. Brand extensions and cobranding
   c. How are brands best rolled out globally?
   d. Store brands

5. How is brand equity determined?

Chapter Discussion Questions

1. What is one of your favorite brands (why)? What is a brand you hate (why)?

2. Which brand personality best describes you? Your business school? What about these images do you like? What about these images would you like to change to something even more desirable (and how would you do so)?

3. Read the methodology of Interbrand.com for brand valuations. How might you improve its methods and the sorts of measures it uses to assess brand equity?

Mini-Case

6MD

A biotech firm creates bone replacements that have been used successfully for about 5 years in a variety of applications—joint replacements, trauma, etc. The parts are primarily titanium, a metal that has a decent track record for such uses because it is strong yet lightweight. It is also said to be biocompatible (i.e., rarely causes rejection problems).

None of that is new. What's new to the firm's technology is that the titanium is calci-plated. Bones wear down faster than titanium, and, in fact, titanium is so strong that it causes further wear on surrounding tissue. The calcium-like plating surrounding the bone pieces offers the advantage of not only slowing down that friction, making the pieces last longer, but also greatly slowing the onset of any returning aches and pains. A by-product of the calci-treatment is that it also does not set off security systems at airports.

The firm is obviously happy about its products' successes, but it is regretting its status as a component piece. They wish to begin branding their pieces. Much like the success of the "Intel Inside" advertising campaign for its microprocessing chip, the biotech firm draws an analogy and wants people to understand that they are offering an excellent ingredient brand.

The firm is pretty set on calling the product lines by the brand name 6MD. It began as a skunkworks project nickname, representing the bioengineers' respect for the Six Million Dollar Man. It had even hoped to get Lee Majors to be its spokesperson, but initial contact made clear that he was too expensive. He was also looking a little long in the tooth. The name also stuck because the "MD" piece of the brand name should resonate with one of the constituencies who would use the brand.

Mini-Case Discussion Questions

1. Who is/are the biotech firm's customers?

2. How should it position this brand?

3. Will the customers appreciate the brand's USP (unique selling proposition)? Why?

4. What directions might you suggest to the biotech firm for brand or line extensions?

Video Exercise: *Method* (7:43)

Eric Ryan and Adam Lowery, cofounders of Method, a line of household cleaning products, discuss how the product concept came into being and subsequently was developed into a premium line. Ryan and Lowery saw an opportunity to create a premium brand from the observation that the lucrative $20-billion-a-year household cleaning products category suffered from product sameness that was uninteresting and uninspiring. Method's philosophy of branding stresses that "the brand is the promise that the consumer gets from the product you are selling and the product itself delivers on that promise." Ryan and Lowery created a line of nontoxic, high-performing cleaning products that would make a home feel fresher, more livable, and more beautiful. These products were packaged so attractively that they would market themselves on stores' shelves. They sought to extend the reach of the brand by focusing on audience segmentation rather than product segmentation, wherein Method cultivated customer loyalty to the brand across all the company's cleaning products rather than cultivating loyalty to a particular cleaning product.

Video Discussion Questions

1. What are the key product features or qualities that define the Method brand of household cleaning products?

2. What value accrues to customers who purchase the Method brand of household cleaning products? What value accrues to Method itself?

3. Is Method's line of household cleaning products a luxury brand? Explain your answer.

Chapter 8
New Products

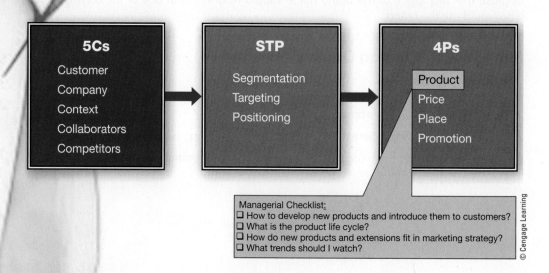

5Cs	STP	4Ps
Customer	Segmentation	Product
Company	Targeting	Price
Context	Positioning	Place
Collaborators		Promotion
Competitors		

Managerial Checklist:
☐ How to develop new products and introduce them to customers?
☐ What is the product life cycle?
☐ How do new products and extensions fit in marketing strategy?
☐ What trends should I watch?

© Cengage Learning

Marketing Management Framework

8-1 WHY ARE NEW PRODUCTS IMPORTANT?

"New and improved!" You see it everywhere. Why? New products are fun for customers, they're fun for employees to work on, and they fuel the company's income.

Companies, like people, are ever evolving. The primary way that companies make changes is by offering "new and improved!" goods and services to customers. Companies seek to *improve* their current products for numerous reasons: a simple point of corporate pride, to be consistent with an image as being innovative, as an effort to better satisfy current customers or attract new customers, or to stave off competition. With *new* product introductions, the company has achieved some success with its existing portfolio and reflects "What else can we do that might appeal to customers and that is something we're likely to be able to do well and better than our competitors? How can we leverage our strengths and technical advantages? How can we serve new markets?"

Change is inevitable. The macroenvironmental context continually shifts, and trends in demographics create predictable transformations in markets and customer demands for new and different products (discussed later in the chapter). For example, the availability of natural resources—even simple supply-side basics such as oil, wood, sugar—have implications for many companies.

122

Change is good. New products increase a company's long-term financial performance and the firm's value.

And change is fun! Customers who like cars can't wait to see next year's new models. Those who like fashion eagerly anticipate every new season. Movie lovers can't wait until Friday. From the marketing manager's point of view, it's fun to work on a new project, to be a part of offering something new in the marketplace and watch the customers respond, ideally, positively!

In this chapter, we'll look at the process of new product development and the stages of the product life cycle. We'll examine strategies to maintain strong product portfolios, and, as we've already implied, we'll need to keep a close eye on our classic Cs: change in the business context, strengths of our company, our customers' desires, and possible collaborator and competitive actions.

8-2 HOW DOES MARKETING DEVELOP NEW PRODUCTS FOR THEIR CUSTOMERS?

Companies differ in their approaches to designing new products. Some pride themselves on being innovative, whereas others are more conservative, launching me-too products after other companies break new ground. We'll see that one of the primary philosophical differences is in how and when companies involve their customers. We'll then see how the process typically unfolds.

8-2a Philosophies of Product Development

Ideally, new product development involves conversations and interactions with customers, but companies differ in how much they draw from customers relative to how much they emphasize their own assertions. These differences are referred to as *top down* when a company thinks up a new idea, develops it, and doesn't involve the customer until somewhat later in the process. They are called *bottom up* when the ideas spring from the customers themselves and are then developed by the company. The top-down approach is often favored in companies with technical expertise (e.g., engineering and medical), but both approaches have their strengths, as we shall see.

Being Culturally Sensitive

Mattell's Barbie entered India with great aplomb.

She got a cold shoulder when she entered China. The Chinese target segment prefers cute to sexy (á la Hello Kitty).

Different strokes!

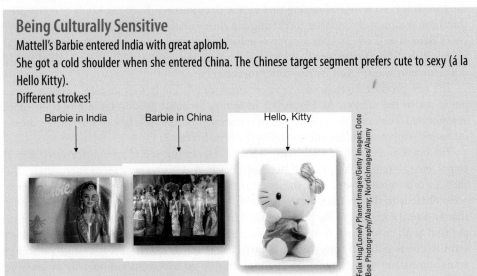

Barbie in India   Barbie in China   Hello, Kitty

Felix Hug/Lonely Planet Images/Getty Images; Oote Boe Photography/Alamy; NordicImages/Alamy

Topdown. The process of developing new products depends first on a company's culture. Some companies take a nearly exclusively top-down approach, beginning with idea generation, proceeding to design and development and then to commercialization. Marketing is essentially an afterthought, to help with the final launch phase to introduce the product to customers.

A top-down approach is found frequently among companies with strong engineering orientations, pharmaceutical and biomedical firms, financial services, and many high-technology companies. The internal R&D team has expertise that the end users lack; thus, it creates cutting-edge products (e.g., a new computer, pill, mutual fund, TV) with such advanced technological benefits and advantages that seem so obvious to the experts that the team believes the product will sell itself.

This approach is the build-a-better-mousetrap philosophy, and it has facilitated zillions of successful new products. It's not necessarily a simple process, nor a particularly quick one (e.g., drugs take years of development). Furthermore, the process can be top down for poor reasons, such as a CEO with a pet project who won't let it go.

Top down is sometimes also called *inside out* because the idea comes from within the company. Feedback from the outside (customers, suppliers, etc.) is sought later in the process. As long as any feedback is obtained from customers, this can be a perfectly fine approach. It is indeed usually the case that such companies can envision more cool new products than their customers could have articulated.

Cocreation. If this process is called top down (or inside out), its opposite should be called bottom up (or outside in), but these days it's referred to as *cocreation* (with the customer). The truth is, in the real world, neither extreme occurs—where the engineers or IT guys are consulted, but the customers are not, or vice versa. So the difference between these styles is just a matter of when and how frequently feedback from customers and business partners is sought.

8-2b Marketing

In marketing-oriented companies, customer feedback is sought at most phases in the process. As is true of most marketing phenomena, consumer packaged goods companies (and those that provide some simple services) excel in the iteration between thinking up what the company can create and testing that idea with customers. Even the kinds of companies that have traditionally ignored marketing are increasingly aware of its importance. Mercedes Benz says, "Here's our new car; you're lucky if you can buy it." And it's right. Whereas Honda says, "We can configure all kinds of features and services for our cars. What would our customers want?" And it's the better marketer.

The new product development process might sound simple: Get an idea, develop it, and put it out in the market. As Figure 8.1 indicates, for most products, the process is more complicated. For example, a great deal of refinement occurs throughout the entire process, including winnowing ideas and tweaking them in-house.

The figure is also a little misleading because it looks linear and straightforward (step 1, step 2, etc.), where, in fact, a lot of iterations occur. A decision may seem appropriate, and then, in subsequent stages, it becomes clear that the earlier decision is untenable. It may seem obvious in the abstract that we shouldn't continue to push forward with something that is already known to be problematic. Unfortunately, that happens a lot (e.g., people tout sunk costs, want to meet preannounced launch dates for PR or investors, don't want to create political waves, etc.). Clearly, it's better to revisit decisions and get things straightened out even if it may be disappointing to go backward temporarily or seeming to slow down.

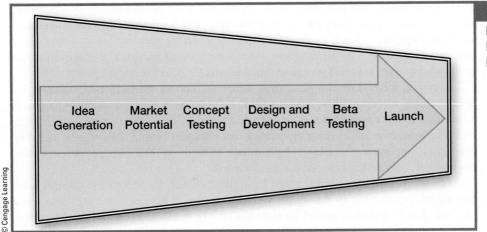

Figure 8.1

New Product Development Process

Marketing management is involved throughout the process. In the early stage of idea generation, the knowledge of customer needs and wants interact with corporate and marketing strategies to see what potential new products makes sense for the firm. Marketing research should also be involved in all the refinement phases and in the decisions about the marketing mix that must be made as the launch approaches. Ideally, all the marketing components (e.g., pricing, packaging, channels) are treated holistically from the beginning of the process through to launch; thus, as the product concept is refined, so are decisions about retail outlets, price points, etc., in order to offer the customer a consistently positioned product. Next we look at the new product development process in greater detail.

8-2c Idea Creation and Market Potential

Ideas can come from anywhere (Figure 8.2). Per the expression "Necessity is the mother of invention," one source of new products is that marketers observe the world around them. This nonsystematic, qualitative form of marketing research helps marketers identify problems that customers have that might be solved with products the firm could offer. For instance, your kids don't like brushing their teeth? No problem. Our toothbrushes light up like a game.

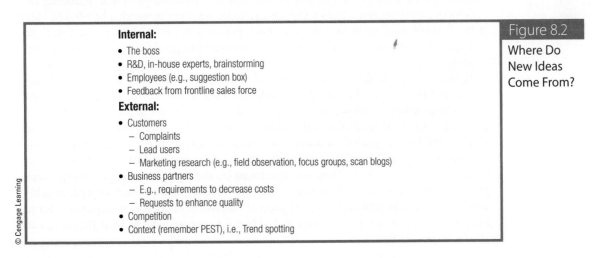

Internal:
- The boss
- R&D, in-house experts, brainstorming
- Employees (e.g., suggestion box)
- Feedback from frontline sales force

External:
- Customers
  - Complaints
  - Lead users
  - Marketing research (e.g., field observation, focus groups, scan blogs)
- Business partners
  - E.g., requirements to decrease costs
  - Requests to enhance quality
- Competition
- Context (remember PEST), i.e., Trend spotting

Figure 8.2

Where Do New Ideas Come From?

Ideas can come from observing social (or cultural or economic) trends, from listening to customers, from your sales force or your frontline service workers. Ideas are often somewhat serendipitous; as Louis Pasteur said, "Chance favors the prepared mind." For example, Viagra was originally created to relieve heart pain. It wasn't particularly effective for that symptom, but users reported an interesting side effect … and the rest is history.

The typical method of idea generation begins with good, old-fashioned, coffee-fueled brainstorming meetings. These sessions are the classic generative discussions—"No idea's a bad idea; let's get everything up on the whiteboard." Companies that pride themselves on being innovative are increasingly putting real resources behind their claims, including supporting employees' allocating a day a month to work on their own pet projects, to be assessed later and perhaps funded for development.

After many ideas have been generated and sketched out, the next step is in-house winnowing and refinement. In this phase, we acknowledge, "Okay, maybe some ideas are in fact bad ideas." Ideas are screened for their plausibility in construction and provision, their compatibility with corporate and marketing goals, and their likelihood of success with customers. At this point, the expertise of the designers, engineers, chemists, etc. are being balanced with the marketers' knowledge of the target customer segment(s) and management's guidance about the firm's identity (e.g., Rolex doesn't want to make an affordable watch, and Disney needs to stay wholesome).

While feasibility assessments and business analyses are somewhat fuzzy at this stage, they are valuable exercises in making assumptions explicit: Who is the target segment? What is its size? What competitors already seek their dollar? What products of our own might we cannibalize? Do we have channels already in place for the distribution of this product, or should we be studying those issues as well? How does the new product initiative fit with our organizational goals and our marketing objectives? Teams can be assembled to investigate answers to these component questions as the product development process continues.

8-2d Concept Testing and Design and Development

At this stage in the new product development process, the company has a number of ideas that it thinks might work, and it's time to get customers' feedback as to which ideas sound most promising. The form of the marketing research at this stage is usually focus groups and increasingly Web surveys (especially for technical target audiences). The particular marketing research techniques used aren't half as important as the fact that marketing research is conducted at all. This stage is the first of several during which marketing research can save a company from a bad idea, yield information to tweak a half-baked idea, or result in encouragement that the company is pursuing an idea with true potential. Time and again, new product success (vs. failure) is attributed to good (vs. poor or nonexistent) marketing research.

If focus groups are the vehicle of choice, 2–3 groups (per segment) of 8–10 target customers are invited to see the concepts and offer feedback. These (1.5- to 2-hour) discussions can begin as broadly as asking the customers to describe their uses of products in this category (e.g., household goods, foods, their driving habits, etc.) to get background information that can inform the product development or the positioning of the product via communications materials developed subsequently. The concepts might be described verbally, but visual cues are very helpful. These visual aids can be as simple as artist's renderings, sleek photos, or mock prototypes. Still more complex is a rendering via virtual reality. Competitors' products can be provided also, as a point of discussion, to get the customers to react to tangible, existing goods. Descriptions and photos (of proposed and existing products) can also be shown via Web surveys.

In either a focus group or online study, a conjoint procedure can be run. In a conjoint study, different combinations of attributes are put together and compared, and the customer is simply asked which product combination sounds best, next best, and so on. From those overall evaluations, the conjoint analysis derives which attributes matter more than others (e.g., the company may learn that it's important for laptops to be light and powerful, and less important that they're encased in color). For the attributes that customers care most about, what are the levels sought? For example, for qualities like a laptop being "light" and "powerful," clearly lighter is better, and more powerful is better, but for those in a segment who care about color, what do they want? Hi-tech gray? Neon blue? And if an important attribute is that the laptop be "preloaded with lots of software," what programs in particular do customers want to see?

Conjoint is great because it gets at customers' trade-offs. It's not unusual for customers to say they want the best of everything, and—oh, by the way—at a really cheap price. Typically a company cannot offer all of that profitably, so a conjoint allows the detection of what price a customer is willing to pay for the loaded laptop. Or, if customers aren't willing to pay a high price, what are the features that all of a sudden become less important—that they're willing to trade off?

After the marketing research conducted in this concept testing stage, the marketing manager has a better sense of which products and features seem to be those most attractive to customers. Internally, the second major winnowing-and-refinement phase critically assesses the paths that no longer appear to have potential and should be discarded or tabled (e.g., those that require advances in technology or societal acceptance) and those that customers find appealing or might find appealing with further modifications.

Insights from customer feedback are often quite eye-opening. In-house experts assume they know what's best and are frequently surprised at customers' reactions. When customers do not like the proposed products, the experts can be dismissive, regarding the customers as stupid. Nevertheless, those unenlightened souls comprise the target purchasers, hence the difficulty lies in the product or the vision, which apparently isn't being communicated clearly. For example, it is not unusual for creators of high-tech gadgetry to overload their new products with all kinds of whiz-bang features, but customers' reactions can be lukewarm because the multitude of options and capabilities seems overwhelming and the product seems difficult to use.

Another round of refined concept testing might occur if any ambiguities remain or if sufficient changes were made such that the reactions to the initial concept are likely to be no longer relevant. When the company is confident it has a handle on which product to develop, it begins to do so. Usually only a single prototype is developed, rather than multiple prototypes, in part because development can be expensive, but, more humanly, because the issue is more about narrow attention spans. It's just easier for the product development team to focus on one product at a time. If one product development goes forward, great! Otherwise, it's back to the drawing board to work up the next one serially rather than process several in parallel.

8-2e Beta Testing

At this point, a beta version of the product is made available for trial and consumption. Ideally, the product is used in the consumer's home or in as similar a setting as possible to simulate a real-world purchase decision and evaluation, for more accurate forecasting later.

While the product is being developed, so should the marketing materials be in the works. Their early development and refinement help make certain the consistency in the positioning information being absorbed by the customer. Thus, while products are being shown to customers for their reactions, advertising copy is also shown to them, price points are made clear, distribution and availability are explained, etc. Showing customers the marketing information both helps clarify the image of the product and allows the company to get feedback on the marketing information itself.

The marketing manager now has evidence of customer potential, and the product has been repeatedly refined. It's time to try the product in the market, on a small scale, before a more expensive full-scale commercial rollout.

Thus far, the marketing research has been comprised of fairly tightly controlled stimuli: A product and an ad and a price are shown to a set of customers, and their reactions noted. Even if competitors knew of the new product development efforts, they cannot interfere with the tests being conducted. Yet when customers are sitting in a focus group or answering questions online, they know they're doing something weird; their behavior isn't likely quite the same as what it will be in the natural marketplace environment (e.g., at a grocery store, at the mall, or at amazon.com). So the idea underlying test marketing is to try to simulate a real-world setting to help customers' reactions be more predictive of their subsequent actual purchasing behavior when the product is launched.

Area test markets are a neat idea. Some 40–50 small metropolitan areas throughout the U.S. are known to marketing research firms as having characteristics (e.g., demographics, socioeconomic status) representative of the country as a whole. A few (2–3) of these areas are randomly sampled to be test markets, in which the product is made available for purchase (and the remaining areas serve as control markets). Ads are run in the test markets, deals are made with the local retail chains, etc. Sales are observed through the test period (3–12 months) and compared to sales in the control markets to give the company a sense of how well the product is likely to sell.

Area test markets aren't used that frequently any more, mostly because they're expensive. They require setup that, while small-scale, nevertheless requires manufacturing, machines, personnel training, etc. They also signal to competitors living and observantly watching in those test markets just what might be coming down the pike, and many a lawsuit has been filed over a product that has been scooped by a competitor. Finally, each of those areas, while chosen for being fairly representative of the broader target population, can have their own local flavors and oddities that can bias the results in unpredictable ways. For instance, if sales are high in one area but low in another, did something about the markets spuriously inflate or suppress sales?

Electronic test markets are also a cool idea. A sample of metropolitan areas is selected, and, within each market, some households are designated as test and others as control. All the local context is therefore equated (local TV stations, newspapers, local stores, local brands, cultural interests, etc.), so whatever differences exist between the households' purchasing is more cleanly attributable to some households having exposure to ads (e.g., via cable transmissions not sent to the control households) or access to the product (e.g., in stores closer to their homes), etc. Given the tighter constraints, the validity of the electronic test market dominates that of the area test market.

Today, *simulated test markets* are the popular means of pre-market launch tests. A customer is recruited (e.g., via a mall intercept or e-mail) to go to an office in the mall (or to a website), where they are given a budget and have an opportunity to buy the new product, which is offered among competitors' or related products. Virtual grocery store aisles are displayed (sometimes in 3-D or virtual reality but, as often as not, just a flat view) that provide the same information the customer would see on a typical trip to the grocery. There would be row after row of pictures of competitors' products, and the new product embedded, on the shelf as it would be when eventually launched. The marketer is looking for how often the new product is selected in this pseudoreal context.

The advertising materials would be available with competitors' ads and offered subtly, e.g., in the context of a popular magazine or TV ads inserted into natural commercial breaks of shows the customer might be asked to view. Marketers would watch the purchases of the new product, and the customers would be asked to fill out a litany of survey questions. All of this customer data would be used as inputs to sales forecasts.

8-2f Launch

In the final steps toward commercialization, both time and money matter. Let's consider money first.

Forecasting. Upon completion of the test marketing, the marketing manager takes the customer data and tries to predict the product's likely success. If the predictions of sales are not promising, this stage is the last opportunity for the company to abort before launching (and likely failing). If the predictions are promising, the company proceeds to commercialize. The forecasting numbers are useful throughout the organization—to accounting and finance for budgeting purposes, to the sales force for setting goals, to production and logistics for planning regarding equipment, storage, and transportation, etc.

Forecasting can be highly technical, but here's a simple formula to get a sense of the basic logic. The goal is to estimate the sales potential, $SP (not the same as estimated sales but more like a ceiling).

The first estimate we need is the market potential (MP); i.e., how many units might possibly be sold. Recall the chaining model approach from Chapter 4 on targeting. We might start with secondary data (e.g., the size of the target potential by census demographics) or other relevant in-house benchmarking data. For example, if the new product is somewhat like a current offering, as with a brand or line extension, then the company would know its numbers for the existing product.

The next piece is the estimate of the purchase intention (PI), or the likelihood that the target segment will buy the product. This number comes from the most recently conducted marketing research. Let's say that among the customers sampled from the target population, the average stated purchase intention was $p = 0.7$. It is important to know that customers predictably overstate their purchase intentions. Companies with databases of past new product launches can look to see what the PI vs. realized sales were and adjust accordingly. For companies without such experience or data, research has suggested ratcheting the estimate downward by a factor of ¾. Thus, if the data said $p = 0.7$, the estimate to be used in the forecasting would be PI = ¾(0.7) = 0.525.

Finally, the component that is under the company's control is the price (Pr) the company intends to charge. (Of course, as economics would tell us, the components in the equation aren't entirely independent; PI is likely to increase a smidge as Pr drops. That's why the marketing mixed should be tested with customers along with the product itself.) These pieces come together in this equation:

$$\$SP = MP \times PI \times Pr$$

For example, businessweek.com reports that Verizon is test marketing a TV video game for young teenage boys. Verizon is testing in an affluent Dallas suburb, but it wants to extrapolate the findings to the broader U.S. The population estimate for the U.S. is about 300mm; the U.S. teen population is 33mm, approximately half of whom are boys, and let's say that roughly one-third of the boys are in the 13- to 15-year-old age bracket. From gaming industry statistics, say Verizon learns that about 20% of eligible target customers are likely to purchase the cable game subscription. Based on those gross secondary statistics, an upper limit estimate for MP is some 1.1mm (= 33mm ÷ 2 ÷ 3 × 0.2) teen boys to whom a new video game is targeted. If testing suggested that PI (with the correction factor already included) is 0.525, and the company plans on charging $9.95 for the DVD or download, then the estimate is

$$\$SP = 1,100,000 \times 0.525 \times \$9.95 = \$5,746,125$$

That number is not profit; it's (potential max) sales, with no development or production or marketing costs factored in yet. Is that number good news, or is that barely enough to bother? If corporate decides that's a worthy goal, then the next step is to launch the product, which means that, finally, after months and sometimes years in development, the product sees the light of day.

Timing. New product development can move along fairly speedily for straightforward brand or line extensions in the context of a mature consumer packaged goods company, but in other settings, the development process can seem torturously slow. For example, pharmaceutical testing begins on animals (for months to years), then the drug is tried on 20–100 healthy patients (for months) to check basic safety (e.g., side effects). Next, the drug is tested on several hundred patients with the particular disease (from 3 months to 2 years) to continue to check safety and to add checks on efficacy. Finally, 100s to 1000s of people (healthy and sick) are observed (1–4 years), to check safety and efficacy and to tweak dosage.

Time is indeed money, and to recoup this extended testing and investment, pharmaceuticals spend $20 billion annually on promotional efforts, e.g., providing retail samples to doctors. D2C (direct to consumers) pharma advertising is growing like crazy (doubling every two years) and is interesting to marketers and salient in business news because of its novelty, but as yet it is actually still fairly small in size (e.g., 5–10% of sales). There can also be external, regulatory delays to product launches, such as

- The FDA (Food and Drug Administration) is trying to reduce the length of time to market with shortcuts on clinical trials. Yet every action is met with an equal and opposite reaction, and the FDA is under investigation for pushing drugs to market too quickly (arising from problems with drugs that produced rare but serious side effects).

- Other industries voice complaints about delays by analogous approval agencies, such as patent offices. Some big companies ask for court intervention to speed things up so that they don't lose millions of dollars in opportunity costs.

- Comparable issues occur with copyright registrations for intangibles like software, movies, video games, music, and architectural plans (seriously). A controversy about when a copyright is official has recently been resolved (at least for now) in favor for simple filing and application, not for when material copyrighted is registered.

8-2g What Is the Product Life Cycle?

Another reason that new products are important is that the company's product portfolio may be aging. The product life cycle is a popular metaphor in marketing to describe the evolution and duration of a product in the marketplace (Figure 8.3). Just as people are born, grow, mature, and eventually die, products are thought to go through a similar life span. The stages are market introduction (the new product development phase we've been discussing), market growth, maturity, and decline. Sales and profits behave predictably during the different phases (indeed, these indicators usually determine the phase in which a product exists), and the marketing actions that are thought to be optimal during each phase are also clearly prescribed.

Anatomy of a Product Life Cycle

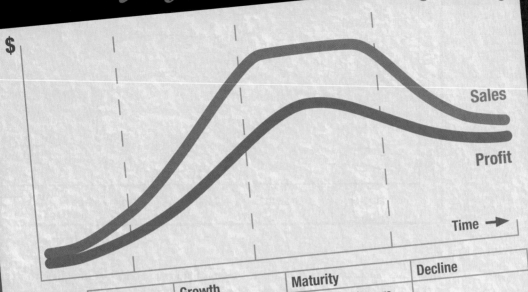

	Intro	Growth	Maturity	Decline
Goals	First-time buyers	Encourage loyalty	Attract new buyers	
Product	One product	Tweak product	New features	Reduce number of products
Price	High	Reduce to compete	Maintain share	Lower if still profitable
Promotion	Give Information	Compare to competitors	Reminders	Cut to stay profitable

PLCs are different for brands, industries, technologies, markets . . .

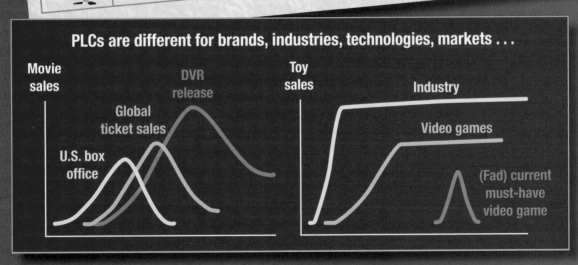

Movie sales — U.S. box office — Global ticket sales — DVR release

Toy sales — Industry — Video games — (Fad) current must-have video game

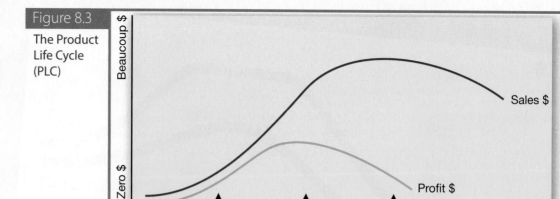

Figure 8.3

The Product
Life Cycle
(PLC)

© Cengage Learning

During *market introduction*, a new product (good or service) is brought into the marketplace with heavy marketing spending (e.g., communications to spark awareness). In addition to advertising to provide information and attempts at persuasion, promotion can include samples and coupons to spur trial. Strategically, prices might start low (penetration), but they often start high (skimming) in part to recoup development costs and in part because there is little competition early on. Distribution is somewhat limited in these early phases, and all of these factors contribute to the typical result that sales are low and slow in the beginning.

The second phase is one of *market growth*. Sales accelerate and profits rise at first. Customer awareness is stronger, and there may be some buzz in the marketplace. Distribution channel coverage is greater, so access also contributes to stronger sales. The firm might be able to begin increasing prices (resulting in higher margins and greater profits). At the same time, competitors observe the pioneering company's successes and start sniffing profit potential, so they enter the game. Competitors either kill off each other, or they begin to specialize a little, identifying emergent segments to which their products can be tailored and targeted. The initial firm can sustain the competition if it had had enough foresight to have launched a product with some reasonable edge of a competitive advantage and if the product can be slightly altered to maintain distinctiveness (and supporting possible price maintenance for interested segments). At this stage, advertising is intended to persuade customers as to the brand's superiority compared to competitors.

Some point later brings a product to *market maturity*. Advertising continues to try to persuade customers about a brand's relative advantages and serves as a reminder to buy in the product category. Products may proliferate to a fuller product line in order to satisfy more segments of customers. Industry sales have leveled off, so competition is intensifying; there is more competition than in any other stage in the life cycle. The stiff competition has induced higher marketing costs and likely lower prices; thus, while sales are stronger than ever, profits have declined. In addition, the pie is no longer growing in size, so strong competitors gain market share or increase their sales only by taking it away from other competitors. Hence, weaker firms begin to fall out of the marketplace. In addition, because firms are going after each other, their product offerings often begin to homogenize to the point that customers see fewer distinguishing characteristics. Instead of swirling into price drops with competition, it's smart to try to find new benefits and either to increase or at least maintain current prices.

The final phase in the product life cycle is that of *market decline*. Sales and profits are both dropping, and new products are replacing older generations. The firm needs to decide what to do with the old product.

1. Sometimes it is divested. If this is the route to be taken, the decision should be made as early as possible, because the best sales price is obtained if it is sold off early, while the product still looks attractive to another firm. Unfortunately, early timing for divestment is difficult to judge; often companies aren't sure when the product has hit the decline stage and aren't willing to give up on it. They hold onto it until it is probably too late to be sold off because it is no longer a desirable investment for another firm.

2. An old product can be harvested. The firm reduces supportive and marketing expenditures to extract more profits. They're merely milking the product, and they know that demand will continue to drop.

3. Perhaps the happiest prognosis for a dying product is when a firm wishes to rejuvenate it as "new and improved!" The product is refurbished to have new beneficial features that the target customer might desire.

While the product life cycle is an intuitively appealing metaphor, critics point out that it is just that, a metaphor. They point out that brands and products are not organic; therefore, they don't have to die. They argue that the life cycle is actually a self-fulfilling prophecy, e.g., when a firm determines that a product is mature, it might lessen the advertising support, in effect causing the product's decline.

The lengths of product life cycles vary a lot. Researchers point to the short lifespan of movies (years and millions of dollars spent in development for only a few weeks in theaters). Yet movies get reborn in the form of international box office, cable, DVD rentals and sales, each bringing a reinvigoration to the product and sales, albeit in a different guise and to a different target audience. Other products and brands, such as Coca-Cola or Tide or Sears or Holiday Inn, seem to stay in that juicy sales phase of maturity for an extended life.

Finally, the length of product-category life cycles tends to be longer than those of individual brands; that is, a particular movie might not "live" a long life, but the category of movies is 100 years old. Or the macro-level category of sports is a healthy and very mature product, but one could point to NASCAR as an example of a recent, younger subproduct with explosive growth.

8-2h Diffusion of Innovation

In addition to the marketing actions underlying the product life cycle, marketers have also developed a theory about what customers are doing during these phases as well. The concept is that new products are like contagious diseases. A high-tech-loving friend who gets some new electronics gadget shows it to friends, and some of them are inspired to buy the gadget and tell their friends. Or the movie-loving friend naturally reads more and knows more about forthcoming movies and is likely to be among the first to see the new show and perhaps then to recommend it—or not. This word of mouth, or viral marketing, helps activate the process of the diffusion of innovations.

The model itself is pretty simple. Marketers posit a normal curve (Figure 8.4) and partition the customer base into groups. The *innovators* are the first 3–5% who like to try new ideas and are willing to take risks. They tend to be relatively educated and confident in assessing information about a product on their own. Note that you might be an innovator with electronics and not movies, or vice versa, and some people are innovators across

Figure 8.4

Diffusion of
Innovation

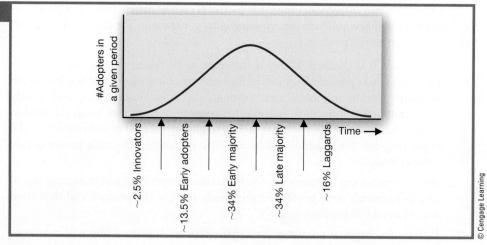

multiple categories. You tend to be an innovator in the product categories in which you have greater involvement unless you have an overwhelming risk-aversion streak that just dampens everything.

The *early adopters* are the next group (10–15%) who are even more influential as opinion leaders, primarily because they are a bigger group. This group is so influential that the loss of one of these early adopters costs the firm more than the loss of later adopters.

The *early majority* (34%) are more risk averse than the first two groups. They're waiting to hear that the early adopters have had favorable experiences with the new product. The *late majority* (34%) are even more cautious, often older and more conservative, and they wish to buy only proven products.

The final group, the *laggards* or *nonadopters* (5–15%), are the most risk averse, skeptical of new products, and stereotypically lower in income (and so perhaps cannot afford to be risky with their purchases). Sometimes the product category has no relevance to them (e.g., your grandfather probably doesn't appreciate the features on your new MP3 player).

The curve of new adopters at each point in time (Figure 8.4) can be recast to show cumulative sales—the number of adopters thus far at each point in time, such as the S-curve in Figure 8.5. The point at which the sales rate increases rapidly, i.e., when sales take off, is determined via calculus as the point of inflection in the curve. In contemporary parlance, it's referred to as the tipping point—the point at which the product or idea catches on and moves like wildfire throughout the marketplace.

Figure 8.5

Cumulative
Diffusion

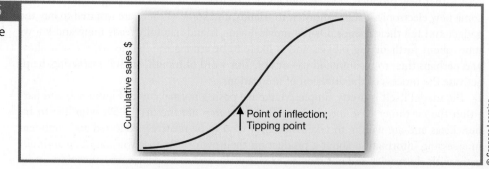

Marketers have forecast sales using this logic. In the equation in Figure 8.6, we are trying to forecast n, the number of units we will sell during time period, t. The prediction is a function of several components: N_{t-1} represents the number of units we have sold so far (cumulative sales in units). M is the max on the likely market potential. The term on the right, $(M - N_{t-1})$, means how are we doing so far: What's the difference between what we could sell (M) and what we've sold so far (N_{t-1})?

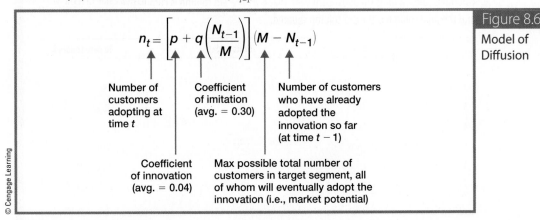

Figure 8.6

Model of Diffusion

Traditionally the pieces that interest marketers are the parameters p and q. The first, p, is called the coefficient of innovation; it's the likelihood that someone will buy or adopt the new product due to information obtained from the marketer. The second, q, is the coefficient of imitation—the likelihood that someone will buy or adopt the new product due to word-of-mouth information obtained from another consumer, e.g., an innovator.

The diffusion model has been used two different ways. First, we can observe early sales data, fit the model, and make predictions about the future. For example, once sales begin, we'll have numbers for n_t and N_{t-1} (t can be yearly data, quarterly, weekly, hourly, etc.). We conduct market sizing exercises (Chapter 4), to obtain an estimate for M. We then solve for estimates of p and q. Alternatively, we can use past results on products similar to ours and plug in those numbers to make predictions about the future even before launching the product.

The imitation effect, q, is usually bigger ($p{:}q$ is about 1:10), and if you consider the massive size of the majority in Figure 8.5, it's easy to see why. The percentage of innovators and early adopters (the customers who are driving p) is about 10–15% of the market, whereas the remainder of the market (the majority, etc.) is 85–90%, and they're driving q. Marketers can speed up innovators (make p bigger) by introducing price decreases early or speed up imitators (make q bigger) by introducing price decreases later.

Marketers are interacting with customers throughout these phases. The first job in a new product launch is heightening awareness, traditionally done through advertising.

Diffusion of Innovation

Forecasting sales can be accomplished via the Model of Diffusion. Forecasted sales for a given period, n_t, are calculated using several elements:

- M is the maximum possible market potential.
- N_{t-1} is the number of customers who have already adopted the innovation.
- The coefficient of innovation, p, is the likelihood that someone will buy a new product based on information provided by the marketer.

- The coefficient of imitation, q, is the likelihood that someone will buy a new product due to information obtained by another user.

The full equation $n_t = [p + q(N_{t-1}/M)](M - N_{t-1})$.

To demonstrate, we'll use a classic data set that everyone uses: the Zenith HDTV sales. The 1st column is some unit of time (it could be weekly sales, quarterly, etc.); here it is annual sales. The 2nd column is sales of units (in 000s) each year, that is n_t. The 3rd column is cumulative sales to date, N_{t-1}, and the final column is the 3rd column squared.

	Year	Units to date	To date squared
1	14	0	0
2	121	14	196
3	648	135	18,225
4	1,460	783	613,089
5	2,536	2,243	5,031,049
6	4,102	4,779	22,838,841
7	5,705	8,881	78,872,161
		14,586	

1. Fit a regression with units as the dependent variable and with the 3rd and 4th columns as predictors. That yields the model:

    Predicted units = 298.32 + 1.09*todate − 0.0000552*todate2

2. Call these values $c = 298.32$, $b = 1.09$, $a = -0.0000552$.
3. Solve for:

    a. $M = [-b - \text{sqrt}(b^2 - 4ac)]/(2a) = 22{,}098.$*
    b. $p = c/M = 0.0135.$
    c. $q = b + p = 1.1035.$

Note: Alternatively, try M as the cumulative sales to date and 14,586 (as a likely minimum) to see if there's convergence on p and q. Here, $p = 298.32/14{,}586 = 0.0205$, and $q = 1.09 + 0.0205 = 1.1105$. Indeed, this p and q are fairly similar to those estimated from the model estimate of M.)

Advertising can be expensive, and marketers have long known that if they have a hot product, word will spread like wildfire, and the buzz will do the job of advertising—for free. In diffusion, word of mouth increases the size of q, the imitation effect. The question is how to identify the opinion leaders, or market mavens, and activate their networks. This topic is so important that we'll focus on it in Chapter 13, when we consider social media.

8-3 HOW DO NEW PRODUCTS AND BRAND EXTENSIONS FIT IN MARKETING STRATEGY?

We've been examining the new product development process, the product life cycle, and the diffusion of innovation. Let's zoom back out and check in on the marketing Cs. A company can begin its new product plan internally by identifying the corporate and marketing missions and objectives to be achieved with the new product or service. Applying SWOT analysis, the marketer asks of the company, "What are our strengths and weaknesses?" and of the industry, "What are the opportunities and threats?"

It should be clear that customers are important in the feedback they provide in the new product development process. A number of factors influence customers' acceptance of new products and the diffusion of the innovation throughout the marketplace. Customers will ask, "What is the benefit of this new thing?" and "Why should I buy it?" Consumer acceptance tends to be higher when the new product

- Has a clear relative advantage over existing products.

- Is compatible with the customer's lifestyle.

- Is not overly complex, or the complexity is masked by a user-friendly interface.

- Is easily tried or sampled in order to facilitate initial assessment.

The customer is important from the beginning, when marketing identifies the target and conducts market analyses to make sales forecasts (e.g., estimating size, growth, customers' unmet needs, trends, etc.).

Competitor analysis is integral to the mission planning in that the benefits of the new product that are points of differentiation (sustainable competitive advantages in the value proposition) must be clear, (Customers can ask, "How is yours better than the competition?" and competitors can ask, "Why don't we offer the same thing, even better?!") Competitor analyses also take the form of identifying which industries and companies are truly competitors and guesstimating their likely reactions.

Most companies offer multiple product lines, so they're constantly balancing the strategic needs of products at different points in their life cycles. Different stages in the life cycle require different investments, e.g., periods of growth need cash, whereas periods of slower growth might generate cash to be reinvested to maintain share. For new service innovations, some of the R&D investment is the training of employees before the service is launched as operational.

Much like the personalities of people in the diffusion of innovation process, companies vary in whether they desire to be known as cutting edge. Some companies value their reputations as innovators, and their business relies on new product market growth. Other companies are more comfortable in their roles as reactors. They might not be the innovators, but they can be quick responders, coming to market soon with slightly different attributes or better price points, for example. Finally, later companies may be more risk averse or not aggressive marketers and offer a product only when it's clear the customer demand exists.

Much research has been generated investigating each of these strategies. Market pioneers have difficulty with really new products. The first to market is often the first to fail. A new concept takes a while to sink into the minds of customers. By comparison, first movers may have advantages in launching incrementally new products because there is less risk. In either case, after the first firm, the next few early follower firms have approximately the same survival risks when launching either the really new or the incrementally new products. Next-generation products (e.g., smartphones, desktops, video games) are easier to launch because there is an existing customer base, channels of distribution, and much more predictability.

8-3a Strategic Thinking About Growth

Marketers have to be smart about where all these new products fit into their marketing and corporate portfolio. It's true that some things in life are serendipitous and that we might occasionally behave opportunistically, but as a company gets bigger and bigger, lots of people are counting on its success. The top folks need to show they have some vision, to know where the company is going, and to not to react to random events.

The strategic paths to growth that marketers typically talk about may be classified by whether you stick to your current product mix and take it to new target segments or generate altogether new products. That's all it comes down to new stuff or new peeps. Figure 8.7 shows the matrix of growth opportunities.

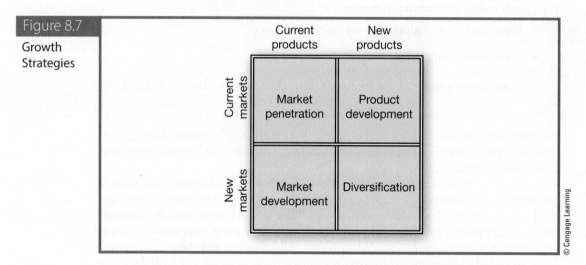

Figure 8.7

Growth Strategies

Market penetration means we're hunkering down and trying to sell more—same stuff, same customers. If the customers are not completely tapped, this is certainly the easiest of all the strategies; we don't have to make anything new, and we know how to reach these customers. Companies strive for more sales (via this strategy) by suggesting new ways to use the product; they might open more stores or improve the marketing mix or turn to more intriguing advertising, better pricing, better reward programs, better in-store service, better store ambience, etc.

Product development is for the company who wishes to be innovative. New or modified products are offered to the current customer base to keep them happy. These new products may be as dramatic as brand and line extensions, but often they are modest extensions (e.g., larger sizes, new flavors, different packaging, etc.).

Market development is the path to take when we're settled on our product mix and we think there are more segment opportunities to target. This path can be dramatic when we launch our brand internationally, but it also is more often subtle, e.g., trying to appeal to a slightly younger or older crowd, trying to appeal to men if the product mostly sells to women, etc. The product may remain the same, but, to reach the new target, we might need to expand our channels and modify our promotional communications to create a new image for that new target.

Finally, *diversification* is the toughest—we're going after new customers with new products. If you think of the 2×2 matrix in Figure 8.7 as a game board, the company can start in the upper-left corner (market penetration), moving to the right (product development) or down (market development), is relatively straightforward. From either of those places, it is easier to move to diversification. But it's just too big a jump for most companies to go from doing what we know how to do for the customers who like us (upper left) to doing something we don't have a clue about for customers we don't know and who don't know us (lower right). Baby steps: Go right or down. Then go down or right.

8-4 WHAT TRENDS SHOULD I WATCH?

It's important to keep an eye on how the world is changing and the directions of things because trends form the context in which all the new products forecasting is occurring. Demographic, lifestyle, and cultural trends can boost or constrain the success of a new product.

Perhaps the most stunning demographic trend in America and Western Europe is the aging of the population (e.g., more elderly, fewer kids and teens). In 20 years, 20% of Europeans will be 65 years old or older. Sheer age carries both health and wealth concerns. Aging brings greater health care needs because the populace will experience predictably more rheumatoid arthritis, osteoporosis, prostate problems, etc. Supplemental health enhancement industries will also grow. For example, in the vain attempt to delay the aging process, witness the growth of botox and health spa consumption. And to help with old bones, people in the U.S. are retiring to the Sunbelt (southern and western states), a trend that has huge real estate and retail implications.

A wealth implication of aging revolves around whether retirees have prepared to be financially independent. For example, in the U.S. and Japan, people spend what they earn (or more), so retirees are going to be hurting. Italy's citizens are among the oldest in Europe, but they're good savers. Germany's age demographics and savings habits are somewhere in between.

Among other large-scale demographic shifts are the facts that, in the U.S., 1 in 7 persons is Hispanic and that this subpopulation is growing faster than any others. The power of the Hispanic consumer is therefore a substantial trend: Hispanics control nearly $1 trillion in spending power, a number that cannot be ignored by any firm except the most nichey or naïve of players.

Beyond simple demographics, numerous lifestyle trends should also be salient when companies are considering new directions. For example, there are more wealthy Americans than ever before, accompanied by an expectation that that number is still rising. Baby boomers are in their peak earning years, and they're becoming empty nesters and hence will have more discretionary funds. Worldwide financial wealth is also tremendous; the top five countries for numbers of millionaires are the U.S. (5.1mm of them), Japan (1.6mm), China (1.4mm), the U.K. (0.4mm), and Germany (0.3mm). In terms of a country's population percentages, the story is a little different: Singapore (17%), Qatar (14%), Kuwait (12%), Switzerland (10%), and Hong Kong (9%).

There is also a growing concern for the environment and corporate social responsibility. For example, consumers are concerned about air pollution from transportation and in B2B land, industrial equipment by-products are a concern. Companies are learning that green marketing can be profitable, e.g., the use of agriculture for fuel would help pollution and farmers simultaneously.

A final class of trends to watch would be cultural differences, across countries or even sometimes within. For example, university students take their online access for granted, but consider these Internet penetration numbers: about 80% in the U.S., Japan, Germany, the U.K., France, and Korea, but less that 40% in China, India, Indonesia, Vietnam, and Egypt.

Clearly China's sheer numbers are going to drive a lot of near-future phenomena. They've been a strong manufacturing force for years, but their role has primarily been behind the scenes. Now they are trying to break out into their own global branding presence in order to demand better margins and as a point of national pride (e.g., Beijing's cooperative with IBM to produce Lenovo). Yet, to put things in perspective, Japan's per-capita GDP is about $46,000; the U.S., $48,000; and China at a different level, $5,000.

Lastly, other countries to watch would certainly start with the BRIC countries (Brazil, Russia, India, China) fast growing economies. Less prominent but perhaps even more promising (given that U.S. and Western European companies are getting tired of the issues they have to deal with in India and China) are Egypt, Mexico, Poland, South Africa, South Korea, and Turkey.

Trends

Smart marketers watch trends to identify opportunities in the marketplace. Here are trends about people and products.

- *Aging:* In the U.S., circa 2010, 40 million people were 65 years old or older. In just 20 years, by 2030, 72 million people will be 65 years old or older. While the government sorts through sticky wickets like funding Social Security and Medicare, marketers can spot numerous lucrative opportunities. Marketers should not seek to induce hip replacements or heart transplants, but they can produce easy-to-open pill bottles and tastier-to-eat assortments of bran and such. This group is known to appreciate warmer climates, and they'll also need access to long-term care and insurance, if well off, so they will travel, etc. Any entrepreneurial efforts to make their newly relevant purchases more affordable or user-friendly or exciting or interesting could pay handsome dividends.
- *Global Markets:* Marketers spend a lot of time considering the thriving young markets of Asia and South America, but the European nations should not be overlooked. Researchers Gaston-Breton and Martin classified market opportunities in two dimensions: (1) market size and potential and (2) market development. Market size was characterized by countries with larger populations, energy consumption, GDPs, and volumes of imports. Market development was constructed as levels of Internet access, indices of perceptions of corruption, gross domestic spending on R&D, and per-capita GDP. Countries like Germany, the U.K., France, Italy, and Spain were seen as having large market potentials and development. Countries like Denmark, Sweden, Luxembourg, Finland, the Netherlands, and Austria were seen as highly developed but smaller in market size and potential. (See the article, "International Market Selection and Segmentation," *International Marketing Review*, 28 [3], 267–290.)
- *Apps:* Apps are making many market transactions smoother and more fun. Some apps let you try on a new haircut, change the device voice, ask questions to do a mood check, and wake you with gentle sounds. Trendwatching.com highlighted several new apps:
  - WordLens lets travelers aim their phones at a sign or a menu to get a translation.
  - Leafsnap uses visual recognition so that while you are out and about, nature hikers can take pictures of a leaf and get their phone to identify the species of tree to which it belongs.
  - Google's Skymap lets astronomers and dreamers aim their phones at the sky to learn details about the constellations they're viewing.

Pretty soon, if you're trying to estimate market size or fit a diffusion model, there will be an app for that!

Managerial Recap

New (and improved!) products are fun to create, and they are crucial to a company's growth. To develop new products, marketers go through a process:

- From idea generation to testing the market potential, to concept testing, design and development, then to beta testing, and ultimately to the launch (review Figure 8.1).

- Reinvigoration along product lines is important because products evolve through a life cycle:
  - From introduction, to growth, maturity, and decline.
  - Each stage is recognizable by its sales and profitability.
  - And each stage carries standard recommendations for the 4Ps.

- Models can be used to forecast sales. Most include factors that reflect word of mouth or buzz marketing. Information technology is facilitating viral marketing.

- A manager who wants to be seen as innovative and foresightful would do well to study trends.

Chapter Outline in Key Terms and Concepts

1. Why are new products important?
2. How does marketing develop new products for their customers?
   a. Philosophies of product development
   b. Marketing
   c. Idea creation and market potential
   d. Concept testing and design and development
   e. Beta Testing
   f. Launch
3. What is the product life cycle?
   a. Diffusion of innovation
4. How do new products and brand extensions fit in marketing strategy?
   a. Strategic thinking about growth
5. What trends should I watch?

Chapter Discussion Questions

1. Consider the trends described in the chapter (e.g., aging, heightening environmental concern, or, say, China). How will each affect the business you are in (or were in before coming to b-school)?

2. Make a list of 3 of your most favorite brands. What would be a great brand or line extension that you would like to see developed as a new product?

Mini-Case

Wild Foods

A huge, highly regarded consumer packaged goods firm wishes to branch into pet food. The company knows a lot about packaging, communications, and pricing. It has a great reputation in trade so the channel partners should be supportive. It figures that selling pet food can't be all that different from their current strengths.

The company is beginning with cat food. It is developing product lines currently and plans to launch within 6 months. About a year after that, it'll follow with its canine line. The company has talked about developing foods for other animal pets (ferrets, snakes, and hamsters), but, to date, no firm plans have been made.

The brand is going to be called Wild Foods and the new-to-the-world feature that the brand will offer is that these canned goods will comprise wild animals. Instead of cat food being the same meats eaten by their owners (e.g., beef, turkey, chicken, tuna), the foodstuffs will be squirrel, mouse, pigeon, and crow (the company's first recipes).

The company expects their new pet food line to be wildly received by pet owners. They expect that pet owners will say, "Finally! A company that knows what my cat wants to eat!" The company also thinks it will earn huge points from people concerned with the environment, given that it's creating a useful by-product of large populations of some unpopular animals.

Mini-Case Discussion Questions

1. In the company's projection of its product line's likely success, what assumptions do you believe the company's made, and do you agree with all of them?

2. What kinds of prelaunch marketing questions do you have about any of the 4Ps?

3. What kinds of marketing research would you suggest for them to address your concerns?

Video Exercise: *Smart Car* (12:52)

Smart USA, headquartered in Bloomfield Hills, Michigan, sells the Smart Fortwo, a two-passenger vehicle that is produced in France by the Mercedes Benz car group. Smart Fortwo is the smallest car sold in the United States, and it is the most fuel-efficient vehicle outside of the hybrid cars. Smart Fortwo offers three different vehicle models, each with a different price point and a different package of standard equipment and options. When the Smart car entered the U.S. market in 2006 and before a full network of dealerships was established, Smart USA discovered that it needed to connect with prospective customers in a different way. The company essentially took the Smart Car to consumers by (1) using a reservation program so they could move ahead in the sales process as the dealer network was being established and (2) conducting a 50-city road tour in 2007 where the vehicles were displayed and promoted. The Smart Fortwo defies traditional target marketing, and it appeals to all socioeconomic strata and cuts across all age groups. The reasons the Smart car appeals to different customer groups are related to price, size, and serving as a second or third vehicle.

Video Discussion Questions

1. What methods did Smart USA use to test-market the Smart Fortwo car among prospective customers?

2. What trends are influencing the market potential of the Smart Fortwo car?

3. How does Smart USA utilize buzz marketing?

Chapter 9
Pricing

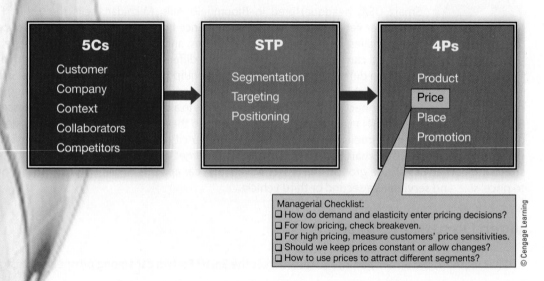

Marketing Management Framework

9-1 WHY IS PRICING SO IMPORTANT?

Our mantra is that marketing is the exchange of benefits and costs between a customer and a company, yet most of the marketing 4Ps are focused outward, with the company attempting to deliver value to the customer by making a good product, making it available through accessible channels, and communicating the product's benefits clearly. It's price, though, that provides the company a mechanism for obtaining value back from customers.

Marketers need to know how to set prices. Whether the brand positioning is at the low end or high end, prices must be set accordingly. Marketers have to understand how customers perceive prices and price changes like promotions to know how prices will be received and affect demand. Finally, we'll see how to use price as a segmentation tool.

144

9-2 BACKGROUND: SUPPLY AND DEMAND

If you know supply/demand charts like the back of your hand, you might wish to skip this section and go right to reading about low prices. If you're not an econ whiz and could use a refresher, read on.

You learned in econ that demand tends to fall off as price goes up (Figure 9.1). If a firm prices its brand too low, it could probably raise prices and pull in more money (better margins and profitability). If the brand is priced too high, generally sales drop off, so if prices were adjusted downward, then the volume of sales would pick up, and, again, the company could pull in more money (better demand and greater volume in unit sales).

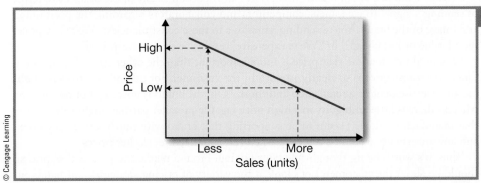

Figure 9.1

Demand Curve/Line

© Cengage Learning

Pricing is easier to change than the other marketing mix variables (e.g., imagine changing the product itself, the communications, or the partners in the supply chain), but it is still more complicated than it sounds. We'll talk about the major approaches to pricing, and acknowledge that, while it all can sound very precise, there is always an element of trial and error. The question is which contributes to your pricing policies more: thoughtful systematic planning or random-ish wiggle room.

One way to think about pricing is to simply price: low, medium, or high. Figure 9.2 illustrates these three simple—and most frequently employed—pricing strategies. The lowest sensible price is set by covering costs and then adding some margin. The highest possible price is set by figuring out just how much a customer is willing to pay and pricing near that mark. Competitive pricing is at a medium level, somewhere in between, using competitors' prices as a starting point and adjusting from there.

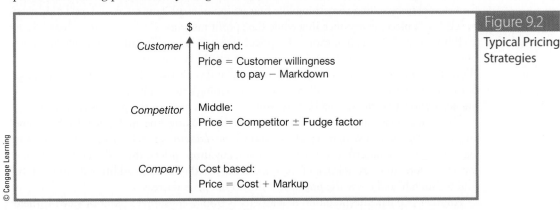

Figure 9.2

Typical Pricing Strategies

© Cengage Learning

Note that the 5Cs of marketing directly affect pricing: The costs inherent to the *company* help determine the low price point, the *customer's* sense of the product's value help determine the high price point, and noting what the *competition* charges helps determine a sensible intermediate price point. Once you establish these 3 benchmarks for your brand, it is a strategic move to choose among them.

There are numerous other considerations in setting prices, and we will examine them as well. For example, pricing typically varies over the course of product's life cycle. Willingness to pay varies across segments, so a firm might offer differential prices to those different segments. Prices can have multiple elements that can be tweaked, and so on.

Pricing is unusual among the marketing 4Ps in how easy it is to change, and thus, it is frequently tempting to do so. The impact of changing price is also easier to measure than modifications of the other Ps. However, it is important to resist dropping prices to enhance a quarterly sales bump because this is short-term thinking.

Pricing is not just about making money. It's as important as any of the other Ps in terms of sending a signal to customers, competitors and collaborators regarding the positioning and image of the brand. You're sending a message to these constituencies: "We're low price" (good value or just cheap?) or "We're expensive" (exclusive or just overpriced?).

One might even argue that price is more important than the other Ps in this signaling function because price is so clearly assessed by the customer. For example, customers might see an advertisement or a retail shop and think, "Oh, the brand is upscale," but not be sure, whereas there is little ambiguity in a high price tag. Or a retailer partner might think, "Gee, that manufacturer doesn't seem to be supporting that brand with much service anymore," and any uncertainty would be removed when the manufacturer slashes prices.

Thus, it's worth being thoughtful about pricing. From a marketing perspective, pricing should be about the customer. Let's look at the variety of pricing strategies and figure out how to choose among them.

Clearly your price point affects your profitability. If we define profit as

$$\text{Profit} = \pi = (\text{Price} \times \text{Demand}) - (\text{Fixed Costs}) - (\text{Variable costs} \times \text{Demand})$$
$$= [(\text{Price} - \text{Variable costs})] \times \text{Demand} - (\text{Fixed costs})$$

then profits increase as price increases. Per the demand function in Figure 9.1, however, demand typically falls off with those price increases. So we have to find a happy medium.

In another kind of marketing paradox, note that profits also increase as fixed or variable costs decrease. Yet sometimes companies do things to enhance their brands, such as by providing special services, that raise costs. When companies cut costs instead, it can often result in perceptions of reductions in quality in the minds of customers, thus indirectly causing a drop in demand.

As the demand line in Figure 9.1 implies, at the extremes, we could get stinking rich by either selling something like gum for a really cheap price and selling it to everyone (i.e., go for volume) or by selling something like fine art for an exorbitant price, and we'd only need to sell 1 or 2 pieces every once in a while (i.e., profit margin).

But what is that cheap or exorbitant price? If our gum is selling like crazy, why not raise prices and make more money? At what point would customers get annoyed and think, "Forget it, it's just gum. It's not worth that price," and walk away? For that matter, paintings don't fly off the walls at art galleries, so if something's not selling, how does the gallery manager know that the special buyer is still to come vs. perhaps the piece is overpriced?

These questions suggest that the oh-so-precise-looking line in Figure 9.1 has some wiggle room. Officially, that wiggle is known as *elasticity*, or *price sensitivity*. One way elasticity has been described is this: If the company drops prices, there should be a volume increase (more units are sold), and the question is whether enough additional units will be sold to "stretch" and cover the profits lost due to the price decrease.

Another popular interpretation of elasticity is from a consumer's point of view: If there is a price drop (or increase), just how much does demand (units sold) increase (or decrease)? If demand is barely affected, the demand is inelastic, whereas if demand bounces around, it's stretchy and elastic.

More technically, in Figure 9.3, we see two demand scenarios. In the left-hand plot, demand is relatively elastic (the slope is flatter than in the right-hand plot). When the price is $7, the number of units sold is 10, for a total revenue of $7 × 10 = $70 (boxed areas 1 and 2). If we drop prices to $4, we'd sell 40 units (areas 1 and 3), for $4 × 40 = $160. So yes, with the price drop, we more than made up (with the $160) the original revenue of $70. We'd say that demand is elastic.

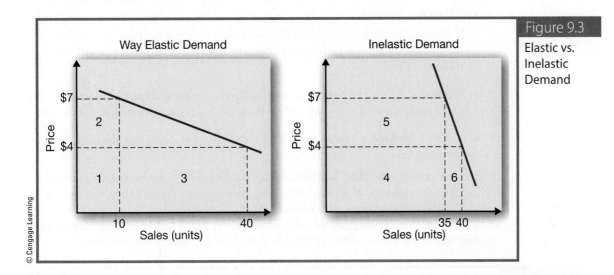

Figure 9.3

Elastic vs. Inelastic Demand

Conversely (to get facile with these plots), stay with the left-hand scenario, but now imagine that we began at $4, bringing in the $160, then we raised the price to $7, watched sales drop off, to $70; thus, again we see that consumers' demand is elastic, (Duh, it's the same plot,)

In contrast, in the scenario at the right, demand is more inelastic. If we simulate the same scenario, we begin with a price point of $7, sell 35 units (areas 4 and 5), for $7 × 35 = $245. Dropping the price to $4 results in 40 units sold (areas 4 and 6), taking revenue down to $4 × 40 = $160. Demand is inelastic. We changed price a bit, and demand didn't change much. We lost margin (the $3 price difference), and we didn't make it up in volume (an increase of only 5 units). Thus, the margin wasn't made up by the too few additional unit sales. IRL, "inelastic" means that many customers will purchase this item even if we raise prices (e.g., sporting events, musical concerts).

In Figure 9.3, we see that elasticity is characterized differently depending on the slope of the lines. Indeed, elasticity is defined by the slopes. Elasticity (E) is defined as the proportion change in quantity (Q) compared to the proportion change in price (P):

$$E = \frac{\dfrac{Q_2 - Q_1}{Q_1}}{\dfrac{P_2 - P_1}{P_1}} = \frac{P_1(Q_2 - Q_1)}{Q_1(P_2 - P_1)}.$$

Thus, for the examples depicted in Figure 9.3,

$$E_{left} = \frac{\dfrac{40 - 10}{10}}{\dfrac{4 - 7}{7}} = \frac{3}{-0.429} = -7$$

and

$$E_{right} = \frac{\dfrac{40 - 35}{35}}{\dfrac{4 - 7}{7}} = \frac{0.143}{-0.429} = -0.334.$$

Elasticity is always computed to be negative, so the negative signs are just ignored (they're a given). Then E is assessed:

- If $E > 1$, as in the left-hand plot, demand is said to be elastic. Price and revenue go in opposite directions; with a price drop, revenues shoot up, with a price increase, revenues fall off.

- If $0 \leq E < 1$, as in the right-hand plot, demand is inelastic. Revenue follows price in the same direction; if price goes up, revenue goes up, if price goes down, so do revenues.

- If $E = 1$, demand is said to be unitary. Prices go up or down, but revenues remain about the same.

That was econ-speak. Now let's talk marketing. Figure 9.4 depicts typical marketing findings. For the purchase of almost everything, there are very likely to be these two segments. Brand-loyal customers are inelastic, less price sensitive; they'll buy our brand no matter what the price. In contrast, the price-sensitive segment is quite elastic and deal prone, and they will run to a competitor (or even drop out of the category) when we raise prices.

Figure 9.4

Elasticity Varies with Customer Segments

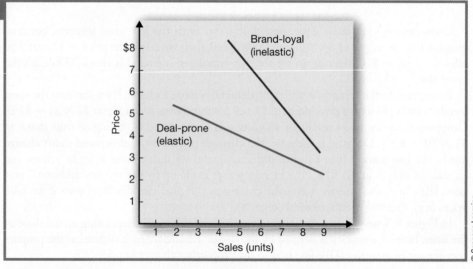

© Cengage Learning

So if we can raise prices as demand goes up or as supply dries up, what factors drive demand? Demand goes up as a function of a customer's desire, i.e., the more customers who want the brand or the more any individual customer wants the brand. Demand goes up with perceptions of the product's benefits or brand image. Demand goes up if competitors' brands aren't great—if there are few good substitutes, or if they're priced even higher.

Alternatively, instead of considering demand, which is focused on the brand or product or company, consider the flip side: the factors that drive a customer's price sensitivity. Customers are more price sensitive (price is more elastic for them) when they don't care that much about the purchase, purchase category, brand, when their preferences aren't strong, when they feel no particularly brand loyalty. Price sensitivity is greater when the item is a luxury good rather than a necessity, when many substitutes are available, when the purchase

Elasticity and Price Sensitivity

If a price decrease (increase) leads to a big increase (decrease) in the number of units sold, demand is *elastic*. If demand barely moves with a price decrease (or increase), it's *inelastic*.

$$\text{Price elasticity of demand} = \frac{\%\ \text{change in quantity demand}}{\%\ \text{change in price}}$$

For example, last quarter, we sold blue sweaters at $65 each. We sold 50 of them. This quarter, we raised prices to $75, and we sold only 40.

$$\text{Numerator} = \%\ \text{change in quantity demand}$$
$$= \frac{\text{quantity time2} - \text{quantity time1}}{\text{quantity time1}} \times 100\%$$
$$= \frac{40 - 50}{50} = -20\%$$

$$\text{Denominator} = \%\ \text{change in price}$$
$$= \frac{\text{price time2} - \text{price time1}}{\text{price time1}} \times 100\%$$
$$= \frac{75 - 65}{65} = 15.4\%$$

$$\text{Elasticity} = \frac{-20\%}{15.4\%} = -1.299.$$

Elasticities are always negative (given the econ curve), so the signs are just ignored. Then,

- If $E > 1$, demand is elastic, and price and revenue go in opposite directions. With a price drop, revenues shoot up; with a price increase, revenues fall off.
- If $0 < E < 1$, demand is inelastic, and revenue follows price in the same direction. If price goes up, revenue goes up; if price goes down, so do revenues.
- If $E = 1$, demand is unitary. Price goes up or down, but revenues remain about the same.

If you raise prices and demand is inelastic, your margin and profitability are greater and your customers are *price insensitive*. If you cut prices and demand is inelastic, you may be in trouble if the units sold don't compensate for the revenue lost by decreasing price in the first place.

is relatively a big one (compared to a customer's household income). And finally, it's no surprise that price sensitivity is generally greater for customers with lower household incomes.

Price sensitivity should increase when price information is easily available to customers to compare across competing brands. Thus the Internet is having an interesting effect on prices for many items. Price comparisons are easier online than driving from store to store, and, in particular, shopping bots (such as bizrate.com) facilitate easy and quick comparisons.

9-3 LOW PRICES

Regarding low prices, there are two issues: First, how do we determine whether costs are covered? To address this basic question, we will compute a variety of breakevens—simple math that determines how many units we have to sell to start making money.

The second pricing issue is whether low prices are a strategic choice that is constant, such as everyday-low-price providers (EDLPs) who position themselves around good value in the minds of consumers, or should we pulse the market with price fluctuations, offering and rolling back temporary price discounts. We discuss breakevens first (and EDLPs later).

Covering costs, to make sure you can stay in business, sets the absolute minimum floor on pricing. Cost-plus pricing is simply computed per unit, as:

$$\frac{\text{Unit cost}}{1 - X\%}$$

where $X\%$ is the intended return "(say, 30%), so we'd" compute:

$$\frac{\text{Unit cost}}{0.7}$$

Rules of Thumb

Low price points come from

- *Cost-Plus Pricing:* Mark up above average cost.
- *Loss Leaders:* Sell below cost to bring in customers for other products.
- *Market Penetration:* Price low to attract volume:
  - Early in the product life cycle to generate buzz and demand.
  - Late in the product life cycle to milk profits before the brand dies.
- *Nearly Predatory:* Price low enough to discourage competitors.

Midpoint prices come from

- See what competitors price at, and adjust according to corporate and brand strategy:
  - Price a bit higher if you offer more benefits or brand equity, wish to enhance image.
  - Price a little lower if you wish to be perceived as good value.

High price points come from

- Determine customers' willingness to pay, then price right below that sensitivity point.
- *Market Skimming:* Price high for margins, not worrying about volume (a strategy often used early in the life cycle of a high-end brand to heighten its sense of exclusivity).
- *Prestige or Status Pricing:* Price high for image appeal.
- Price high due to real quality differences or true rarity.

B2B pricing tools are the same, even if they're called different things:

- *Trade Discounts and Price Discrimination:* Discounts for cash, quantity, bulk, seasonality
- *Trade Allowances:* Prices to intermediaries cut based on the functions they perform, such as participation in advertising or sales support programs
- *Differential Prices Based on Geography:* Based on distance and transportation costs
- *Transfer Prices:* Pricing passed along through the channel network
- *Barter and Countertrade:* Making full or partial payments in goods, services, or buying agreements rather than in cash

If your fixed costs (including marketing, advertising, R&D, depreciation, etc.) are high relative to variable costs (which include labor or unit components), the strategic objective is to maximize sales volume (to spread the fixed costs over as many units as possible). If instead, variable costs are relatively high, the strategic objective is to maximize per-unit margins (we can't bring down price in hopes to build sales volume because volume drives up variable costs).

9-3a Concept in Action: Breakeven for a Good

So what is a breakeven (BE)? A breakeven analysis is a mean of figuring out how many units you'd have to sell before you make back your costs. Here's a thought experiment to illustrate. Say you're heading out of town to meet a client. You can take a cab from your place, or you can drive to the airport. Say a cab costs $20 + $5 ($1 airport fee and $4 as 20% tip) vs. $20 a day to park in your city's airport parking lot (pretend gas is free). For trips of what length is it smarter (cost-efficient) to take a cab vs. drive and park at the airport?

- If the trip is 1 day (i.e., you're flying to a nearby city and back the same day), and you take a cab, it would cost $50 (roundtrip). If you parked, it would cost $20.

- If the trip is 2 days, the cab costs $50 still, and parking now costs $40.

- For 3 days, the cab is $50, and parking is $60.

- For d days, the cab is, yes, still $50, and parking is $20d$.

So, if the trip is 1 or 2 days, then the smart thing is to park. If the trip is 3 days or longer, take a cab.

You do breakevens intuitively like this all the time. Now we have to make it official. Let's also be clear up front that we're pricing for a onetime transaction. If the marketer is long-term focused, as in relationship marketing via CRMs, they might be willing to not quite break even on the first purchase because they expect to breakeven shortly thereafter. The early hits on the company are investments in the customers.

A breakeven can be computed in terms of the number of units sold or monetary values. We'll look at BE in terms of units sold first. As the term *"breakeven"* suggests, we can look at how many units we'd sell before we make any money. Our profits are defined as

$$\text{Profit} = [(\text{Price} - \text{Variable costs}) \times \text{Demand}] - (\text{Fixed costs})$$

If we just broke even, that would mean that profits would be zero, at a level of demand that we will call BE:

$$0 = [(\text{Price} - \text{Variable costs}) \times \text{BE}] - (\text{Fixed costs})$$

Rearrange terms to solve for BE:

$$\text{BE} = \frac{\text{Fixed costs}}{\text{Price} - \text{Variable costs}}$$

And there you go. The last term, Price − Variable costs, is also called *contribution per unit to fixed costs.*

Let's turn to an example slightly more complicated than the taxi-vs.-parking issue. Imagine you have a friend who is following the e-book industry closely, has a lot of knowledge, and wants to help consumers choose the right e-book reader. Figure 9.5 breaks down the basic costs. The fixed costs include a modest income for your friend, some marketing and administrative costs, and rental space (likely a small office in a shopping mall). The variable costs are listed as well: $75 for the e-book reader (on average) and $5 for an e-book reader cover. The bottom figures show how much it would cost to set up a shop to sell 30, 60, 90, or 120 e-book readers per month.

Figure 9.5	
Costs for e-Book Reader Business	**Fixed Costs** for 1 month:

Your friend's salary	$1,000
Marketing, admin	350
Space rental, utilities, part-time help	650
Total	$2,000

Variable Costs per e-book reader:

e-book reader	$75
e-book cover	5
Total Unit Variable Costs	$80

Total Costs for quantity of e-book readers sold:

30	2,000 + (30 × 80) =	$4,400
60	2,000 + (60 × 80) =	$6,800
90	2,000 + (90 × 80) =	$9,200
120	2,000 + (120 × 80) =	$11,600

© Cengage Learning

Figure 9.6 begins with income, which is, as you keep hearing, a function of price and demand! So at the max (lower right of the top table), if we could sell about 4 e-book readers a day (can we?), and if people would pay $140 for it (would they?), we could make $16,800. Woohoo!

Figure 9.6	
Breakeven for e-Book Reader Business	**Income:**

e-book readers sold:

Price	30	60	90	120
100	$3,000	6,000	9,000	12,000
120	3,600	7,200	10,800	14,400
140	4,200	8,400	12,600	16,800

Recall Total Costs:

	30	60	90	120
	4,400	6,800	9,200	11,600

Income − Total Costs:

	30	60	90	120
$100	−1,400	−800	−200	400
$120	−800	400	1,600	2,800
$140	−200	1,600	3,400	5,200

© Cengage Learning

But wait. Now we have to subtract our costs. In the table at the bottom, we see that there are many scenarios of price and demand combinations where we lose money!

In this example, we use the BE equation for each price we're considering:

$$BE = \frac{\text{Fixed costs}}{\text{Price} - \text{Variable costs}}$$

$$BE100 = \frac{2,000}{100 - 80} = 100,$$

$$BE120 = \frac{2,000}{120 - 80} = 50,$$

$$BE140 = \frac{2,000}{140 - 80} = 33.3.$$

That is, if we priced at $100, we would need to sell 100 units to break even; if we priced at $140 dollars, we would need to sell only 34 units.

Now that we can compute a breakeven, let's face it, breaking even isn't a great business goal. It's simply how low can we go? Here's a better idea: Let's look at the scenarios in which we would actually make money! If we charged $100 and sold at least 120 readers, or charged $120 (or $140) and sold at least 60, we'd make at least a little bit of money.

These are daunting scenarios. The prices seem high, and who knows if we could really move 2 to 4 e-book readers a day? Alternatively, could we cut costs and become more productive? Could we ask our friend to take less in salary? Could we find a hardware supplier that offers a better discount? But these are managerial questions to ponder, separate from the issue of the breakeven.

9-3b Concept in Action: Breakeven for a Service

Let's look at a BE scenario that involves pricing for a service. Services are tricky because they are notoriously disproportionately high in variable costs. As a result, the cost numbers move faster with an increase in demand. So let's say your e-book aficionado friend is considering a store where it's not the e-book reader itself that is sold, but a service in which the customer's favorite software is loaded, the machine customized, new apps put on, etc. We'll keep the fixed cost for consistency.

Breakevens

Breakeven for a product is calculated by dividing fixed costs by contribution per unit to fixed costs. Contribution per unit to fixed costs is determined by subtracting variable cost from price. It is the point at which revenues, or the number of units sold, give you a monetary profit (and loss) equal to zero.

How many units do we need to sell to cover our costs and then start making money? Define profit:

$$\text{Profit} = [(\text{Price} - \text{Variable costs}) \times \text{Demand}] - (\text{Fixed costs})$$

If we just broke even, that would mean that profits would be zero, at a level of demand that we will call *BE*:

$$0 = [(\text{Price} - \text{Variable costs}) \times BE] - (\text{Fixed costs})$$

Solve for *BE*:

$$BE = \frac{\text{fixed costs}}{\text{price} - \text{variable costs}}$$

The last term, Price − Variable costs, is also called "contribution per unit to fixed costs."

For example, say you sell doodads. Your fixed costs (administrative, salaries, rent) are $2,000 a month. Variable cost is $100 per unit. How should you price the doodad?

$$\text{Price at \$110? } BE = \frac{2,000}{110 - 100} = 200$$

$$\text{Price at \$120? } BE = \frac{2,000}{120 - 100} = 100$$

$$\text{Price at \$130? } BE = \frac{2,000}{130 - 100} = 66.67$$

$$\text{Price at } \$140? \; BE = \frac{2{,}000}{140 - 100} = 50$$

$$\text{Price at } \$150? \; BE = \frac{2{,}000}{150 - 100} = 40, \text{etc.}$$

Thus, if we price as low as $110, we'd need to sell 200 units just to break even.

Breakeven for a service is calculated in the same manner as breakeven for a good. Contribution per unit to fixed costs is determined by subtracting variable cost from price. The main difference is simply that services tend to have relatively high variable costs compared to those of goods.

Now there are additional costs. It costs the store's staff time to load the software (say $30 a reader), and the store must maintain legal licensing fees on a variety of software packages (say this is roughly $3 a reader).

The question remains, how much should or could be charged for the service? How many customers would be needed before making money?

In Figure 9.7, the first row reminds us of the fixed costs, the next rows capture the variable costs, with the totals at the bottom. Figure 9.8 shows possible income, depending on price and demand. Figure 9.9 contains the differences, or profits. This analysis could be refined, using continuous numbers rather than our rougher numbers (15, 30, etc.). Similarly, the prices charged could be assessed in a more refined manner, with a continuous scale ($0 to $500 a machine), but, again, the discrete price points gives us a sense of the breakeven problem.

Figure 9.7
Costs for e-Book Software Service Business

Fixed COSTS	2,000	2,000	2,000	2,000
Number adapted				
Variable costs	15	30	45	60
Labor ($30)	450	900	1,350	1,800
Licensing ($3)	45	90	135	180
Total monthly variable costs	495	990	1,485	1,980
Total costs (fixed and variable)	2,495	2,990	3,485	3,980

© Cengage Learning

Figure 9.8
Breakeven for e-Book Software Service Business

Number served:		15	30	45	60
Cash inflow	$30	450	900	1,350	1,800
Revenue	$50	750	1,500	2,250	3,000
Sales	$100	1,500	3,000	4,500	6,000

© Cengage Learning

Figure 9.9
Breakeven for e-Book Software Service Business

Sales − Total Costs	15	30	45	60
$30	−2,045	−2,090	−2,135	−2,180
$50	−1,745	−1,490	−1,235	−980
$100	−995	10	1,015	2,020

© Cengage Learning

In Figure 9.9, let's take a look at the money we'd make (or not). First, note that $30 is just a totally ridiculous baseline. We'd lose money fast, and, as we service more machines, we'd lose even more money. If we charged $50, we're still not doing well. Increase the charge a little more to $100, and we can make money if we customize 30 e-book readers or more.

So how do we decide on pricing? We will compute this in a more refined manner in a moment, but just looking at this table, to break even, we'd have to charge at least $100 (and service at least 30 e-book readers). Later, when we talk about the value to customers or their willingness to pay, we can figure out whether we could charge just $100, or could we charge even more? Depending on the zip code of the mall, $200 may be quite tolerable, and if that's the case, why would we charge the mere $100?

Once more, return to the *BE* equation. Fixed costs are $2,000, and variable costs are $33 (the $30 labor and $3 licensing, per e-book reader). For a price of $100 for the service,

$$BE = \frac{\text{Fixed costs}}{\text{Price} - \text{Variable costs}}$$

$$= \frac{2{,}000}{100 - 33} = 29.85$$

Round up to 30 because e-book readers are integers.

Those were *BE*s in terms of quantity we need to sell.

How about calculating BE in terms of revenue? We modify the equation slightly to

$$BE\$ = \frac{\text{Fixed costs}}{1 - \text{Variable costs per unit price}}$$

$$= \frac{\text{Fixed costs}}{1 - (\text{Variable costs} / \text{Price})}$$

$$= \frac{2{,}000}{1 - (33/100)} = \frac{2{,}000}{1 - 0.33} = \frac{2{,}000}{0.67} = \$2{,}985.07$$

Finally, we can, of course, have a profit target, not just the breakeven point where profit = 0. To incorporate that goal, we would say:

Target profit = [(Price − Variable costs) × Demand] − Fixed costs

so

$$BE = \frac{\text{Fixed costs} + \text{Target profit}}{\text{Price} - \text{Variable costs}}$$

Figure 9.10 shows the breakeven goal in terms of linear functions from which we may interpolate. The number of e-book readers forms the horizontal axis, and money—both costs and revenue—form the vertical axis. The first horizontal line in the graph itself shows the fixed costs, steady across all number of units; of course, it's fixed. The line Total costs line includes these fixed costs and have an increasing slope because they also reflect the variable costs, which increase with numbers of units produced and sold. The Revenue line is our income, and the point marked where this line intersects the Total costs line is our breakeven point, as we just computed, right at 30.

BE analyses should be performed for every price decision to understand the lower bounds. Let's turn now to the upper bounds.

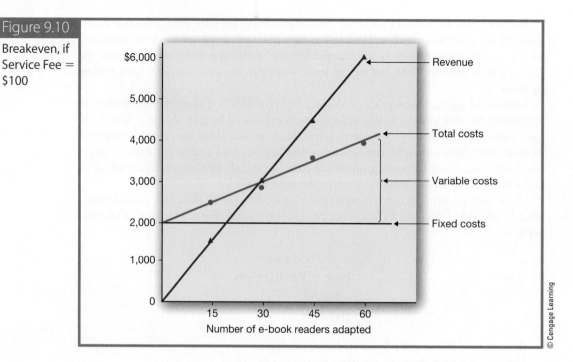

Figure 9.10

Breakeven, if Service Fee = $100

9-4 HIGH PRICES

The MasterCard commercials that end with the word *"priceless"* are great fun, but, most of us have an upper limit on what we'd pay for many items. The trick for marketers is to discover that upper bound and price just below it.

We've discussed the concept of price elasticity and can compute it (for any brand or segment) to answer the question, just how much would sales drop off in the face of a price increase? In markets that are fairly stable (e.g., mature products, with few technological introductions), marketing managers might see that their price sensitivity estimates are also fairly stable. If that's the case, we can turn the elasticity or price sensitivity (*PS*) equation inside out. The price changes are under our control, and if *PS* is largely stable, we can plug that estimate in and solve for a decent forecast as to what the sales change might be:

$$\% \text{ change in sales} = \frac{PS \times (P_2 - P_1)}{P_1}$$

This is an estimate that would be very useful in budgeting. If we have no good estimate for price sensitivity, or if the recent historical data move around a lot, we should get current estimates. There are several means of obtaining the data require to make good guesses of price sensitivity. Let's see.

9-4a Scanner Data

Any marketing manager working on consumer packages goods has the luxury of working with scanner data, which can yield very precise estimates of demand and price sensitivities at numerous price points. Scanner data include indicators of which brands are bought, the quantities bought, the shelf price of the objects, the paid price (e.g., if a coupon was used), the price of competitors' brands that week, a flag for whether any of the brands were featured in local weekend newspaper flyers or in end-of-aisle displays in the store, advertising exposures to panel households, etc.

If all these variables remain constant, a firm can run an experiment by randomly selecting some outlets as a test market and dropping prices, say by 20% in some stores, 33% in others, while allowing still other outlets to serve as a control group, a benchmark for comparison (in case anything like the displays or competitor prices change). For example, the effect of a 20% decrease would be estimated to be

$$PS = \frac{(S_{@20\%off} - S_{benchmark})/S_{benchmark}}{(P_{@20\%off} - P_{benchmark})/P_{benchmark}}$$

where the benchmark might be initial sales or the sales averaged over the control group outlets.

If this PS is large, then the 20% discount was effective in stimulating sales. If it is small, then either the discount wasn't big enough, or these customers just aren't price sensitive.

Even firms not interested in conducting experiments per se can use the scanner data and run straightforward regressions to forecast expected changes in sales. For example, to see the effect of price, we can forecast sales as a function of price and include any other marketing or market information we might have as control variables:

$$Sales\ estimate = b_0 + b_1 Price + b_2 Ad + \cdots + b_k Factor_k$$

9-4b Survey Data

Even without scanner data, several marketing research tools can be used to assess a customer's willingness to pay (WTP). For one, we can simply ask our customers, "What are you willing to pay?" (Radical!) Imagine a survey in which some annual online banking service was described, and consumers are asked:

Q1—$25.00: Definitely would not buy 1 2 3 4 5 6 7 Definitely would buy
Q2—$35.00: Definitely would not buy 1 2 3 4 5 6 7 Definitely would buy

Even if we're not price-sensitive types, most of us prefer to pay as little as possible. So it wouldn't be surprising if the average score for question 2 was lower than that for question 1.

Still, the items can convey information. Some people simply aren't interested in the banking service no matter what the price, so their scores would look something like Q1 = 2 or 3 and Q2 = 1 or 2. At the other extreme, some people might be really keen for the service, so their scores would be Q1 = 6 or 7 and Q2 = 5 or 6. A final segment might be sort of interested in the banking service, if the price was right, and these people's scores would be something like Q1 = 4 or 5 and Q2 = 3 or 4.

Price studies can also be tested using different samples. Some customers would be randomly assigned to fill out survey form A, and others would fill out form B. The surveys would be identical except the price in form A would be higher than that in B. More versions than two could also be used to obtain a finer estimate of demand sensitivity to prices.

9-4c Conjoint Analysis

More than surveys, marketing managers' favorite tool to study pricing is the conjoint study. In a conjoint study, customers are shown products with various combinations of features and attributes, price being one of them. The customers are asked, "Which combination do you prefer most?" then, "Next most?" etc.

For example, in Figure 9.11, a Red Bull kind of caffeine energy drink is offered in a 4-pack for $2.99 or $3.99, and a store brand drink of the same variety is offered at the

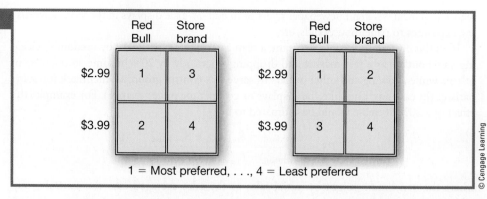

Figure 9.11

A Conjoint Experiment

1 = Most preferred, . . ., 4 = Least preferred

© Cengage Learning

same price points. Two different kinds of segment preferences are represented in the figure. Both segments say their most preferred choice would be the Red Bull at the cheaper price, and both would least prefer the store brand at the higher price. What distinguishes these segments is which they value more: the brand or the price. On the left is a consumer who wants the brand and is willing to pay more. On the right is a consumer who appreciates a good deal and gives up the brand to retain the lower price.

What's neat about the conjoint approach is that customers aren't ever directly asked about price, so the method obviates the customer's natural inclination to say, "I want to pay less." We also know that customers are indeed willing to pay more for what they want, and the conjoint technique helps detect those attributes. Customers are asked for a simple judgment: "Which one of these do you like most? Next most?" etc. They can do this easily and quickly. We derive from the conjoint analyses the attributes that customers seek, including what price they're willing to pay (we'll do a conjoint in Chapter 15). The analysis allows us to infer their price sensitivities.

Part of the point of developing a brand is to charge a premium price. If brand associations go beyond the basic features, customers will pay higher prices accordingly. For example, generic spandex sells for $8 per pound whereas Lycra costs twice as much. Some marketers define a good brand by whether the customer is price insensitive because the customer is determined to buy the brand regardless of its cost.

9-5 UNITS OR REVENUE, VOLUME OR PROFITS

There is, of course, a difference between maximizing the number of units sold to produce volume vs. objectives to maximize revenue and profits. Figure 9.12 illustrates the comparison among smartphone platforms. Apple leads on the number of phones that rely on its system (45%), whereas RIM (BlackBerry) and Google have similar shares. As BlackBerrys decline in favor, RIM is charging less than Google, and both charge far less than Apple. Thus, for revenue, the picture is that Apple's lead is extended and that Google does better than RIM because it charges more.

If profit = revenue − expense and revenue = price × quantity sold, then to maximize profits we need to find a price where any further increase in price would lead to a large falloff in demand. Specifically, profit maximization occurs when marginal revenue (*MR*, the extra money brought in by selling one more unit) equals marginal cost (*MC*, the extra cost incurred by selling one more unit); that is, P_{max}: $MR = MC$.

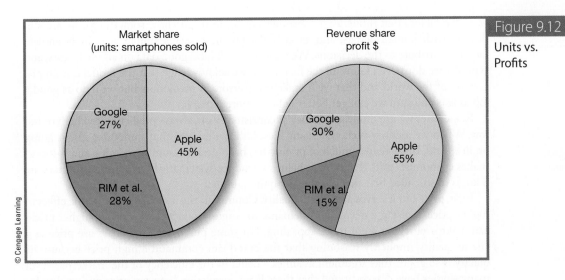

Figure 9.12

Units vs. Profits

© Cengage Learning

In Figure 9.13, we see where this matching occurs. Prices are listed from $1 to $2 for, say, a soft drink from a vending machine. Naturally, as price goes up, fewer customers partake (as price in column 1 goes down, quantity sold in column 2 goes up). The third column represents the variable (or marginal) cost of $1 a unit, and the fourth column shows revenue (price × quantity).

Figure 9.13

Profit Maximization

© Cengage Learning

Price	Quantity	MC $1/unit	Revenue	Marginal Revenue
$2.00	100	$100.00	$200.00	
1.75	200	200.00	350.00	$1.50
1.50	300	300.00	450.00	1.00
1.25	400	400.00	500.00	0.50
1.00	500	500.00	500.00	0.00

The final column presents marginal revenue. These numbers are computed as follows: the $1.50 is [($350 − $200)/(200 − 100)], the $1.00 is [($450 − $350)/(300 − 200)], and so on. Marginal cost was stated to be $1, and marginal revenue achieves $1 when we price at $1.50, thus covering costs nicely.

Okay, so pricing is never simple. In this example, the same profit is also obtained at $1.75 (350 − 200) as at $1.50 (450 − 300). Apparently there's a flat spot in the demand curve. Thus we could price at 1.50 or 1.75, so the final decision is one of strategy (go high for an upscale image or low for customer reviews as good value).

9-6 CUSTOMERS AND THE PSYCHOLOGY OF PRICING

Our pricing discussion thus far has involved some strategic thinking and a lot of number crunching. Yet any model you'll ever see (marketing, statistical, economic, etc.) will be of the form

$$\text{Our prediction} = \text{Our model} + \varepsilon$$

where ε (epsilon) is the error term, also referred to as noise, variability, heterogeneity, a fudge factor, or beats me. The idea is that no matter how well we think we know a system (e.g., the factors that influence a consumer's decision to purchase something), we are still dealing with human beings, and, even if the purchase seems simple, seemingly endless factors contribute to the decisions. We typically don't have good data on all the factors, and typically we don't even know all the factors. So we acknowledge that the model is a simplification of the world and that we'll make some errors in prediction, but we'll do as good a job as we can (until we can get better data on more factors).

Sometimes we use models, and they're consistently off, always predicting too high or too low. When we identify such systematic biases, then we know that something else is going on in ε-land. In particular, much of pricing has been derived from economics, and it sort of makes economists nuts that human beings introduce systematic variation into ε. There are 8 kinds of so-called bias that are actually quite rational.

First, price often serves as a cue to quality. Counter to the anticipated economic effect of higher prices causing a decrease in demand, for some products and services, higher prices can make a purchase seem more appealing. For some purchases, customers use price as a cue to quality, implicitly reasoning that the brand can command a high price because its quality is so good. That argument assumes a belief in the efficiency of the marketplace, yet many studies have demonstrated that there is no correlation between price and quality for most product categories. But our beliefs persist.

A price's role as a cue is so strong that prices are known to contribute to the formation of expectations prior to a purchase. A price is a clear, tangible cue, and higher prices set higher expectations.

Price differentials can reflect different product functionality, but different prices can also reflect mere cosmetic differences. To say that the product differences are superficial is not to say that they are not relevant or rational, if they contribute to brand image differences. Further, if an ad claims that a brand is superior due to the presence (or absence) of some feature, customers frequently trust that somehow that feature is thereby important. A high price point almost becomes the sought feature, as when basic Visa cards can be obtained with no annual fee, but AmEx charges $2,500 for their elite Black card.

Second, consumers process absolute numbers and relative numbers differently. Say you receive some e-mail coupons for Office Max. Your Office Depot is much closer. Would you drive to the Office Max for $15 off a box of printer toner (that costs $49)? What about if the coupon was for $15 off a new tablet (that costs $199)?

In both cases, the coupon offers the same face value, a $15 discount, but for the toner, $15 off is a larger proportion ($49 vs. $199), so it seems like a better deal. Rationally, we'd assess the absolute value, but there's a logic to assessing the relative value as well.

Psychology of Prices

You can count on some reliable behaviors by your customers:

1. Price is often used as a cue to quality.
2. %price differences can have more impact than absolute price differences.
3. Customers feel happy if they think they got a deal.
4. Without even knowing they do it, customers tend to process $49.99 as closer to $40 than $50.
5. Customers like to think they're smart shoppers, so give them a good compromise purchase (a product line of 3 items: a low-price and basic-quality item, a moderate-price and -quality option, and a high-price and -quality item).

Third, the contextual frame in which information is expressed matters—the spin, if you will. Imagine you're planning a spring break trip with a friend, and you've narrowed your choices down to two vacation packages: One is priced at $499, the other at $599 with a $100 discount when you book. Which choice seems more appealing? In either case, your credit card is going to be charged $499, but the second choice starts at a higher price, so it's not unusual to assume that maybe the trip package is of better quality (e.g., nicer hotel, more activities). You'll feel like a smart shopper by getting more value, a $599 trip for just $499. A price of $499 is $499, but it's not irrational when we have a rationale.

Fourth, price discounts serve as mood inductions. Temporary price discounts are not only an economic lever. Customers think they're smart shoppers when they get a good deal. People feel good when they get something for a price that's better than usual. The experience is about feelings of happiness, pride, appreciation, confidence, etc., not about money per se.

Fifth, there's a reason the prices of many things—groceries, books, clothing, cars—end in 9, such as $4.99 or $49.99 or $4,999.99. Wouldn't you think that their whole number counterparts ($5, $50, $5,000) would be easier to understand and advertise? Well, it's reliably known that $4.99 is far more attractive than $5, much more than the penny difference. Why? Apparently because we read from left to right; we process and internalize the 4 before we hit the 0.99, so we're thinking, "Oh, the price is $4-ish," not, "Wow, the price is $5!"

Sixth, consumers keep track of their spending; it's called "mental accounting." They also rationalize compensatory or future purchasing. Just as we speak in financial terms of discounting future sales for the time value of money, we do this mentally also. If we buy a case of wine for an upcoming party, the current purchase is seen as an investment, not spending. And the later consumption of that wine at the party is seen as free because it's not tied closely in time to when it was purchased. This concept of an immediate vs. future cost-benefit analysis has also been used to explain why we don't do things in the short term that are good for us (as individuals or collectively as a society) in the long term (e.g., engage in healthy behaviors or in sound environmental ones). We simply pay less attention to future consequences.

Another form of mental accounting is how we think of categories of money. You might think that money is money because it's fungible; money spent on one household item comes from the same budget for a competing item. However, we often classify money as if it were nonfungible, meaning that we categorize our purchases and budget within the categories. For example, just because we splurged at a great restaurant last weekend doesn't mean we will cut corners on spending as we plan next month's vacay.

A relatively new phenomenon is the customer processing of alternative currencies—no, not the euro vs. the yuan. Rather, all the zillions of companies' loyalty programs are generating additional currencies, which usually have fairly transparent monetary values (and can be traded or given away). The airline mileage programs are the most mature, and it is not infrequent to see customers behave in seemingly inconsistent manners, e.g., refusing to pay for business class seats but having no problem redeeming points for upgrades.

Seven, marketers frequently observe the compromise effect in consumers. To illustrate, consider the following: One group of consumers was given the choice of buying two professional basketball tickets for $250 or two tickets several rows up for $200. On an order of 2:1, most (67%) went with the cheaper seats ($200).

Next, an entirely fresh sample of consumers was offered two tickets for $200, two slightly better seats for $250, or two even better seats for $300. About 10% went for $300. Of the remaining 90%, the preference for the $200 and $250 reverses the 2:1 ratio of the first scenario, with 60% of the sample asking for the $250 seats and 30% for the cheaper $200 seats.

This effect is called a "compromise" because the middle choice in the second scenario is an attractive compromise between the two extremes. The seats are probably better than the $200 seats, but the tickets are not as expensive as the $300 ones. It's thought that this effect occurs because ultimately, whether we can articulate it explicitly or not, we apparently believe in an efficient market. In other words, if a company charges more, we assume that they must be providing something better or more of something. If they were not, eventually consumers would figure it out, and the company would have to drop prices. Note that the company doesn't really care how many $300 tickets it sells; it introduces the $300 tickets to make the formerly higher price of $250 seem more enticing.

Eight, consumers work with referent pricing. When we evaluate a product's price to determine whether we think the price being charged is fair, we compare the price to some reference, either an externally available price or an internally, mentally stored price. Sometimes a product's price tag will offer this comparison to encourage the consumer to believe that the current price is a good deal, such as "MSRP is $49.99, now available for $35.99!" Other external reference forms are popular during sales, e.g., "Now $14.99—regular price $35.00!" or by companies who position themselves as EDLP when they state, "Our price $34.99. Compare at $45.00!" Whenever we refer to someone experiencing sticker shock, the idea is that the price (on the sticker) is much higher than the referent.

The reference price point can also be internal. The expectation regarding how much the product costs comes from a variety of sources, including the buyer's experience. For example, if the product being purchased is one that consumers buy a lot, they would be familiar with the product's typical price. Internal references can, of course, be faulty or not very relevant, e.g., how much you paid for your last car (even though that was 5 years ago, and it was an economy car vs. the luxury model you're now buying). Internal references can also be based on inferences (e.g., is the store an upscale one), lending themselves to the belief that perhaps the prices are a bit inflated (e.g., paying for the store's service, yet also perhaps implying high-quality brands).

Legal Stuff Related to Pricing

- *No Price Fixing:* Two or more firms agree on what price to charge, to reduce the effect of competition that drives prices (and profits) down (Sherman Antitrust Act 1890 and Federal Trade Commission Act 1914).
- *No Vertical Price Fixing:* A manufacturer cannot force a retailer to charge a certain price; hence, we see "MSRP" (manufacturer-suggested retail price). Retailers need to charge the manufacturer's minimum price in order to provide consistency with the brands' images and to ensure the manufacturer gets some profits, not just the retailers (fair trade laws).
- *No Predatory Pricing:* You cannot price unreasonably low to drive out competition (unfair trade laws). Yet grocery stores routinely sell certain products cheaply, e.g., below costs, calling them "loss leaders" and counting on their attracting traffic to the store. Also, huge companies routinely drop prices to discourage new competitors (then the lawyers define "unreasonable").
- *No Price Discrimination to Consumers or Channel Partners:* You cannot charge different prices to different customers for the same product (Robinson-Patman Act 1936). Different prices must reflect a difference in costs, e.g., the loyal segment gets a deal because it costs less to process them, or they're charged more because they require more services.
- *No Deceptive Pricing (a.k.a. Bait and Switch):* You cannot mislead customers by advertising one product but only making another, usually more expensive, product available for purchase or by posting one price but scanning and ringing up another.

We know that customers vary, and that's why we consider segmentation. They also vary in these psychological profiles of reactions to prices, and we can use that information to price smartly, as discussed next.

9-6a Price Discrimination, aka Segmentation Pricing

Price Discrimination, with a capital "P" and a capital "D," is not legal. We're not allowed to charge different prices to different people for the same goods or services. However, marketers frequently speak of price discrimination, with a small "p" and a small "d." Let's instead call it segmentation pricing.

Good marketers do their homework and inevitably find customer segments who value different things. Then it is perfectly acceptable to charge different customers different prices for different goods and services. In most markets, there is almost always a price-sensitive segment, and another that seeks quality (remember Figure 9.4). There is nothing wrong with a company offering a stripped-down product at lower prices to the former and a souped-up version at a higher price to the latter.

For example, there are periodic deals offered on soft drinks, for oil changes, for local restaurants, and so forth. Some customers will buy their favorite brands and hardly pay attention to the deals. How can a marketer price when there are different segments?

In Figure 9.14, we see that as price goes up (in column 1), demand falls off for both the deal-prone and brand-loyal segments (columns 2 and 3). The difference is that there is a high volume of buyers in the deal segment at the low prices, whereas the brand-loyal segment is willing to pay more. Column 4 sums these purchases in units and revenues. Column 5 shows that, if we offer just one price, contribution is maximized at a price of $4.

Price ($)	Segment Deals	Segment Brand	Total Units ($)	Contribution (−1$ per unit)	Just Deal Segment	Just Brand Segment
2	9	0	9 ($18)	$1 × 9 = 9 = $18 − $9	1 × 9 = 9	1 × 0 = 0
3	7	9	16 ($48)	2 × 16 = 32 = 48 − 16	2 × 7 = 14	2 × 9 = 18
4	5	8	13 ($52)	3 × 13 = 39 = 52 − 13	3 × 5 = 15	3 × 8 = 24
5	2	7	9 ($45)	4 × 9 = 36 = 45 − 9	4 × 2 = 8	4 × 7 = 28
6	0	6	6 ($36)	5 × 6 = 30 = 36 − 6	5 × 0 = 0	5 × 6 = 30
7	0	5	5 ($35)	6 × 5 = 30 = 35 − 5	6 × 0 = 0	6 × 5 = 30
8	0	4	4 ($32)	7 × 4 = 28 = 32 − 4	7 × 0 = 0	7 × 4 = 28

Figure 9.14

Pricing for Brand and Deal Segments

© Cengage Learning

The final two columns separate out the segments. For the deal-prone customers, $4 remains the optimal price. For the brand-loyals, we maximize at a higher price, $6 or $7, and as long as they don't seem price sensitive, we might as well charge the higher of these two choices, $7. Now, what do we do with this information? We can either determine that a high-end image is our strategy, price at $7, and let the deal-prone group fall off. Or we can price $7 during a "regular" season and get the purchases of the brand-loyal segment, and then price around $4 for the deal-prone segments during promotion times.

It is important to keep these distinct segments separate. Customers can get irritated if they learn that they've paid more than others. Web designers need to be sensitive to this issue also: When a checkout process prompts customers to enter promotional codes (a digital coupon), some customers may be a little annoyed to realize they don't have one. A suggestion is to offer the customers a back-door part of the website to obtain the deal.

9-6b **Quantity Discounts**

Another completely legitimate and accepted form of segmentation pricing is to offer quantity discounts—as in "The more you buy, the more you save!" Figure 9.15 works through the numbers of an Internet offer. We begin with sales or survey data, determining how many customers want 1 month of Internet access for $15, or 2 months for $25, or 3 months for $30. Customers are used to seeing these offers; they can compute the average price per unit, and demand falls off with higher prices. None of that surprises us. In the $ column of the figure, it looks like we should go for the 3-for-$30 because $960 is the biggest number. However, the per-unit sales registered in the last column show us that we would do best to use the 2-for-$25 deal.

Figure 9.15								
Pricing with a Quantity Discount			Consumers, interested in buying:					
			1 month for $15?	25 said yes				
			2 months for $25?	35				
			3 months for $30?	40				
Number Bought	Price	Average Price	Net (−$2 cost)	Net Profit	Demand	$	Per Unit	
1	15	15.0	13.0	13.0	25	325	325.0	
2	25	12.5	10.5	21.0	35	735	367.5	
3	30	10.0	8.0	24.0	40	960	320.0	
a	b	$c = b/a$	$d = c - 2$	$e = d \times a$	f above	$g = e \times f$	$h = d \times f$	

© Cengage Learning

9-6c **Yield or Demand Management**

You know the expression "Time is money." Just as customers can be divided into segments that are more or less price sensitive, customers can also be more or less time sensitive.

In particular, services are said to be perishable if there is no such thing as storing inventory or excess capacity. All the customers rush a system when they want to be served, and, if they overload capacity, it can be a problem for the service provider, and the quality of service can deteriorate. So another example of segmentation pricing is to vary prices during peak and nonpeak seasons.

For example, if you're willing to go to the movies during the day, when most people are working and the theater owners would like encourage better attendance, you get a price break. You can also frequently get price breaks by making airline or hotel reservations far in advance of your needs, which these service providers appreciate so that they can plan better. (If your plans are flexible—that is, if you're not in the time-crunch segment—you can also get price breaks at the very last minute because they wish to operate at full capacity.) Some restaurants recognize different segments by pricing differently during the weekdays vs. weekends.

Whether a customer experiences a price or time shift, it's important that the company manage perceptions of fairness. With regard to time, FIFO (first-in/first-out) seems universally fair in queuing, but customers also tend to be understanding when there are exceptions (e.g., larger parties wait longer to be seated at restaurants).

These practices of yield management are popular in services, many of which are characterized by high fixed costs and lower variable costs (e.g., airlines, hotels, rental cars) to enhance revenue and capacity utilization. The systems have also gotten very complex, but an advantage of this approach to pricing is that it is based on the market, not on costs per se.

9-7 NONLINEAR PRICING

If it's not complicated enough to set a single price, marketers further complicate things by trying to coordinate the pricing of multiple pieces of their product offerings. Some prices are set using a so-called two-part tariff, meaning that a customer pays some amount for one part of the service (usually a fixed fee, such as an entry fee at a night club or a ticket to enter a theme park) and another amount for another part of the service (usually this fee is a charge per unit of usage, such as drinks at the club, or food, T-shirts, and memorabilia at the theme park).

For example, in Figure 9.16, we see an illustration that cell phones charge a monthly fee with some basic coverage, but data plans are charged extra. The plot to the right illustrates the theme park, with an initial charge (the admissions ticket) and additional fees for whatever consumption is enjoyed in the park (e.g., beverages, T-shirts). Part A of each graph shows the base fee, and part B shows the extra fees, so the total amount charged per customer depends on how much the customer wishes to buy.

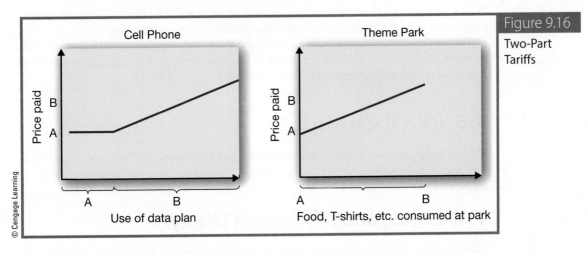

Figure 9.16

Two-Part Tariffs

© Cengage Learning

Figure 9.17 depicts data sampled from patrons of local upscale restaurants responding to survey questions about the fees proposed for a newly opening wine bar. The wine bar plans to offer wine classes during which customers would sample triplets of wine as the sommelier describes them. For access to this instruction, the wine bar hopes to charge a

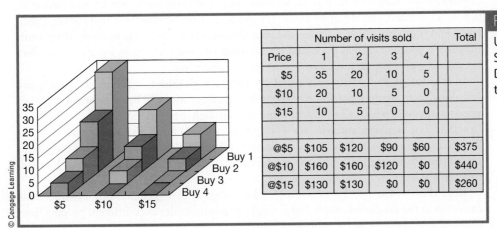

Figure 9.17

Using Self-Reported Demand Data to Set Prices

	Number of visits sold					Total
Price	1	2	3	4		
$5	35	20	10	5		
$10	20	10	5	0		
$15	10	5	0	0		
@$5	$105	$120	$90	$60		$375
@$10	$160	$160	$120	$0		$440
@$15	$130	$130	$0	$0		$260

© Cengage Learning

cover fee (like a bar charging a cover for live music). The entrance fee is the first tariff, and the glasses of wine that the consumer drinks comprise the second part of the price structure. The graph (or table) tells us that 35 respondents said they'd go to the wine bar once (in a month) if the cover charge was $5, and slightly fewer (20) said they'd go twice if the entrance was priced at $5. Ten said they'd go once (a month) if the cover charge was as high as $15, and no one said they'd go 4 times (once a week) if the price was that steep.

Let's weight the number of sales by the profitability. Say we take $2 as a variable unit cost. The values in the lower part of the table are computed as follows:

- *Column 1:* $105 = 35 \times (\$5 - 2), 160 = 20 \times (\$10 - 2)$, and $130 = 10 \times (\$15 - 2)$.

- *Column 2:* $120 = 2 \times 20 \times (\$5 - 2), 160 = 2 \times 10 \times (\$10 - 2)$, and $130 = 2 \times 5 \times (\$15 - 2)$.

- *Column 3:* $90 = 3 \times 10 \times (\$5 - 2), 120 = 3 \times 5 \times (\$10 - 2), 0 = 3 \times 0 \times (\$10 - 2)$.

- *Column 4:* $60 = 4 \times 5 \times (\$5 - 2), 0 = 4 \times 0 \times (\$10 - 2)$, and $0 = 4 \times 0 \times (\$15 - 2)$.

When we aggregate these values to get the row sums of $375, $440, and $260, the results suggest the $10 price point would lead to the greatest overall profitability.

With two-part tariffs, you price items separately even though you know customers will probably purchase both pieces. Price bundling is sort of the opposite. It aggregates prices of 2 or more complementary products for a single price.

9-8 PRICE CHANGES

A smart company doesn't just set a brand's price and forget about it. There are a number of reasons to think about changing prices, including the product life cycle, coupons, and price discounts.

9-8a Pricing and the Product Life Cycle

Like any of the 4Ps, a firm needs to revisit the strategic questions about pricing from time to time. Two contrasting strategies are referred to as pricing for market penetration and skimming. If you want to disperse your brand quickly and widely throughout the marketplace, that is, *penetrate the market*, the brand would be priced low at the time of its introduction to stimulate sales and to encourage trial and word of mouth. This approach is intended to capture a large market share. It is a little risky because if many customers immediately start buying your brand, you better be ready. The product better be good (no beta testing, thank you!), and your production capacity and your channels better be ready to serve. With time, the price is usually raised as the brand reaches maturity and finds its segments; the product is adorned with more features that customers care about, etc.

In contrast, market *skimming* is a strategy where a high price is set because the company is seeking profit margin, not volume. The only customers who will buy this brand at a high price are the ones who really want it. Think of your digit-head friends who want the latest in software or hardware and who are willing to pay (a lot!) for it. Think of the authors you like so much that you buy their new books in hardback, rather than waiting for the lower-priced paperback or e-book to come out months later. Over time, price is usually lowered, to make the brand accessible to more customer segments.

Regardless of the starting point, high (skimming) or low (penetration), modifications can occur as the product matures. For example, as segments develop, different product lines could be priced differently. As the brand matures, a drop in prices might restimulate sales, but if a firm believes in the brand, sales would also be restimulated by maintaining (or raising) prices, and adding features and benefits. Finally, when the brand has one foot in the ground, prices often tumble as the firm dumps inventory.

9-8b Price Fluctuations

Another element of changing prices is a price promotion through temporary price cuts or the issuance of coupons. These techniques are reliable in generating a modest short-term uptick in sales, but there are also equally predictable side effects that aren't as positive.

First, competitors can imitate price cuts immediately, so whatever market share increase in volume you were aiming for gets negated, and you (and your competitors) have shot yourself in the foot by squeezing your own margins. Second, price drops attract disloyal customers, and why not? Customers are savvy and often price sensitive, and they are quickly trained to buy when brands are on deal. Indeed, one motivation for your price drop was probably to widen the circle of customers who will purchase your brand and perhaps come back with future repeat purchasing. However, certainly some proportion of those newly attracted customers will be fickle and not return. You're betting on your brand and true product differentiation to retain customers. If your brand and product are similar to competitors, however, customers will switch back to cheaper substitutes when you reraise your prices.

Another dirty little secret is that price discounts are often not profitable. Yes, demand increases with deeper discounts, but only to a point. And, even if the temporary price discount is profitable in the very short run, it may come at the expense of longer-run profitability. For example, for many consumer packaged goods, the uptick in sales due to a promotion is due to some households who accelerate their purchasing, stock up and inventory their goods, and wait to buy again only during the next sales promotions. Hence, sales may dip a bit postpromotion.

A final cause for concern of occasional price fluctuations is the deleterious effect on the image of the brand. From the company's point of view, price promotions are intended to increase sales. From the customer's perspective, the occasional savings are appreciated, but there is also some question as to why the brand would need a sale. Brands that are of sufficient high quality shouldn't need the gimmick of a promotion.

9-8c Coupons

Coupons are a slightly different vehicle. They're more temporary or ethereal because by definition they're relevant only to the segment of customers who are coupon clippers. For these customers, it's likely that price is more important to them than brand image, so the concern of temporary price drops reflecting poorly on the brand is less an issue for coupons.

Coupons are big business; by some estimates, 350 billion are available yearly in the U.S. alone, with an average value of about $1. Potential savings thus is $350 billion, so it's good for companies that the redemption rate is less than 1% (annually and across SKUs). Coupons are especially effective at encouraging new (current) customers to try current (or new) products and brand extensions.

9-8d Competitive Strategy and Game Theory

In addition to concerns about the impact of price points or price changes on our own brand image, marketers must consider that the competition won't just sit idly by while we enjoy increased sales due to a price cut. Marketers frequently use game theory to try to estimate likely results of various actions, most frequently price cuts and competitive response. Say a competitor such as the market leader initiates action by dropping prices. We must then decide whether to cut prices also in order to convey to our customers our equitable value or to maintain prices and emphasize to customers that our brand is based on nonprice features. Or, further, do we offer a line extension to diminish the brand confusion but risk cannibalization, and so forth.

Game theory isn't a theory about Nintendo; it's just a structured way to think about the behavior of interdependent players, like two (or more) firms. The point is to get each player to think about the broader market, rather than optimizing only his or her own needs. Although it may seem counterintuitive at first, and it is important to avoid collusion or appearances thereof, the point is to find a solution to avoid price wars. Mutual cooperation can yield even better outcomes than both parties acting selfishly on their own accord. Go figure.

For example, Figure 9.18 illustrates a price-cut game. Current prices are $5 per unit (or $349 for a flight from L.A. to New York, whatever). Both firms are tempted to drop price to $4. Why? Currently, with us both at $5, we're selling 100 units each. That's fine. But if we drop the price and our competitor does not, more customers would flock to us. We'd sell 300 units—woohoo!—and our competitor would sell only 50. Well, unfortunately our competitor isn't stupid, so they're thinking the same thing. If they drop prices and we don't, they'd get 300 and we'd get 50. But if we're both so motivated, and we both therefore drop prices, we're back to splitting the pie, 50:50, but at worse margins. Brilliant.

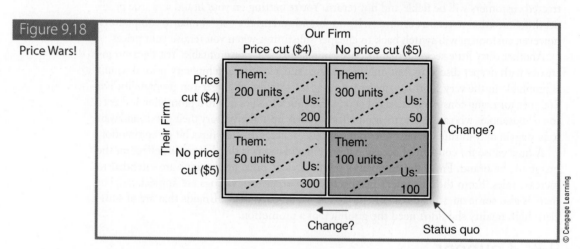

Figure 9.18
Price Wars!

© Cengage Learning

9-8e Auctions

As long as we're talking about changes, let's talk about dynamic pricing. The idea is that there isn't a fixed price; rather the price is negotiated between the buyer and seller. In a sense, auctions have always been around, and they are interesting in part because they continue to grow in popularity online.

The factors already discussed that increase or decrease demand are analogous to factors that give bargaining power to a buyer or a seller. Buyers have strength if they account for a significant portion of the seller's sales or if they have multiple options for meeting their procurement needs. When products are in short supply and high demand, sellers have strengths if they have differentiated products or simply during good economic times. Prices stay down when there is high supply relative to demand, intense brand competition, etc. Prices are boosted by controlled supply, high product value, product differentiation, high buyer dependency on suppliers, high switching costs, etc.

The defining characteristic of an auction is that the price point isn't set or fixed, nor is it even negotiable between a seller and one buyer. Rather, buyers/bidders compete to obtain the item. As in any marketplace, sellers want to yield high prices, and buyers want low prices. There is a particularly odd sense of efficiency in that whoever bids the highest

Auctions

Auctions have always been around as a mechanism of competition, pricing, and distribution. They have been a common means of sale for fruits and vegetables, tobacco and timber. Contemporary auctions are numerous and financially voluminous, selling:

- Fish at Tokyo's Tsukiji market (founded 1923, $5.5b annual, tsukiji-market.or.jp)
- Real estate at williamsauction.com (f. 1957, $.75b)
- Antiques at teppergalleries.com (f. 1937)
- Thoroughbreds at, keeneland.com (f. 1935, $1b)
- High-end artwork and other SKUs at Christie's (f. 1766, $5b, christies.com)
- Ditto, Sotheby's (f. 1744; $5B, sothebys.com)
- And, of course, anything on eBay (f. 1995; $8b)

Fun fact: In an old (1949!) issue of the *Journal of Marketing*, Kitchen described the challenges of auctions for perishables and the huge advantage of (then) new *refrigerated-carriers"* known as "reefers."

is very probably indeed the customer who values the item the most. Everyone else would have fallen out of the auction when the price exceeded their reservation price. This is the point of indifference at which you say, "If you raise the price, forget it. I won't buy. If you drop the price, okay, I will." So, a reservation price is really a good estimate of the customer's willingness to pay. Naturally, this price cap varies by segment and product category.

An auction can be comprised of very few bidding participants, such as when B2B suppliers bid for projects (e.g., an architectural design for a new office building, territorial rights for energy and minerals, etc.). In consumer bidding, the numbers of potential buyers can be quite large.

Many nonprofits hold sealed auctions, during which attendees at the event offer to pay a certain some for a desired item (a sculpture, exotic travel, etc.), and no bidder knows any other bidder's price offers. (Oh, to reveal such *c'est très gauche!*).

In contrast, many large-scale consumer bidding systems (e.g., online) are open auctions in which all bids are transparent to all participants, and the bidding proceeds in a sequential manner. In so-called English auctions, bids increase among the players over time. As the price surpasses the value to a customer, that customer drops out of the auction, and with time, whoever remains standing pays the last, highest bid, to obtain the item. In contrast, so-called Dutch auctions begin high, and prices drop over time (though not below the seller's reservation price). When the price finally drops low enough that a buyer is willing to buy the item at that price, the item is sold and the auction is concluded.

Markups vs. Margins

The difference between a markup and a margin is one's point of view. If you're a retailer, you buy a sports watch for $100, and you sell it for $200, then your markup is ($200 − $100)/$100 = 100%. The markup is the price you're adding going forward into the channel toward the customer.

Now change perspectives. You're still the retailer, but you look at what proportion of the customer's price is profit coming back to you. That's the margin, and it's ($200 − $100)/$200 = 50%.

We can add channel members and more price changes, and it will look more complicated, but the concept is the same:

From the manufacturer's point of view:

$50 = cost of manufacturing (raw materials, labor, etc.)
$150 = the manufacturer's price to the retailer
→ Markup = $(150 - 50)/50 = 200\%$.
→ Margin = $(150 - 50)/150 = 66.67\%$.

From the retailer's point of view:

$30 = cost of retailing (rent, salespeople, ads, etc.).
$40 = retailer wants to build in a profit of $40.
$270 = price to customer.
→ Markup = $(270 - 150)/150 = 80\%$.
→ Margin = $(270 - 150)/270 = 44.44\%$.

Whether you are interested in auctions, or price changes, or price as a driver of image, if you can't remember the math of pricing, take away this: Competing on price is nearly always dumb. Find a benefit that your target segment values, and play that up and charge for it. Value is an assessment of what the customer gets (e.g., quality, psychological benefits) compared to what the customer gives up (e.g., cost, time, effort of driving to a store). Customers can be taught to value many benefits; then the costs incurred seem worth the value. So be a smart marketer and teach them what your brand's benefits are!

Managerial Recap

The key concepts of pricing for a marketer are these.

- Pricing strategies are basically low, medium, or high:
  - The company and its costs can dictate the lower-bound price, where price is a function of the costs and some markup (thus, we calculate breakevens).
  - Customers' willingness to pay marks the upper bound, where price is a function of the customer's value of the item, minus some markdown (thus we learn techniques such as conjoint to try to obtain high-end price sensitivities).
  - In the middle, price is tweaked up or down relative to competitors' prices, depending on our firm's and brand's pricing strategies and goals.

- Pricing can be used to shape a brand's positioning and can attract (repel) different target (nontarget) segments, e.g., through tactics such as quantity discounting.

- There is a yin and yang in pricing between economic and psychological approaches to studying consumer behavior. Seemingly irrational behavior (so says an economist) may nevertheless be perfectly logical (so says a psychologist). Part of the reason marketing is interesting is because real life is not simple.

Chapter Outline in Key Terms and Concepts

1. Why is pricing so important?
2. Background: supply and demand
3. Low prices
   a. Concept in action: Breakeven for a good
   b. Concept in action: Breakeven for a service
4. High prices
   a. Scanner data
   b. Survey data
   c. Conjoint analysis
5. Units or revenue, volume or profits
6. Customers and the psychology of pricing
   a. Price discrimination, aka segmentation pricing
   b. Quantity discounts
   c. Yield or demand management
7. Nonlinear pricing
8. Price changes
   a. Pricing and the product life cycle
   b. Price fluctuations
   c. Coupons
   d. Competitive strategy and game theory
   e. Auctions

Chapter Discussion Question

1. Lawyers are changing their pay structures. It used to be that they would bill hourly (top dollar for top lawyers, and less experienced helpers had cheaper rates). Now they're beginning to price like consultants—per project. Thus, they must begin assessing the value-added to the client firm of the legal expertise and assistance. What advice would you give a law firm to proceed fairly and profitably?

2. Why do you think the fashionista segment pays such high prices for designer clothing with the knowledge that it will be passé after the current season?

3. What are the kinds of purchases for which you'll spare no expense? What kinds of purchases do you want to buy spending as little as possible? What are the major differences between these two categories that drive your attitude regarding price?

Mini-Case

Inexpensive Leather Portfolios

Impress4Less is working with a nearby b-school's entrepreneurial club in proposing to roll out a national launch of their nice-looking but inexpensive portfolios for $50. This past year served as a test market at the b-school. Given the friendly partnership and as a learning opportunity for the students, Impress4Less shared some information on basic cost structures. Their fixed costs on this project were $3,000, and variables costs were $10 a folio.

Currently at the b-school, the situation is as it looks in the next figure (on the left); that is, 200 folios were sold during the last academic year at the $50 price. But the club members get regular feedback (from classmates) that the $50 price tag seems steep, so they're asking Impress4Less for a price cut of 10%, essentially going to the figure at the right.

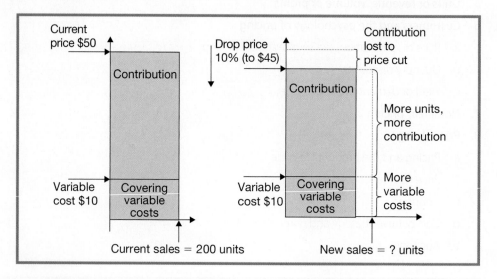

Mini-Case Discussion Questions

1. How many portfolios would they have to sell at $45 to at least meet last year's profits?

2. Should Impress4Less drop prices further? Could they raise prices above $50?

3. What assumptions are you making?

Video Exercise: *Washburn Guitar* (7:02)

Washburn Guitar has been a maker of fine musical instruments since the company's founding in Chicago in 1883. The company promises, "Each guitar [it produces] represents the finest quality at the best possible price." Washburn has four price points: (1) entry level at $349 and below; (2) intermediate level at $1,000 and below; (3) professional level at $1,000 to $3,000; and (4) collectors level at $3,000 and above. Amid the evolving perception that lower prices indicate lower quality, Washburn has taken steps to ensure the quality of its products at all price points. Interestingly, guitars made in the United States typically are of better quality and workmanship than are guitars made offshore. Consequently, U.S.-made guitars command higher prices. Indeed, most musical artists demand U.S.-made guitars. Washburn uses a manufacturer's suggested retail price (MSRP) as the pricing guideline for retailers selling its guitars. If discount and online retailers offer Washburn guitars for sale at under a minimum advertised price (MAP) that is set by Washburn, these distributors are warned to cease the practice. If the practice of violating the set MAP continues, the retailers lose their distribution rights for Washburn products.

Video Discussion Questions

1. How does the concept of segmentation pricing relate to Washburn Guitar's four different price points?

2. How does Washburn's four different price points reflect customer wants and needs?

3. Are Washburn's four price points an accurate indicator of differential quality? Why or why not?

Chapter 10
Channels of Distribution and Logistics

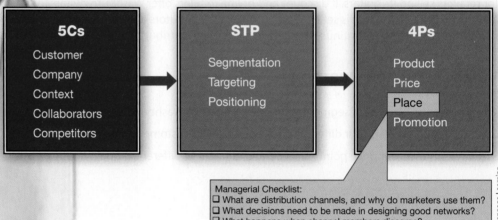

Managerial Checklist:
- ❑ What are distribution channels, and why do marketers use them?
- ❑ What decisions need to be made in designing good networks?
- ❑ What happens when channel members disagree?

© Cengage Learning

Marketing Management Framework

In just about Anytown, U.S.A., on Saturday mornings during seasons when the weather is nice, the town holds a farmers' market (Figure 10.1). Local farmer Eli brings a portion of his week's corn haul, and local baker Emma brings her famous apple pies. Eliot's selling his asparagus and squash, and Eliza, flowers freshly cut from her garden. Emery's selling his chili, and Emily sells her oatmeal cookies. Each of these providers registers with the community center and pays a small fee to set up a booth to sell their wares.

Figure 10.1

Farmer's Market

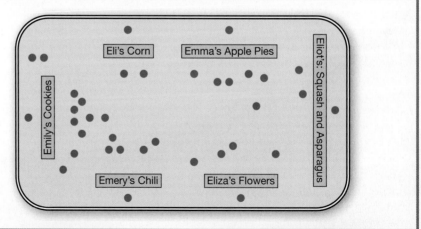

© Cengage Learning

The buyers are yuppie gentry who fill their SUVs with (reusable) bags of this very fresh, unbranded produce. During the week, these buyers shop at national chains, where the food is perfectly fine (it is fresh, and there is a good variety), and they shop at upscale groceries (where the food might be fresher still and perhaps organic or exotic, and probably more expensive). Still, Saturdays beckon buyers to this marketplace of old.

Providers have large quantities of their goods; e.g., Eli has more corn than his own family could possibly consume, so he'd like to sell some of it. Buyers wish to pick up only a few of any one particular item, e.g., several cobs of corn (but not Eli's whole stash), a bunch of flowers (but not more than one vase full), etc. The different needs of the buyers and sellers can be met nicely in the market.

In marketing, we talk about realigning the discrepancies between the quantities and the selections that the sellers and buyers offer and desire. Given that it is more efficient for any particular seller to produce a large quantity of a limited number of goods, and yet most buyers wish to purchase a smaller quantity of a wider variety of goods, the large supply of the sellers' goods must be made available to be sold in smaller batches (this process is known by the charming phrase of "breaking bulk"). It might be a little hassle for the farmer to stand around all Saturday morning until all his corn gets sold in batches of 2 or 3 ears at a time (that is, there are some "costs" involved), but he'd wait forever until someone was willing to buy his whole truckful.

The market has benefits for the buyers too. The central location of the market allows a buyer to go to purchase fruit and vegetables and homemade baked goods all in one convenient stop (it's an old-fashioned mall!). Otherwise, the yuppie in the SUV would track mileage up to Eli's farm for the corn, over to Emery's for the chili, back to Emily's for cookies, etc., and, before you know it, the morning is shot (and car emissions have contributed to global warming!). As a compromise, a consumer might hire a professional shopping agent to go to these locations to pick up these goods, saving the consumer time but almost certainly incurring some service fee. Similarly, farmer Eli might hire a helper to meet him at his farm and haul away some corn to be delivered to consumers or grocers, and here, too, the convenience of the helper relieves Eli of some hassle but will cost him for the assistance.

10-1 WHAT ARE DISTRIBUTION CHANNELS AND SUPPLY CHAIN LOGISTICS, AND WHY DO WE USE THEM?

These scenarios are different forms of *channels of distribution*, each of which is trying to solve the age-old problem "How do I get my stuff to where consumers want to buy it?" A *distribution channel* is a network of firms that are interconnected in their quest to provide sellers a means of infusing the marketplace with their goods, and buyers a means of purchasing those goods, doing it all as efficiently and profitably as possible.

The actors in the distribution network include manufacturing firms, distributors or wholesalers, retailers, consumers, and other players with other names. The names aren't as important in the end as the functions of all the parties. These functions include customer-oriented activities such as ordering and handling and shipping, product-oriented activities such as storage and display, marketing-centric activities, such as promotion, financial activities such as, well, financing, etc. The links among these actors include the movement and ownership of physical products, the flow of payment and information, and assistance in promotions and other marketing activities. When managers speak of *logistics*, they're talking about coordinating the flow of all those goods and services and information throughout the channel and among the channel members.

In the spirit of the saying, "No one is an island," it's hard to do business without partners. But as soon as you start taking on partners and forming a network of distribution channel partners, not surprisingly those partners want to make some money for their services. So the tension in channels is always of the form does this channel member contribute value? Does the member provide more benefit than it costs? This is the classic make-or-buy decision that firms constantly address: "Should we do this [some function] ourselves [i.e., make it] or ask someone to do it for us [buy it, outsource it]?"

One view of how channel members can make a marketplace more efficient and cost-effective is depicted in the contrast between Figures 10.2 and 10.3. In Figure 10.2, the manufacturers are delivering their goods to the consumers directly. In Figure 10.3, they go through an intermediary player, such as a common retail outlet. In the first scenario, the number of contacts in the network is the number of manufacturers *times* the number of consumers; in the second, the number of links is the number of manufacturers *plus* the number of consumers. Presumably some cost is associated with each link (e.g., managing that marketing relationship), and, as a result, if the costs are roughly the same, it follows that

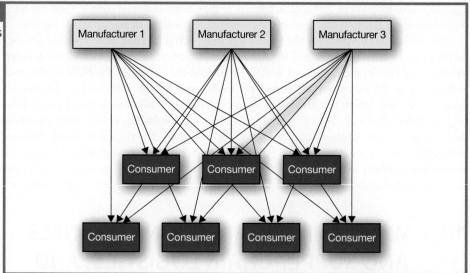

Figure 10.2

Manufacturers Direct to Consumers

© Cengage Learning

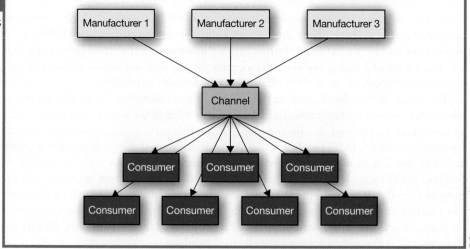

Figure 10.3

Manufacturers Through a Channel

© Cengage Learning

the marketplace with the fewest links, or costs, is more efficient. Thus, the system with an intermediary channel member (Figure 10.3) is more efficient than all firms going direct to consumers.

The channel member in Figure 10.3 is not well defined, so Figure 10.4 shows explicitly the three general classes of distribution channels. For example, many laptop and cell phone companies make their products and sell them directly to consumers online (as well as through a channel), and these companies do so because they can make (or save) money doing both.

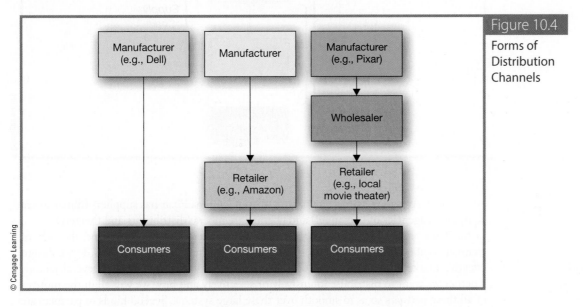

Figure 10.4

Forms of Distribution Channels

© Cengage Learning

Next we see the template for companies that collect stuff from manufacturers to sell and to serve as a touchpoint to consumers. For example, book publishers (and zillions of other SKUs) can sell through Amazon.com, which provides a coordination service for consumers. It's handy for consumers who can go directly to Amazon to obtain whatever they wish; it's handy for the book publisher who doesn't want to deal with that many consumers. And, of course, it's handy for Amazon. Amazon is not capable or interested in producing all those SKUs. It is simply functioning as the electronic equivalent of the farmer's market: a place where buyers and sellers can meet to enact their desired exchanges.

Lastly, in Figure 10.4 we see that companies can make something and hand it over to an agent who, in turn, hands it over to retail outlets to make the product available to consumers. For example, Pixar is in the business of making fun movies. The company may not be good at or interested in getting its movies to the audiences directly, and so it hires, and expects to pay for, distribution partners. The distributors see to it that the movies are available in theaters, and the theater serves as the retail point of access for the consumer audience.

The three channels systems have to deal with different issues. The PC or cell phone company doesn't have to deal with other companies, yield to their goals, split profits with them, or any of that. But they have to do everything themselves. Amazon has to have cooperation and reliability from its suppliers and then deal with customers. Pixar has to deal with its distributors and then is somewhat removed from its audiences.

Figure 10.5 illustrates these differences. Using the vertical lingo of marketers, when a company is dealing with partners that are upstream, it's called *supply chain management*. The partners that are downstream comprise the *channel members*; i.e., they provide the way to channel stuff to the customer. Referring back to the companies in Figure 10.4, a laptop company's suppliers (e.g., of batteries, hard drives, plastic computer casings) are invisible

Figure 10.5

Channels and Supply Chains

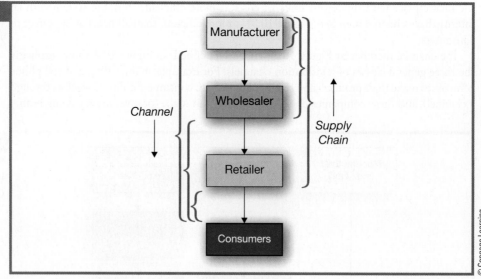

© Cengage Learning

but implied. Amazon's supply chain is the manufacturers. Pixar has suppliers (film, camera equipment, agencies of personnel) and channel members (distributors and theaters).

So if the *what* of channels is a network of suppliers and providers, and the *why* of channels is about efficiency, scales, and consistency in positioning, just *how* do we design effective marketing channels? To optimize delivery systems, we consider several factors: whether we want to distribute intensively or selectively and how we will align the motives of all these partners so as to smooth over these large systems. Several kinds of partners are special (e.g., retailing, catalogs, the Internet), so we will look at their concerns as well.

10-2 HOW TO DESIGN SMART DISTRIBUTION SYSTEMS: INTENSIVE OR SELECTIVE?

While distributor partners add value, there is no question that some companies go it alone and are very successful. So how does a company decide to go direct or indirect or, as most do, choose some combination of both? This first issue in designing a distribution system is that of *distribution intensity*—how many intermediaries will the manufacturer go through to distribute its goods to end-user consumers?

Many consumer packaged goods (CPGs) are distributed *intensively*. For example, many brands of snack foods (e.g., candy, chips, soft drinks), personal care products (e.g., shampoo, mascara), utility goods (e.g., pens, lighters, candles, newspapers, and magazines), and so forth are sold in many kinds of stores: drugstores, supermarkets, discount stores, convenience stores, etc. Why?

- First, as a consumer, consider how far you'd drive for a pack of gum (not very far) because it's a low-cost item and often an impulse purchase. Accordingly, to stimulate sales, gum needs to be widely available to consumers.

- Second, given that CPGs are inexpensive, companies require big-volume sales to make big bucks, hence the extensive distribution.

- These goods are relatively small, so it is easy for manufacturers to box up a zillion units into a still fairly small box, put many boxes onto a truck, and get the goods all over the place to many retail outlets.

- Finally, these goods are simple, so no sales force is required to explain to the consumer, "Okay, this is how an M&M works." Companies advertise directly to the consumer, who *pulls* the goods from the manufacturer.

In contrast, some goods and services are more complicated and expensive, both of which mean the purchases seem riskier to the consumer. So the consumer needs a salesperson to explain the purchase (e.g., choices among brands, features to select, etc.) and to reduce their feelings of anxiety associated with the risk, inducing a greater likelihood that they will buy. Sales people can seem pushy, but, let's face it, they're useful. The salespeople at car dealerships or electronic stores, or those in department stores selling major household appliances, probably know more than you about these SKUs.

For the consumer's part, these more expensive purchases require information and deliberation. They aren't typically impulse purchases, and they aren't typically frequent purchases. As a result, the consumer is probably willing to drive 5 to 10 miles to a dealership or to a department store to buy a household appliance. Thus, the manufacturer doesn't need an extensive distribution system.

Every choice has pros and cons. It's true that sales forces are useful, but they are also expensive to maintain, so manufacturing companies can't afford to staff many retail outlets in a given geographic area. In addition, given that sales-force kinds of goods are expensive, customers don't buy a lot of them; there's no frequent repurchasing, and so there is only a certain level of demand in any given area. Accordingly, such goods are usually available via *selective distribution channels* (i.e., not intensive distribution).

While companies like these advertise to consumers, they're really relying more on their distribution partners to help *push* the goods to the buying consumer (so they advertise and provide incentives to the sales force).

The intensity of distribution is a function of consumer convenience in access, information search, etc. If the goods are simple, inexpensive, easily transported, etc., typically they're distributed widely and intensively. If the goods are complex, requiring assistance in purchasing, relatively expensive (therefore feeling like a somewhat risky purchase), channels are often structured to be more selective.

Selectivity in channels offers additional benefits to the manufacturer; by definition, there are fewer relationships to manage, so the manufacturer has somewhat more control (e.g., over distributors engaging in price-cutting), and costs of interactions are less (e.g., trade discount deals to push new products need to cover fewer parties). The extreme case of selectivity is the *exclusive channel*, e.g., as when a small city might have only a single Infiniti dealership. Exclusive channels can be a little tricky because they can tend to be monopolistic (by definition, there is less competition), creating potential legal problems.

Bottom line: Channels are supposed to make access easier for customers, so think about the customer's buying behavior for your product category. Channel design is an integral part of marketing, strategy, and positioning. If your SKUs are available everywhere, that says something about you ("We're going to be there for you"). If your SKUs are found only in select outlets, that says something else ("We're special, and you're going to have to make the effort to find us").

The channel design needs to be consistent with all the other marketing elements. Recall that certain positioning elements tend to go together: Wide distribution usually goes with heavy promotion, lower prices, and average- or lower-quality products, whereas more exclusive distribution accompanies exclusive promotional efforts, higher prices, and higher-quality merchandise. For example, high-end hair products choose to distribute exclusively through salons to reinforce their positioning and not end up in Walmart.

The extensiveness of distribution channels is also related to the brand's life cycle or the company's maturity in the marketplace. The brand that comprises the sole offering of a new firm is typically sold through very few channels, probably a website and then, beyond that, it's hard to convince a retailer to support an unknown brand. As the company matures, it may go broader if doing so is consistent with the desired corporate and brand image.

10-2a Push and Pull

The terms "*push*" and "*pull*" refer to whether the manufacturer targets consumers or its channel partners with its marketing communications. Consumers are said to pull goods through the channel, whereas trading partners push the goods down the food chain. The manufacturer can use any marketing mix variables to push partners or to encourage pull from consumers, but you'll see some common trends.

We're very familiar with the many pull marketing strategies that assist marketers in encouraging consumer demand because we experience them as consumers (Figure 10.6). A marketer can temporarily reduce pricing, or enhance size or quantity. A marketer can offer trials (small sizes at low prices) or free samples (e.g., bundled onto a complementary product). A marketer can offer coupons (money redeemed at point of purchase) or rebates (money redeemed postpurchase), financing (e.g., buy now and don't pay for 6 months), and points toward rewards in loyalty programs. The marketer still must manage its relations with distributors and retailers, but pull strategies are targeted to the end user to engage consumers' awareness and loyalty.

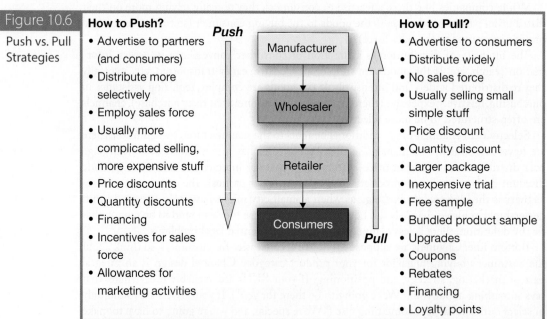

Figure 10.6

Push vs. Pull Strategies

How to Push?
- Advertise to partners (and consumers)
- Distribute more selectively
- Employ sales force
- Usually more complicated selling, more expensive stuff
- Price discounts
- Quantity discounts
- Financing
- Incentives for sales force
- Allowances for marketing activities

Push

Manufacturer → Wholesaler → Retailer → Consumers

Pull

How to Pull?
- Advertise to consumers
- Distribute widely
- No sales force
- Usually selling small simple stuff
- Price discount
- Quantity discount
- Larger package
- Inexpensive trial
- Free sample
- Bundled product sample
- Upgrades
- Coupons
- Rebates
- Financing
- Loyalty points

© Cengage Learning

Push marketing strategies involve manufacturers offering incentives to distributors (dealers, wholesalers, retailers) to sell product to end users. While the manufacturer targets the channel member rather than the consumer, push marketing tools resemble those of pull. For example, a marketer can offer the distributor or retailer temporarily reduced pricing, an allowance to help cover marketing activities, a discount for purchasing larger quantities (e.g., a twofer or a bogo [buy one get one free]), financing a payment for several months, spiffs (incentives for the sales force), etc.

The manufacturer may hope that the retailer will pass through to the end user some of these incentives (e.g., price discounts), but the retailer may or may not. The value of that retailer is still in what they do with the incentives; e.g., a price discount might not be passed along, but the retailer may provide more shelf or floor space to the manufacturer's brands, and the manufacturer might be perfectly happy with that result. In the end, what the manufacturer hopes is that, if they give the trade partners incentives, the partners will support the manufacturer's goods and services and push them to the final customer.

10-3 POWER AND CONFLICT IN CHANNEL RELATIONSHIPS

Whether you're pushing or pulling, distributing intensively or selectively, you and your channel partners want to see happy customers and enjoy profitability, but there are many ways to achieve these goals. When channel partners differ in their opinions on how to do so, conflict can arise. The question is whether strategies and tactical incentives can be designed so that the goals of all parties are compatible. For example, a manufacturer usually desires that a retailer stock its entire line, but a retailer can see that certain SKUs don't sell well, so it doesn't want to waste shelf space or floor real estate with those unattractive items. Channel members also frequently bicker over (negotiate terms on) prices and margins. For example, suppliers will say that the retailers are charging the consumers too much; hence, demand is not as strong as it could be. But retailers will counter that the suppliers' prices to them are also too high and that they must pass along high prices to make some decent margin.

A little bit of conflict can be healthy. Just as people working together can have divergent views, companies can also have diverse perspectives. The question is how conflict is handled when it gets to be too much. In handling conflict, the differences can be useful as motivation to find alternative solutions (e.g., systemic cost-cutting mechanisms) that are both mutually satisfying and superior in optimizing goals than either party had first considered.

Conflict can be squashed if one player is inherently more powerful than another. Perhaps it shouldn't be true that might makes right, but, indeed, power is usually defined by size and it is effective; e.g., if you produce a few lines of a niche product and Walmart doesn't like how you're doing something (your packaging, price points, delivery schedules, etc.), who do you think will blink first? Or if you're the big player and your partner is a little entrepreneur, you similarly expect your "Jump" to elicit the response "How high?" Power isn't a great way to resolve conflict in the long term, however, because the less powerful player can feel resentful and look to leave the channel arrangement as soon as another opportunity becomes available. (Or, for example, they could create a competing product, with knowledge and technology learned from you!) Similarly, sometimes conflict arises between two mighty companies, and then a show of strength is ineffective; it will be a standoff that just generates a lot of hot air and noise.

Transaction cost analysis is a model that considers channel members' production costs and governance costs, both of which are ideally minimized. Costs of producing and bringing products to market are often reduced by having intermediaries because those channel partners operate with economies of scope and scale. Costs of governance are these relational issues incurred by trying to coordinate the enterprise and control one's partners.

Types of Power

When channels marketing people talk about a powerful retailer or a powerful supplier, here's what they can mean.

Type of Power	Quick Image	Definition	Example
Coercive power	Bully	One party can make another do something by taking away benefits or inflicting punishment.	"We're Big-Retailer, and we won't stock your stuff until you give us a better trade margin."
Information (expert) power	Know-it-all	One party gets cooperation because they have information the other seeks.	"We're Big-Online-Retailer, and we won't provide you with your SKUs sales data for the CRM database you wish to build, until you purchase more advertising in our space."
Legitimate power	Great Dane and a Chihuahua	By size or expertise, one party can make claims and threats that encourage the other party to conform.	"We're Big-Pharma-Supplier, and we will not supply you with more of drug X because it's running into testing problems."
Referent power	I want be like you.	One party cooperates with another because the former seeks affiliation with the latter.	"We're Little-Guy, and we cooperate with Market-Leader because they have a great brand name. We're riding their coattails as we establish ourselves."
Reward power	I have goodies for you.	One party has the ability to provide good outcomes for another.	"We're Big-Supplier, and we do what we want > But when Big-Retailer asked us to make our package smaller, we did because they'll stock more and sell more for us."

A concern is that all players will act selfishly and opportunistically, but a more contemporary view is that of transaction value analysis, a perspective that emphasizes the benefits a company brings to its partners (beyond cost reductions). Marketers speak of all these plays and counterplays using human relationship terms: They speak of the communications between a supplier and distributor, the trust between a distributor and retailer, the satisfaction a retailer has with a supplier, etc. As with people, when channels are in conflict, the best way through it is by talking to each other; communication enhances trust and satisfaction. It's also clearly important to deliver on one's promises (e.g., meet delivery dates, quantities, quality, etc.). Channels experts speak of trust as both the willingness and the ability to deliver on promises.

Other ways that channel members have used to strengthen relationships is to exchange some personnel for short stints to learn the perspectives and needs of the other party more intimately. All parties need to feel that they're being heard, and their needs are understood and being met. Sometimes it's helpful to remind all members of the channel network that they have the mutual goal of customer satisfaction. Hence, occasionally, multiple channel members may sponsor joint programs of marketing research in order to see just what it is that the customer values, so that the channel members can determine together how best to respond to those requests.

Anatomy of Airbus' Channel Partners

1. Carson, California: Water engineering and plumbing
2. Irvine, California: Testing in-flight entertainment of 600 seat-back video monitors
3. Perth, Australia: Red clay with bauxite for aluminum to ▶
4. Texas: Smelted into aluminum chunks "the size of mattresses," then ▶
5. Davenport, Iowa: 1.2-mile aluminum mill to make wing pieces, which are ▶
6. Trucked to Baltimore, Maryland, and ▶
7. Shipped to a factory in Broughton, North Wales (Plant can fit 12 soccer fields.)
8. Put on ship, made in China
9. Rendezvous soon with fuselage, built in Germany
10. Shipped to Bordeaux and driven by tractor trailer to Toulouse overnight (French police close roads) for final assembly.

© FREDRIK VON ERICHSEN/DPA /Landov

The final step in preparing the A380 is painting the aircraft for specific customers. Among the airlines purchasing the A380 are Emirates, Quantas, Singapore Airlines, Air France, Lufthansa, and Korean Air.

© HRISTOPHE MORIN/Maxppp /Landov

Several engines are available on the Airbus A380, from suppliers such as Rolls Royce and Engine Alliance, which consist of a General Electric engine and Pratt & Whitney fan.

© ITAR-TASS/Newscom

To give you a sense of size, the big A380 is in the foreground, and the little toy in back is an A340, which is only slightly smaller than the huge 747! The A380 assembly requires • 18,000 suppliers in 30 countries, • 1,000,000 aluminum fasteners.

The plane: • houses 800 passengers, • has a 260-feet wingspan, • has a tail seven stories high.

For more, see Peter Pae's *LA Times* article, "Giant Passenger Plane Requires Giant Supply Chain." Thank you, Professor Mumin Kurtulus (Vanderbilt U) for this suggestion!

When all of these measures are insufficient, there are still other options, including mediation (negotiate through a third party who determines the two parties' utility functions) and arbitration (the third party makes a binding decision for the two). Part of communication, to preclude or abate conflict, is negotiation. Just as differential power affects pricing, buyers and sellers rarely come to the table as equals when bargaining. Suppliers have more power when their inputs are important to the buyer, when their services are differentiated, and when there are no substitutes. Customers have more power when they're large, relatively few in number, and they purchase large quantities.

10-3a Revenue Sharing

Sometimes channel conflict can be about feeling unappreciated and such psychological and interpersonal issues, but it often comes down to money; e.g., the retailer complains, "I want a bigger piece of pie. Look at the great service my sales staff provides!" And the manufacturer counters with, "But it's my brands that the customers are coming for, and, although your service is nice and we appreciate it, it's not what they're buying, so we should get more than you." So let's look at some of the money issues.

First consider the scenario that a manufacturer sells directly to the customer. A price is set to the consumer from which must be recovered the manufacturing costs (producing the good or service) and the retailing costs (for this scenario, the manufacturer incurs the various costs of interacting with the customer). So the manufacturer profit is a function of the customer price, the manufacturing and retailing costs, and demand.

When the manufacturer goes through an intermediary, not surprisingly that player wants to make some money, too, for the services they perform. There's a markup (a profit to be made) when the manufacturer yields product to the retailer, and there's a second markup (more to be made) when the retailer makes the product available to the consumer. If the channel is not managed well, we quickly run into a situation where, in order to recover these markup costs, we'd be tempted to set a rather high price to the end-user consumer. In fact, the price may become so high that demand would start to drop off, and then both the manufacturer and retailer lose. This problem is called "double marginalization" because the manufacturer wants a profit (a margin), and so does the retailer (hence, two margins). So what to do? You learned it in preschool: Channel partners must share.

If you take the D2C scenario, and call the "manufacturer profit" instead "total channel profit" and divvy up the profits in some portion (equitably agreed on by the manufacturer and retailer), then the consumer is not overcharged, the problem of double marginalization is solved, and demand is such that both the manufacturer and retailer can make some serious money. The money is simply reapportioned.

If that was a wee bit abstract, consider an example. Figure 10.7 shows a direct and indirect channel scenario on pricing to illustrate the impact of double marginalization. Say it costs a manufacturer $c_m = \$50$ to make a designer sweater, and the costs to set up retail are $c_r = \$50$ (for whoever incurs the cost—the manufacturer if they sell direct or, in a moment, the retailer when sold indirect). Say the manufacturer marks up $100. If it sells it directly, the consumer would be charged $200.

If instead of selling the sweater directly, the manufacturer hands it over to a retailer to sell, pricing it at $p_r = \$150$ (which is $c_m = \$50$ and $100 manufacturer markup). Then the retailer wants some margin, too—say, $50, so they mark it up, and the price to the consumer is $p = \$250$ (which is $p_r = \$150$ and $c_r = \$50$ and $50 retailer markup). Costs total $100, and the surplus of $150 is split $100 for the manufacturer and $50 for the retailer (Figure 10.8). Say demand is okay, and some 500 sweaters are bought. That gives the manufacturer 500 × $100, or $50,000, and the retailer 500 × $50, or $25,000.

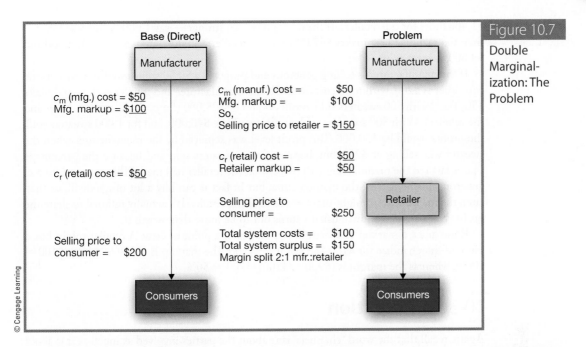

Figure 10.7

Double Marginalization: The Problem

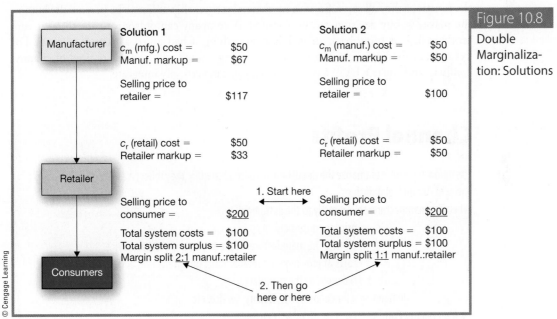

Figure 10.8

Double Marginalization: Solutions

If the channel system could drop the consumer price to $200, demand would presumably pick up, according to the sales of other comparably positioned, but lesser priced sweaters. So lower the consumer's price to $p = \$200$. The costs are still the same, i.e., $c_m = \$50$ and $c_r = \$50$, so the question is what're p_r and the markups.

Say the manufacturer proposes a 2:1 (or 67:33%) split like before. Then $p_r = 117$: The manufacturer makes $67, the retailer $33. These figures are less than before for both parties (the manufacturer had made 100 and the retailer 50). However, let's factor in the pickup on demand, say, to 800, and now the manufacturer would make $67 \times 800 = \$53,600$ and retailer $33 \times 800 = \$26,400$ (which is $3,600 more than before for the manufacturer and

$1,400 more for the retailer). If the demand is even stronger—say 1,000 sweaters are sold—then the manufacturer makes $67,000 and the retailer, $33,000 (an increase of $17,000 and $8,000, respectively).

If the manufacturer is feeling generous and proposes a 50:50 split, and if the price to the consumer is $200, with total costs at $100, the manufacturer and retailer each would make $50. Then, with 500 sweaters sold, profits would be $25,000 (for both the manufacturer and the retailer). With 800 sweaters sold, profits would be $40,000, and for 1,000 sweaters sold, the profits would be $50,000. This profit level was achieved by the manufacturer when the sweater was selling at $250, but, because fewer sweaters sold and because the percentage shares favored the manufacturer, it's twice what the retailer had made. This move might feel generous on the part of the manufacturer, but in fact it can buy a lot of goodwill, so that, later, the manufacturer might make requests of the retailer. It's actually rational to share the profits because the goodwill usually turns out to be more than worth it.

Remember, a markup or a margin is a matter of a point of view. A retailer might buy a piece of merchandise for $100 and sell it for $200. The markup is ($200 − $100)/$100 = 100%, whereas the margin is ($200 − $100)/$200 = 50%.

10-3b Integration

Again, recall that the word "channels" isn't about the parties involved as much as it is about the functions they all serve. So, if some channel relationship seems to be perennially bumpy, the make-vs.-buy decision can be revisited. A company can outsource something it currently makes or bring back an in-house something it had asked a partner to cover. For example, in the latter scenario, if revenue sharing annoys you, and you're tired of channel conflicts, and you're a bit of a control freak, you can vertically integrate.

Channel Profits

The following terms summarize the discussion on revenue sharing. They reflect a means of negotiating win-win channel relationships.

When the manufacturer sells directly to the customer:

p = price to consumer.
c_m = costs to the manufacturer of producing the good or service.
l_r = costs of providing the retailer function, interacting with the customer, etc. (incurred by the manufacturer).
demand = a function of price, quality, service, etc.

→ Manufacturer profit = $(p - c_m - c_r) \times$ demand.

When the manufacturer goes through an intermediary:

p_r = price to retailer (i.e., wholesaler price).
c_m = costs to the manufacturer of producing the good (assume same as in previous entry).
c_r = costs to the retailer of providing the retailer function.
demand = a function of price, quality, service, etc. (assume same as previously—just that a different channel member is providing this function)

→ Manufacturer profit = $(p_r - c_m) \times$ demand.
→ Retailer profit = $(p - p_r - c_r) \times$ demand.

If we've managed the channel properly, the customer shouldn't see any difference in price, and every player gets a piece of the pie. For example:

Manufacturer profit when going direct =

Manufacturer profit when going indirect + Retailer profit in indirect channel or, using the three previous equations:

$$(p - c_m - c_r) \times \text{Demand} = (p_r - c_m) \times \text{Demand} + (p - p_r - c_r) \times \text{Demand}$$
$$= [(p_r - c_m) + (p - p_r - c_r)] \times \text{Demand}$$
$$= [p_r - c_m + p - p_r - c_r] \times \text{Demand}$$
$$= [-c_m + p - c_r] \times \text{Demand}$$
$$= [p - c_m - c_r] \times \text{Demand}$$

A manufacturer could engage in *forward integration* by opening its own retail stores.

- For example, Sony and Apple computers used to only be manufacturing and subsequently (partially) were forward integrated, opening Sony and Apple stores.

- Ralph Lauren took its fashions forward in two retail channel formats; it has a few select flagship stores to carry its entire line (thus offering more SKUs than what it makes available to department stores such as Bloomingdale's).

- Perhaps the most popular means of forward integrating has been manufacturers providing their wares online for direct purchasing.

A manufacturer can also engage in *backward integration* by controlling some of the raw material inputs.

- For example, some booksellers like Barnes & Noble have done some backward integration into warehousing, which is typically a distributor's function, not a retailer's. It has enormous warehouses that stock thousands of books. In addition, B&N has been publishing classics under its own imprint (books published before 1923 are not covered by copyright laws, and so can be reissued).

- Retailers backward-integrate when they set up private labels (e.g., foods, fashions, toys). Private labels offer a number of advantages: (1) If they sell well, they give the retailer negotiating power with the manufacturers; (2) they can offer significant margins; and (3) they can help the retailer differentiate itself (e.g., Kenmore is available only at Sears).

These moves introduce additional forms of competition. Where there was horizontal competition between retailers of different types (e.g., pharmacy vs. discount house vs. department stores), there now can be vertical competition. wherein the manufacturer finds itself competing with its partners. For example, a manufacturer's own branded retail store can compete with an independent channel retailer, i.e., with a retailer's private label brand.

Sometimes it's hard to keep track of all the players in the channel. Although the prototypical channel structures in Figure 10.4 look simple, the real world is, of course, messier. Companies that compete in one industry, even over one SKU, may collaborate in the production and selling of others. The terrible earthquake that Japan experienced and the consequences that unfolded for many businesses reminded us that the network of companies and channel responsibilities are complex and amorphous, given our globally interconnected world (Figure 10.9).

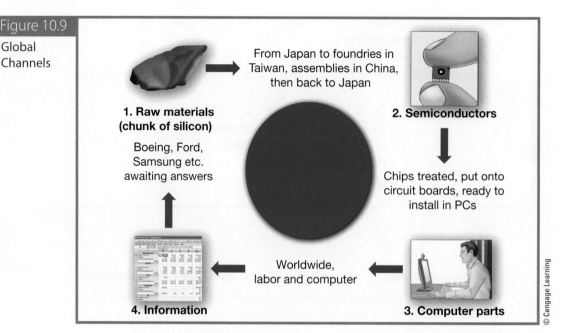

Figure 10.9

Global Channels

1. Raw materials (chunk of silicon)

From Japan to foundries in Taiwan, assemblies in China, then back to Japan

Boeing, Ford, Samsung etc. awaiting answers

2. Semiconductors

Chips treated, put onto circuit boards, ready to install in PCs

3. Computer parts

Worldwide, labor and computer

4. Information

© Cengage Learning

10-3c Retailing

A channel function that has generated a great deal of interest is retailing, in part because it is the most visible element to the end customer, and so it can have the most direct impact on image, positioning, and brand equity. Retailing has also been a topic of discussion because they have been gaining power and momentum over the past 10–20 years. Marketers reliably find that large, powerful retailers can make or break a new product.

Retail outlets are classified along a number of criteria. They can be compared by the extent of the manager's ownership, some being independent retailers (e.g., a local artist's gallery, the town jeweler, the local florist, a village baker), and others being branded store chains or franchises like Jiffy Lube or Subway. Alternatively, we can categorize retailers by their level of service, which tends to be positively related to their price points, from Dollar General to Saks.

Most frequently, though, marketers and industry discussions classify stores along their product lines. *Specialty stores* carry depth but not breadth; e.g., a shoe store may carry only shoes, or only men's shoes, or even only men's athletic shoes, but it does not carry table linens or children's clothing. The product assortment is broader at *general merchandise retailers*, such as department stores, which carry shoes, linens, and kids' clothes, but perhaps not as many brands of men's athletic shoes as the specialty shoe store we just considered. Other general retailers include the monster-sized mass merchandisers (e.g., discount warehouse clubs like Sam's Club hypermarkets) and smaller general stores, such as convenience stores and drugstores.

Marketers and smart CEOs have long recognized the importance of the frontline employees as the primary connection between them and their customers. Unfortunately, some backward CEOs think that it's their merchandise that attracts customers, so retail staff should be paid minimum wage. Clearly the merchandise is important, but so are the employees; they are a salient representation of the brand to the customer.

A lot of research has demonstrated that there is a relationship between employee satisfaction and customer satisfaction. If a retailer isn't selective in hiring employees, and if the employees are not trained or paid well, then the service they provide will be suboptimal, and there are clear and immediate repercussions on customer dissatisfaction. Not surprisingly, this situation isn't particularly pleasing to employees either; they experience the stress of role conflict, i.e., they may want to please the customer but be unable to do so. Sooner rather than later, they resign, and new workers are hired as replacements, and this churn exacerbates poor service because newbies rarely know how to do something in an organization. If, instead, the retailer has foresight, it'll select good people, train them, pay them and reward them well, and trust them enough to empower them to make on-the-spot decisions to make customers happy.

Retailing falls under the general rubric of services, and just as the employees are more noticeable to customers, so are the operations elements, such as IT. A tool that marketers have found useful is to draw a flowchart depicting the front stage, meaning all the elements that a customer sees, as well as the back stage elements of the service provision that the customer does not see but that also must run efficiently to support the front stage. Since services—such as a customer walking into a retail outlet, wandering around, picking up merchandise, putting some back, considering what to buy, finally checking out—all unfold in real time, the flowchart map can give the marketer a sense of the elements that need to be managed: What parts of the process flow smoothly? What parts bog down quickly during peak periods? What parts of the process might be streamlined or eliminated altogether?

One streamlining phenomenon that IT is facilitating is self-service. We take self-service for granted in a number of industries: retail banking, check-ins at airports, checkouts at hotels, pumping one's own gas, buffet lines at salad bars, etc. Internet retailing is also clearly a form of self-service; instead of flipping through a catalog and calling an 800 number to place an order with a customer rep, we go online and click, click, click. Beyond these forms, a number of retailers are experimenting with self-service in places like the checkout. There are personnel, e.g., at hardware stores, as backup in case the machines are too confusing and to discourage theft. IT has made checkout staffing more efficient (e.g., one person supervising six self-checkouts instead of six checkers). It's a development to watch.

Finally, a classic concern in retailing is the old mantra you've heard: "location, location, location," that is, how to identify an ideal site location for one's store. Marketers are hired to study environmental data such as population densities, income and social class distributions, median ages, and household composition if that is relevant to a particular store (e.g., placement of a toy store vs. a dance club).

Site location models essentially predict the likelihood of a successful outlet as measured by predicted sales as a function of those density stats. Starbucks looks for population density and urban, upscale, high foot traffic. Walmart has rural store footprint, and yet it is well placed with respect to car traffic in average or downscale socioeconomic zip codes.

Once it is succeeding, a retailer has multiple growth strategies available. First, a retailer can expand by providing *additional services* to serve its current customers better. For example, it's not unusual for companies known for a particular core service (e.g., a grocery store) to add peripheral services for the convenience of their shoppers (e.g., adding banking, a florist, a dry cleaner, etc.). Alternatively, the retailer can maintain their focus on their current offerings but reach out to attract *additional segments* of customers.

Given the importance of location and channel access, another popular course of action is to go *multisite* and open additional stores. Although this strategy seems easy—after all, you already know how to make one shop succeed—it can be a challenge to oversee quality control in the multiple locations. There are particular risks when companies expand too quickly. *International* expansion is a form of multisite expansion, and it brings additional challenges in terms of tailoring one's brand (and entire marketing mix) to the local markets. International approaches include direct exporting, joint ventures, direct foreign investment, license agreements, etc.

In addition to setting up shop internationally, companies in other countries can serve as very useful channel partners. An important form of international channel support these days is global outsourcing. For example, outsourcing reliance on India is huge for the technical training (engineers hired there are less expensive than comparable talent in the U.S., U.K., Germany, or Japan) and for skills in English, both verbal (call centers) and written (software code and medical records transcriptions). In addition, India's offerings are broadening to include the provision of auto parts, chemicals, and electronics.

China's role in outsourcing is also clearly huge for the size and costs of its nonunion labor force. Employees' roles are less versatile given the more recent heritage of English as a second language. Its capitalistic business environment is also less mature, and it needs to redress its stance on copyright violations before playing with the global companies. Finally, though its infrastructures are improving, they are still relatively weak.

Choices among outsource providers depend on the talent, costs and size of the labor pool, the existence of relevant infrastructures (IT, transportation, e-power, telecom), a hospitable government stance on foreign investment (e.g., local taxation), costs of real estate and travel, and local ethics (e.g., the country's treatment of women). These less experienced companies and countries are also more amenable and motivated to tailor their services to the buyers.

10-3d Franchising

Franchising is a unique format of multisite expansion. It's a means for a company to quasi-integrate; the company can retain some control without complete ownership or capital expenditure. Franchising systems offer benefits to both the franchisor (the company) and the franchisee (the local front line).

For the franchisors' part, they receive some capital, they enjoy some scales of economy, they know they have committed people in their franchisees, their expansion and investments are relatively reduced in risk, and, trusting their franchises in good hands, they can focus on their core functions, such as their expertise in product development. For the franchisees, they immediately inherit a company with a well-known brand and some market awareness, supplier relationships are largely intact, there are templates for training the staffs they hire, and there is central firm support for many business concerns, including marketing.

The two major classes of franchising are product distribution franchising and business format franchising. For product distribution franchising, a supplier authorizes a distributor in some territory (a prescribed geographic area) to carry its products, use its brand name, enjoy the efforts of its advertising, etc. The biggest example of product franchising is the automobile dealership (e.g., Ford dealers are meant to sell Ford cars and trucks). Other product franchises include Mobil gas stations and Baskin Robbins ice cream shops. Business format franchising is an arrangement where the company offers a tried-and-true system in which to conduct business, along with the marketing support, brand name, advertising, etc. to the franchisee—the owner who will run the local arm of that business. Examples include restaurants (e.g., Denny's, Hardee's), some hotels (e.g., Days Inn, Hampton Hotels), and a variety of other businesses, such as H & R Block tax preparers, ServiceMaster cleaners, etc.

In either case, a franchisee pays an up-front fee to buy into the system and then continues to pay royalties to the franchisor. In exchange, the franchisee enjoys an established brand name, corporate support on equipment, training of personnel, and marketing and advertising. Franchises are a low-capital, low-risk means of being an entrepreneur with a safety net. Most owners have some business management experience, and they can see the advantages of the economies-of-scale. The profits earned by all the outlets help finance the operations of the entire system, e.g., marketing the brand name, advertising dollars, operations, capital (buildings, land, equipment), etc. While initial franchise fees can seem steep, these networks provide access and support at a level that an independent entrepreneur typically cannot reach.

The franchise system has appeal to customers also because the brand name implies a level of standardization and predictability in quality across the outlets; e.g., one Jiffy Lube is pretty much like another, or, if you're in a McDonald's, you would be hard-pressed to identify which city you were in. Franchises are popular up and down the channel (for the manufacturer or franchisor, the retailer or franchisee, and the customer), and hence they continue to grow in many sectors, e.g., movie theaters, weight loss centers, ice cream shops, etc.

10-3e E-Commerce

An enormously important channel is the Internet. Retail sales online are about $170 billion and growing about 6% a year, but that's still only about 4.4% of total retail sales (www.census .gov/estats). Who is buying all these books, music, DVDs, and, well, frankly just about any SKU? First, in terms of demography, people online still tend to be younger and more affluent, but gaps are closing toward being representative of general markets. Second, the countries with the largest Internet presences are the U.S., Japan, Germany, the U.K., France, and Korea. The populations in China and India each exceed 1 billion, with relatively few online (31% and 8%, respectively), thus obviously both countries have huge potential for growth.

The Internet is frequently characterized as a tool to empower customers. Figure 10.10 shows the increasing variety of channels through which a consumer might view entertainment programming. Price points and access durations vary, and the business models are still shaking out. As always, it's important to consider the target customer segment(s) when designing or choosing channels: Different channels appeal to different individuals and customer segments. Increasing consumer choice is a central manifestation of empowerment.

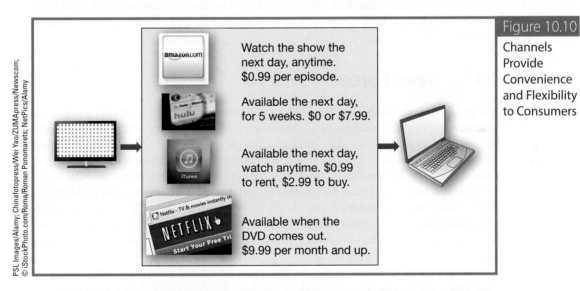

PSL Images/Alamy; Chinafotopress/Wei Yao/ZUMApress/Newscom; © iStockPhoto.com/Roma/Roman Ponomarets; NetPics/Alamy

Figure 10.10

Channels Provide Convenience and Flexibility to Consumers

Watch the show the next day, anytime. $0.99 per episode.

Available the next day, for 5 weeks. $0 or $7.99.

Available the next day, watch anytime. $0.99 to rent, $2.99 to buy.

Available when the DVD comes out. $9.99 per month and up.

In addition, e-commerce offers convenience and sometimes even smarter shopping. For example, the online services of "my lists" and order histories make reorders easier (e.g., Amazon's wish list, NetGrocer's last list, Netflix's ratings), etc. Web hosts' recommendation agents seem to enhance purchasing (but perhaps not lock-in or continued patronage).

10-3f Catalog Sales

The hardcopy predecessor to e-commerce was the direct-to-consumer catalog. The top 10 catalogers are B2B companies, including Dell, Themro Fisher Scientific (lab supplies), IBM, Staples, and the like. The biggest B2C catalogers are Sears, Penney, Williams-Sonoma, L.L. Bean, Fingerhut, and Doctors Forster & Smith (pet supplies).

The advent of any new medium (e.g., the Internet) brings excitement and also naturally some concern that it will displace existing media (e.g., catalogs). But no worries; according to multichannelmerchant.com, 80 of the top 100 catalogers continue to see sales growth. While conducting business via the Internet is dirt cheap, many costs for cataloging, such as color printing, have come down also (however, postage costs occasionally rise).

Marketers have shown that, while the Internet is very well suited for a search, catalogs still dominate when customers are browsing. In addition, the photography in catalogs is beautiful and sensual. Catalogs serve as a prompt, stimulating a customer to go to a website more frequently. Thus, these channels are complementary and not competitive.

The channel synergies extend to retail stores as well. Marketing researchers describe the strengths of each: The Internet is great for the search experience (it's convenient, the information is vast, and comparisons between products and prices are facilitated), catalogs are great for the enjoyment of the browsing experience, and retail dominates for pre- and postpurchase service.

While a hardcopy catalog is, of course, fixed once printed, catalogers are also using technology and customer transaction databases to customize their printed offerings. The types of products and SKUs to include in one customer segment's catalog versus those that are sent to another can be modified, as can the frequency of the catalogs sent, the promotional incentives offered, etc. Catalogs can be used to yield sales directly and also to drive online or retail traffic. Increasingly, these promotional efforts are tracked, as when a catalog insert coupon is printed with an individual barcode, with the coupon redeemable at point of purchase. The redemption data further contribute to the database to enhance subsequent personalization efforts and to continue to test the effectiveness of marketing offers.

10-3g Sales Force

We've talked about machines (the Internet, self-service IT systems) as a channel and about frontline employees at retail shops as channel representatives, but another human element of a channel is a company's sales force. For the companies high on push, such as many B2B channels, the sales force is an enormously important part of the corporate system and contributor to the bottom line. If we look at the performance of highly trained sales teams in industries such as shipping and metals, we see that the highest-educated and longest-tenured sales teams have growth rates in the mid-20% range. Particularly for more undifferentiated products, the quality of the sales force is often the single most significant means of differentiation. Stated another way, for these products, a company's sales force is its most important driver of performance.

The issues regarding sales forces are two: First, how many salespeople should we have (and where will they be deployed), and, second, how should salespeople be compensated for their efforts? The determination of the size of a sales force is usually done via some estimation of expected workload. We'd solve for the optimal number of salespeople by factoring in how many customers we must serve, how frequently we must call on a customer throughout the year, the average amount of time necessary to spend with each client, etc. For example, a particular SKU is sold to 100,000 drugstores and convenience stores, and the brand manager wants each salesperson to visit each account at least once a month, or 12 times a year. Say each visit lasts 30 minutes. The average number of hours worked a year would be 2,000 (50 weeks × 40 hours a week), but not all 2,000 will be face time with clients; say travel and administrative duties take away 500 hours. Then the minimum number of salespersons we'd require for this coverage would be (100,000 accounts × 12 visits per year × 0.5 hour)/ 1,500 hours = 400 salespeople.

Naturally this number and the kind of salesperson most useful to the company will vary with the brand and corporate life cycle: Newer brands and companies might well take advantage of current selling partners. As the brand grows, the sizing issue is easier to clarify, and the salesperson's roles are beginning to be defined and specialized. As the brand matures, the sales people need to be generalists for coverage of multiple products, and with the brand in decline, the sales force might be cut; indeed, the company might return to the use of selling partners.

Each company develops its policies to train and evaluate its salespeople. Sales managers are motivated by the criteria set for their performance reviews, to which their compensation is tied. Sales compensation is salary plus bonuses, but the question is a matter of proportion. The bonuses can be cash, trips, or chunks of wood (plaques).

Work performance criteria need to be clear from corporate so that the sales reps don't get frustrated that their work is for naught, and transparency is important for morale and feelings of fairness throughout the company. Numerous inputs can serve as components of performance evaluations, including sales data, perhaps by segment (e.g., client size), or product line (e.g., pushing a new line), or improvement (e.g., sales compared to last year's or last quarter's sales). In addition to these outcome-based measures of conversion, there can be effort measures, such as time spent with clients, apparent expertise and product knowledge, and training, the sales person's attitude, or there can be time clock inputs such as number of days worked, number of calls placed, keeping selling expenses down, etc.

Just as the front line in retailing is part of the brand image to the consumer, the sales force is part of the brand to the B2B customer. Here are the 3 biggest complaints by B2B buyers about salespeople: (1) "The salesperson isn't following my company's buying process." (2) "They didn't listen to my needs." (3) "They didn't bother to follow up." Avoid these problems, and the account is yours!

10-3h **Integrated Marketing Channels**

As the number of channels proliferates, increasing care must be taken to coordinate and integrate their efforts, data, customer touchpoints, etc. Companies are trying to understand customer behavior, to see what channel attributes are important and what impacts customer choices. Companies are also trying to be strategic, considering how an additional channel would impact sales and profits and therefore how to allocate resources across channels options.

As always, when the decisions seem overwhelming, simplify and remember, the key to marketing is to think about the customer. With a customer focus, the marketer can design effectual distribution channels for the target segments to optimize the benefits it seeks.

Managerial Recap

Distribution channels are important to marketers because they're the link from the manufacturer to the customer.

- Numerous thoughtful decisions must be made in designing the channel networks of partners, including choices of intensive vs. selective channel partners.
- Channel entities are independent yet interdependent organizations; thus, from time to time, conflicts may arise. These are best addressed by employing good communication and trust, revenue sharing, or greater vertical integration.

Chapter Outline in Key Terms and Concepts

1. What are distribution channels and supply chain logistics, and why do we use them?

2. How to design smart distribution systems: intensive or selective?

   a. Push and pull

3. Power and conflict in channel relationships

   a. Revenue sharing

   b. Integration

   c. Retailing

   d. Franchising

   e. E-commerce

   f. Catalog sales

   g. Sales force

   h. Integrated marketing channels

Chapter Discussion Questions

1. Go online and compare three franchises (e.g., franchise.org, americasbestfranchsies.com, or whichfranchise.com). Choose two franchises in the same industry (e.g., fast food) and the third franchise from another industry (e.g., hair cutting). Make a table to report the fee structures (up-front, continued licensing), as well as benefits touted for franchisees of each franchise system. What would tempt you to pitch in with some friends and buy a franchise when you finish your degree?

2. If you were to take your company global, which 3 countries would be your first targets, and why? What kinds of strategies and products fit with those countries' segments of customers?

Mini-Case

B2Buzz

As they head toward graduation, a couple of b-school friends, Jan and Geoff, are building a consultancy to help businesses with their social media. They are confident that there is a huge demand out there. Most companies know that social media are important, and yet most don't know where to start, nor do they have the expertise in-house. So the value proposition that B2Buzz will offer is to work with a company's marketing people for content and with their IT people to design dedicated webspace for some of the media.

B2Buzz has generated nearly a dozen first-round presentations with good- (medium-) sized companies (from many more cold calls than that, of course). The problem is that while the potential clients acknowledge the importance of social media and admit their internal confusion, B2Buzz isn't getting many second-round discussions or bids. Jan's and Geoff's interpersonal styles are not perfect but good enough that they don't think the responses are personal. So they're picking over their business plans, trying to pinpoint why the unique selling proposition isn't quite, well, selling.

Jan and Geoff have done follow-up calls with every set of first-round people they met who have not committed to contracting their service, as an additional sales opportunity and as a means of debriefing and gathering more information. When companies say, "No, thank you," follow-up debriefs are usually vague, polite, and uncomfortable, and the company rep wants to get off the phone. But one inkling that Jan and Geoff have surmised is that the companies find their proposals interesting but eventually conclude that their own IT people could and should serve the social media function.

Mini-Case Discussion Questions

1. What advice would you give Jan and Geoff to help sell their B2Buzz services more successfully?

2. Alternatively, are the companies correct in their suppositions that they will figure out this "social media thing" (like companies did for creating websites 20 years ago), and therefore, B2Buzz is destined to fail? Why or why don't you think so?

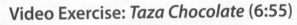

Video Exercise: *Taza Chocolate* (6:55)

Following the Mexican chocolate-making tradition, Taza Chocolate, based in Somerville, Massachusetts, manufactures a unique, stoneground chocolate with a very coarse texture and a very intense flavor. Making its chocolate from scratch, Taza produces chocolate bars, Mexican-style chocolate disks, and chocolate-covered nuts. Taza's products are carried in specialty and health food stores around the nation and on the company's website. Given the nature of the product, distribution is a critical element of Taza's marketing program. Taza markets its products through three distribution channels at different price points. As a manufacturer, Taza must produce a large volume of product in order to be cost-effective; the bulk of Taza's output is sold wholesale. The wholesale channel is an intermediate price point. A second channel occurs through distributors, and this pricing is below wholesale. A third channel is through direct retail, which has the highest price point; most of Taza's direct retailing occurs through the company's website, although it is working on opening a factory store.

Video Discussion Questions

1. What distribution channels does Taza Chocolate use, and what do they contribute to the company's overall marketing efforts?

2. Taza Chocolate prices its products differently based on the channel used for distributing them. Does this approach make good managerial sense? Explain your answer.

3. How does the concept of integrated marketing channels apply to Taza Chocolate's product distribution system?

Chapter 11

Integrated Marketing Communications: The Advertising Message

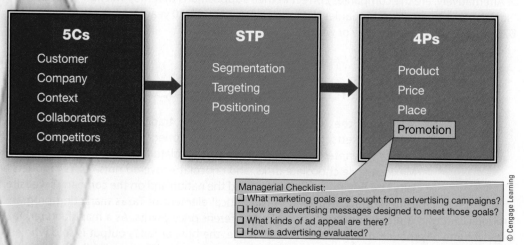

Managerial Checklist:
- ❏ What marketing goals are sought from advertising campaigns?
- ❏ How are advertising messages designed to meet those goals?
- ❏ What kinds of ad appeal are there?
- ❏ How is advertising evaluated?

© Cengage Learning

Marketing Management Framework

Many a CEO has wondered, "Has the money we've been spending on advertising been effective?" It's fair to raise the question of accountability, as long as the CEO does so thoughtfully. The problem is that some ROI questions are a little simplistic.

For example, when the question is posed, "Was the advertising effective," it must be clarified, effective at what? What was the goal of the advertising campaign? Just as the fuller marketing plan must begin with a goal, so too should advertising begin with a clear understanding of what the campaign is supposed to achieve. Typical goals include an increase in near future sales or a longer-term goal of an enhanced brand reputation. To be understood, an ad message needs to be simple, and so it best to focus on achieving a single goal. Most advertising cannot achieve multiple goals (any more than a single financial instrument might, etc.).

In addition, it must be acknowledged that advertising effectiveness can be very difficult to measure. In particular, much of marketing is a long-term game, not intended to pay off immediately. If the goal is to strengthen a positive brand image, then a measure needs to be devised to capture whether that goal was attained. A marketing research project could easily measure the pre- and postadvertising attitudes in the relevant target segment to see if they've improved. But if the CEO is flipping through this quarter's sales figures hoping to

Two beautiful people.

Beautiful clothing.

Her bare shoulders and back (and posture) say she's accessible.

His clutching says he's glad.

RALPH LAUREN R

THE WOMEN'S FRAGRANCE BY RALPH LAUREN

Image-based message to women:
"If you wear this perfume, you will be irresistible."

Cognitive/Rational Appeal

Lots of text to convey technical information.

Cobranding and bonus upgrade not necessary, but adds strength.

Windows®. Life without Walls™.
Dell recommends Windows.

DELL
YOURS IS HERE

£449
from incl VAT &
Delivery

Co-ordinate your laptop with a matching sleeve. £25

Knock 'em dead in a gorgeous gown, or slinky little number – in your choice of colours.
GO ON, TREAT YOURSELF.

The Dell Studio 15" laptop – operating on Genuine Windows Vista® Home Premium. Express your personal style with one of 7 colours and 11 exclusive designs. It comes with 5.1 channel surround-sound and subwoofer and a 512MB ATI graphics card so you get a great multimedia experience too.

Click: dell.co.uk/studio | **Call:** 0844 444 3348

Upgrade Offer
Windows 7

DELL WINDOWS® 7 UPGRADE OPTION PROGRAMME
Buy selected Dell Windows® Vista PCs today and qualify for an upgrade to Windows® 7 (tax, shipping and handling charges may apply). Limited time offer. Go to www.dell.co.uk/windows7 for details.

McAfee™ - PROTECT WHAT YOU VALUE.

Rational-based message:
"You know we're known for good laptops.
Now we help you look good too."

see an increase when the goal was to strengthen the brand image, then there is a mismatch between the goal and its assessment, and it would be unfair to criticize that advertising wasn't working. So, what is advertising, why do we need it, and how do we do it well?

11.1 WHAT IS ADVERTISING?

Advertising is the primary means by which a company communicates to its customers about its products and brands and position in the marketplace. Product, price, and place also signal a brand's positioning, and certainly all these signals need to tell a coherent story. If ads claim that a brand is an exclusive, premium brand, the product needs to be of high quality, priced relatively high, and distributed relatively exclusively. But while the rest of the marketing mix is important, advertising is the most direct communication link.

For many people, the word "*advertising*" connotes television commercials, and certainly this is a fun form of advertising. TV commercials and print ads (in magazines, billboards, online banners) do represent much of the typical advertising budget. But companies advertise their brands in everything they do, including event sponsorship, the packaging that encloses their products, the price points for those products, etc. Thus, many advertising gurus prefer the more general term "marketing communications," which is broader and can include public relations, direct marketing, and the like. Indeed, the current pc term is "integrated marketing communications" (IMC) to remind the marketer to be sure the message has a holistic nature and is consistent and complementary across all media choices and executions. We'll see IMC in action in the next chapter. In this chapter, we focus on the content of the message being expressed in the ad, no matter where that ad will be placed.

11.2 WHY IS ADVERTISING IMPORTANT?

First, advertising facilitates customers' awareness. The company has segmented the market and selected a set of target customers. The company now wishes to provide information to those target customers because the company thinks they will be intrigued by its brands.

Second, advertising attempts to persuade potential customers that the featured brand is superior to competitors' market offerings. A company expresses its brand positioning by emphasizing a feature or benefit that makes it seem better than any other options.

Advertising has both short-term and long-term effects. By short term, we mean both that the effect occurs immediately or very shortly after the ad exposure, as well as the effect being of short duration or short-lived. Several short-term effects can be shown. For example, customers' memory of ads and brands and attributes are easily measured. Attitudes are also easily surveyed and may be compared to prior attitudes (measured previously) to assess any change in valence.

Not unreasonably, advertising is expected to generate sales and profitability, but demonstrating this effect on the bottom line is rather complicated. Occasionally short-term sales increases can be observed during an advertising campaign. But marketers have learned that if your goal is only to increase sales, nothing's quicker than a price promotion.

The reason that the financial impact is more difficult to assess is that advertising is complicated and thought to operate in a longer-term manner. And again, by long term, we mean both that the effects of the ad might not appear immediately and also that the effects are sustained long after the ad exposure. Advertising effects might not appear immediately because they are cumulative and therefore difficult to attribute to a single ad campaign that was run five years ago. Ad results are sustained because, when used in this manner,

Ethics

The American Marketing Association's Statement of Ethics speaks to several issues regarding advertising. Here are two professional standards:

1. *Honesty:* A company should honor its explicit and implicit commitments and promises to its customers.
2. *Fairness:* A company should represent its products in a clear manner, and avoid false, misleading, and deceptive promotions.

Here's a thought question: Is it misleading to claim that a piece of clothing is "Made in the U.S.A."? What does it mean to say that? Was the garment assembled here, but comprised of imported cloth? Were the pieces cut here but sent abroad for sewing? Was the cotton grown or knitted here? It's a complicated, interconnected world...

the role of advertising is to strengthen brand awareness, positive attitudes, perceptions of brand equity, and so on. In turn, these enhanced attitudes will manifest in behaviors: more purchases, more expensive purchases, more frequent purchases, and word of mouth by the target customer. So even though a CMO typically does not see an immediate sales bump from an ad campaign, everyone "knows" that advertising works and that the brand needs it, and so we keep investing in advertising.

We next consider the content of the advertising message. Advertising has rich communication potential; ads can convey rational information as well as emotional imagery. We'll see many types of ad formats. To choose among them, we have to know what our marketing and advertising strategic goals are, and again, to assess the ad's effectiveness, we must measure against those goals. For example, if the goal is to increase awareness, we might run an ad chock-full of information, and then subsequently measure customers' memory for the ad, brand, brand attributes, etc. Let's proceed to creating advertising messages.

11.3 WHAT MARKETING GOALS ARE SOUGHT FROM ADVERTISING CAMPAIGNS?

Advertising could be used to address many goals. One popular model of goals is called AIDA (*a*ttention, *i*nterest, *d*esire, *a*ction). The flow goes like this: We first get the ad recipient's attention, then pique their interest, see if you can get them to be attracted to the brand, and hopefully induce a purchase or intention to purchase.

Other advertisers have other models: Some describe the flow of the ad recipient from a level of awareness to greater knowledge, to more liking and preference, to a sense of brand conviction and then purchasing. Another variant goes from awareness to interest to brand evaluation, to trial and adoption. Another model describes the process as one going from an ad exposure to receiving the message to a cognitive response to a change in attitude to intention to buy, to the behavior of buying. It is currently fashionable to go still further and add levels such as brand affinity, attachment, connection, ambassador, zealot, etc.

Figure 11.1

The Goal of an Ad Campaign: To Affect Consumer Decision Making

Whichever the model, the goals fall into one of three camps (Figure 11.1):

1. *Cognition:* Increase awareness and knowledge about our brand,
2. *Affect:* Enhance attitudes and positive associations about our brand, and, ultimately,
3. *Behavior:* Encourage more buying of our brand.

In advertising, we wish to affect consumers' cognitions, emotions, or behaviors. Marketers talk explicitly about winning "hearts and minds." The pocketbooks usually follow.

These goals are correlated with the product life cycle:

- Early in a brand's life, the job of an ad campaign is to get the word out, inform the consumer of this new or improved market offering: "Here is the brand, here are its features, here are its points of differentiation from the competition," etc.

- When the brand is growing, awareness is already strong, and ad campaigns are developed to enhance the positivity of the target segment's attitudes about the brand.

- At brand maturity, awareness has pretty well permeated the market, and customers have pretty set attitudes (some people don't care for the brand, but hopefully many people in the target segment do), and so at this point, ads are intended to be reminders, "Hey, we're still here," "We're offering a twofer," etc. Advertising hasn't dropped off yet, but sales are strong so less ad budget (as measured by percentage of sales) is required to maintain a steady presence (sales, market share, etc.).

- Finally, when a product is in decline, ad spending is usually reduced greatly, and eventually the brand is pulled from the market.

And, of course, it's best if the elements of marketing are integrated, thus, if a brand manager can keep the product fresh, the advertising would always have something new to say. For example, a laundry detergent might morph from powder to liquid to detergent with built-in fabric softeners. Then the ads follow the product changes and continue to inform consumers.

As you might imagine, these goals aren't equally easy to achieve. Increase awareness? Easy. Enhance attitudes? Check. Encourage more buying? That goal is more challenging. Consider a thought experiment. Say you're online, and a banner ad pops up, and it's about a new movie that's about to come out: *Toy Story 14*! You'd think, "Oh, I hadn't heard about that yet." With that one simple message, the communication achieved the goal of informing you, offering you awareness about a new product. You now know something you hadn't known just a moment before. Awareness: Check.

Let's say the banner ad continues with a picture and a few lines like, "Just as fun, same Woody, same Buzz, saving the world again!" You might think, "That sounds pretty good." So the ad succeeded in making you think positively about the movie. Enhanced attitudes: Check.

Finally, say the banner ad closes with the tagline, "Click here to buy a ticket for this Friday, now!" Will you? Perhaps, but probably not. Even if it sounds like a fun movie, maybe you're busy Friday, or maybe you prefer watching movies on your computer rather than at the theater, whatever. Your response doesn't mean the advertiser didn't succeed. You might add the movie to your mental must-see (eventually) list. That is advertising success, but it is difficult to measure.

In general, the goal of getting the consumer to purchase is not easily achieved or measured, but that doesn't necessarily render an ad ineffective. Even though a product may be simple (familiar, inexpensive, etc.), nevertheless most purchases are complicated. A simple ad message cannot easily propel a customer to go buy. In addition, many product categories show buying inertia, and many of our purchases are low involvement, meaning, we just don't care about the product or the brand choice, and we buy whatever we typically buy and we don't even "see" ads for other brands, much less spend any cognitive effort in processing the messages. As this example illustrates, a zillion (well, at least several) factors go into even the simplest purchase decision.

11.4 DESIGNING ADVERTISING MESSAGES TO MEET MARKETING AND CORPORATE GOALS

Advertising is a means of communication. A company says to its potential customers, "Buy our stuff!" "We have a new service!" "Look at our low, low prices!" and "We're better than the competition!" As a result, marketers must understand the basic model of dyadic communication. In the classic model, there is a source (e.g., the firm), a message (e.g., the ad) and a receiver (e.g., customer). The source intends to send out certain information, which is encoded (i.e., expressed in a certain way), and then transmit. The receiver then decodes the message. Hopefully, the receiver interprets the content of the message in a manner similar to what the sender had intended. But there can be errors along the way. Think of communicating with a friend; it can happen that you intend to say something, but it comes out wrong, or you say it right, but your friend takes it the wrong way. All of that can happen with advertising as well. That's why copy testing (marketing research examining the content of the ad) is important, before launching the full ad campaign, to learn whether the intended target segment understands the message as the company intended.

M&Ms

If marketing is said to be the 4Ps, here are the 6Ms of advertising:

1. Who is the *market* being addressed?
2. What is your *mission*, the objectives of the advertising campaign?
3. What is your *message* to be communicated?

In Chapter 12, we'll turn to the next three Ms:

4. How much *money* will be spent?
5. What *media* choices will be implemented?
6. How will the effectiveness of the campaign be *measured*?

There are many kinds of ads, or ways to communicate, and most may be mapped pretty cleanly onto one of the first two goals of advertising, that is, with a message that is primarily cognitive (e.g., increasing awareness and knowledge) or emotional (e.g., enhancing attitudes and preference). Cognitive or rational appeals can be further distinguished into arguments (one-sided vs. two-sided, comparative vs. noncomparative ads), product demonstrations, and dramas. Emotional ads rely on humor, fear appeals, so-called subliminal ads, image appeals, and endorsements. We'll look at each.

11-4a Cognitive Ads

A cognitive or rational appeal engages the consumer's brain. The ad gives the consumer a reason to buy the product that is practical or functional. It's a utilitarian (as opposed to hedonic) appeal. The ads tend to be informative, featuring the product's attributes and their benefits.

A *one-sided argument* means that the company focuses on expressing the benefits of its product to the consumer. This approach is a common one among advertisers, so many examples exist, e.g., Brookstone featured a "motorized grill brush with steam cleaning power!" as an ideal Father's day gift with the pitch "The ultimate power tool for your grill." One-sided ads are straightforward; they offer an explanation of the anticipated benefits.

In a *two-sided argument*, the company describes the pros and cons of its brand. Two-sided arguments are used when your target customers already know that your brand has some weakness. Thus, you might as well acknowledge it (earn some points for honesty) and then argue why your brand is nevertheless excellent. For example, direct-to-consumer ads by pharmaceuticals companies make claims for drugs that will help alleviate symptoms, but possible side effects must be acknowledged. (In contrast, if the product weaknesses are not known to customers, companies don't usually point them out via this kind of ad.) There are two benefits to two-sided arguments: (1) They stand out; most ads are one-sided with everyone claiming their brand is great, so two-sided arguments get attention because they are different. (2) Two-sided ads are seen as more objective or neutral because you're getting the pros and cons, and hence, they seem more credible.

In a *noncomparative ad*, a brand is mentioned, and its features and attributes and image portrayal, etc. are conveyed in the message. The ad features a single brand (Figure 11.2). The brand's benefits, imagery, and positioning are highlighted, and no competitors are featured or implied.

In a *comparative ad*, the featured brand name is mentioned, as is the brand name of a competitor (Figure 11.3). On the face of it, this sounds irrational: Why would you pay to

Figure 11.2

A Noncomparative Ad: One Brand Featured; Very Popular

Lucas Jackson/Reuters

Figure 11.3

Comparative Ads

RODNEY TURNER/MCT/Landov

advertise for the competition? The rules of thumb are these: If you're the big player (i.e., the market leader), you treat your competition as irritating little gnats that you wouldn't bother to acknowledge in an ad. However, if you're a new brand or the brand with a small share, you might mention the big brand in your ad for the purposes of gaining an association to all the good qualities that consumers seek when they purchase the market leader brand.

So, for example, it is asymmetric in that Lexus would never mention Hyundai, but Hyundai ads for their luxury car Equus might liken the car to a Lexus. However, Hyundai needs to be careful about mentioning Lexus because it is reliably shown that if you're the small player and you use a comparative ad, your ad budget helps you, but it also helps the brand against which you're making comparisons. (To the victor go the spoils.)

Where would the advertising industry be without *product demonstrations*? Whether an ad shows a laundry detergent that can clean kids' mud-caked clothes, or Dan Aykroyd pulverizing a fish in a Bass-o-Matic on *SNL*, we love to see stuff in action. Demonstrations are vivid, they make our expectations clear, we see precisely what we'd get for our money. All ads try to persuade us that the product is great, but demo ads show the product and consumers can decide for themselves as to the validity of the claim (Figure 11.4).

Figure 11.4

Product Demonstration Ad

Image Courtesy of The Advertising Archives

A TV commercial is often a narrative *drama* or a slice-of-life vignette. Often a problem is depicted, and the brand is featured as the perfect solution. For example, a guy finds dandruff flakes on his shoulders, buys the right shampoo, and then all the women in his world think he's hot. A nice by-product of story-based ads is that they easy to communicate from the advertiser to the viewer, and also from the viewer to friends via word of mouth. Dramas are more memorable than sheer listings of product features and claims. The stories give the brand a context and show the viewer how the brand could be helpful in their lives.

11-4b Emotional Ads

Another type of ad that elicits emotions uses *humor*. Ad execs count on humorous ads to break through the noisy media clutter (Figure 11.5). Humorous ads are popular because they're fun, and they win a lot of awards in the advertising industry because they're seen as clever.

Figure 11.5

Humorous Ad

LUCASFILM/PhotoShot, Inc.

Unfortunately, humorous ads are not all that effective. Part of the problem is that people remember the joke, but they don't necessarily remember the brand being advertised. In addition, not everyone has the same sense of humor, and it is easy to insult some people with an ad that other people think is funny.

The final major problem of humorous ads is inherent to humor itself: Humor is based on the element of surprise, but once you know the joke (whether it's verbal, a visual gag, or whatever), the second time you see the ad, you already know the punch line, and pretty soon you begin to ignore the ad and the message. Thus, humorous ads inevitably have quick wear-out (the ad campaign can't last long because the audience will become bored quickly). If you couple an ad's short life with the fact that ad creation and media placement is expensive, then it quickly adds up that funny ads just aren't cost-efficient.

Yet the life of a funny ad can be extended, if the ad execution varies, e.g., the Geico insurance company's talking gecko appearing in different scenarios. People also enjoy sharing humor, so the ad may generate buzz, be posted online, etc., perpetuating free word-of-mouth communication.

Fear and embarrassment are negative emotions that have been used to sell both products and social marketing ideas: "Buy this deodorant or mouthwash so you won't smell," "Stop smoking so your lungs won't turn black." The problem with negative emotions, and fear in particular, is that its effect is nonmonotonic. That is, if the ad overdoes it, and it's seen as so fear inducing as to be creepy or horrifying, we cope with that kind of message by blocking it out, and therefore the ad would have no effect on propelling the consumer to the desired behavior. For a fear appeal to be effective, the ad must provide a solution to reduce the consumer's fear, resolving both the problem and emotion by the end of the ad (Figure 11.6).

Figure 11.6

Fear-Appeal Ad

Subliminal ads have long been a curiosity. Long ago, a print ad for an alcoholic beverage, which featured the bottle and some of its contents poured over ice in a glass, was claimed to contain the letters "*s*," "*e*," and "*x*" embedded in the ice cubes. The thought was that on some subconscious, precognitive level, people would be turned on and therefore favor this brand and go buy it. About the same time, movie theater owners experimented with flashing ads at millisecond speeds on the screen during the movie with messages like "Go buy popcorn!" so fast that no viewer could point to the moment of having explicitly seen the message, yet the message was thought to have an effect on the subconscious, propelling the audience member to mindlessly go to the lobby and buy a bucket of popcorn. (Most marketers believe this was an urban legend.) These mind games were thought to be quite disturbing and unethical, and they are banned. The odd thing is that they were never shown to be effective. Indeed, more than one cynic in the advertising industry has remarked, "We don't use subliminal ads not because we're not supposed to. We don't use them because they don't seem to work."

Yet it's a fine line. Many retailers play nondescript background music to set an ambience. It's known that music with a faster tempo seems to induce more energy, excitement, and people buy more. The music is audible so it is not subliminal, but the effect is sort of sneaky. Some product placement in movies is rather overt, e.g., an actor drives a particular brand of car or uses a Dell or an Apple. But much of product placement can be rather subtle. The question is whether the brand left an impression that can affect a viewer's subsequent purchasing. The brand is visible, not subliminal, so strictly speaking, not forbidden.

11-4c Image Ads

When advertisers talk about emotional appeals, they often mean that the ad conveys an image. The ad message is more abstract than a list of features and attributes (Figure 11.7). Usually these are feel-good portrayals: "Use this brand and you'll be more attractive," or "Buy this and you'll be able to emulate this cool person's lifestyle."

Figure 11.7

Image-Based
Ad

Many products in many purchase categories are seen as nearly commodity-like in the eyes of customers, and the category is so competitive that firms struggle to distinguish their brands from each other. Image is closely tied to branding; e.g., all soft drinks are sweet and bubbly, but this is the one for young people; every restaurant has tasty food, but this one is family-friendly; every theater shows a variety of films, but this is the arts theater, etc.

Image is about perceptions, and advertising imagery is extremely malleable among the marketing mix variables for creating perceptions regarding a product's positioning. Elements of the product itself, its price, and distribution outlets all certainly contribute to perceptions of a brand's image. But advertising is the most amenable vehicle for persuading customers and potential customers as to a brand's relative strengths.

11-4d Endorsements

Endorsements are ads that feature a spokesperson on behalf of the brand (Figure 11.8). These ads can feature celebrities or experts or even seemingly regular people offering testimonials as satisfied past customers.

Figure 11.8

Celebrity
Endorsement

When a celebrity is used to endorse a product, the hope is that the positive associations attached to the celebrity would transfer to the brand (this is literally known as "affect transfer" or "association transfer"). The star's endorsement basically says, "This brand is cool. Be like me!" The celebrity is typically attractive and successful, and the idea is that a regular consumer can achieve part of the celebrity's appeal and lifestyle by purchasing the item in the ad.

There are risks associated with, well, pretty much anything in life but particularly here, with using a celebrity endorser. We've all seen when a celebrity goes a little wonky, and then the brand they've been endorsing could be affected by those new, bad associations. As an alternative, some brands have spokes-characters, like the Jolly Green Giant who looks over his vegetable garden, or Buzz, the Honey Nut Cheerios spokes-bee, or the Keebler Elves baking cookies in their hollow tree, or PepsiCo's Cheetos character, Chester Cheetah, who surfs and skateboards while wearing cool sunglasses, and so on. These characters bring the brands to life, and you will never catch them doing bad things (at least not in public).

Experts who are not celebrities frequently serve as spokespeople for high-tech products, such as computer equipment or pharmaceuticals, e.g., doctors recommending drugs. Here, we don't expect mere transfer of positive affect but rather a signal that the expert is offering credible information, so this otherwise possibly risky purchase for the consumer is made to seem less risky by the endorsement of someone who is more knowledgeable than us.

Testimonials are sometimes provided by regular people. They're not celebrities and they're not experts; they're just satisfied customers, with the claim that if the product worked well for them, it will for you too. These representatives tend to convey credibility too, due to their similarity to us, the target audience of regular people. In addition, we know celebrities are lending their names to products for cash—in fact, doing so can hurt their persona-brand (that they're a money-grubber), which explains why many celebrities are more likely to do endorsements abroad but not in their home markets. In contrast, even if the "regular people" providing testimonials are paid, we can guess they're not paid as much as celebrities; plus, there is just something about their being like us that makes their voice sound more authentic and trustworthy.

There are several conceptual ideas about how endorsements (and a lot of other advertising tactics) work. One theory is ELM (elaboration likelihood model), which basically posits there's two ways into your brain: a central path or a peripheral path. An ad's central message is thought to be the content of the persuasion itself, and it is processed by the target segment because these customers are highly involved in the brand and product category, so they are motivated to process all the details of the information the ad was providing. In contrast, other information is classified as peripheral cues, including the celebrity endorser, their attractiveness, their credibility to be speaking on behalf of the featured brand, the style of the ad, etc.—pretty much anything that is not the central ad argument. Both sorts of information may be processed. If the central message is complicated, people who don't care that much about the brand may just look to the peripheral cues when judging the ad or the brand.

Another theory is source credibility, which means the consumer interprets the message as the most important piece of information but also processes the credibility of the source as a cue to the likely validity of that message. So doctors touting pills sound credible; they're a convincing source of information (but note how often we've been fooled even with the disclaimer "I'm not a doctor, but I play one on TV," and we believe them anyway). But a super model is unlikely to be credible in praising the technology in a new computer.

One more theory describes the so-called sleeper effect, whereby a piece of information is conveyed by some source, maybe a celebrity, maybe an expert, maybe not. Maybe you read something in *The Wall Street Journal* or in the tabloids, or maybe you remember it from a conversation with a friend. Over time, we forget the source of the information, so whether the original source had been credible or not, it doesn't really matter. We encoded the information, but disassociated the source. As a result, even if the cute actor or actress couldn't possibly know anything about the product they're touting, the consumer is affected by positive associations with the attractive, famous person.

There are many kinds of ads, and we've been discussing the major classes. The one- or two-sided ads, comparative or noncomparative ads, product demonstrations and dramas tend to be rational in content and are processed cognitively. In contrast, emotional responses are triggered by humorous ads, fear-appeals, image ads, endorsements and even so-called subliminal ads (because they don't quite reach cognitive processing). Different combinations are possible; e.g., a humorous product demonstration. Different content (e.g., comparative or image) may also be mixed with different executional styles (e.g., drama or humor).

In most industries, different players try to attract their customers with different appeals, consistent with their distinct position. However, in some industries, all the players use the same kind of appeal, e.g., product demonstrations show how fast or roomy a car is, and experts are used as spokespeople in ads for investments.

The choice among these options is facilitated when we return to the question, "What is our advertising, marketing, corporate goal?"

- For example, companies trying to increase awareness and create positive attitudes and buzz about a brand extension need to express the new features and benefits clearly in an ad. That goal might be less achievable in a humorous ad, than in a straightforward, one-sided, noncomparative ad.

Slogans

Has your message gotten through to your customers? In a recent study, "Are You in Good Hands?" reported in the *Journal of Advertising Research*, marketers Kohli, Thomas, and Suri studied the characteristics of brand slogans that heighten their memorability.

In a large-scale interview study, 220 consumers were asked to name any advertising slogans that came to mind. When the consumer completed this elucidation, the interviewer went through the list asking the consumer to identify the brand for each slogan.

On average, respondents generated 9.72 slogans, forming a master list of 649 slogans. The top ten most frequently recalled and properly attributed brand slogans were

1. "Just do it!" for Nike.
2. "I'm lovin' it" for McDonald's.
3. "Have it your way" for Burger King.
4. "Melts in your mouth, not in your hand," for M&Ms.
5. "Got milk?" for the National Milk Processor Board.
6. "Eat fresh" for Subway.
7. "M'm! M'm! Good!" for Campbell's Soup.
8. "You're in good hands" for Allstate.
9. "Think outside the bun" for Taco Bell.
10. "The ultimate driving machine" for BMW.

Next, the researchers sought to understand what makes slogans more or less memorable. They found that the slogans that were more memorable as a function of age (older slogans are better), advertising spending (more is better), and length of slogan (shorter is better).

Several creative design elements did not matter. The complexity of the message didn't matter, though the slogans that had tested better were shorter, and length in turn nearly necessitates or implies that a message is simpler.

Whether the slogan was associated with music, in a jingle, didn't matter. And whether the slogan rhymed didn't matter. Not surprisingly, these two features often coincide, so if one didn't matter, it wouldn't be unusual to find that the other didn't. Yet for people who have had the experience of not being able to get a jingle out of their heads, it is perhaps surprising that jingle and rhyming didn't matter.

Given their findings, the marketers suggested that if a brand has a decent slogan, maintain it. Do not change slogans simply for the sake of changing them (e.g., a brand's new manager's whim). If a slogan can be shortened or a brand has undergone some change, then a slogan may be required nonetheless. Once a decent (short and sweet) slogan has been created, use it, keep it, use it again.

- Companies pulsing out reminder ads to reinforce its target customers' attitudes might wish to get their attention via an emotional appeal.

- When a competitor initiates a price war, rather than meeting the price cuts, a company would be better off to launch comparative ads to show the benefits of its (higher-priced) brands.

Finally, ads are likely to change throughout the product life cycle, with comparative ads used to launch a new product, and mature brands advertised via image-based communications.

11.5 HOW IS ADVERTISING EVALUATED?

Whether the strategic goal of an ad campaign is cognitive (awareness, knowledge), affective (image, preference), or behavioral (trial, repurchase), there are methods of measuring the results. For cognitive tests, the primary consideration is memory. Advertising researchers call random samples of households and ask first a *recall* memory test ("Which brands do you remember seeing advertised last night on TV?") and note which ads are mentioned. In the advertising industry, this test is called "day after recall" (DAR), and it is a stringent test. Did the ad so make an impression that the consumer remembers it, unprompted, a day later? DAR scores are a particularly big deal the day after the Super Bowl or any other huge event, during which air time was charged at high rates, as an assurance or test that the ads did as well as anticipated.

When the respondent can think of no more ads, the advertising researcher turns to memory tests of *recognition* ("Do you remember seeing an ad for Ford last night?"). Recall and recognition tests of memory can also be applied to assess the impact of online banner ads or magazine or billboard advertising, etc., e.g., "Which brands have you seen advertised online during the past week?" or "What ads have you seen on the metro recently?"

Traditionally, marketers and advertisers have believed that, while memory is not the same as persuasion, it's a necessary starting point. The assumption is that an ad can't affect your attitude if you can't even remember having seen it. That seems sensible, but recently this assumption has been under question. The recent thinking does not negate the very likely effective path of memory to persuasion to buying, but now it is suggested that perhaps cognition and persuasion could also function implicitly. That is, even if consumers can't quite remember having seen an ad, it doesn't mean they didn't see it, and it doesn't mean that the ad won't impact their attitudes and possible subsequent buying patterns.

Conceptually, this implicit processing is thought to work along the lines of what's called "mere exposure"—the idea is that sheer familiarity due to repeated exposure to a brand name or logo or ad will in time enhance the viewer's favorability toward the ad and brand. Billboards are thought to operate in this manner; no one really wants you reading these signs while you're driving. Yet every day, to and from work or school, you see a picture, a brand name, maybe a brief message, and with time, the sign is part of your life, and it gains some positivity. The same principle operates for the ads in the frames of websites; we don't even know they're having an effect.

While the cognitive goals (awareness, knowledge) are primarily tested via memory measures, whether affective goals (image, preference) have been achieved is tested with numerous measures of attitudes and behavioral intentions. Tests of the persuasive powers of the ad are usually tested prior to launching the ad campaign to tweak the content or ad execution details. Creative types (in ad agencies) will say that you cannot tell a priori which ads will do well. That's nonsense; they just don't like having their work evaluated (in part because the feedback will involve at least a little tweaking to what the creative had considered art and also because creative types are more interested in the creative, not strategic, aspects of advertising). Ad copy testing is done in two stages: First, the overall concept is tested, and, second, the preliminary flow of the ad is tested.

Ad *concept testing* is usually conducted in a focus group setting. Focus group facilities recruit 8 to 10 consumers who may be screened on criteria such as relevance to the target segment or usage in the product category but who are otherwise random consumers. The ideas underlying the ad are explained, and illustrative props show the basic idea of the ad.

Rarely are completed ads shown and tested at this stage (they're too expensive, ca. $500k). Instead, the ad is somewhere in preliminary development ($10–20k). It can be mocked up as a drawing like a cartoon strip—a storyboard, with each scene and possible dialog unfolding. Or the ad may be animated graphics shown on a computer. (Just FYI: Finished commercials cost $100,000s, but animatics cost only about a tenth of that, and it's even less for storyboards. While these draft forms can seem rough, research indicates that the correlation between customer reactions to animatics and a finished commercial are very high; marketingpower.com.) Research has shown that an audience's reactions to the ads even in their rougher, proposal stage are correlated with real, completed ads. The consumers respond to the ad, to the brand and to whatever else the company asks the focus group moderator to cover in 1.5 hours. After 3 or 4 focus groups concur that the ad agency is heading in a good direction, the ads are further developed, and copy testing begins.

Copy testing is usually conducted via surveys. Larger random samples of consumers are recruited by advertising researchers to attend a "screening for possible new television programming"; that's the typical cover story, and it's a load of hooey. The consumers travel to a relatively central location, such as a hotel near the city's airport. The supposed pilot TV series is shown, with several ads aired in natural TV show breaks. After 30 minutes, the attendees fill out dozens of pages of questionnaires asking about the TV show, the ads, their buying habits, and the like. Increasingly, copy testing is done online, with invites sent over e-mail, requesting participants to go to a website, to view the materials and answer the questions.

The survey items include measures of attitudes on stimulation ("The ad made me curious, enthusiastic"), information ("It gave me useful, credible info"), negative emotion ("The ad irritated me"), transformation ("The ad gave me enjoyment, gave me a pleasant, satisfied feeling"), identification ("I recognized myself in it, I felt involved with it"). An ad's scores on these measures is compared to the ad agency's extensive data base to determine how well the current set of ads might do, since the agency has other data indicating how well previous ads had done. There are basic scores that any ad must surpass: Does the ad evoke positive feelings? Is the ad remembered for the correct brand? And so on.

11-5a A_{ad} and A_{brand}

There are two basic attitudes that marketers are measuring in evaluating ads: attitude-to-the-ad (A_{ad}) and attitude-to-the-brand (A_{brand}). A company and ad agency can pride itself on creating cool ads, ads which customers like, ads whose scores on A_{ad} are strong and positive, but marketers care (and if the ad agency wants a long-term relationship with the marketing company, it should care too) that the ad is effective in making strong positive brand attitudes, the A_{brand}. And, of course, most marketers believe that the brand attitudes trigger sales, i.e., ultimately $A_{ad} \rightarrow A_{brand} \rightarrow$ likelihood to purchase.

Another sort of measure of an ad's impact on a viewer is the dial procedures intended to capture moment-by-moment processing. In an ad copy test, a viewer is given a dial (or a mouse) to control by turning it from the left ("I hate this") to the right ("I think this is great") continually while viewing the ad. This idea is useful in editing ineffectual sections of an ad and identifying which positive sections might be played up. Critics say that viewers' reactions to an ad have a natural lag, and measures taken after the ad or by accumulating and integrating all the moments across the ad duration, predict ad and brand liking better than any particular moment. The technique is in its infancy, and, given its potential, perhaps the kinks will be worked out.

Big TVs

Large-screen televisions—consumers love them. Marketers and advertisers should too!

Marketers conducted a national online survey and obtained the opinions of 1,328 consumers. In the sample, 475 of the respondents owned large-screen TVs (40 inches or larger), 378 owned traditional TVs (29 inches or smaller), and 475 owned TVs of an intermediate size.

- *Demographics:* Large TVs were more frequently found in houses of married couples and those with young children. Large TVs were also more often owned by households reporting higher incomes, and there was a modest effect that large TVs were more often owned by those with higher educational levels. There was no relationship between size of TV and age or race.
- *TV Viewing:* participants were asked to report on several aspects of the viewing behaviors. First, they were asked about the extent to which they paid attention to TV programs and ads, rating each from 1 ("pay no attention") to 5 ("pay full attention"). The consumers with big TVs reported paying significantly more attention to TV programs (4.01 of 5) than consumers with standard, smaller TV screens (3.74 of 5). All consumers reported paying more attention to the TV programming than to the TV ads, but even for advertising, those with big TVs reported paying significantly more attention to ads (2.36 of 5) than consumers with smaller screens (2.12 of 5).

  Next, consumers were asked to rate the extent to which they "get absorbed in the programming." Big TV viewers were significantly more involved in their viewing (3.88 of 5) than were viewers watching smaller TVs (3.31 of 5). Perhaps much like a viewer is enveloped by a large screen (and dark audience) at a movie theater, the large TV screens, even while viewed at home, in well lit rooms, with all of the usual domestic distractions, also captivate viewers more completely than smaller TVs. Viewing a smaller, traditional TV screen, probably at approximately the same viewing distance, is easier to contextualize because the viewer can so easily look past the smaller box to take into account the large environment.

  While this news about TV viewers being more involved with television programming is interesting, it is perhaps even more surprising, and good news for advertisers and marketers, that TV viewers are more engaged by the ads as well. In addition, the consumers were asked about their overall attitudes about advertising, and their levels of skepticism about advertising. The effects were modest, but indeed significantly in favor (for the advertiser) of the big screen TVs. Specifically, attitudes toward advertising were significantly more positive for consumers watching big-screen TVs (3.4 of 5) than for consumers with smaller TVs (2.4 of 5), and consumers with big TVs were less skeptical about advertising (3.5 of 5) than those with smaller TVs (3.7 of 5).

The researchers refer to these effects as a larger-than-life experience. Such an immersion seems to imply a stronger conviction on the part of the advertiser.

For more information, see the article by McNiven, Krugman, and Tinkham, "The Big Picture for Large-Screen Television Viewing," in the *Journal of Advertising Research.*

If advertising is intended to address the heads and hearts and wallets, we can check diagnostics that measures these objectives. In Figure 11.9, the data for the bank indicate that there is a problem with awareness, at only 25%. But of the aware customers, a full 80% like the brand. Generating awareness is an easy problem to fix via advertising: Spend more money, and choose media that reach more broadly.

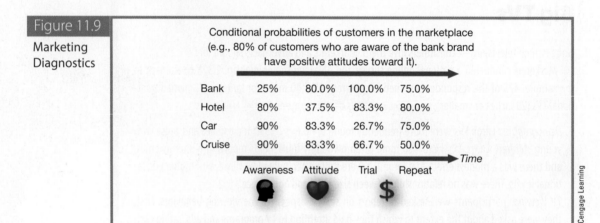

Figure 11.9

Marketing Diagnostics

Conditional probabilities of customers in the marketplace (e.g., 80% of customers who are aware of the bank brand have positive attitudes toward it).

	Awareness	Attitude	Trial	Repeat
Bank	25%	80.0%	100.0%	75.0%
Hotel	80%	37.5%	83.3%	80.0%
Car	90%	83.3%	26.7%	75.0%
Cruise	90%	83.3%	66.7%	50.0%

Time

© Cengage Learning

The hotel has a different story. Most people are aware (80%), but only 37.5% of them hold positive attitudes toward the hotel brand. If the hotel itself is not great, then the attitude measure will be sticky. Otherwise, advertising can help the hotel by generating more favorable attitudes via more positive and more persuasive advertising.

The car scenario is different still. Awareness is strong. Attitudes are favorable. But the proportion of the same who have taken the car for a test drive is only $0.90 \times 0.83 \times 0.27 = 20\%$. This problem might not be one that advertising can resolve. The product might be priced out of reach (think Ferrari), or perhaps it's a channels issue (e.g., few dealerships).

The cruise scenario is one in which awareness is high, attitudes are positive, there is good trial, but people aren't coming back. This profile might suggest a problem with the product itself. If that's the case, we can advertise till we're blue in the face, but we have to deliver on our promises. On the other hand, for cruises, customer may simply wish to try something different for their next holiday. In such a scenario, the company would need to extend its product line.

Initiates media planning.

Sends creative brief (outline of what client wants).

Account Services (client interface)

Relies on research group for customer feedback.

Creative Department (develops concepts to present to client)

Feedback used to tweak concepts and execution.

Advertising Research (tests copy on customers)

Sends approved idea.

Production (gets it made: hires photographer, directors, etc.)

Media Services (buys TV time, magazine space)

Coordinates for IMC.

Social Media

May outsource to boutique agencies.

© Cengage Learning

Managerial Recap

The key concepts of advertising communications messages are these:

- Goals must be set before ads can be evaluated.

- There are several classes of advertising communications messages:
  - Rational or cognitive ads include one- and two-side arguments, comparative and noncomparative ads, product demonstrations and dramas.
  - Emotional ads include humorous and fear-inducing appeals, image, and endorsements.

- Advertising is tested via concept testing and copy testing. The content of what is measured depends on the corporate strategic goals of the ad campaign, and those assessments can include
  - Memory tests (recall and recognition).
  - Attitudinal tests (enhancement of the favorability of the product and brand).
  - Behavioral measures (likely to purchase the brand or generate positive word of mouth).

Chapter Outline in Key Terms and Concepts

1. What is advertising?
2. Why is advertising important?
3. What marketing goals are sought from advertising campaigns?
4. Designing advertising messages to meet marketing and corporate goals
    a. Cognitive ads
    b. Emotional ads
    c. Image ads
    d. Endorsements
5. How is advertising evaluated?
    a. A_{ad} and A_{brand}

Chapter Discussion Questions

1. Rip up your favorite magazine, and classify any 5 ads according to whether you think they're aiming to achieve a cognitive, emotional, or behavioral goal. Which ad do you like the most? Did any stimulate you to learn more about the brand?

2. Imagine you were designing an ad for a (choose one): car, laptop, health clinic. What would your ad look like if you were targeting (a) old people, (b) kids, (c) super-rich people. (d) What celebrity would you have endorse your brand? Why?

Mini-Case

Celeb Relief

John Russell, who goes by Jack, is a busy exec by day, but he likes to volunteer at a local, no-kill animal shelter at least one weekend a month. He helps by walking dogs and feeding them, and, given his business acumen, the shelter calls on him to do more administrative tasks as well, anything from animal intake to giving the shelter advice about their website. At the shelter's board meeting 6 months ago, Jack was asked to propose a low- (very low-) budget advertising campaign. He's supposed to present his proposal next week.

Jack's been thinking about how to pull off an ad campaign on a shoestring budget. It helps that animal shelters tend to be local businesses (and every locality having one or more of its own). So far, his proposal includes 2 billboards: one to be located on a highway downtown that runs N-S, the other on one that runs E-W. He hopes they can afford 2 or 3 radio spots of advertising, but if they can't pop for the radio ads, he might be able to use one or two of their upcoming events as an opportunity to get a PR announcement on the radio, at the least. The main part of the campaign would be the development and dissemination of brochures about the shelter's good work that would be sent to homes as direct marketing and posted in local grocery stores and other high traffic venues, as their respective managers permit.

In terms of the content of the campaign, Jack was flipping through a recent issue of *Newsweek* and noticed an article on how many "stars" lend their names to causes, from George Clooney shedding light on genocide in Darfur, to Sean Penn helping to rebuild Haiti, and, of course, Bono's perennial fight against world poverty. Jack thinks the same principle could hold here. Next week, Jack Russell will propose to the shelter's NPO board that a celebrity become their spokesperson. One question is what celebrity would make sense? He has several slides, listing several options. Discuss each.

Mini-Case Discussion Questions

1. Jack wants to reach out to a star of Clooney's or Penn's or Bono's status. It would be cool.

2. Another option might be the shelter's manager-in-chief.

3. A third option is the town's mayor.

4. A fourth option is one of the state's representatives.

5. A fifth option is a guy named Alex Green, who graduated from a local high school and went on to be really successful, and who has given money to local charities since making it big.

Video Exercise: *L.L. Bean* (8:04)

L.L. Bean left an enduring legacy for the company that bears his name. Bean fervently believed in testing a product to make sure that it delivers what is promised, in terms of the value of honest advertising and of keeping customers satisfied at all costs. This legacy is infused into all of the company's marketing activities, including promotion activities. L.L. Bean's corporate marketing department uses a variety of promotional tools to drive consumer traffic to the company's retail stores, website, and phones. Promotional activities include the use of catalogs; television, online, and radio advertising; e-mails to customers; alternative promotions such as with the tarp covering the Boston Red Sox playing field; and outfitting meteorologists around the nation. The objective of using a variety of promotional venues is to create many so-called advertising touch points to keep the L.L. Bean brand in front of consumers. Consumer interactions are increasingly shifting to the Internet, so L.L. Bean is challenged to provide a superior customer experience online and to effectively use catalogs and television advertising in conjunction with online ads. The company uses data-based analytics to refine the integrated use of catalogs since that medium is very expensive.

Video Discussion Questions

1. What purposes do promotional activities serve at L.L. Bean?

2. Describe L.L. Bean's approach to integrated marketing communication.

3. What are some useful indicators of the effectiveness of L.L. Bean's approach to integrated marketing communication? Why are these indicators useful?

Chapter 12

Integrated Marketing Communications: Media Choices

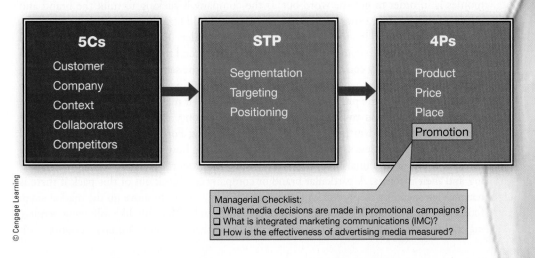

Marketing Management Framework

© Cengage Learning

Advertising is about shaping a message and getting it to the target audience via some optimal combination of media. This chapter focuses on the media decisions. Many media choices are available to the marketing manager, and each can optimize the achievement of different kinds of goals. Ad budgets are usually fixed, so choices must be made and the resource allocation across media can be complicated. With the proliferation of media came the notion of IMC, integrated marketing communications—the idea that marketing planning should ensure that a company's various advertising efforts send a coherent story across the different customer touch points.

12-1 WHAT MEDIA DECISIONS ARE MADE IN ADVERTISING PROMOTIONAL CAMPAIGNS?

There are several media questions to answer: How much do we spend? What's the schedule of expenditure? Which media do we use as channels of our communications? Take the first question, how big should the ad budget be? Most companies spend on their entire communications package (i.e., advertising in all its various forms including the purchase of the necessary media) an amount determined by one of three methods:

1. The advertising budget is a percentage of last year's sales.
2. The company spends approximately what it believes is parity with competitors.
3. The company can use its strategic advertising goal (e.g., enhance awareness or positive attitudes) and work backward to calculate necessary expenditures.

The first method is easy. The only challenge is what should the actual percentage value be: 7%, 10%, 15%? Most companies would begin with their past numbers or an estimate of the industry norm and then adjust: If the marketing goal is merely to maintain brand share, then roughly the percentage that they (and competitors) spent last year should suffice. If the company has done something newsworthy with the brand, an increase in advertising monies is in order to get the word out. If the company is seeking to milk the brand and redirect funds to their other brands, the percentage would be adjusted slightly downward.

The second method is also relatively easy. Service providers (e.g., Schonfeld, saibooks.com) keep tabs of how much companies in various industries tend to spend (e.g., beer companies spend 8–10%). If every competitor spent approximately the same percentage on advertising, then their market shares would be proportional to their ad spending shares; indeed, the ratio for each company of the proportion of ad spending to their market share proportions would be approximately 1. As you can see in Figure 12.1, among major car manufacturers, GM spends the most on advertising and has the greatest sales; Ford, Toyota, and the rest spend less and their sales are less as well. It's somewhat surprising how many industries in which the companies fall along a line, indicating a fairly constant proportionality between their spending and their incomes. A particular brand or company can break out of this pack if there is reason, e.g., spending disproportionately more ad dollars to try to move up the market share food chain or spending less because they're a niche brand with a cult-like following, rendering traditional advertising less necessary, etc. Note too that we're not claiming causation with

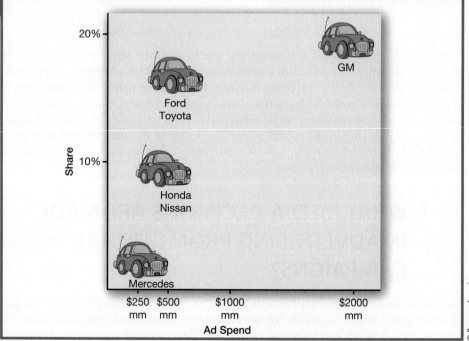

Figure 12.1

Proportion of Ad Spending to Sales

a correlation plot: Marketers hope that larger ad budgets enhance sales (i.e., ad budget ➜ sales), but big companies have more money to spend (i.e., sales ➜ ad budget), and for that matter, big companies have more dealerships or retail outlets (e.g., distribution ➜ sales), etc.

While these methods are easy, they are a bit simplistic. When sales decline (for reasons of a soft economy or a decrease in the brand's popularity), each approach would suggest cutting the ad budget. Smaller ad budgets would mean less presence in the marketplace, further perpetuating a cycle of decreased sales.

Another approach is to be more strategic and treat advertising expenditures as an investment (in the brand and company), with the expectations that an investment should return sales and profits. This approach can be somewhat challenging because advertising effects are difficult to measure, and often they intended to produce long-term effects such as brand building. But let's see how it's done. To set an ad budget, we need to understand how advertising exposures are measured, then we set our exposure goal, and then we can estimate how much to spend to achieve that goal.

12-1a **Reach and Frequency and GRPs**

First, let's discuss the jargon. Advertising agencies work with a unit called *GRP, gross rating points.* Whether we're talking about placing an ad on TV or in a magazine or on the side of a bus, a GRP is a simple function of reach and frequency:

- *Reach* is the share (percentage) of your target audience that has seen your ad at least once.

- *Frequency* is the average number of times your target audience saw the ad (within some set duration, say the 3-month period during which the ads were in circulation or a 3-month testing period within a longer ad showing).

- GRPs, then, are defined as the simple product: *GRP = Reach × Frequency.*

For example, if your ad reached 25% of your target audience on average 3 times, the ad is said to have delivered 75 GRPs. If your ad reached 75% of your target, on average once, the ad would have delivered 75 GRPs also, but the results look different. For the first, the frequency was greater, so we'd expect the small portion of the target who saw the ad to be really familiar with the brand. For the second, the reach portion was bigger, and while we might have hit a basic level of awareness, one ad exposure probably was not hugely effective in changing attitudes yet, if that was a goal.

So, if the marketing goal was (at least minimal) awareness among a larger segment (i.e., greater reach than frequency, as in the second scenario), the ad would need to be run during a highly viewed TV show (for example), which would likely be quite expensive. If the goal was deeper knowledge and more favorable attitudes in the smaller segment (i.e., greater frequency than reach), the ad could be run 3 times during a specialized TV show with a smaller viewer audience (which would also likely be less expensive).

For reach, the goal is to expose as many of the target customers as possible to the ad. The challenge is to find the media that are most cost-efficient for finding as many of those and primarily only those, customers. Note that it is the business of firms like Arbitron and Nielsen to collect these data so you can imagine they're continually working to improve these measures; e.g., marketers care that measures of reach and frequency are unduplicated, not capturing the same eyeballs twice.

For frequency, there used to be a rule of thumb that an ad needed to be seen and processed three times to be persuasive. This notion that 3 repetitions is a magic number is now recognized as simplistic. The good news is that sometimes seeing an ad once or twice can be sufficient, and the bad news is that sometimes a customer needs even more exposures than 3. The fundamental question comes down to the usual: What's the goal? Awareness and memory can probably be attained with few ads. Persuasion might take longer, if the product is complicated or the viewer is unfamiliar with it. In addition, sometimes more is not better. If the product and ad are pretty readily understood, then it is known that there is wear-out and a reduced effectiveness of subsequent exposures to the ad—people start disassociating from the ad, thinking random thoughts and attitudes toward the advertised brand start to drop.

In general, regardless of the budgeting method, it is important to acknowledge that while working on ads can be great fun, they can be very expensive. The cost to produce a finished (and fairly simple) 30-second television commercial is at least $500,000. Companies spend this money because they believe in advertising and know its value as a communications tool. Research has shown a positive relationship between levels of advertising and promotional spending and the market value of the firm but, of course, the direction of causality is unclear: Do the heavy levels of ad spending by these companies ensure their continued success, or are these companies the only ones with pockets deep enough to advertise a great deal. The big spenders on ads are cars at $2b, movies $1b, pharma $500mm, and big banks on credit cards, $350mm.

12-1b Media Planning and Scheduling

Marketers have long tried to answer questions regarding ROI or ROMI (return on marketing investments), essentially estimating a breakeven for an advertising expenditure. Again, with the caveat that no measure is perfect, here's how to approach this estimation.

In Figure 12.2 we see a number of television shows, plotted by their ratings or their popularity with the viewing audiences, and by the costs for 30 seconds of airtime during the shows. There is naturally a positive correlation between these two indicators; you pay more to get more. But the relationship is not perfect; some TV shows are bargains, delivering more audience exposure than they charge, and others are a little costly, charging a bit more than they'll deliver in terms of audience viewership.

Let's say you advertise during the show *Person of Interest*; its rating is 15.6, which translates to 17.5 million TVs tuned into the show in the marketplace households. (One ratings

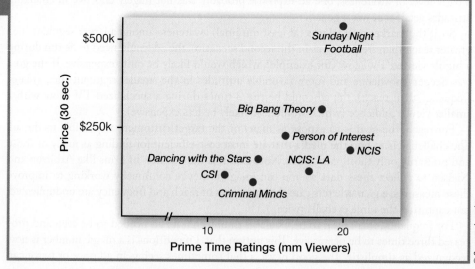

Figure 12.2

Advertising Time Costs More During Popular TV Shows

© Cengage Learning

point is 1% of all households with TVs. Currently the number of U.S. households measured is approximately 112,000,000, so 1% or 1 ratings point is 1,120,000.) The show charges $235,000 per 30 seconds. If you're McDonald's, and you're trying to encourage people to go pick up breakfast tomorrow on their way to work, how many meals would you have to sell to make the advertising charge worth it? If a meal contribution is $0.50, then you'd need $235,000/0.50 = 470,000 purchases (tomorrow, this week, whatever your timeline). That number is only 2.7% of the viewers who had been exposed to the ad (470,000/17.5 million). It seems achievable.

In terms of timing, or media planning, there are basically three kinds of media schedules: continuous, occasional, or seasonal. For *continuous* schedules, there is a regularity in ad exposure; it doesn't have to be a perfectly predictable schedule (e.g., every Friday, a half-page in *The New York Times*), or even all that frequent, but the idea is that you're fairly constantly reminding the consumer that you exist. The periodicity depends on the length of the buying cycle (advertise frequently for soft drinks, less frequently for tires). You want to advertise a little more frequently than the object is purchased, to keep it top of mind, but not so much as to risk overexposure and boring your customers (not to mention the costs of the advertising).

In *occasional* media scheduling (sometimes called "flighting" or "pulsing"), you are not omnipresent but you pop up from time to time. Given that you're advertising less frequently, this approach will be less expensive, therefore possibly more cost-effective. Obviously, one should advertise in synch with purchase cycles. During times when ads aren't aired, competition can swoop in, but you're probably doing the same to them during their downtimes. Furthermore, if you're building brand image, you'll be less vulnerable to competitors' poaching.

Seasonal ads are simply those that are infrequent and focused on the preterm season for the product (e.g., school supplies advertised in August, candy advertised before Valentine's Day and Halloween, outdoor grills advertised in April and May). Advertising outside the season is not done because it will not induce additional purchases.

Media scheduling goes beyond simply counting the number of times an ad was aired in a household whose TV set was on and tuned to the appropriate channel. Advertising agencies are savvy about capturing psychological processes of advertising effects. For example, agencies factor in the recency of the ad exposure when examining subsequent purchase behavior (reasoning that ads viewed last week will have less of an impact on the contents of grocery cart than an ad you saw last night). We'll return to issues surrounding measuring advertising effectiveness later in the chapter.

Types of TV Shows

ESPN Research identified 4 personalities of TV channels:

TV Channel Personality	TV Channel Exemplars
Integrity and information	History Channel, Discovery
Relevance and involvement	Lifetime, HGTV
Entertainment and fun	HBO, NBC, ESPN
Personality and rapport	Lifetime, ESPN
And PS, viewers liked the ads most on these channels:	ESPN, Lifetime, HGTV

12-1c Media Planning and Scheduling

Media planning and scheduling executives carefully follow television ratings. Ratings measure the popularity of a program among viewing audiences. A 1% rating indicates that 1,120,000 households viewed a program. Share differs from ratings. Share is the percent of television sets turned on that are tuned into a desired station. Together these two variables, ratings and share, are usually reported as ratings point/share and indicate the percentage of households watching television/percentage tuned into a particular program.

12-2 INTEGRATED MARKETING COMMUNICATIONS ACROSS MEDIA

With a sense of how much to spend and when to schedule the advertising, we face next the choice of communication outlets. This choice used to be TV, radio, newspaper, magazine, or billboard? Now the choice is even more complicated with so many more media (e.g., more TV stations, radio stations on XM, the Web), and audiences are fragmented across those many media and using technology to zip past ads.

To try to capture these splintered audiences across the varied media that engage them, marketing gurus have encouraged the strategy of *integrated marketing communications* (IMC). To make informed choices and select the appropriate media outlets, the marketing manager needs to understand the strengths of the various individual media available. It is ultra-important that the marketing messages are seamlessly integrated across the media selections.

The philosophy underlying IMC is totally logical: Keep in mind the company's overarching strategy, and ensure that all marketing activities send a consistent message, beginning with the communications (i.e., consumer and trade advertising and promotions, product placements, personal selling, direct and database marketing, etc.), as well as other marketing mix elements (e.g., product design and packaging, pricing, channel availability).

Research suggests a positive relationship between IMC practices and good brand outcomes: high levels of awareness, brand loyalty, and sales. Yet, even if the IMC goal sounds great, it's not that easy to execute in practice, in part because traditional advertising agencies aren't that good at PR, direct marketing, or certainly nontraditional advertising tactics as when using social media. To resemble full-line service providers, some ad agencies acquired smaller specialized agencies, and others outsource part of their overall IMC plan. Ultimately, regardless of how it is achieved, the integration across media is the responsibility of the marketer and brand manager.

Early suggestions were that all the IMC messages across all the media should be the same, to affect a common strategy. More recently, marketers recognize that, while some elements should be consistent (e.g., the brand name, logo, general flavor and positioning), the varied media have varied strengths, and the message should play to the medium's strengths. For example, a TV ad is vivid and dramatic, but the message needs to be kept simple, whereas complicated products can be explained better in print (magazines, online, direct marketing). The goal is consistency in the general positioning, but the different media offer supplemental information.

IMC gurus say that 1 + 1 can equal 3. Advertising in a consistent yet complementary manner across two or more media can have the impact of having spent even more in a traditional single-medium budget. As an example of such synergy, research has shown that websites haven't made catalogs obsolete; instead, their roles are changing. Specifically, online

Creative Communications

- Flashmobs took off with T-Mobile's train station events, choreographed to look spontaneous, with the tagline "Life Is for Sharing."
- Whirlpool donated appliances for houses built by Habitat for Humanity.
- To get in better touch with Hispanic consumers, Kleenex sponsored a contest for amateur artists to submit ideas for package designs. Winners received cash prizes, and the top 3 designs were in distribution during National Hispanic Heritage Month.

shopping is (1) easy for purchasing, (2) efficient for search, and (3) suited to goal-oriented purchasing, whereas direct mail catalogs (1) are colorful and vivid, (2) facilitate browsing, and (3) drive consumers to the website!

12-2a Media Comparisons

Figure 12.3 indicates the relative strengths of popular media—TV, radio, newspapers, magazines, billboards, the Web, and direct mail—on some business criteria. TV ad spots are by far the most expensive (e.g., $5–100k for 30 seconds during prime time), yet even with today's TV channel fragmentation, this medium still yields the largest reach numbers (sheer audience size). While reach is strong, frequency can be challenging to achieve because of the expense. In addition, reach via the mass media is relatively broad, not targeted.

Medium	Cost	Reach	Frequency	Targeted
TV	$$$$$	★★★★★	★★	★★★
Radio	$$	★★	★★★	★★★
Newspapers	$$	★	★	★
Magazines	$$$	★★★	★★	★★★
Billboards	$$	★★	★★★	★★
www	$	★★★★	★★★★	★★★★
Direct mail	$	★★★★	★★★	★★★★

Figure 12.3

Media Choices: Relative Strengths on Business Measures

© Cengage Learning

Traditional TV is considered a mass medium, but special TV and cable channels serve more focused audiences. Similarly, some magazines have broad appeal, but others can hit a target segment quite efficiently (i.e., with little excess expenditure). Radio spots and newspapers are often planned and purchased nationally, but alternatively each can also certainly be planned and purchased for local markets. These media can capture known segments, e.g., radio by genre, or in-flight magazines for the flying audience. Billboards and other urban methods (e.g., subway ads, ads on buses, ads before previews in movie theaters) are relatively inexpensive but are effective in covering good local numbers.

Radio, newspapers and magazines are certainly less expensive than TV (e.g., $250 for 1 minute of radio, $5k for one page, 1 day in a decent paper, $5–15k for 1 page, 1 issue in

TV Tidbits

- Even in households that receive 100+ channels, on average consumers watch only about 14 channels.
- When we sit down to watch, we (1) first go to one among our 14 favorite channels, (2) next we check listings, (3) next, we zone out, surf the remote, and select nearly randomly.
- TV segments of customer media choices (based on research by ESPN Research and Quirks.com):

Segment	Watch their TV shows primarily:	Because:
1	On-demand	It's convenient; they can control the experience (e.g., pause, rewind); they can watch any episode; the shows don't take up space on their DVRs.
2	Live	They're ardent fans; they schedule their lives around their shows; they want to be cool and talk about the show at work the next day; right after it's aired.
3	via DVR	It's convenient, and they're busy; they like high-def; and they can keep episodes they like.

a magazine), but, of course, they also deliver smaller audiences. Bigger magazines (where bigger implies greater reach) naturally cost more (e.g., a full-page color ad in *BusinessWeek* is roughly $100k; in *Newsweek*, it's $200k; back pages cost still more). Particular costs and GRP delivery depends on whether the radio station is local or the newspaper a national.

Each medium has its own personality. For example, newspapers have the advantage of extreme timeliness. Magazines require longer lead times for production, but they have nice reproduction quality. So-called beauty shots of products in magazine photos are as high quality as TV. Newspapers and magazines also have the advantage of being nonintrusive because readers choose to pick up the magazine at a time of their convenience, and can flip past a print ad quickly if they wish to do so. Each medium has drawbacks as well, cf. the flipping past the ad.

The media with the best customization options are online advertising and direct mail. The varieties of ads on the Internet are still very inexpensive, and data-based profiling enhances the technology's ability to target. Still, online penetration isn't yet 100%, and users have to actively find the brand and company; hence, reach is not yet a strength of this medium.

Direct mail is relatively inexpensive, but it is not terribly efficient. That is, some of the direct mail appeals will be received as junk mail by the recipients. With better database programs, the reach of the particular target audience can be quite focused.

Figure 12.4 displays the relative strengths of these media in terms of the content they can deliver. TV messages need to be simple and straightforward, and radio messages even more so, given that fewer sensory modalities are engaged in receiving the message. TV allows for vivid, dramatic portrayals, including humorous and emotional appeals, much of which gets lost in the more impoverished media. On the other hand, print vehicles (magazines, papers, direct mail, online, etc.) are the perfect outlets for conveying detailed product information.

© Cengage Learning

Medium	Information	Product Demo	Vivid, Emotional
TV	★★	★★★★★	★★★★★
Radio	★★	★★	★★★
Newspapers	★★★★	★	★
Magazines	★★★	★★	★★★
Billboards	★★	★	★★
WWW	★★★★★	★★★★	★★★★
Direct mail	★★★★★	★★★	★★★

Figure 12.4

Media Choices: Relative Strengths on Ad Content

12-2b Beyond Advertising

IMC is about integrating a brand message across any media, not just traditional advertising outlets. In addition to advertising—whatever personal selling staff a company has at its disposal, their sales promotions, their public relations, and so forth—all should be expressing a consistent, complementary message. All of these media (broadly defined) are supposed to work as a team on behalf of the brand.

The key advertising concepts are still applicable. For example, the AIDA process (attention, interest, desire, action) works in selling too: A salesperson must first get the attention of the potential customer (by prospecting a database, qualifying the potential customers, and approaching them), then his or her interest (through a sales presentation), desire (e.g., through a product demonstration, being ready to handle the customer's objections), and action (closing the deal and following up with service).

Personal selling and a company's *sales force* are essential communication vehicles for many companies and industries. Personal selling is huge; the Department of Labor estimates that some 14 million jobs (over 10% of the work force) are in selling. These sales-related positions include the guy or girl doing road trips selling machine parts or insurance, as well as the counter help at Nordstrom's, as well as the order takers at 1-800-cataloger.

While we've said direct marketing and Internet are media that can be tailored, nothing beats a face-to-face conversation to try to figure out what a customer wants and how a company can deliver. Sales forces are clearly high cost, all due to labor (salary, training, etc.), but they're nevertheless important, especially for the sale of complicated, expensive goods and services. So while sales forces exist for consumer products (e.g., Avon, Amway, etc.), they're ginormous in B2B. It's thought that an expensive piece of medical equipment or a high-volume photocopier or a new eco-friendly chemical or a new cholesterol-reducing medication are all too complicated to just sell online or via a catalog; it's helpful to have a salesperson explain all the product features, as well as other details such as service and leasing agreements.

Marketers face three primary questions in designing a sales force: (1) How many sales people do I need? (2) where do I deploy them? (3) How do I compensate them? Sale forces are larger when a company wants an aggressive product launch and when a company wants to protect its territories from encroaching competition. Sales territories are determined not only by existing sales and competition but also from strategic assessments of future desired markets. Compensation is always some proportion of salary and commissions; the proportions tend to have more to do with tradition and competition than any psychological assessment of the motivating factors.

Ads vs. Salespeople

Advertising	Personal Selling
Customers can be anywhere.	Need geographic concentration.
Product is simple to understand.	Product is complicated, technical.
Product is fairly standard.	Product can be customized.
Relatively inexpensive, less risky	High-priced, B2B items
Advertising can be expensive.	Sales force can be expensive.
Results can be difficult to establish.	Quick feedback, measurable results

Costs of sales forces include more than compensation. Salespeople are partners, members of your distribution channel, and just like your end users, they want deals. So while consumers might think they're bombarded with advertising, Figure 12.5 indicates that companies' expenditures on advertising and sales promotions directed to consumers is only a small piece of the pie. The largest portion of their marketing communications budgets is directed to trade—their channel partners (according to a recent A. C. Nielsen study, "Annual Survey on Trade Promotion Practices").

Figure 12.5

Allocation of Communication and Promotion Budget

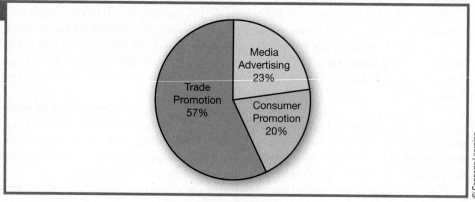

© Cengage Learning

Recall the concepts of push and pull in channels of distribution, push being a top-down effort, selling to customers through a sales force and retail partners, and pull being a bottom-up drive from customers seeking their products. Pull (advertising to consumers) is important to a brand manager when the company's intermediaries stock a large number of competing products, and the partners don't care about supporting any of them in particular. Then, advertising and sales promotions are necessary vehicles. Direct-to-consumer (DTC) pharma ads are a very popular and effective example of pull.

Push relies more on personal selling, and a brand manager needs to direct promotional efforts to members of the channel, more than to the final user. Channel members don't care about ads per se as much as money, and so trade allowances are frequently used. These are price reductions offered by the manufacturer to the intermediary (wholesaler or retailer) in exchange for their doing something such as allocating space to a new product (so-called slotting allowances) or buying more product during special periods. Sometimes these trade bonuses are passed along to the retailer's salespeople in the form of cash or training and product demonstrations, free merchandise, or conventions and trade shows.

Inc.com and Money.CNN.com track the largest sales forces in the world: In computers, the greatest numbers of salespeople work for Microsoft, Xerox, and Cisco. In consumables, the big sales forces are at PepsiCo, Sysco, Interstate Bakeries, Coca-Cola, and Anheuser-Busch. And the largest medical sales forces work at Schering Plough, J&J, and Pfizer. These days, most sales forces are facilitated by CRM databases (cf., vendors: SAP, Oracle, and Salesforce.com). Customers' purchases and preferences are stored, so the salesperson can refresh his or her memory of the buyer and company before a sales meeting, and update the database immediately after each contact.

Public relations (PR) is another means of providing information and building brand attributes. PR lines of communications are the attempt of an organization to reach its customers, suppliers, stockholders, government officials, employees, or the general community. PR can be conducted from within the company, its advertising agency, or (most often) outsourced to PR specialists.

PR people issue press kits—news releases (used to be in print, now via video clips)—whenever anything newsworthy is happening. The information features a blurb on whatever's going on (e.g., a new product launch), as well as background propaganda about the company, bios, history, whatever's needed to round out the edges. That background information is also available on a website they'll maintain for year-round inquiries. PR people arrange events such as speaking engagements (e.g., CEO Joe to speak at this year's new bank opening), sponsorships (e.g., a poster and coffee at a professional conference or trade show), or community philanthropy (the bank's name on Little League uniforms, or the bank sponsors a walk for charity).

Most companies use PR in recovery mode, in an attempt to smooth over some complicated or embarrassing event, such as when a product is reviewed critically or when customers boycott a brand. Company reps communicate to the customers, shareholders, and press to counterargue the criticisms and to enhance and strengthen positive images and brand and corporate equity.

It's even smarter to practice continual (albeit pulsing) proactive PR, which can be brand building and also inoculate the firm from possible subsequent criticism. Positive PR can be large scale, such as ingredient menus for restaurant chains, or local, such as a company sponsoring a community event or, say, a Little League team.

PR

Part of the utility of PR is its versatility. It has been exercised in the wake of oil spills, brake failures, package tampering, political and sports figure misbehavior. Newsweek.com identified several cases:

Company	Problem	PR Spin
Johnson & Johnson	Recalls.	Customers can trust them. The company is transparent in owning up to problems and addressing quality control issues.
Boeing	Delay unveiling the 787 Dreamliner.	It's Boeing, for heaven's sake. They're strong in many businesses. We need to sit tight.
Glaxo	Lawsuits re: a drug's side effects of heart attacks and strokes.	They are settling cases quickly and proceeding with business as usual—developing vaccines to grow in emerging markets.

For more, see Public Relations Society of America (prsa.org) or Council of Public Relations Firms (prfirms.org).

The intent of PR is to convey a positive image and to educate a constituency about the company's objectives such as recent innovations. In general, the job of a PR firm is to generate goodwill on behalf of the company.

Publicity is another tool of communication; it's not paid for by the brand's company and so can carry the appearance of objectivity, e.g., some new brand feature praised by a third party, such as a newspaper or a website that provides news coverage. Press releases are, of course, constantly prepared by a company, but there is no guarantee than any influential media will bother to pick up on what a company deems newsworthy.

Sometimes the publicity indeed comes from a third party, such as when a popular press business magazine such as *Fortune* publishes its annual "100 Best Companies to Work For" issues. Companies included in these listings are celebrated, and you just can't buy that kind of attention. On the other hand, the company has no control over the spin on the story, and publicity can be negative, requiring some recovery on the part of the company's own PR group.

Product placement is more subtle than most advertising. It's been around awhile but has become increasingly popular (over $1 billion annually) as brand managers struggle to find creative means of getting in front of viewers who are increasingly zapping ads. In movies (e.g., James Bond's cars), TV (*Survivor*), and video games, products and brands are being integrated into the show. The product is integral to the scene, so the viewer can't zap past it, and the inclusion of the product carries an implicit endorsement by the actors on-screen.

While ads are more useful than product placements in providing information, both can result in the transfer of positive associations. (Negative emotions can transfer too, so many brands [e.g., Coke, Pepsi] don't advertise during news broadcasts; the viewing experience is a bummer, and the brand managers don't want to inherit the negative baggage.) Both ads and product placement are also met with some viewer skepticism, since it's known that both are paid for. A somewhat related phenomenon is the placement, or plant, of a brand advocate in chat rooms. When a brand is talked up and the chat is thought to be authentic, it is very powerful and persuasive, but if the rest of the chat room attendees smell a plant, the tactic can backfire.

Event sponsorship, usually of sports but sometimes other cultural or artistic endeavors, has a long tradition. The event is exciting, and the brand draws from its positive valence and energy.

NASCAR racing is a popular "vehicle" for sponsorship (17 of the 20 biggest spectator sports are NASCAR races). Big crowds attend (average attendance per race is 100,000; the average ticket price is $90), TV audience sizes and ratings are soaring (Fox, NBC, and TNT have a multibillion-dollar deal for coverage), merchandise exceeds another $2b, and corporate money is pouring in through sponsorship (already over $1.5 billion; fortune.com).

Working for a company whose brand helps sponsor an event is exciting, but it's not entirely clear that sponsorship is cost-effective in apportioning advertising budgets. For example, when companies like Coca-Cola, GE, Kodak, Omega, Panasonic, and Visa sponsor events like the Olympics or the World Cup, do they need the exposure? When companies like Atos Origin or Manulife sponsor these events, does the exposure help them (e.g., achieve heightened brand name awareness)? Yet so-called ambush marketing is frowned upon (companies that try to associate with such prominent events without obtaining and paying for sponsorship rights).

By the way, if you want to find the tough demographic audience of 35- to 40-year-old white-collar men with bachelor's degrees making almost $100k, help sponsor Fantasy Football. These guys are into FF big time, and, P.S., they're checking their teams' performance while at work.

Sales promotion is still another tool in the IMC mix. The best known form of sales promo is the coupon—a newspaper or magazine cutout to take shopping for a small discount on a future purchase.

Coupons are very popular, so there are many forms; e.g., there are FSIs (freestanding inserts in newspapers, magazines, and direct mail), printouts at the checkout, coupon pop-outs at point of purchase (on the shelves on which the products are featured), Internet printout coupons to take to retail shops, etc. In addition to coupons, sales promos include rebates, promo prices, trade-ins, deals for loyalty programs, free trial-sized (i.e., small) products, contests and sweepstakes, etc.

Sales promotions activate purchase interest, thus effecting short-term sales boosts. Sales promotions are also thought to be effective devices for enticing customers to switch brands.

12-2c The IMC Choices Depend on the Marketing Goals

There are many media, any of which could be useful and all of which should be coordinated. Advertising can be carried via print (magazines, newspapers, mailing, billboards, point of purchase signs), TV, radio, the product's packaging, movie product placement, sales promo-tion (coupons and rebates, loyalty cards), the sponsorship of events and experiences, public relations and publicity, personal selling, direct marketing, etc. For each element, the brand manager and CMO need to answer two questions: (1) Who is the target audience? And, of course, (2) what is our goal—awareness, provision of information about features and ben-efits, enhancement of brand attitudes, the strengthening of preferences, the stimulation of purchase trial, the encouragement of repeat purchasing, the attraction of brand switchers? The effect of the ad campaign on that target segment with respect to the select goal can be and should be measured. Other effects might also result, but one should not expect that all of those goals could be met with a single blip of advertising and IMC.

Let's review the choices and decisions that must be made. If you sell something that is seasonal, you'll advertise just prior to that season. Otherwise, you have a choice of advertis-ing continuously or occasionally. Big companies with big ad budgets can advertise contin-uously, but little brands can advertise continuously if the less expensive media are used. So the choice between continuous vs. occasional is not just budget.

Further, if the marketing goal is brand awareness, occasional ads won't cut it. The adver-tising needs to be fairly frequent until that basic knowledge has nearly saturated the target market. Note that the target needs to be defined well to be able to send media to it and to test it later. In addition, the level of saturation needs to be defined: Do you want 90% awareness? 60%? To be profitable, the saturation percentage can be smaller if the target market is large.

Once there is awareness, to prompt continued purchasing, correlate the frequency of advertising with the customers' purchase cycle. If the item is purchased frequently, then advertise frequently.

Modify all these actions depending on your marketing strategy; if the brand in question is a cash cow at the end of its product life cycle, you're likely to be advertising less frequently. If the brand in question is one the company wishes to grow aggressively, ramp up above previous years' budgets and above competitors' spending.

Regarding media choices, there are two questions: (1) What can you afford? (2) What fits best for your target segment? If yours is a little brand with meager budget, you're pre-cluded from national TV or sponsorship of big sports event. Big deal—there are plenty of other options. Even local TV or local sports events are fine alternatives. Be creative with buying (or, better, creating and maintaining) databases to target your audience. Find out what magazines they read and what websites they visit, and advertise there.

Regarding the IMC across the message pieces, draw up a pie-in-the-sky message—all that you want to convey to your customers—from the facts of the features to the benefits and images. Then put the images in the visual media and the facts in the written media. Use a common tagline and design appearance to tie the messages together. Doing so will ensure a sense of consistency as well as complementary, both of which reinforce brand equity.

Figure 12.6 is an example IMC schedule encompassing timing, media selection, and message for integration. Many companies make most of their money during the Christmas holiday season. Thus, this example company hypes up for December. The ads in the winter (March) and spring (May) feature the brand and the company (to maintain its reputation). The messages are reminders in content: "We're here, and we're good quality, and here are some reasons you should like us." Media selections are targeted (magazine ads, specialized cable TV ads) as well as broad (online), and price promotions (coupons) are used along with the advertising.

Figure 12.6

An IMC Schedule

Jan	Feb	March
		Brand promotions magazines ads, online coupons
April	**May**	**June**
	Company ads, target segment cable TV ad	
July	**Aug**	**Sept**
	Brand; back-to-school online deals, local paper inserts	Attitude brand ads via local radio spots, refer-a-friend
Oct	**Nov**	**Dec**
Top-of-mind ad; 3 TV ads say go online for more information	Spur purchase; events: parade float, 3 ads during college football games	Pre-Christmas: 3 local TV ads & paper inserts. Post-holiday deep discount

© Cengage Learning

At the end of August, a slight shift in message occurs. Kids are going back to school and this event prompts another coupon and a referral program.

Things get really heated right around Halloween and November. Messages that had simply been nice reminders are getting more focused, keeping the attitudes enhancing aspects, but encouraging a salient top-of-mind readiness in recall, and, of course, encouraging purchase. Advertising expenditures are growing, as the ads are placed in more numerous and more expensive media outlets (e.g., large metropolitan radio spots, national TV ads, etc.).

Thanksgiving kicks in some novelty, with the sponsorship of two highly televised events: a float in a popular Thanksgiving Day parade and 3 announcer-mentions during a big college football game. In the second week of December, local TV ads are aired in three large markets

Ad Ethics?

Is it okay when Miller produces and advertises Plank Road beer as if it's from a small brewer? Is it okay when squeaky clean Disney produces R-rated movies under the name Miramax?

Isn't it impossible to tell customers everything about products and how they're made?

(For more, see Davidson's *Moral Dimension of Marketing*.)

and on the weekend between the second and third weeks of December, city newspaper insert ads are bought for those 3 markets, plus the next 20 in size. Prices are also cut 15%.

Whatever product is left after the big Christmas rush is sold at 50–75% discount (depending on the retailer relationship). The company sits back to recover from the activities of the last few weeks of the year to regain energies to start the game all over again the next March.

The company is thoughtful about varying media choices, scheduling and planning, and the overall content of the communication pieces that fit together. This is IMC as an integral whole—across message and media.

12-3 HOW IS THE EFFECTIVENESS OF ADVERTISING MEDIA MEASURED?

Depending on the goal sought, advertising effectiveness can be assessed in a number of ways. In the previous chapter, we discussed measures of memory (recall and recognition), attitudes and propensity to purchase, and so forth. Coupling that ad content with this chapter's concerns over media, it should be clear that things get both more complicated, and yet there are some synergies.

For example, if the marketing goal is enhancing awareness and memory, then reach is the more likely media goal (than frequency), and this can be measured by viewership, readership and circulation numbers, traffic indices, and many measures of exposures. If brand awareness is already pervasive in the target segment, and the goal of the ad campaign is an attitude adjustment, then surveys (even quick 3-item smartphone surveys) will be necessary.

Advertising research (on memory or attitudes) ask respondents whether they can remember the source of the ad (did they see something on TV, hear something on the radio, receive a piece in the mail, etc.). Consumers aren't typically accurate in their identification of the media sources, which further underlines the importance of exposing consumers to your messages via multiple media. The marketing concern is primarily that the message reaches the consumer via any medium, but the fact that consumers can't tell you where they saw the message means it's more difficult to assess an ROMI on the radio portion of the ad budget vs. the direct mailing piece, for example.

The ways to test advertising are many. The same kind of scanner data that allow marketers to run experiments in stores on price points are also used to assess ads in the marketplace. For all households in a zip code, advertising researchers can find out what national or local ads have been running on TV, radio, newspapers, etc. For the households in certain research companies' panels (e.g., such as those run by A. C. Nielsen or Information Resources Inc.), finer measures of advertising exposure are possible, e.g., was the household TV set on during the ad showing, etc.

Many studies have been conducted with such data. For example, to address the question, "If you spend more on advertising, do you see more in sales?" a huge real-world marketing research study was conducted, and researchers found that increasing ad budgets, relative to the competition, doesn't increase sales in general. Think about it: Sometimes an ad might not seem to predict something like sales or share because there is little variance in the system. That is, if everyone in the industry tends to advertise a lot, then the relative market share positions wouldn't shift much. On the other hand, if all companies advertised less, they'd all be more profitable because advertising is costly), and, again, presumably market shares wouldn't change much, but this is not a good idea for the long term. Companies are supposed to be advertising to communicate with customers, but sometimes it almost appears as though they advertise because competitors are doing so.

While varying ad weight (budget expenditures) may have limits in affecting sales and shares, research has found that qualitative differences, such as better ad copy, or strategies to reach current noncategory users, etc., can increase the likelihood that TV advertising will positively affect sales. As another indicator that content matters, researchers have also found that an increase in media weight (i.e., advertising budgets) is related to sales for ads that both evoked positive feelings and failed to evoke negative feelings. Finally, some marketers would say, why bother spending ad dollars on retaining customers who already have a strong positive preference for the featured product? Instead, eliminate these wasted (or redundant) dollars, and spend on consumers who are more ambivalent to prevent their switching to the competition.

Different Media

Marketers have lots of fun media choices:

1. *Celebrities:* Whenever it's announced that another celebrity has struck a deal to be paid megabucks to endorse some brand, it raises eyebrows. Can the celeb possibly be worth it? Research suggests yes, at least for sports stars. When the athlete signs on, there is a boost in sales in an absolute sense and relative to competitor brands. Furthermore, there are lifts in sales and stock returns every time the athlete meets some major achievement. The effects on stock enhancements seem long lasting, but sales bumps begin to decline over time. (See Elberse and Verleun, "The Economic Value of Celebrity Endorsements," i*Journal of Advertising Research*, 52, 2.)

2. *Sponsorship:* Speaking of athletes, what about the prices of the real estate of soccer jerseys? The cost of renting these human billboards ranged from $40.9m for FC Barcelona and $35.7m for FC Bayern Munich to $3.5m for LA Galaxy and, well, $0 so far for Colorado Rapids. Is it worth it? Brand exposure in the presence of such adrenaline and excitement? You bet. (See the *Bloomberg Businessweek* article, "Full Frontal Sponsorship," by Roger Bennett.)

3. *Product Placement:* The product types that use TV and movie placement the most are cars (especially Mercedes, Chevy, BMW, Cadillac), beer (Miller), and soft drinks (Coke, Pepsi); placements for liquor have declined. In video games, Pepsi, Siemens, Burger King rule. When the content of the TV, movie, or video game programming is coded as being positive, neutral, or negative in tone, product placement is split almost perfectly 33% across. Strange—wouldn't you expect that the product placement dollar would specify a positive context? When the product presentation is coded as full-frontal vs. partial product displays, the full-on dominates, but only 2:1. (See Galician's, *Handbook of Product Placement in the Mass Media*.)

Online advertising is new enough that advertising researchers are still trying to determine just what should be measured. Click-through rates (from banner ads) are a simple no-brainer, but they also track downloads, inquiries, purchases, returns, etc. Then costs can be assessed against these measures: cost per click, cost per download, cost per acquisition, etc. On the face of it, costs of online advertising are low, but click-through conversion rates are also low, so online "costs per" aren't terribly impressive. That is, cost-effectiveness of online advertising may not be great, but cost per se is so extraordinarily low that the inefficiencies are ones that most advertising managers are willing to live with.

Finally, it's important to note that just as advertising media need to be integrated, à la IMC, messages and media themselves may be optimally integrated. Consider the following example. A national electronics firm that produces hearing aids was interested in learning how to get its message to people who have various forms of hearing loss, as well as what they should say. Hearing aids are a tricky product because, while there are young people with suboptimal hearing, for many people, hearing loss first occurs as they begin to age. So wearing a hearing aid is an admission of aging, and it's seen as somewhat embarrassing. So what to do?

In this example, a test market was run in which public media were tested against private media. An example of the public media was a videotape of what a TV ad would look like. An example of the private media was a direct marketing piece sent to the home that could be read in the privacy of one's own home. In addition, different messages were created: One was a supposedly humorous ad (sort of making fun of the confusions that hearing losses can create), and one was an ad that essentially promised the hearing aid would help the wearer interact better with his or her family, friends, and coworkers. The funny ad worked better on the video, and the promise ad worked better on the direct marketing materials, and the latter combo worked better than the former. The bottom line is not that one message was better than another or that one medium was better than another. It's that certain messages are conveyed more effectively via certain media. The challenge is to find the fit that works for your brand and product. The integration "I" in IMC needs to be across media and messages.

Managerial Recap

Media decisions about both expenditure and timing are integral in running advertising promotional campaigns.

- Marketing managers must oversee the media choices to integrate the marketing communications so customers hear the company's message in one clear voice.

- The effectiveness of advertising is measured using long-term and short-term measures.

- Gross rating points (GRPs) are calculated by multiplying reach × frequency. Reach is the percentage of the target audience that has seen an advertisement at least once. Frequency is the average number of times the target audience saw the ad in a given period (e.g., 3 months).

- Don't forget: There's a difference between ratings and advertising measures of share. Share is the percentage of TV sets that are turned on to the desired show. Together, measures are usually reported as ratings points/share. For example, Nielsen ratings may indicate that some TV show received a 10/15 during its broadcast, meaning that 10% (or 11,200,000) households were watching TV, and 15% of them were tuned into this program.

Chapter Outline in Key Terms and Concepts

1. What media decisions are made in advertising promotional campaigns?
    a. Reach and frequency and GRPs
    b. Media planning and scheduling
2. Integrated marketing communications across media
    a. Media comparisons
    b. Beyond advertising
    c. Choice between advertising and a sales force
    d. The IMC choices depend on the marketing goals
3. How is the effectiveness of advertising media measured?

Chapter Discussion Questions

1. Choose an ad you like, from the Web, radio, a magazine, wherever, and design an IMC campaign for the other media; that is, if you heard a radio ad you liked, design what a complementary Web ad and magazine ad might look like. What gains might the company enjoy by the added media and supplemental messaging?

2. If you had to reach a customer segment of "tweens" (kids between 8 and 13), which medium would you choose? What about for men in their 30s? Men in their 60s? In which medium would you advertise if you ran one of your city's performing arts centers?

Mini-Case

Where Should We Place Our Ad?

A software company that is fairly well regarded for 2 large product lines has TurboTax in its sights. It's developed a tax package that it thinks its current customers will like, and it thinks this software will give them a chance to bring new customers to their products.

The company has developed an informative yet succinct, and even somewhat humorous ad. One of the top managers is saying the company ought to ship out the ad in brochure form along with a DVD with a demo file on it, as a form of direct mail. Another guy is saying that because the product is hi-tech, they should reach out to customers through an e-mail campaign with the brochure essentially in PDF form, with an embedded link to the same demo file as the direct mail recipients would receive.

The boss is indifferent (doesn't know much about marketing, history, biology, or what a slide rule is for), but he cares about costs. So a third manager called up some media providers and compiled the following prices.

	New Customers		Current Customers	
	Direct Mail (list rental)	e-mail (list rental)	Direct Mail (list in CRM system)	e-mail (list in CRM system)
Cost per 1,000 (CPM)	$1,750	$500	$750	$50
Click-thru rate	—	10%	—	20%
Rate of purchase	2%	3%	4%	5%
Cost per sale	$88	$167	$19	$5

Mini-Case Discussion Questions

1. What did we learn from the cost assessment manager?

2. Which of the first two managers' directions (direct mail or e-mail) would you support?

3. What is the strategy? If the company wants to emphasize customer acquisition, what would you recommend? If the company wants to emphasize customer retention, what would you recommend?

4. What else would you like to know for a more thorough assessment?

Video Exercise: *Ogden Publications* (7:48)

Ogden Publications, a publisher of a variety of magazines, uses integrated marketing communications to coordinate and achieve consistency across all aspects of its marketing efforts. Ogden's marketing department—consisting of a circulation team, a creative services team, a merchandise and events team, and a public relations team—searches for ways to collaborate more effectively with each editorial team so that there is consistency of key brand imagery and marketing messages across the company's various magazines, websites, and marketing materials. The circulation team is responsible for managing overall readership by using touch points such as direct mail, magazine insert cards, e-mail campaigns, and newsstands. The merchandise and events team is charged with developing new products and identifying new events to attend. The creative services team provides creative development for marketing as well as for the rest of the company. The PR team is responsible for gaining media exposure for Ogden. The overall message across Ogden's various magazines is that Ogden provides "cool information that is relevant."

Video Discussion Questions

1. What are some of the key customer touch points for Ogden Publications?

2. How does Ogden Publications use integrated marketing communications to provide a consistent message across these customer touch points?

3. How does Ogden Publications benefit from using integrated marketing communications?

Chapter 13
Social Media

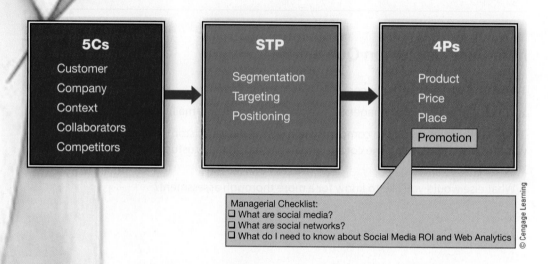

5Cs	STP	4Ps
Customer Company Context Collaborators Competitors	Segmentation Targeting Positioning	Product Price Place Promotion

Managerial Checklist:
❑ What are social media?
❑ What are social networks?
❑ What do I need to know about Social Media ROI and Web Analytics

© Cengage Learning

Marketing Management Framework

13-1 WHAT ARE SOCIAL MEDIA?

Once upon a time, there were only ABC, CBS, and NBC. No MTV, no HBO, no Fox. You had to be near a wall to talk on the phone. Amazon was a river, google was a number, and byte was a typo. How primitive. The enormity of today's media choices—the Internet alone—makes it a wonderful time to be alive. The media are obviously part of the social media story. Computer technology continues to get smaller, more powerful, and less expensive. It seems omnipresent.

Mobile marketing is growing because our cell phones are particularly convenient: They contain our identities and those of the people we talk to frequently. They are our portals to e-mail and Facebook, our primary means of sharing information and entertainment. We engage in simple social conversation, forward funny e-mails, and share videos, links, and music. We are both voyeurs and exhibitionists in sharing photos and evidence of recent behavior. The GPS units embedded in our phones help us find destinations and help marketers find us.

At the same time that electronic and information technologies are becoming more accessible and pervasive, traditional media are experiencing their own changes:

- Newspaper circulations are declining, and, while optimists continue to launch new magazines every year, their overall sales and circulations are down as well.

- The number of radio stations has grown, boosted by satellite servers such as XM or Sirius, but listeners are tuned in for less time each day than just a few years ago.

- Television channels also continue to grow. The bad news about this fragmentation is that with more TV channels, the audience for any given show is typically smaller (consumers are spread thin across the multitude of options). The good news is that targeting is a facilitated when the segments of viewers are somewhat more homogeneous.

The other part of the social media story is, of course, its social or human element. People enjoy connecting with each other. Belonging to different communities and interacting with different people in our social roles is part of our self-identity.

The most fundamental means of interaction is a dialogue. In social media, customers have become participants in a dialogue with marketers or brands. Traditionally, customers had been mere recipients of one-way messages that had been shot out by marketers, but now they have means of talking back. Customers post positive endorsements about brands, and they also use the Web to vent. Marketers are realizing that they're losing control, and they are scrambling to reinsert themselves into the conversation and steer it in fruitful directions. Let's see what new vehicles are available.

13-1a **Types of Social Media**

The phrase "social media" is usually applied to people interacting and connecting with others via online software or alternative electronic access technologies (e.g., their smartphones). There are so many variations that it is more useful to consider their properties rather than their particulars. First, some social media offer very rich, vivid sensory experiences, such as virtual worlds or video games, with their dynamic sights and sounds that compel the user to interact and engage. By comparison, other social media seem relatively simple, even impoverished, such as blogs and forums, which tend to resemble little more than protracted strings of e-mails.

Second, social media differ in that some are primarily social in nature, such as social network sites, which serve as places to asynchronously hang out with friends. On spaces like Facebook, friends chat, share photos, music, and videos. Sharing slices of life with friends is the goal. Other media have more industrious goals, such as collaborating wiki content, seeking jobs via professional sites like LinkedIn, or reading technical blogs to extract advice from experts.

Third, social media vary with regard to whether the interactions are pointedly commercial. On this dimension, there are not many pure forms; for example, *Facebook* may seem to host noncommercial gatherings, and yet ads are floating about, and retail links have begun to sprout. Online brand communities for BMW or Lego hosted by their respective companies obviously have purchase as their ultimate goals, but their brand communities—bimmerfest and lugnet—are built by user groups who are more interested in simply celebrating the brand experience.

13-1b **Word of Mouth**

A particularly important phenomenon for business is that social media facilitates word of mouth (WOM). Long before social media technology, marketers have known that customer word of mouth is very powerful. Consumers view ads with some skepticism, knowing that the point of the message is persuasion. By comparison, if a customer hears the endorsement of a brand from a friend, that message is seen as more objective because the friend presumably has nothing to gain from making any claims. As Figure 13.1 illustrates, you might tell several friends about a new brand, and they in turn tell several friends of theirs.

There are a number of metaphors to describe this phenomenon of people talking about a brand, e.g., people will say that a YouTube video about a brand has gone viral or that a new Groupon issuance is generating a lot of buzz. What makes a product or event newsworthy?

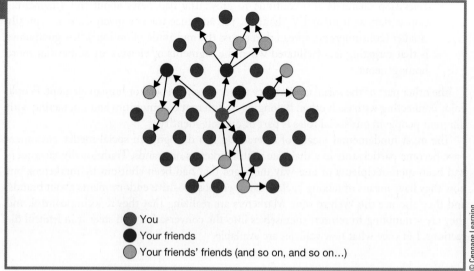

Figure 13.1

Word-of-Mouth Networks

○ You
● Your friends
○ Your friends' friends (and so on, and so on...)

© Cengage Learning

What makes an opinion leader tell their friends about the latest products they've found? How does word of mouth work?

Harris Interactive polls regularly show that the most WOM occurs for restaurants, movies, and computers. For restaurants and movies, WOM helps because consumers seek novelty and variety, and for computers, WOM helps reduce perceptions of risk due to the products' expense and most consumers' lack of technical expertise. Much less WOM occurs for medicines and financial products (they're personal) and for simple or inconspicuous goods (WOM isn't necessary or exciting). Similarly, Twitter is said to be popular because, with it, people never feel out of touch, lonely, or bored, and sources that are popular are those that are informative, interesting, or funny.

It seems intuitive that word of mouth would work on inherently exciting products, where the notion of buzz makes sense. Yet creative brand managers have launched clever ad campaigns that get talked about even for pretty mundane products too, the key being that the product and the message are meaningful to the customer. The hook can be humor, or promotions, or support of social causes. For example, insurance may seem a little dry, but the Geico Gecko has many friends on Facebook. Mash-ups of real brand material with nostalgic TV commercials and irreverent content are another way to pique some interest and heighten buzzability. Distinct from whether the product category seems WOM-worthy, it is also the case that some consumers are extraverted in generating more word of mouth (positive and negative) than others. Word of mouth travels via communication in social networks, so let's understand those structures.

13-2 WHAT ARE SOCIAL NETWORKS?

Networks have been studied in many realms—epidemiology (e.g., contagion), transportation (e.g., hub and spoke), and now business (e.g., word of mouth). The key is a focus on connections. A network is defined as the set of actors (or nodes) and the relational ties that link them. Actors may be customers, firms, brands, concepts, countries, etc. The connections between the actors are relational ties (or links). Ties can be symmetric ("X is a coworker of Y") or directional ("X likes Y"), and they can be binary or vary in strength.

Networks are often depicted in graphical form (called a sociogram), but their analysis requires tabular representation (called a sociomatrix). Figure 13.2 shows a network for

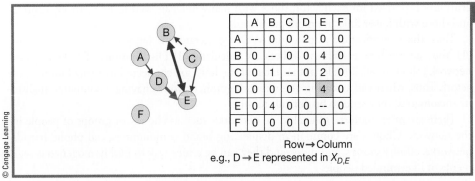

Figure 13.2

A Sociogram
and a
Sociomatrix

6 actors and its corresponding matrix data. There is a strong mutual link between actors B and E and a weak unidirectional link from C to B; F is isolated, and actors B, C, and E form a group. While the graphical depictions can be impressive for large networks, the information is converted to matrices for analysis.

13-2a Identifying Influentials

There are many kinds of influential voices in many industries—experts whose opinions can affect the preferences and purchase choices of many customers. For example, the wine connoisseur Robert Parker, who writes a weekly column in *BusinessWeek*, is trusted because he's objective and not beholden to the wine industry or any particular vintners; also queue up John Cleese's television show, "*Wine for the Confused.*" Similarly, *Vogue*'s September issue is an annual occasion, celebrating and influencing the fashion for the coming season (the issue is fatter than most of its models). Or consider Ted Allen, whose appearance on the Food Network influences food choices and presentations for family and socializing.

In network data, it is easy to identify influential parties. There is a natural intuition that in social networking sites, as in any social circle, some members are more connected and influential than others. Marketers would like to leverage these interpersonal group dynamics, ideally locating the highly connected influential members, to induce their trial of products, in turn initiating and propelling the diffusion process. To do so, network marketers study how actors are embedded in their network to locate those who are relatively central or in the thick of things. Centrality indices are computed for each actor in the network to describe the position of that actor relative to the others.

The easiest and most common way to characterize centrality is to count the number of connections each actor has with the others in the network (Figure 13.3). An index of degree

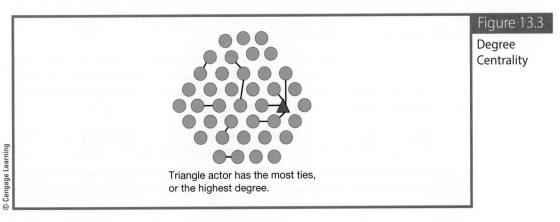

Figure 13.3

Degree
Centrality

Triangle actor has the most ties, or the highest degree.

centrality is derived for each actor; those with many links are said to be relatively central, and those with fewer links are more peripheral.

Thus, the identification of potential WOM-generators is fairly easy for two reasons: (1) You can see how easy these indices are calculate. (2) Distributions of links in most network follow an 80/20 rule, in that most of the links are connected to a small number of actors. Thus, when you're staring at a network graph, or you're having a computer analyze its sociomatrix, they tend to be difficult to miss.

There are other patterns to analyze in networks, such as cliques, or groups of people in the network. Cliques are common in delineating brand communities, cell phone friends networks, affinity groups, and more, and they can be a nice way to find homogeneous segments of like-minded people.

13-2b Recommendation Systems

Structural equivalence is another pattern sought when analyzing networks; two actors are said to be structurally equivalent if their links to others are the same (Figure 13.4). Structural equivalence is the logic underlying recommendation agents employed by big SKU-offering sites like Amazon. Two customers are essentially equivalent if their purchase patterns are similar; hence, whatever one buys, the other might also find appealing. Thus, a recommendation is made based on similarities between the SKUs bought by one customer compared with others.

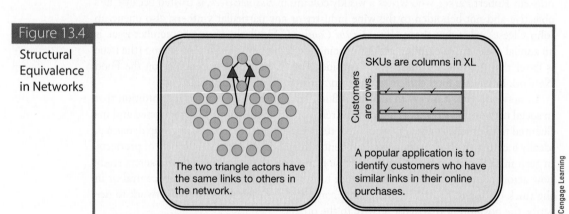

Figure 13.4

Structural Equivalence in Networks

The two triangle actors have the same links to others in the network.

SKUs are columns in XL

Customers are rows.

A popular application is to identify customers who have similar links in their online purchases.

© Cengage Learning

Recommendation systems are social in that the data of purchase patterns or ratings are aggregated over many people, but ultimately these endorsements come from strangers. Yet indeed, consumers trust online recommendations:

- When consumers read an endorsement in a chat room dedicated to a sport they follow or a health condition they are monitoring, they usually make the assumption that others who visit the website, reading and posting, are similar to themselves and hence have some credibility and relevance.

- When consumers read a rating of a book or piece of music online, they usually make the assumption that the majority of people can't be too far from wrong.

These scenarios share the fact that while the word of mouth originates with strangers, it nevertheless seems spontaneous and not paid for and therefore authentic in a manner not easily achieved in advertising.

Recommendation Agents

Recommendation agents are another form of CRM. Companies keep track of your purchases and then match you with other customers whose purchases have had some overlap with yours. The implication is that you and these other customers are probably in the same segment, with similar preferences. Thus, things they've bought and you haven't form the system's recommendations to you, and things you've bought but they have not are recommended to them.

Geek squad: How's it done? Imagine a huge spreadsheet with millions of customers as rows and hundreds of thousands of SKUs forming the columns. There's a "1" in a cell if that customer-row purchased that SKU-column. Otherwise, the database is mostly full of zeros. Cluster analyses are conducted in an iterative fashion: first clustering the rows (customers), then the columns (SKUs). When the clustering converges, there are segments of customers and purchase groups of products. Every customer in each segment can be sent a prompt recommending every SKU in the product grouping.

As you can see, social media seem to have exciting potential for marketing, social networks are fairly easy to track, and recommendation agents are a boon as a systematic means of cross-selling. What's the resistance? Many CEOs are conservative in spending money on something they can't understand, and many CEOs are old enough that they can't understand the attraction of social media. On the other hand, some companies are lead users; these brands have some 15–20mm Facebook fans each: Coca-Cola, Disney, MTV, Oreo, Red Bull, Skittles, Starbucks, and Victoria's Secret. Certainly most CEOs share a desire to know the ROI for social media. Never mind that marketers hadn't completely cracked the nut of being able to measure ROI for traditional media. It's a fair question to ask, so let's see.

13-3 SOCIAL MEDIA ROI, KPIS, AND WEB ANALYTICS

The question, "What's the ROI if we do this social media thing?" sounds eerily similar to the question posed some 20 years ago when companies asked, "Should we have a website? What can it do for us? How can we make money from it?" We know how that turned out, and for social media also, companies will figure out what makes the best sense for them.

As seen in the previous chapters on traditional media, we can begin to answer ROI questions only if we know the goal that the marketing action was intended to achieve. Once we know the goals, selecting the media and measures is rather straightforward. We'll assess whether resources have been well spent by comparing costs to measures intended to track the effectiveness of the investment.

Early on, social media held the allure that they looked to be nearly free. The approach is certainly less expensive than advertising via many kinds of traditional media. And perpetually there seems to be something that goes viral, yielding vast reach essentially for free, that fuels the hopes that marketing efforts will be extremely cost effective. But managers know now that marketing via social media is not free. At the least, their 24/7 maintenance requires thought and labor. Thus, when estimating ROI, the primary expenditures might not be media buys or explicit budgetary contributions, so much as salary equivalents of people's time allocations. In this sense, time is indeed money.

If the costs are mostly labor, what are the measures of effectiveness, or the key performance indicators (KPIs)? KPIs for social media are analogous to traditional measures for advertising effectiveness. Specifically, marketers are always interested in quantifying reach, frequency, monetary value of customers, customers' behaviors, attitudes, memory (recall, recognition), and so on. In social media, measures for these marketing goals simply take on slightly different forms.

13-3a Prepurchase: Awareness

Let's track the usual suspects for marketing goals. In the prepurchase phase, marketers want customers to be aware of their brand and consider their brand for purchase. Reach is a classic measure of the size of the audience that has been exposed to some brand information and who might therefore have some familiarity with the brand. Reach can be achieved via traditional media and measured via online capture, e.g., as in a magazine ad that tempts the reader to learn more by going online and landing at a particular page associated with the magazine source. Reach can also be achieved wholly online, as a function of ads on popular sites, purchased status on search engines, even via click-thrus on banner ads.

If we wish to enhance awareness, we seek media that optimize reach, ideally fitting our target audience, if possible. Tweets are fine. Facebook postings, contests to submit videos of user-proposed jingles on YouTube would all work. They're all brief and intended to be a bit more fun than informative. In contrast, lengthy expert blogs, webinars, podcasts, and such would remain untapped; the customer isn't ready for that detail.

If there is an existing customer base (i.e., for anything other than a brand new product), marketers can reward current customers with incentives to generate word of mouth. WOM in customer networks is very rewarding to firms because they are usually bringing in new acquisitions. Completely new customers are the most difficult for a company to find.

13-3b Prepurchase: Brand Consideration

Next, still in the prepurchase phase but moving on to getting customers to consider our brand, marketers want to offer more information to build customers' knowledge of the brand and more persuasion to make their opinions as favorable as possible. To do so, marketers need to use media that convey more content. Marketers pay for search engine ad placement, post some information teasers in related brand communities, and provide podcasts containing product information and customer testimonials. By comparison, brand consideration goals aren't achieved as readily by providing information on social networks—people use Facebook or MySpace to socialize or be entertained, not to conduct product research.

Many of the measures in this phase fall under the broad category of search engine optimization (SEO). When customers have a preferred brand, they can go directly to purchase sites. When they don't, they'll do a search. The search key words depend on where they are along the knowledge continuum. If they have heard of the brand, they will search the brand name to learn more about it; if they are vague about the brand name, they will search the product category to see the scope of competitors; and if they're even less familiar, they will search the general benefits they are seeking to see what products and specific brand names pop up.

To narrow the search for consumers, search engines used to measure the relevance of a website or an information page by counting the number of times the searched words appeared on that webpage or document. Unfortunately, this criterion of relevance was easily (and frequently) manipulated. The innovation of Google's Page Rank algorithm was to count the number of incoming links, weighted by the importance of the sending site. SEO gurus say there are two important paths to enhancing the likelihood that a brand pops to the top of the search results:

1. Put the most meaningful keywords in the Web page title (they're very important to SEO).

2. The order of those words also matters, so lead off with the most relevant words.

At the stage of brand consideration, several measures are prime Web analytics: frequencies, rates, or durations. Frequencies include the sheer number of visits and estimates of the number of unique visitors; that is, the second number is an attempt to remove the duplications from the first number. Even the second number has its limitations, however; e.g., imagine a couple trying to choose which car to buy next—both parties may visit several websites, from their home computers and from those at work (only during lunch, of course). That's at least four computers, even though the search is one.

Durations are usually measures of times spent per page, and overall time spent on the site. Rates include bounce rates; these are the percent of sessions for which a visitor lands on the website and needs only one page viewing to decide "I'm so out of here!" and click off the website altogether. Rates also include conversion rates—capturing when a visitor transitions from a looker to a doer, and we'll discuss those next.

13-3c Purchase or Behavioral Engagement

Ideally, customers are moving toward purchasing. However, just as any salesperson knows, a number of steps serve as precursors that nevertheless are hopeful signals of ultimate purchase. Thus, marketers speak of inducing any kind of action that begins to engage the prospective customer. For example, once customers visit a Web page:

- What do they open? What do they download?

- Do they watch demos that may be available?

- How much time are they spending on which purchase-related pages?

- Do they register to subscribe to newsletters?

- Do they sign up for RSS or other timely news sends?

Web analytics experts disdain the Contact Us buttons, instead recommending that a Web visitor has to fill out a form so the company can capture at least basic information on this customer and a possible sales opportunity.

Companies can provide exclusivity to Web visitors, e.g., preordering a product not yet available to others. Brand fans may be asked to post opinions and reviews. Sales promos may be made available from site visits or Tweeted out to followers. Customer service can unfold in real time, e.g., announcing flight cancellations as a courtesy or sending a map to a customer's phone who has clicked on a product online (or scanned a bar code in a store) to find the nearest retailer (who doesn't have a stock-out).

KPIs are pretty clean when measuring behaviors—they happen or they don't—it's not a gradual or subjective thing like "How positive is a customer's attitude toward my brand?" Thus, metrics include numbers of posts regarding the brand on blogs or social networks, audience build as measured by incoming links and the speed of that growth. Conversion rates are straightforward to compute. They consist of frequencies of Web visitors to engage in the focal behavior (purchase, sign up for e-mail distribution, etc.) relative to the number of visitors who come to the website. That is, the rates compare the desired outcomes to the number of visits or to the number of unique visitors.

It should be coming clearer how easy ROI will be to compute. Costs of the actions depend on the marketing goals: estimates of acquisition costs, payment for placement in search engines or banner ads, sending e-mails from a rented address database, etc. On the KPIs side, the effectiveness of those actions can be assessed by these frequencies, rates, and durations. Web analysts track the number of visitors coming via different routes, and they follow the customers' traversal to the particular engagement behavior of interest.

13-3d Postpurchase

The wise companies care about their customers long after the purchase. The online environment offers more direct data about what happens postpurchase than we've had thus far IRL. If customers are satisfied, they may post positive reviews. If they're ecstatic, they may post extremely happy endorsements. The company may wish to reward these so-called brand evangelists (or brand ambassadors or brand advocates).

If the customers are unhappy, the company can at least read the nature of the complaint and work to address it. Companies can intervene to try for service recovery, bringing the customer back on board. Even grumbling customers respond to incentives; company apologies, problem solutions, and restorative benefits can help in retention, preventing customer defections, and turning a bad situation around.

In the same way that the marketing media activity differs slightly from pre- to postpurchase, they will also vary over a product's life cycle. It is not unusual for blogs, wikis, lead user communities to be essential during product development and generating enthusiasm in the marketplace prior to launch. Webinars might then pick up the product introduction. Networks might capture troubleshooting issues that the company's customer support can readily handle.

What's especially fun about this day and age is the enormity of the data to play with—all of which are captured easily and tracked in some form of dashboard. Then the analytics are up to you: Do you want your data compared geographically, e.g., state by state, or by time zone? Do you want to watch performance over time, e.g., the number of brand share mentions today compared to yesterday, this quarter vs. last, this week vs. prior to the ad banner launch, etc.? What can be done is limited only by your strategic creativity.

13-3e How to Proceed?

Anything that is new and anything that is growing as quickly as social media tends to throw managers for a loop. Where do we begin? It's true; there are many social media, and the choice of an initial medium can be difficult. Social media can be so exciting that managers believe they must engage via all possible channels. This goal is obviously impossible and also not desirable. As we have seen, some media fit some marketing goals better than others. In addition, some media fit the target market better than others; tweeting about twofer drinks at a popular bar works for 20-year-olds, but not 60-year-olds. In addition, being selective about the social medium is important because they do require maintenance and constant activity; otherwise, followers lose interest. Trying to keep current on many media would keep the marketer spinning.

It's true that the explosion of media is great for consumers but more challenging for marketers. Even prior to social media, marketing decisions about how to allocate advertising budgets were complicated, as marketers tried to find attractive viewer profiles. Resource allocation decisions have become more complex than ever.

What Are Companies Doing?

- Health care:
  - Mayo Clinic has a news blog, a YouTube channel, and a Facebook page.
  - Merck supports a physician portal.
- Munchies:
  - Doritos solicited ideas for new flavors via videos.
  - Domino's Pizza attracted customers to try a new recipe.
- Miscellaneous:
  - UPS recruits drivers.
  - Threadless T-shirts, with its slogan "Nude No More," hosts online design contests for cash and the chance to see their creation produced and sold.

Yet, with the right attitude, marketers can embrace social media as heartily as many of their customers have, once they see the potential in doing so. Word-of-mouth conversations or other customer-to-customer information flows have become a rich new source of consumer insights. Marketing researchers learn a lot from lurking or Web crawling and scraping:

- Tweets, blogs, discussion forums are monitored to make predictions about new product launches more accurate. A great deal of data results from categories with many releases, such as music, books, or movies.

- Marketers use text analyses on Facebook to get a read on customer opinions about their brands. These comments may be on the brand's own Facebook page, or they may come from an easy search of the brand name throughout other, seemingly unrelated postings.

- Beyond the brand itself, content analysis has been useful in detecting developing consumer trends. Posted musings give insights into what people consider important. What are people talking about? What do people care about?

- Brand managers check websites for misinformation, to try to nip bad grassroots PR in the bud.

In addition to passive listening, marketers can actively create interventions:

- Marketers enter online communities and ask for (paid) volunteers to be user groups to beta-test products and offer feedback. Online lead users are easy to find.

- Marketers conduct experiments. In the so-called A/B split tests, one group is exposed to one ad or new product description or whatever element of the marketing mix the marketer is testing. The other group is either a control group, or they see a different version of an ad, new product description, etc. The marketer then compares brand attitudes or subsequent sales in test markets to detect some lift due to the marketing intervention.

- More complex experiments are obviously possible also. A company may wish to measure comparative click-through rates, or member sign-up rates, or purchase

Wiki

Wikipedia itself says that "*wiki*" means "fast" in Hawaiian. Mahalo.
   Other fun wikis:

- *wiktionary.org:* A collaborative, multilingual dictionary
- *shopwiki.org:* Guides and suggestions in many product categories
- *wikiquote.org:* For your upcoming presentation

How to Do It?

In a recent white paper, McKinsey suggested that managers need several key abilities to use social media wisely.

- First, any content uploaded and posted must be compelling, necessitating skills like an excellent screenwriter and director. What is posted must also be professional-looking, which requires the production values of a good film editor.
- Second, social media must always be managed with an eye toward the goal of business functions and business outcomes. The firm is relatively formal in structure, at least compared to the social media dialogs, but the latter must continue to reflect the goals of the former. In addition, while the immediate goal of social media may not be a purchase, that goal is of primary importance to the enterprise.
- Third, social media must be coordinated across channels of marketing activity. Doing so may put the social media person into roles as varied as teaching older, less savvy colleagues about the utility of social media and how each is best utilized, to advising to and contracting from colleagues who are responsible for other, traditional marketing communications purchases and implementation.

   Marketing researchers were trying to determine which brands played well on Facebook and why. They found the following:

- Facebook users often profiled hedonic activities, those that are fun or adventurous, or their participation in volunteerism. The particular activities tended to be golf, tennis, wine class, cooking class, shopping, fund-raisers, and mission trips. The brands that tended to be featured were Callaway golf clubs, William Sonoma, Polo, Brooks Brothers, Saks Fifth Avenue, Chanel, Chateau Margaux, Red Cross, and the American Cancer Society.
- Users also profiled their personal interests and goals, such as eating right, exercising, going to the movies, socializing with friends, and traveling. The brands they found in these categories of mentions included brands like Nabisco 100-calorie snacks, Nike, Star Wars, Starbucks, Whoopsie Daisy Designs, Hampton Inns.
- See "Consumers' Use of Brands to Reflect Their Actual and Ideal Selves on Facebook," by Hollenbeck and Kaikati, in the *International Journal of Research in Marketing* (29: 395–405).

   Finally, everyone advises being authentic, i.e., don't sound like a script. (See Kerpen's *Likeable Social Media*.)

valuation, as a function of whether the ad appeal is more rational or emotional, whether video or script endorsements are featured, which price is posted, and whether a discount is available, etc.

- GPS data function much like live cookies, storing information for your convenience upon return (and still protecting your privacy). The purpose of GPS units in phones was originally consumer service for mapping (e.g., "How do I get where I want to go from here?" Or, "Where is my 15-year-old daughter [and her phone]?"). GPS units are becoming georetailing units, and they will soon offer extremely timely (intrusive) opportunities for marketers. A motivated company will know where its customers are at all times. The company's claim will be, "When you walk near my product, I can send you a promo."

Finally, if it still seems overwhelming, many companies are willing to help. They can help collect data, store it, provide simple but quick—indeed nearly instantaneous—analyses, help you figure out what to measure, etc. Two big brand providers in the market space are Google and Omniture (with Adobe), but many other software providers exist purporting to do the same, e.g., see the software tab at toptenreviews.com.

In general, social media pundits advise that any corporate postings or representations have to start by being interesting; otherwise, they won't even be read. The content needs to be honest, not defensive, and not too corporate. There needs to be transparency for customers, employees, stakeholders, where transparency usually means honesty, building trust, and opportunities for two-way dialog. Social media have sufficient variety and prevalence that they can be a tremendous marketing tool—if the company can offer something that provides value to those customers and reaches them in a way that matters to them.

Managerial Recap

Social media offer abundant opportunities for marketers. Word of mouth feels objective and authentic to consumers, compared to advertising, and that makes social networks an important and provocative channel.

- Social media are a Web-based means of interacting with friends and strangers by posting opinions, pictures, and videos.
- Social networks are the structures of interconnections among customers that propagate word of mouth. Networks can be drawn and analyzed, and the actors measured on indices of centrality to assist the marketer in finding opinion leaders and influential consumers.
- Social media ROI and KPIs can be computed with the help of online analytics, as for any marketing effort, once the marketing goals are understood.

Chapter Outline in Key Terms and Concepts

1. What are social media?
   a. Types of social media
   b. Word of mouth
2. What are social networks?
   a. Identifying influentials
   b. Recommendation systems
3. Social media ROI, KPIs, and Web analytics
   a. Prepurchase: awareness
   b. Prepurchase: brand consideration
   c. Purchase or behavioral engagement
   d. Postpurchase
   e. How to proceed?

Chapter Discussion Questions

1. What would you do to enhance the chances that a video you post will go viral?

2. Do you post personal photos or videos on your Facebook page? What do you think about companies that research their job candidates' Facebook pages before hiring them?

3. What would you do if you found out that a colleague had posted your slides to a recent presentation on a public slide-sharing platform? How do you define intellectual property rights? When is something yours?

4. Do you ever read product recommendations before buying? You don't know these people. How do you discern which ones to believe? What cues do you use to figure out who knows what they're talking about?

5. Choose a program from the reality TV genre. How is it that a person with no apparent talent becomes famous? Are these societal mechanisms a good thing or a bad thing?

Mini-Case

Google's Page Rank

Google's Page Rank is an algorithm that attempts to inform you where people are coming from when they land on your website and which are the most frequent sources. Note that, as its name suggests, a page rank is an index estimated page by page. It's not an overall website assessment.

Nevertheless, say you're trying to determine the rank of your home page, you figure that's a good start and customers can navigate more precisely once they're in your domain. The ranking model begins by checking all the incoming links to the home page over some given duration (say the last 24 hours or the last week, depending on the site traffic and the extent to which the information must be current). Customers can land on the home page starting from many links, and those links generating traffic to you differ in their importance. In particular, those incoming pages are differentially influential, as weighted by two factors: (1) What is the page rank of the source link (higher is better)? (2) How many outbound links does that source page contain (a lower number is better, in that the link to your home page is therefore more selective)? Thus, if page A contains a link to your home page and has a high page rank of its own and relatively few outreaching links, it carries more weight than page B that has lower page rank and more outreach links.

This algorithm is obviously iterative because we need to estimate the ranks of pages A and B, before we can bring them into the estimation of the rank for your home page. In theory, the iterations could continue ad infinitum. In the actual algorithm, there are starting values, and about 100 iterations bring most estimates to the convergent approximation. Finally, Google then exercises the universal modeling prerogative of also including a term for wiggle room or a fudge factor.

Mini-Case Discussion Questions

1. How would you describe this algorithm in network terms? Would you use the same network principles if you were to design a competing algorithm?

2. Critics say this method doesn't account for the fact that many websites are not managed well—they might not be updated, links might not work, etc. How would you improve upon this algorithm to address these concerns?

Video Exercise: *RogueSheep* (5:59)

RogueSheep is a software development company formed by a group of people who have had considerable experience in developing software for the Macintosh computer. When Apple came out with the iPhone, this group's experience translated directly into developing applications for this smartphone. One such application is Postage, an idea that was conceived when two members of the group were traveling on business and one of them wanted to send his wife a postcard. Postage is a digital postcard application that preserves the sense of a real postcard through a computer. Recognizing that success—and business profitability—depends more on the execution of an idea than on its generation, RogueSheep continually seeks to expand usage of its Postage app. The company keeps Postage fresh by adding new designs and content, which are automatically signaled to users who have already downloaded the app. Other promotional methods include partnering with other businesses to develop themed postcards that also can promote those businesses, providing free app downloads to a certain number of customers, and getting Apple interested in the app.

Video Discussion Questions

1. Social media can be described with three properties: (a) very rich, vivid sensory experiences versus relatively simple, even impoverished sensory experiences; (b) primarily social in nature vs. more industrious goals; and (c) commercial versus noncommercial. How would you describe Rogue Sheep's Postage application in terms of these three social media properties?

2. What segment of the population do you think might be most likely to become avid users of the Postcard application? Explain your answer.

3. Rogue Sheep's Postage application contains various postcard themes. How can the volume of digital postcard traffic on these different themes help Rogue Sheep to identify different groups (or network cliques) that may be viable target markets for given products or services?

PART 4

Positioning: Assessment
Through the Customer
Lens

Chapter 14

Customer
Relationships

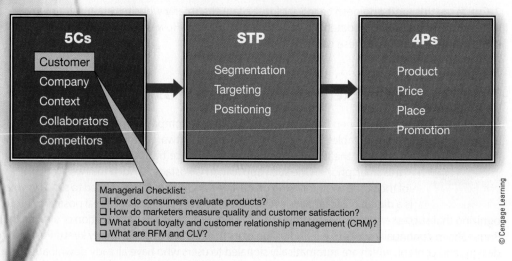

5Cs	STP	4Ps
Customer	Segmentation	Product
Company	Targeting	Price
Context	Positioning	Place
Collaborators		Promotion
Competitors		

Managerial Checklist:
❑ How do consumers evaluate products?
❑ How do marketers measure quality and customer satisfaction?
❑ What about loyalty and customer relationship management (CRM)?
❑ What are RFM and CLV?

© Cengage Learning

Marketing Management Framework

14-1 WHAT ARE CUSTOMER EVALUATIONS, AND WHY ARE THEY IMPORTANT?

Marketers are interested in their customers' assessment of how their company is doing. Customer evaluations come in many forms: customer satisfaction, perceptions of quality, customers' intentions to repurchase the same brand or from the same provider, the likelihood that a customer will generate word of mouth, speaking favorably to friends and family and coworkers, etc. In this chapter, we'll see how customers' evaluative judgments are formed.

Marketers don't track customer evaluations just because they're interesting. Marketers know that satisfied customers contribute to the bottom line. Given the hierarchy of customer behavior, from awareness to trial to repeat and loyalty, the hope is to satisfy new customers so that they become loyal. Truly loyal customers love the brand, purchase frequently, are zealous in telling others about it, and are even willing to pay more for the brand and all it means to them. In this chapter, we'll look at customer evaluations and see how it translates to customer relationship management (CRM) and customer lifetime value (CLV).

14-2 HOW DO CONSUMERS EVALUATE PRODUCTS?

When you buy something—whether it's toothpaste or athletic shoes, a travel package or dental services—marketers think that you evaluate the goodness of the purchase against some sort of expectations. This comparative evaluation process is depicted in Figure 14.1. There are three possible outcomes:

1. If customers' experiences surpass their expectations ➔ customers are delighted!
2. If customers' experiences meet their expectations ➔ customers are satisfied.
3. If customers' experiences fall short of their expectations ➔ customers are dissatisfied.

This comparative model is intuitively appealing, and it has captured the minds of marketers, as evidenced by the many ads which state, "We wish to exceed our customers' expectations."

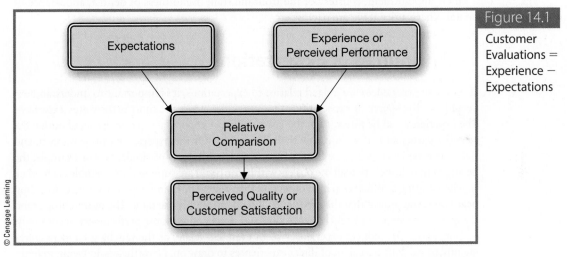

Figure 14.1

Customer Evaluations = Experience − Expectations

© Cengage Learning

The comparative evaluation process is thought to operate whether the purchase is low or high involvement. For the *low-involvement* purchase, such as a routine repurchase of your habitual brand of toothpaste, the process may be nearly instantaneous and equally quickly forgotten. Even so, when you got the toothpaste home, if it was somehow different (e.g., it cost more (or less), or the packaging looked different, or the taste seemed extra minty), it would prompt you to think about your toothpaste more than you normally do. Your expectations for toothpaste are usually latent (i.e., you don't obsess over your toothpaste attributes normally), but those expectations would now become more explicit as you think about whether you like the toothpaste that you just used that seems different. Your expectations, while normally tucked away, come to the forefront and serve as the basis for the comparison.

For *higher-involvement* purchases, the comparison process is typically quite deliberative and conscious. These are purchases someone cares a lot about or those that are more expensive or complicated. For example, brands of athletic shoes have some very loyal segments of customers because in our society, the shoes aren't just shoes; they're a means of self-expression. Athletes purchase the shoes because they want high performance, whereas fashionistas seek attractive styles. Each segment thinks about the purchase and holds certain expectations, and the shoes need to hold up to those expectations.

The comparison of a purchase to expectations is also thought to occur whether the item purchased is comprised primarily of search, experience, or credence characteristics. As discussed briefly in Chapter 6, for *search* goods, such as the athletic shoes, more of the qualities sought are obvious from visual examination, objective, and concrete, e.g., the color, size, style, price, and the evaluation process is thought to be straightforward (e.g., a holistic, or attribute-by-attribute comparisons to expectations perhaps weighted by attribute importance).

For *experiential* purchases, such as the purchase of a travel package, where the evaluation cannot be completed until there is some trial or consumption, marketers acknowledge that prior to purchase, expectations might not be fully formed. The experience itself simultaneously shapes the evaluation as well as the expectations. For example, a customer might hold rather generic hotel expectations when checking in, but when they check out, they might muse, "Gee, the pool near the hotel could have been nicer." This process is referred to as constructing counterfactuals (on the spot, you think of how things might be different). Many purchases have these kinds of experiential elements.

Finally, expectations also form a basis for comparison in *credence* purchases, such as dental services or many professional services. Most consumers don't have the expertise to evaluate their dentist's abilities, so we instead evaluate what we can, e.g., the ability to book a timely appointment, courtesy of the frontline staff, friendliness of dentist, appearance of dental offices, price if we are paying, etc.

14-2a Sources of Expectations

If purchase experiences are judged relative to expectations, it is important to understand expectations. The source of expectations that consumers trust the most is their *own experience*. The experience can be direct, as in the last time they shopped at a particular retail outlet, the visited a particular coffee shop, saw their dentist, etc. Or the experience can be indirect, and then the experiences we draw from range along a continuum of similarity. For example, the beauty of franchises is that all the outlets within the chain are supposed to resemble each other, so when visiting a coffee shop in another city that shares the brand of your favorite coffee shop near home, you project that the experience should be roughly the same. The overarching brand is supposed to lend consistent expectations, and we benchmark the performance accordingly.

Sometimes the indirect experiences seem even less relate, or the purchase happens infrequently, so we don't have a lot of direct experiences to draw on. Nevertheless, in trying to function as quasirational beings, we draw from what we can. For example, in the first-time visit to a realtor, most new home buyers don't know what to expect, but they might think, "It'll probably be something like dealing with a bank account manager and a salesperson." So their expectations are extrapolated from a general category of past experiences with professional service providers.

If we have little personal expertise on which to make brand choices, our next favorite and trusted source of information is our friends. We seek people whose judgments we trust. Our friends usually have somewhat similar value systems and often similar preference structures, and they have no commercial gain in expressing an opinion for one brand over another. Sometimes we seek opinions from people who are experts, perhaps coworkers, who are not as close to us as friends, but they are people we acknowledge as having more information than we do about the category we're about to enter. And as seen in Chapter 13, social media are exerting a good deal of influence on customers' behaviors.

The third class of information that contributes to our expectations is any *marketing mix* element originating from the company, including positioning claims made in advertising, suggestions of quality inferred from the price point, or the frequency of sales and coupons—inferences we draw from the exclusivity (or not) of the distribution outlets in which the merchandise is available, product performance descriptions from retail sales-people, and so on. This class of information is tricky: It is simultaneously usually the most detailed and in many ways more objective than our subjective personal experiences or those of our friends. Yet consumers trust this source of information the least because they expect the company to be biased; i.e., of course, it will say good things about its products.

Finally, third-party communications help consumers form expectations. Customers can get ideas from movies and television, books, the Internet, *Consumer Reports*, and other third-party objective rater services about quality and value and how service procedures are supposed to unfold. The bad news for the marketer is that these sources of information are usually beyond their control. However, that neutrality is also why this information seems especially valid and objective to customers.

14-2b **Expectation and Experience**

Next, let's examine the nature of experiences. In particular, marketers have found that cus-tomers routinely evaluate the *core* of the purchase itself (e.g., reliable performance, tangible cues to quality including the appearances of the facilities, the employees, the firm's com-munications materials), and, when applicable, the interpersonal aspects of *service* that may surround the purchase (e.g., a front line that is responsive and able to offer personalized attention to a customer's unique needs, employees who seem competent in their knowledge of the organization, and employees who express empathy and who are courteous).

What's interesting is that both the core components (e.g., dinner at a nice restaurant) and the peripheral, value-added supplemental components (e.g., the service or wait time at the restaurant) contribute to customer satisfaction and dissatisfaction, but in slightly differ-ent ways. Specifically, if the core is good, it doesn't enhance satisfaction much because it was anticipated to be good; it should be good, and the customer expects any provider to be able to meet this commodity-like requirement. But if the core is bad, it can affect dissatisfaction. For example, if dinner at the restaurant (the core) was not good, the customer can be dis-satisfied, but the place doesn't get points if the dinner was good. By comparison, the supple-mental services can affect satisfaction or dissatisfaction. If the dinner is fine but the service is extra great or extra bad, even though it's not as important, it affects the customer's judgment.

Just FYI, this distinction is analogous to that between so-called hygiene and motivating factors. Hygiene attributes or goods or services are the must-have features (so if they're missing, customers are dissatisfied). For example, a hotel room should be clean; if it's not, the customer would be dissatisfied. At the same time, if it is clean, the hotel chain doesn't get brownie points toward customer satisfaction because it didn't do anything unusually good. Motivating factors are those that that can show the company is going above and beyond (customer expectations), thereby enhancing customer satisfaction. For example, a mint on the pillow before retiring is not expected, so that extra touch contributes to sat-isfaction. Note that if the mint had been missing, it wouldn't contribute to dissatisfaction.

It is also important to know that customers evaluate companies and brands based on every data point they see, every so-called moment of truth or point of interaction between the com-pany and the customer, from the search effort (online or trying to find a retailer's address while driving) to the shopping experience, apparent quality of the purchase, its price, the checkout process, etc. To gain a better understand of all that makes up the customer experience, mar-keters have suggested mapping the shopping experience as a flowchart (as you learned in ops). Doing so forces one to be explicit in depicting, from beginning to end, the myriad interactions between the customer and company. A flowchart allows us to understand the company from the eyes of the consumer and makes us understand what corporate elements must be in place to support the front line in their attempts to provide superior service. Flowcharts have been used to generate quality measures at each stage (e.g., "We answer 95% our calls within 2 rings"), identify pressure points of likely repeated problems (e.g., queues, inefficiencies), and suggest system redesigns to streamline and make more efficient for both customers and employees.

As difficult as it seems to some companies to satisfy customers, the good news is that most customers' expectations aren't terribly unrealistic (e.g., customers expect hotel rooms to be clean, safe, and ready at check-in). Marketers talk of three kinds of expectations: *ideal* levels of quality, *predicted* or expected levels of quality, and levels of quality that are merely *adequate*. Some customer segments are demanding, but for most purchases, most segments have an average predicted level of quality as their expectation marker. The wiggle room between the low, adequate level of expectations, and somewhere slightly exceeding the middle predicted levels of expectations is referred to as a "zone of tolerance," a range of performance that would be deemed acceptable in the eyes of the customer.

Expectations depend on price or, more generally, any cost incurred to the buyer (e.g., having to drive farther for a sale, engage in a more protracted search online, etc.), and, as a result, some marketers would say that firms should seek to enhance not customer satisfaction but rather customers' perceptions of value. *Value* is defined as the trade-off between the quality of the purchase received and the price paid and other costs incurred. For example, we all would agree that a consumer has a right to have higher expectations of performance when buying a brand new Ferrari compared to another consumer who is just buying a beater for their 15-year-old kid to learn to drive.

Expectations are dynamic, and the purchase experience that pleased a customer last year may no longer suffice this year. Marketers lament this what-have-you-done-for-me-lately attitude among customers, but it's a phenomenon for every industry.

Expectations also vary cross-culturally, as when defining good value or beautiful design. Marketers have also found that individualistic cultures, in which personal success and achievement are valued (e.g., the U.S., Europe) are more likely to be satisfied when the quality of reliability and service provider responsiveness are strong. Customers in collectivistic cultures, in which social ties are highly valued (e.g., Asian, Latin American countries), appreciate the relational aspects of frontline employees (e.g., assurance and empathy). Different cultures even expect different things from websites—their appearance and information provided. As a result, rolling out products to new customers in new markets should be done thoughtfully (e.g., beginning with conducting local marketing research).

14-3 HOW DO MARKETERS MEASURE QUALITY AND CUSTOMER SATISFACTION?

Manufacturers have gone through the total quality era, with programs such as 6sigma (i.e., only 3 or 4 errorful parts per million produced) or ISO9000 compliance, and marketers are facing an even tougher challenge. How can we measure customers' perceptions of quality and satisfaction and expect such precision? The answer is simple. We can't.

There are occasionally objective measures of quality, such as the risk a passenger incurs by flying a particular airline carrier, based on ratios of the number of accidents to numbers of passengers safely served. However, rarely can we set precise measures of quality standards and expect to conform. For example, a cereal manufacturer can decide, "I want 10.2 ounces of cornflakes in each box—no more and no less. I don't want more flakes to go in the box

Anatomy of a Customer Satisfaction Survey

1st Screen (or Page), brief intro:
- Promise confidentiality.
- Promise not to sell data.
- Say their opinion matters.

2nd Screen:
- Get more detail on focal attributes.

http://www.ourhotel.com/survey2.html

Restaurant	1	2	3	4	5
High-quality food:	❑	❑	❑	❑	❑
Good selection:	❑	❑	❑	❑	❑
Reasonable prices:	❑	❑	❑	❑	❑
Not too crowded:	❑	❑	❑	❑	❑
Friendly service:	❑	❑	❑	❑	❑
In-room entertainment	1	2	3	4	5
Good selection:	❑	❑	❑	❑	❑
Reasonable prices:	❑	❑	❑	❑	❑
Fast download:	❑	❑	❑	❑	❑
Website	1	2	3	4	5
Easy booking:	❑	❑	❑	❑	❑
Good availability:	❑	❑	❑	❑	❑

◀ Previous page   Next page ▶

http://www.ourhotel.com/survey1.html

We're Interested in Your Opinions!

Please help us improve our service to you! We will not sell your information and we will keep your responses confidential.

Reflecting on your most recent stay at our hotel, how satisfied were you, overall?

Extremely dissatisfied	1	2	3	4	5	Extremely satisfied
	❑	❑	❑	❑		

Specifically, how satisfied were you with:

Extremely dissatisfied	1	2	3	4	5	Extremely satisfied
Check-in	❑	❑	❑	❑	❑	
In-room entertainment	❑	❑	❑	❑	❑	
Restaurant	❑	❑	❑	❑		
Meeting rooms	❑	❑	❑	❑		
Value for price	❑	❑	❑	❑		

Next page ▶

Progress bar 33% complete Page 1 of 3.

3rd Screen: Demographics go at the end.

Always include at least one open-ended question.

http://www.ourhotel.com/survey3.html

Gender		Age	
❑	Male	❑	18-29
❑	Female	❑	30-49
		❑	50-64
		❑	65+
Education		**Household income**	
❑	Some high school	❑	< $30,000
❑	High school graduate	❑	$30,001- $49,999
❑	Some college	❑	$50,000- $74,999
❑	College grad or more	❑	$75,000 +

Is there anything else you wish to tell us?

|

Send

◀ Previous page

Be nice!   Thank you for your time!

because in the end we'd lose money. I don't want less because I want my customers to be happy." Precluding a glitch in the machine, each box will have 10.2 oz of cornflakes. Now imagine creating a comparable standard for much of marketing: "I want my ad to be seen by 10.2 million viewers; I want my revenue-sharing offer to incent cooperation from 75% of my suppliers." It's not clear how we could measure these achievements, and it's not clear that human beings are capable of such standardized and perfectly consistent behavior.

Satisfaction?

- Quality and satisfaction are not the same thing. For example, experts may create excellent technology, but if the customer doesn't get it, the customer will be dissatisfied. Conversely, some product may lack bells and whistles, yet customers may be perfectly happy with it (perhaps due to its simplicity).
- Customers' expectations are a basis of comparison to judge their levels of satisfaction. They come from customers' own experience, their friends' advice, and companies' marketing information.
- Luckily, most customers are pretty realistic. They seek reliability, tangible cues such as retail appearance and price, service that is responsive and ideally customized, competent, and empathetic.
- If a purchase or service encounter goes badly, what disturbs customers most? (1) Frontline people were incompetent or rude. (2) The initial complaint wasn't handled well, heaping insult upon injury. (3) The purchase was too expensive.
- When customers are dissatisfied, what do they do? They (1) switch brands and/or (2) complain to friends. Few dissatisfied customers complain directly to the company because (1) they figure it won't make any difference, (2) it's not worth their time or effort, (3) they couldn't figure out where to go to complain.
- If the purchase or service encounter has gone badly, the state of the art in recovery is three simple steps: (1) Empathize with the customer. (2) Compensate for the mistake. (3) Give the customer some sort of freebie.
- Companies can also enhance satisfaction and subsequent chances of loyalty if they simply tried to solve the customers' service problems, such as no one wants to have to re-explain an issue to multiple sales reps; no one wants to have to switch from the Web to the phone and back; no one wants to give a company heads-up about a problem more than once. (see HBR's "Stop Trying to Delight Your Customers," by Dixon, Freeman, and Toman.)
- When things are going well, that's great, right? Life is always more complicated. There's a paradox in success. As customer satisfaction results in more sales, the segment of buyers gets larger. By definition, a larger segment is more heterogeneous, and it is difficult to please all customers with a single market offering, which is why marketers segment in the first place. A larger market share, with more customer differences in expectations and experiences, can then result in customer dissatisfaction. If this happens, resegment, launch another product line, repeat.
- Contrary to the age-old mantra, we know that customers are not always right. Yet right or wrong, they often have big mouths, e.g., via blogging. Lots of consumers express customer dissatisfaction through social media, but over 90% of companies polled said they don't gather customer feedback through these channels. It's human nature not to want to hear negative feedback, but if the company doesn't facilitate hearing it, then customers can leave and switch brands. Social media, even complaints, are a source of good info (see research by quirks.com). Use the information to see if something can be fixed or whether the brand has not found the right customer segment.
- Finally, don't be surprised if customer satisfaction hinges on, or they complain about, the so-called little things. Consider, for example, that customers come to a dentist or a lawyer or a consultant or a medical

clinic because they need the professional's expertise. Customers assume the professional will be proficient and charge fair prices. Yet most customers are incapable of judging either. What customers can understand, however, is how the waiting area compares to other similar services, whether the receptionist was helpful and friendly, and whether the professional's demeanor seemed competent, engaged, and approachable. If they're having a bad day and being rude, it affects the customer's opinions about you! So be selective in hiring your receptionists, and pay them well. They are essential to a client's first impressions. Those little things loom large in customer evaluations in part because they cannot judge the pro's core proficiencies.

Surveys are ideal instruments to obtain customers' perceptions. Critics may wish we had 10.2 oz of cornflakes standards and complain that we seek softer numbers, like "90% of our customers check the 'top two' boxes" (satisfied and very satisfied)." Yet consider what we'll do with the numbers; our ratings data would be no more subjective than those of our competitors or than our numbers from a comparable survey conducted last quarter, etc. So while these may be imperfect measures, the numbers nevertheless allow us to gauge our performance relative to benchmarks (past or competitive performance).

Marketers have made peace with the fact that the numbers represent customers' perceptions; that is no longer the issue. But there's a popular management adage, "If you can't measure it, you can't manage it." So marketers want customer data.

Some marketing gurus claim that just one or two indices can reflect the overall health of an organization. However, survey results are more actionable if they measure multiple facets of the customers' thoughts about the firm. Look at it this way: If everything is going well, you can have one or many indices, but if things aren't going well and marketing managers are trying to assess and improve performance, they need more information.

For example, say a department store just received its annual "Happy Stats" but found, to its dismay, the customer satisfaction score dropped from last year. The store was able to glean more diagnostic information from the survey because it had been structured to cover several contributing factors. The scores on the questions about the store's prices and the quality of the staff were stable from last year, but there were drops in kitchenware and children's clothing regarding their assortment selections. The store could make a decision to pull out of one of these lines of businesses, but customers would be happier if these areas were more fully stocked. In other words, a managerial decision has to be made, but at least the data are clear and helpful.

In terms of customer dissatisfaction, when things go wrong, research suggests that the primary means to regaining the customer is through an empowered frontline employee. That employee needs to be capable of immediately redressing the problem, empathizing with the customer, and offering a perk for the customer's troubles. We worry about recovery because if customers are dissatisfied, they can go to the competition or drop out of the category altogether. Instead, as we consider in the section that follows, marketers seek customer retention and long-term relationships with customers, at least the ones we find to be valuable.

14-4 LOYALTY AND CUSTOMER RELATIONSHIP MANAGEMENT (CRM)

Customer satisfaction isn't a goal in itself. Companies are in business to make money. You could perhaps be a monopoly and make money even with unhappy customers, but most industries attract competition, so your sole provider status won't sustain for long. Plus, who

Ethics

Customer Ethics: There's always a segment of customers with whom we do not want to encourage relationships. For example, companies like Nordstrom's and L.L. Bean have had to scale back their formerly generous return policies because customers had taken advantage of them. And in a somewhat backward form of CRM, companies like Walmart and Home Depot flag customers who return 3 or more things in 2 months.

Company Ethics: From a company's perspective, how do we determine fair prices? Econ tells us that a market agreement will be met where supply and demand curves cross. (Oh, that helps.) Do customers understand sellers' costs, when providing, say, wireless phone service or health care? If buyers and sellers are both looking out for their own interests, how often or how easily could they arrive at a price they both considered to be fair? Finally, marketers want something more than a onetime sales transaction. Marketers seek long-term relationship with customers. How does that modify the definition of fair?

really wants to be in business with unhappy customers? Companies and employees, from CEO to frontline workers, take pride in providing good products to customers, and they enjoy having customers who appreciate them and want to return, customers who are enthusiastic about their brands and who tell their friends about their good experiences with the company and its products.

In addition, we need to push beyond customer satisfaction. Many measures capture customer evaluations from opinions such as preference, or satisfaction, or purchase intentions. We want to see positive reinforcing behaviors such as repeat purchasing and customers generating word of mouth. In addition, for true loyalty, we want to see customers who have positive attitudes toward the company or brand, not just repeat purchases.

If marketers want to be taken seriously and have input at the executive C-level, they need to translate these marketing metrics into money metrics to impress the finance guys. A popular means of attaching a financial value to a customer is via the assessment of lifetime customer value, per customer or at least per segment.

Customer satisfaction is thought to be the first step in a longer-term relationship. Early, primitive efforts at customer relationship marketing (CRM) were frequently driven by price discounts, reasoning that a company could buy a little loyalty by locking in their customers (e.g., "Buy 9 coffees, get the 10th free"). There are certainly debates (e.g., is it true loyalty or is it merely inertia or ingrained purchasing habits, or how do we keep the members of loyalty programs separated from the nonloyal segment of customers?), but the bottom line is that loyalty programs can keep customers from defecting, as well as induce additional purchasing.

Recently, the loyalty pendulum has swung in the opposite direction, with companies charging their loyal customers more, figuring that the loyals like the brand so much that they're price insensitive. It's not unusual, for example, for companies to entice new customers with special deals, while not rewarding current customers with comparable promotions. These extremes are just another indicator of how frequently price is used as a knee-jerk lever. But just because price is easy to change doesn't mean it's the best element in the marketing mix to change. And whether the loyals pay more or are rewarded with lower costs or more benefits, plenty of research supports the clear tie between satisfied returning customers and bottom-line corporate financials.

14-4a Recency, Frequency, and Monetary Value (RFM)

A loyalty program invites customers to become members to enjoy certain benefits for frequent or heavy purchasing, and a CRM (customer relationship management) program is a tool in the company that tracks spending, regardless of whether customers are segmented into loyals or disloyals and rewarded or not. CRM systems collect customer identification and contact information, and some form of RFM, that is, information on the Recency, Frequency, and Monetary values of the customers' purchase history.

Figure 14.2 represents these three dimensions as a cube, and the most desirable customers, e.g., those we might wish to send premium offerings via e-mail direct marketing efforts, are those in the "recent/frequent/high value" area of the cube. Traditionally, these three factors comprise the key ingredients to "scoring models." To find the most desirable customers, the RFM behaviors are recorded, coded, and weighted using expert systems judgments of the importance of each component.

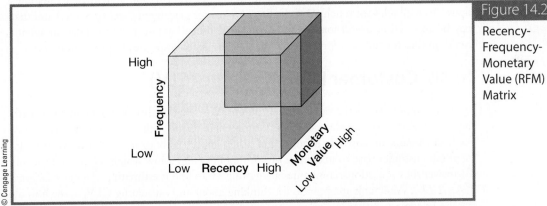

Figure 14.2

Recency-Frequency-Monetary Value (RFM) Matrix

© Cengage Learning

Regarding the first step, codes might be assigned like these: "If the most recent order was placed within the past 3 months, then $R = 3$ points; if the most recent order was between 3 and 6 months, $R = 2$; if the most recent order was between 6 and 12 months, $R = 1$; and any customer that hadn't purchased within the past year receives a code of $R = 0$. Frequency and monetary values are coded similarly.

In the next step, R, F, and M are multiplied by weights judged to reflect their importance, such as 5 for M, 2 for R, and 1 for F. A single score is obtained for each customer, as the simple function $[(5 \times M) + (2 \times R) + (1 \times F)]$. Customers with the highest scores are deemed most worthy of special attention. RFM models are still used, and still useful, but they emphasize past customer behaviors (purchasing, Web surfing, etc.), whereas more sophisticated models allow us to extrapolate into future earnings of customer segments, as we'll see in a moment.

In addition, the best CRM programs begin with the RFM behaviors but go beyond these data to learn more about their customers. With better customer knowledge, companies can provide specially tailored offerings through cross-selling efforts; i.e., the product assortment itself is modified, or the channels through which the goods and services may be accessed are made more flexible, etc. Specifically, CRM databases typically contain

- Contact information (name, address, phone, e-mail, permission status).

- Demographics (economic worth, age, marital status, partner's name and age, children [name and ages], region of country).

- Lifestyle and psychographic data (home owner or renter, car ownership [type and year], media preferences, payment preferences, relevant product ownership, recreational preferences).

- Internet info (type spent on websites, number of visits to site).

- Transaction data (source and date of first transaction, R, F, M, what was purchased, form of order [Web, phone, etc.], mode of payment).

- Rate of response to marketing offers (promos and other incentives redeemed).

- Complaints.

- And so forth, pretty much anything the company can get its paws on to compile.

Finally, expenditures are cross-tabbed with everything to try to find patterns.

Good CRM programs take planning and money, and they require ongoing monitoring of customers. Even just the coordination and maintenance of the database is nontrivial; companies are still struggling with how to design an information system that integrates inputs from all relevant touchpoints (call centers, order placements, websites, etc.) and that may be accessed in useful formats for managerial usage (system recommendation agents, useful profiles for call center recipients, predictions about responses to promotions, etc.).

14-4b Customer Lifetime Value (CLV)

Just as customers assess the value of their purchases—what quality do I get compared with the price I paid?—companies can assess customers in terms of their worth to the company. Some customers are costly to acquire, and others more costly to retain. How can we segment our customer base to maximize our profitability and know which segments to serve? To answer these questions, companies are getting smart about estimating *Customer Lifetime Value (CLV)*. We'll look at a process for thinking about and estimating CLV, to see how all the pieces come together in a reasonably good and yet fairly simple model.

Figure 14.3 shows conceptually how CLV unfolds. Models require 3 kinds of components: (1) numbers about money, (2) numbers about time, and (3) a financing finesse. The money inputs we need are (a) estimates of acquisition costs, (b) estimates of retention costs, and (c) average contributions (for the segment[s] under consideration). The time inputs include (a) a decent guesstimate at the likely retention rate from year to year and (b) a sense of the average life span duration for the particular product or brand. Finally, if the estimates are to be useful in forecasting and budgeting, a simple financial adjustment of a discount rate is important.

Gerber

Gerber has fabulous brand equity in the baby food category. Its problem is that bambinos grow up! So Gerber's extending the lifetime—in CLV—of relevance to its parental customers. After a newbie progresses from infant formula to cans of pureed fruits and vegetables, crawling kids get foods that are mostly pureed but with some chunks to exercise their baby teeth. After that, toddlers are offered chicken and carrot ravioli, with kiddie spoons, and when the kids' are preschoolers, Gerber has full meals and snacks that emphasize convenience and nutrition—all foods that parents can trust. (For more, see research by Professor Karel Cool Insead.)

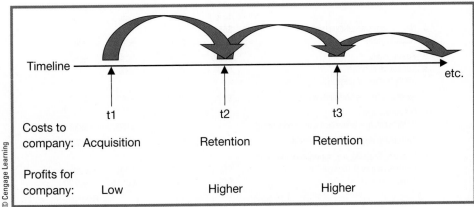

Figure 14.3
Customer Lifetime Value (CLV) Conceptually

To see the model, let's consider an example: MobiMed is a mobile health care provider of health care consultation and services for all but the most complicated conditions, e.g., screening and physicals, annual vision and hearing tests, immunizations (e.g., kids going back to school, travelers going to exotic locations), diagnostics via portable X-ray, ultrasound, cardio EKG's, even some basic lab work. Business is booming for several reasons: (1) Health care costs are disturbing, and, while people pay cash for many of MobiMed's services, customers don't have to wait for appointments, and the retail exchange is very pleasant. (2) Some technology is portable, e.g., X-ray and ultrasound machines. (3) Most health complaints that motivate customers to seek advice are fairly simple and can be handled by a variety of health care staff.

The MobiMed founder, an MD/MBA, attracts new customers via advertising and coupon promotions. Once a month, the company takes out an ad in the local paper, alternating between a weekend flyer @$50 each and a half-page ad @$200 each. The acquisition costs thus are ($50 × 6) + ($200 × 6) = $1,500 per year. Both kinds of ads contain a nominal coupon embedded in them, which helps MobiMed track how the customer came to hear of their services and to measure the effectiveness of the ad money. Approximately 60 customers redeem coupons in a year, or just over 1 patient a week. Thus, acquisition is $1,500/60, or $25 a head.

In addition, MobiMed has a sales manager who works part-time (20 hours), with no benefits (other than health!), but is loyal because he's paid $45,000. When he's on duty, he's supposed to spend 10% of his time, or 2 hours a week, logging sales calls. Thus, note that the sales call budget is essentially 10% of $45,000, or $4,500. In any given week, while many calls are placed, the yield is approximately 1 customer a week, or about 50 a year. Personal selling is almost always more expensive, but the belief is that customers contacted via a salesperson is already beginning to develop a relationship and therefore is more likely to convert to being a loyal customer. In this scenario, the cost is $4,500/50 = $90 per capita.

We could track these groups separately to test the comparative effectiveness of the two acquisition approaches, but our goal at the moment is simply to compute LTCV. Thus, we'll take the average acquisition cost to be (60 × 25 + 50 × 90)/(60 + 50) = $54.55. This $55 is the first number entered into the spreadsheet in Figure 14.4.

Next, MobiMed estimates retention costs. Each customer who has ever been treated is issued $100 worth of coupons throughout the year, and, on average, $20 of those are redeemed. The retention figure is represented in row b in the spreadsheet.

Retention rates begin at 0.75 and decline slowly thereafter. Row c in the spreadsheet lists the loyalty rates per segment, and row d shows how those numbers multiply and accumulate.

Average contributions begin at about $100 a year and grow. These values form row e in the CLV computation.

Figure 14.4		Time 1	Time 2	Time 3	Time 4...
Crunching Customer Lifetime Value (CLV)	a. New customer acquisition cost	$55			
	b. Retention costs		$20	$20	$20
	c. Retention rate	100%	75%	70%	65%
	d. Cumulative retention (multiply adjacent rates)		75%	52%	34%
	e. Average customer contributions	$100	$150	$200	$250
	f. Net contribution (contribution e − acquisition a or − retention b)	$45	$130	$180	$230
	g. Expected average contribution (f × d)	$45	$97.50	$93.60	$85.00
	h. Financing finessing, e.g., for discount rate of .07, Divide each g by [$1.07^{(t-1)}$]	1.0	1.07	1.145	1.225
	Today's value	$45	$91.12	$81.75	$69.39
					Final sum: $287.26

© Cengage Learning

You might think the life span for lifetime customer value is 80 years or something, but obviously that's not likely to be true for any brand. For example, people are mobile, moving about every 7 years. Once MobiMed goes national, the customer could take their membership with them, and loyalty to the chain could last throughout the patient's life. In any event, for the ease of computation, we're going to pretend the life span is a mere 4 years.

We now have all the components to crunch the CLV numbers. (We'll tweak the financial discount at the end.) In Figure 14.4, the net contributions begin with the averages in row e, and the acquisition costs of time 1 or the retention cost of a subsequent time is subtracted, as noted in row f. Row g figures the expected contributions, based on the net contribution in f, and the cumulative retention rate in d. Row h takes the time horizon out on the discount rate. At the bottom right is the sum, the CLV for a customer (over 4 years).

The basic CLV calculation is very simple. Once the basic template is in a spreadsheet, you can extend it to other scenarios and make it more sophisticated. For example, costs and revenues, even retention rates, usually vary across segments, so, at the least, there could be multiple versions and different resulting estimates per segment. There is obviously a lot of flexibility in capturing CLV. The important thing is to get the assumptions as right as possible and to use the numbers as guides regarding which segments to continue to target, which customers to try to please, and which customers to let defect.

To close this chapter on customer evaluations and keeping good relationships with customers, let's broaden the view to CRM, not just models of computing CLV.

- Marketers can think of CRM as a holistic strategic approach in managing customer relationships to create shareholder value. From this view, CRM is core business, and the firm is customer-centric. The strategy is to win and retain profitable customers.

- Marketing gets more analytical about CRM as plans are enacted to route and analyze data and store information appropriately.

- Marketing gets quite operational, when implementing plans to capture and create those databases. Customer information must be collected, automated, and integrated to be useful to the firm, such as in turning around and sending out messages or products to customers.

What's important is to keep an eye on the goal. It's fun to calculate CLV, but we do it because it fits a strategic initiative to serve certain segments of customers better, as well as our corporate goals for growth and profitability.

Finally, consider a couple of ways that firms demonstrate their implicit knowledge of CLV. Figure 14.5 shows a Honda product line that begins by appealing to young customers with

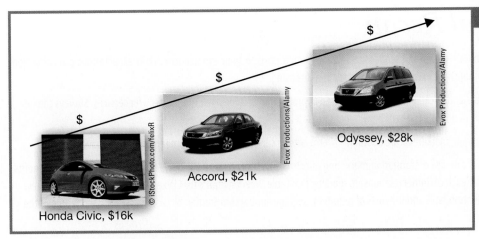

Figure 14.5

A Product
Line to
Extend
Customers'
Lifetime with
Honda

Odyssey, $28k

Accord, $21k

Honda Civic, $16k

limited budgets and who Honda hopes will grow into customers whose lifestyles and wallets might appreciate subsequent Honda incarnations. The product line is a classic means of a company trying to extend the duration of its customers' lifetime, as well as contribution margins, in CLV. A newer development in loyalty programs is the transference from physical cards to mobile technology. Customers are rarely without their smartphones; hence, they might use their loyalty programs more frequently, hiking up the contributions as well (see Figure 14.6).

Figure 14.6

Loyalty Cards
Made Easy

Myrtle Beach

Golf is big business in South Carolina; by rough measures, it is some $3b and 40% of the state's tax revenues. The Myrtle Beach Area created an affinity program, available to locals (year round) or out-of-town visitors (good for December, January, and February). The program affords the member discounts on golf fees, discounts at partner restaurants, retail, and other local attractions. The program is considered relatively successful, with 10,000 members and 75% renewal rates. (For more, see "Driving Improvements" by Latta et al. at quirks.com.)

Managerial Recap

Customers are thought to evaluate goods and services by making comparisons to their expectations. Their expectations can come from previous experience, word of mouth, or marketing efforts such as advertising.

- Quality and customer satisfaction can be precisely measured in production of goods, but not as easily for services. Surveys can be used to ask customers for their evaluations of any kind of purchase.

- Beyond customer satisfaction, marketers care about long-term criteria such loyalty and customer relationship management.

- Customer lifetime value is a means of translating marketing efforts in financial results. CLV allows firms to match customer benefits to revenues to ensure that each customer relationship remains profitable. Needed inputs for CLV: estimated cost of acquiring new customers, customer retention rates and the costs of retention, average annual contribution by customers, and the lifetime of the customer.

Chapter Outline in Key Terms and Concepts

1. What are customer evaluations, and why are they important?
2. How do consumers evaluate products?
   a. Sources of expectations
   b. Expectation and experience
3. How do marketers measure quality and customer satisfaction?
4. Loyalty and customer relationship management (CRM)
   a. Recency, frequency, and monetary value (RFM)
   b. Customer lifetime value (CLV)

Chapter Discussion Questions

1. New businesses are frequently launched as a means to smooth over dissatisfaction with a current glitch in the industry. Pick some industry, and solve its customer dissatisfaction problem(s). For example, if you find flying annoying or you're not happy with your dentist (or professor?), what changes could you make to enter that industry and enhance customer satisfaction (and be profitable)?

2. Go online and find the average length of a "lifetime" for purchases in the categories of houses, cars, gym memberships, baby diapers, birth control pills, Viagra prescriptions.

Mini-Case

Happy Global Customers: Cultural Differences on Surveys

Joe Pike is a CMO in a consulting firm out of Miami that specializes in creating loyalty programs for its clients. As a first step, he gathers customer satisfaction data, and the results for an international hotel chain follow. These data draw from three samples: Brazil, Japan, and England.

Brazil:

	Strongly disagree								Strongly agree	
Overall, I was satisfied with the hotel.	1	2	3	4	5	6	7	8	9	
The hotel prices were good value.	1	2	3	4	5	6	7	8	9	10
The hotel exceeded my expectations.	1	2	3	4	5	6	7	8	9	10
I will recommend this hotel to others.	1	2	3	4	5	6	7	8		10

Japan:

	Strongly disagree								Strongly agree	
Overall, I was satisfied with the hotel.	1	2	3	4	5	6	7	8	9	
The hotel prices were good value.	1	2	3	4	5	6	7		9	10
The hotel exceeded my expectations.	1	2	3	4	5	6	7	8	9	
I will recommend this hotel to others.	1	2	3	4	5	6	7		9	10

England:

	Strongly disagree									Strongly agree
Overall, I was satisfied with the hotel.	1	2	3	4	5	6	●	8	9	10
The hotel prices were good value.	1	2	3	●	5	6	7	8	9	10
The hotel exceeded my expectations.	1	2	3	4	●	6	7	8	9	10
I will recommend this hotel to others.	1	2	3	●	5	6	7	8	9	10

The hotelier's response to seeing these data: "Wow, we're doing great in Japan, and pretty good in Brazil except their perception of value. Maybe the English don't care that much about hotels."

Marketing managers of global multinationals frequently gather customer satisfaction data from their customers all over the world. The question is how to make sense of the data. When the Japanese customer satisfaction ratings look higher than those in England, does that mean the Japanese customers are truly more satisfied, or is something else going on?

Joe's got a lot of experience with international data, and knows the cross-cultural literature. There are known response tendencies found in different countries. These are stereotypes, of course, but here are the generalities typical in such data:

- Some cultures are said to be "enthusiastic," meaning that the ratings display high variance. Thus, customers in the U.S., Brazil (and many other South American countries), France, Italy, and Australia will produce data that indicate when customers are happy, they're really happy, and when they're not, they're really most sincerely not.

- Other countries, such as England and Germany are more reserved, which translates into numbers on surveys that show less variability. Ratings tend to be near the midpoint, which means customers won't indicate liking or disliking anything all that strongly.

- Some countries have an acquiescence, or courteousness, bias, saying things look favorable when maybe deep down that's not quite what they think, e.g., Japan (and some other Asian countries). Thus, when the Japanese ratings appear more positive, giving the impression they're happier, it's more likely that they're just being polite on the survey.

Mini-Case Discussion Questions

1. How would you interpret the data? Where is the hotel chain doing a good job?

2. How could you tease out the effects of customer satisfaction vs. cultural biases?

Video Exercise: *Jordan's Furniture* (15:44)

Jordan's Furniture sells home furnishings in the middle and upper-middle price range, but in doing so it provides customers with much more than a product. The fundamental business philosophy of Jordan's Furniture is to do things differently and better than competitors rather than being similar to their competitors. In addition to the products, display, and service, Jordan's creates a fun experience, and as a result the company generates more foot traffic than other retailers. The Jordan's Furniture difference incorporates an upbeat attitude, excitement, fun and interesting people, customer appreciation, and postsale follow-through. Jordan's has a different kind of store environment that creates very different customer expectations. Jordan's strives to give people a reason, other than buying furniture, for coming to the store. Many people come into Jordan's just to have fun, and they end up buying furniture.

Video Discussion Questions

1. Customers have expectations of the businesses that they patronize. What expectations would someone entering a Jordan's Furniture store for the first time likely have? What expectations would a loyal repeat customer of Jordan's Furniture likely have?

2. Sometimes companies approach customer relationship management differently for new customers than they do for loyal repeat customers. Does Jordan's approach to customer relationship management differentiate between new customers and loyal customers? Explain your answer.

3. Using the concepts of recency, frequency, and monetary value, explain the impact made by the "Jordan's Furniture difference."

Chapter 15

Marketing Research Tools

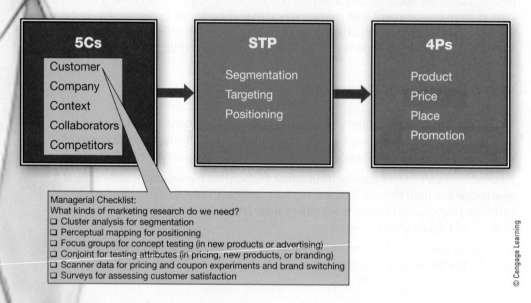

5Cs	STP	4Ps
Customer	Segmentation	Product
Company	Targeting	Price
Context	Positioning	Place
Collaborators		Promotion
Competitors		

Managerial Checklist:
What kinds of marketing research do we need?
❑ Cluster analysis for segmentation
❑ Perceptual mapping for positioning
❑ Focus groups for concept testing (in new products or advertising)
❑ Conjoint for testing attributes (in pricing, new products, or branding)
❑ Scanner data for pricing and coupon experiments and brand switching
❑ Surveys for assessing customer satisfaction

© Cengage Learning

Marketing Management Framework

15-1 WHY IS MARKETING RESEARCH SO IMPORTANT?

Every marketing decision should be based on facts. Marketing research is about gathering those facts.

The smartest marketers are always monitoring their customers, the environmental context, their competitors' actions, their relationships with their collaborators, their own company strengths—yes, the 5Cs. And the smartest marketers make decisions about their products, place, promotion, and price—yes, all 4Ps, based on marketing intelligence. As Figure 15.1 indicates, marketing research methods can be used to obtain many insights about marketing and customers.

Marketing information should be gathered constantly so that the company can be knowledgeable and poised for action. Customer relationship management databases are an important example of ongoing data collection and management systems. In addition, occasions frequently arise that require periodically pulsing of the market with specific marketing research projects. Whether the assessments are continuous or periodic, they require knowledge of marketing research techniques.

- STP:
  - Cluster analysis for segmentation
  - Multidimensional scaling for perceptual mapping, targeting, and positioning
- 4Ps:
  - Conjoint for new products
  - Scanner data for pricing
  - Surveys to assess customer satisfaction with Internet as a distribution option
  - Experiments to verify ad testing
- 5Cs:
  - Secondary data to understand context
  - Observational data to check on competitors
  - Networks to study collaborators
  - Interviews to study company's employees
  - Surveys for customer satisfaction

Figure 15.1

Examples of Relevant Marketing Research

Figure 15.2 depicts the typical flow in the research process, from formulating the marketing and marketing research problem, to data collection and analysis, to reporting the results. Data collection can take quite a number of forms, as Figure 15.3 suggests. Marketing research is tremendously flexible; it can be used to address just about any business question, and there are many ways to do so. This chapter focuses on 6 popular techniques:

1. Cluster analysis for segmentation
2. Perceptual mapping for positioning
3. Focus groups for concept testing (in new products or advertising)
4. Conjoint for testing attributes (in pricing, new products, or branding)
5. Scanner data for pricing and coupon experiments and brand switching
6. Surveys for assessing customer satisfaction

- Define marketing and marketing research problem.
- Try to answer questions with secondary data.
- Design primary data collection.
  - Sample (e.g., random sample, stratified sample by segment)
  - Technique:
    - Qualitative: Interviews, focus groups, observations and ethnographies
    - Quantitative: Surveys, experiments, scanner data analysis
  - Instruments (e.g., questionnaire, focus group moderator guide)
  - Mode of Administration (e.g., Web survey, mail, personal interview)
- Data collection
- Data analysis
- Communicate results (white paper, presentation, recommendations).

Figure 15.2

Marketing Research Process

Figure 15.3

Kinds of Data

Kind of Data?	Definition?	Examples?	Advantages?
Secondary	Already exist	Library, online	Quick and cheap to get
Primary	Design, collect, analyze	Focus group, surveys	Can be quite precise

Kind of Study?	Used for?	Examples?
Exploratory	Formulate marketing questions	Focus groups, interviews
Descriptive	Obtain large-scale stats	Surveys, scanner data
Causal	Study effects of manipulating 4Ps	Experiments

15-2 CLUSTER ANALYSIS FOR SEGMENTATION

A couple of MBAs who are feeling a little broke are thinking they could start a NPO to fund young people to go to college. There are many nonprofits, but not many, or no particular branded ones, seem to support the goal of offsetting these costs. The team wishes to first verify or test its assumptions by looking at people's perceptions on these issues. They figure there must be a segment of customers who will be sympathetic.

The results of their study are presented in Figure 15.4; it's a typical executive summary of a segmentation study. The segment names are catchy titles that the marketer creates to label the segments and summarize the qualities that the customers have in common, e.g., people who give charitably to medical associations, the arts, environment societies, etc. The Size column reflects the proportion of customers in the database who belong to each segment. The right column contains the questions from the survey that each group resonated with the most.

Figure 15.4	Segment Name	Size	Beneficiaries
Segmentation of NPO Supporters	Health and medical	30%	e.g., American Cancer Society
	The arts	20%	Ballets, museums, operas
	Greenies	15%	Nature Conservancy, World Wildlife Fund
	Children	10%	Make-a-Wish, St. Jude's Charity, UNICEF
	Other	25%	Religious, local (e.g., Animal Shelter, Food Bank), etc.

© Cengage Learning

Let's see what's behind the segmentation summary and how the marketers got these results. Figure 15.5 shows the survey that gave rise to the data. The marketers asked customers about their charitable giving behavior, as well as their opinions about higher education—its importance in society and its cost.

Figure 15.5

Survey used to Interview Customers

How important is it to support these nonprofit causes for a better society?

	Not very Important 1 2 3 4 5 6 7 Very Important
Medical causes like American Heart Association	1 2 3 4 5 6 7
The arts, like ballet or museums	1 2 3 4 5 6 7
Environmental concerns, like WWF	1 2 3 4 5 6 7
Children's charities, like Make-a-Wish	1 2 3 4 5 6 7

To what extent would you say that you agree with these statements?

	Strongly disagree 1 2 3 4 5 6 7 Strongly agree
Higher education is very important.	1 2 3 4 5 6 7
More college educated people make for a better society.	1 2 3 4 5 6 7
My success in life was largely due to my going to college.	1 2 3 4 5 6 7
People don't really need to go to college.	1 2 3 4 5 6 7
Only the very privileged can go to university these days.	1 2 3 4 5 6 7
Higher education is too expensive.	1 2 3 4 5 6 7
I would help sponsor a kid (not my own) to go to college.	1 2 3 4 5 6 7

© Cengage Learning

Figure 15.6 contains part of the data set. For example, the first customer tends to give money to environmental and medical causes but not a lot to kids' causes and is not overly concerned with the price tag on colleges.

Figure 15.6

NPO DataSet

Customer ID#	Med	Art	Envir	Kids	Imp	More	Suc	No Need	Priv	Too Exp	Spons
1	5	4	7	1	4	2	4	2	1	1	1
2	3	7	3	5	4	7	3	4	1	1	3
3	3	5	2	4	5	4	2	4	7	7	4
4	5	5	1	3	7	2	2	2	4	2	7
5	6	5	3	3	4	3	4	3	3	1	3

Next the marketer imputes the data into a cluster analysis. Clustering methods form groups of customers who are similar within the groups with regard to what the group is seeking and who are different across groups in that each group looks for slightly different attributes. Thus customers should be homogeneous within a cluster and heterogeneous across clusters. In these data, there are 11 variables, and, while clustering techniques have no problem with processing even more variables, it is difficult for us to imagine what 11-dimensional scatter plots look like; so in Figure 15.7, the problem is simplified a bit.

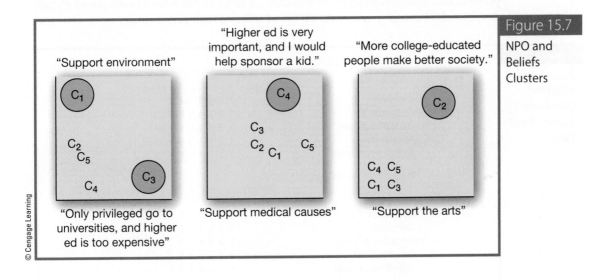

Figure 15.7

NPO and Beliefs Clusters

In the left plot, we can see the pretty clear patterns of the 1st and 3rd clusters, people who support environmental concerns and people who are concerned that higher ed is so expensive that only the privileged can attend. The customer segments are near the origin, meaning they don't really care that much about either issue. In the middle plot, we see the 4th cluster pop, where customers tend to support medical causes, and they acknowledge the importance of higher ed and even indicate a willingness to help contribute to such a fund. In the right plot, we see the 2nd cluster identified as those who support the arts and believe that education enhances society. The intuitions of the MBA team seem to be valid; they may be onto something in creating a NPO to support scholarships, and there seems to be at least one segment of people who would be willing to help.

That's it. That's all there is to it. Get data from your customers, and process it through a cluster analysis. There are many clustering techniques, so you will have to hire a marketing researcher for the fine points. But this example shows you the essence of how to find segments. Note, of course, that a cluster analysis helps you identify segments (and their sizes), but it does not tell you which segment to target; that's dealt with in Chapters 4 and 14.

15-3 PERCEPTUAL MAPPING FOR POSITIONING

Positioning studies are used to understand customer perceptions of brands in the marketplace. Marketers and executives find perceptual maps extremely appealing; they are pictures of competing brands as well as attributes, which together offer a sense of competitive strengths and weaknesses. There are two approaches to creating a perceptual map: an attribute-based approach and multidimensional scaling (MDS).

15-3a Attribute-Based

To create a map based on attributes, customers complete a survey that looks like that in Figure 15.8. The customer makes two kinds of ratings: (1) How does our brand rate on a number of attributes? (2) How important is each of these attributes? This particular study was motivated by Ford's frustration that its Fiesta wasn't perceived more favorably, or so they thought. They solicited a positioning study of that car and some recent appealing competitors. They asked customers how well each car fared on the bases of value, comfort, fun, design, and the extent to which the car brand reflected their personalities.

Figure 15.8			
Perceptual Mapping (Attribute-Based): Ford Fiesta	**How does {our brand} rate?**		
		Not as good as others	Better than others
	Good value	1 2 3 4 5 6 7	
	Comfortable	1 2 3 4 5 6 7	
	Fun to drive and own	1 2 3 4 5 6 7	
	Attractive design	1 2 3 4 5 6 7	
	Reflects my personality	1 2 3 4 5 6 7	
	How important are these qualities to you?		
		Not very important	Extremely important
	Good value	1 2 3 4 5 6 7	
	Comfortable	1 2 3 4 5 6 7	
	Fun to drive and own	1 2 3 4 5 6 7	
	Attractive design	1 2 3 4 5 6 7	
	Reflects my personality	1 2 3 4 5 6 7	

© Cengage Learning

The analysis begins by merely taking simple averages over these questions. Doing so results in a pair of means for each attribute; e.g., there is a mean on whether the Fiesta is good value and a mean for how important value is to this customer.

These pairs of means are used to plot the 5 attributes in a 2-dimensional space (or chart) as in Figure 15.9. The higher the mean on performance on an attribute (in the first 5 ratings) translates to how far to the right the attribute will be plotted. The importance of the attribute (in the second 5 ratings) is the coordinate on the vertical axis of the chart.

Along the horizontal axis, these data indicate that the Fiesta is perceived to be good value and comfortable, relative to the other cars tested, but not as strong on the other attributes. Along the vertical axis, these data indicate that value, comfort, and design are the most important features of the cars, whereas "Fun to own and drive" is less so.

This very simple construction (simple in the survey, data analysis, and plotting) of an attribute-based perceptual map yields pretty helpful insights. The car has strengths, including some in areas that are important to customers. Unfortunately, the car is seen as

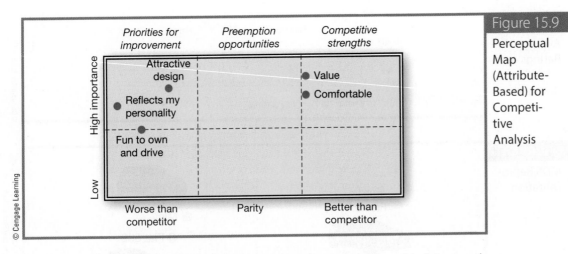

© Cengage Learning

Figure 15.9

Perceptual Map (Attribute-Based) for Competitive Analysis

weaker in some areas that are also important. Attributes on which a brand is doing poorly and yet are important to the customers would be priority 1 for fixing.

15-3b Multidimensional Scaling

Multidimensional scaling (MDS) takes a slightly different approach. Rather than asking customers, "What's important?" MDS simply starts by asking, "How similar are these 2 brands for every pair in the set?" So, in Figure 15.10, the first ratings are the similarities judgments for all pairs of the 4 cars. The next ratings cycle through each car and ask how each brand rates on each of a number of attributes.

Figure 15.10

Perceptual Mapping (Multidimensional Scaling)

© Cengage Learning

How similar are these cars?

	Very similar Very different
Ford Fiesta & Mini	1 2 3 4 5 6 7
Fiat 500 & Smart	1 2 3 4 5 6 7
Smart & Ford Fiesta	1 2 3 4 5 6 7
Mini & Car Fiat 500	1 2 3 4 5 6 7
Ford Fiesta & Fiat 500	1 2 3 4 5 6 7
Mini & Smart	1 2 3 4 5 6 7

How does Ford Fiesta rate on these qualities?

	Not great Really great
Good value	1 2 3 4 5 6 7
Comfortable	1 2 3 4 5 6 7
Fun to drive and own	1 2 3 4 5 6 7
Attractive design	1 2 3 4 5 6 7
Reflects my personality	1 2 3 4 5 6 7

(Then the other brands are rated on the same qualities.)

Figure 15.11 shows what the similarities data look like. The Mini and the Fiat are seen as the most similar, the Mini and the Smart are the most different, and the Ford is rather different from most of the cars in this group.

MDS takes the similarities data to create a map like the result in Figure 15.12. This figure represents cars as points in 2 dimensions such that cars that customers think are similar are points close together, and cars that customers think are different are points that are father apart. Hence, recall that the Mini and Fiat were similar, and here they are close in space.

Figure 15.11		Ford Fiesta	Mini	Fiat 500	Smart
Average Ratings over $n = 75$ **Respondents**	Ford Fiesta	—			
	Mini	5.0	—		
	Fiat 500	4.7	1.8	—	
	Smart	5.1	6.2	5.5	—

1 = "Very similar" to 7 = "Very different"

Figure 15.12

MDS Representation

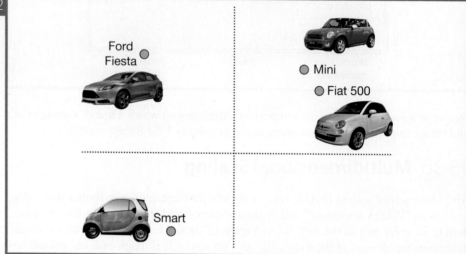

B2B

- U.S. marketing research providers were surveyed, and 56% said they were doing some B2B research. B2B marketing research also seems robust to economic fluctuations, at least compared to B2C marketing research.
- Some industries are bigger users of B2B marketing research (e.g., health care products and services, financial (banking, insurance, credit cards), and technology industries. Other industries use B2B research less; e.g., in consumer packaged goods and retailing, manufacturers tend to overlook their partners and instead go directly to the consumer.
- What kind of B2B marketing research is conducted? Clients ask for attitude and usage studies and customer satisfaction surveys (66% of marketing research companies have conducted these studies within the last calendar year). They commission studies of brand tracking throughout their products' life cycles, from concept testing to later stages of new product development (50%). The next most popular kinds of marketing research projects examine ad copy testing and brand equity and market structure estimations (30%).
- How is the B2B marketing research conducted? Most respondents are contacted via phone and online reaches (42% together, 37% online only, 13% phone only). In-person was rare (4%), and good old-fashioned mail surveys, rarer still (1%).

(For more on B2B marketing research, go to quirks.com.)

Next, the marketer must interpret the north-south, east-west of the map. To do so, we overlay the basic perceptual map with the attribute ratings to obtain Figure 15.13. Now the interpretation is a little clearer. The Mini and Fiat are similar, and what they have in common is that they're attractive and fun and project personality-plus (these two cars project high onto the vectors). Ford does well on comfort and value, as we had seen in the raw data, and it does not fare well on these self-expression sorts of measures.

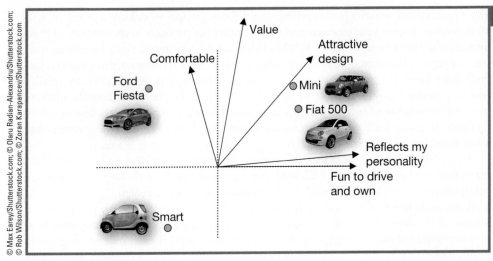

Figure 15.13

MDS Representation with Attribute Vectors

For more information, the overlay is known as attribute vector fitting. Imagine a little data set with 4 rows, 1 for each brand, then 2 columns, 1 for each coordinate (on dimension 1 and 2). Add a column for the means for each brand on how good it is on the first attribute, e.g., value (and then add more columns for the means of all the remaining attributes). Then, run a regression using the 2 dimensions variables to predict the attribute variable (and run another regression for each additional attribute). The resulting beta weights give you the coordinates to put in these vectors. Then, the final step is to overlay respondents onto these maps, in what are called "ideal points." That is, if a brand could have just the right set of features to make the customer perfectly happy, what combination of features would those be? Perceptual maps with ideal points, one point per customer, are frequently used to identify market opportunities.

These perceptual maps offer a great deal of descriptive information about current positions among competitors. It is a strategic question to consider possible repositioning efforts. Thus, for example, Figure 15.14 shows one of the directions Ford is considering. Mini is fun

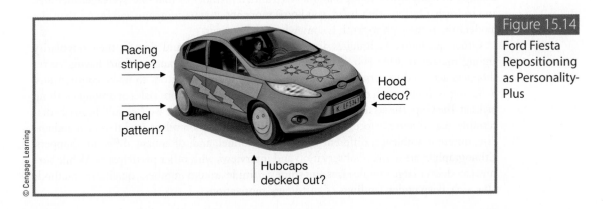

Figure 15.14

Ford Fiesta Repositioning as Personality-Plus

in part because of its looks, so if Ford creates more superficial personalization (and paint is cheap), it figures its Fiesta will be seen as more personal and more fun, as well.

15-4 FOCUS GROUPS FOR CONCEPT TESTING

There's something amazingly compelling about focus groups—watching a group of 8 to 10 consumers discuss your products and your competitors' products in the contexts of their lives, all while you're munching on M&M's behind a one-way mirror and schmoozing with your colleagues. Focus groups are usually used as exploratory techniques, meaning that you don't quite know yet what questions you'd put on a survey. The sample sizes are smaller (running maybe 3 to 4 groups of 8 to 10 customers), so, really, predicting how the market-place will respond as a function of these focus groups is not a great idea. It is best to follow up the focus group leads with a larger-scale survey. But there's just something remarkable about watching a live person say something good, or bad, about your brand.

An exploratory technique is used in the early stages of some marketing inquiries. Most often, focus groups are used as a vehicle for concept testing in the early stages of new product development or working toward the development of an ad campaign.

A person is hired to be a moderator, a person who keeps the discussion going, tries to address all the items on the client's wish list, tries to bring out the quieter group members, tries to control the overbearing group members, etc. If the topic is a sensitive one (e.g., some health issues), it can help to have the moderator be similar to the focus group participants (e.g., age, gender, ethnicity) to put them at ease and establish rapport.

The moderator kicks off the group discussion with some warm-up exercise, e.g., going around the room with brief introductions and an easy, softball question, e.g., "How do you use this product in your lives?" Then questions from the client are introduced, e.g., "Here are two different ads my client is working up. Which one speaks to you more, and why?" Then the discussion is off and running. "I like the sexier one" … "I disagree. I think the whole-some one makes better sense for this product," etc. When the discussion starts dwindling on this topic, the next topic is introduced. After 1.5 hours, the group is thanked, dismissed, and paid.

If you've been an observer, you should jot down notes about your impressions before your work team starts talking about what they think the conclusions are. If you weren't an observer, these sessions are usually taped, and, as often as not, transcriptions are made as well. Moderators are also usually paid to interpret the session. Since they have more experience than you in watching focus groups interact, they are in a better position to tell you whether to really worry about that one disgruntled member or that one overeager member, and so forth. On the other hand, you know more about your company and brand than the moderator, so the path to truth is somewhere in between.

Other qualitative techniques are available, and they ebb and flow in their popularity among marketers. One is a set of observational techniques, ranging from having secret shoppers act as customers, purchasing your brand and competitors' to make comparisons, to having auditors watch consumers make choices in grocery store aisles or among clothing racks at The Gap. The strategy of brands and retail outlets, if done well, should be easily discernible; e.g., different stores' positioning should reflect themselves in different merchandise, different ambience, different frontline personnel, and, of course, different shoppers. Ethnographies are a mix of observation and interviews with other participants. While surveys can deliver large sample sizes and some certitude around numbers, qualitative methods offer rich, deep understandings of customers' motivations.

15-5 CONJOINT FOR TESTING ATTRIBUTES

Conjoint studies are really popular for questions of pricing, new products, and branding. The studies are run to understand how consumers make trade-offs. For example, in the design of a new product, engineers and R&D departments are always keen to add as many whiz-bang bells and whistles as possible, but then, of course, doing so drives up the price. So the question is, "What do customers really want if they can't have everything (all the features and a cheap price)?" Conjoint analyses will help uncover the attributes that are most valued by consumers and provide guidance as to the attribute values to combine for optimal product design.

Figure 15.15 presents all possible combinations of a home delivery service that a grocery chain is designing, trying to respond to the convenience that shoppers enjoy from online stores. The grocery company wants to know if there should be regular monthly delivery of household staples (e.g., bread, tissue, allergy meds), or should deliveries be made only when customers go online and schedule them. Should the grocer promise a "1-day delivery window" or try to adopt a "2-hour window"? Finally, should the grocer charge $30 or $60 a month? The question is, "What do customers want?"

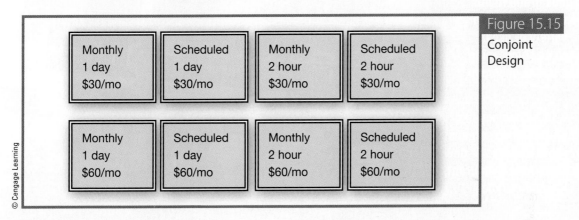

Figure 15.15

Conjoint Design

The 2 (schedule) by 2 (window) by 2 (pricing) design results in 8 combinations (per the 8 boxes in Figure 15.15). Consumers are asked to rate or rank these 8 combos in terms of their most to least preferred.

Figure 15.16 shows one customer's data. The first 5 columns are data that are constant for every customer; they comprise the 8 combinations. The consumer's ratings are in the last column. This customer would most prefer to have convenience in scheduling, a tight delivery window, for only $30.

Row	Column	Schedule?	Window?	Fee?	Rating*
1	1	0	0	0	5
1	2	1	0	0	6
1	3	0	1	0	7
1	4	1	1	0	8
2	1	0	0	1	1
2	2	1	0	1	2
2	3	0	1	1	3
2	4	1	1	1	4

*Like the least 1 2 3 4 5 6 7 8 Like the most
Predictor variables coded: 0 = no, 1 = yes

Figure 15.16

Conjoint Data for 1 Customer

Focus groups are used to elicit qualitative feedback on brand perceptions, testing new product concepts, reacting to "storyboards" depicting a potential ad campaign, etc.

Why are focus groups so popular?
- There is something compelling about watching customers talk about your brand.
- Also, they're flexible, they can probe to see whether something interesting comes up, the resulting data are rich and deep, they get at the why of customer behavior, they help generate some business ideas and clarify others, and the group dynamics can be synergistic and creative.
- On business specs, they're relatively inexpensive, and there is a ready industry of providers.

Focus group rooms can be set up for a variety of uses, such as showcasing products, like shampoo …

… Or technology like high-definition screens to show websites or new designs for a restaurant, retailer, hotel.

Focus groups can also be used to obtain quantitative ratings, but then the focus groups should be followed up on with more extensive surveying on larger, representative samples.

A focus group room as seen from behind one-way mirror. The viewing room is where management gathers to watch the group discussions without interfering with the free flow of ideas and commentary.

Focus groups of the "future" are already here! There are participants in our town (in the room) and participants on the screen are in another city.

FAQs:
- How many in the focus grou[p] Eight to ten.
- How many groups? ~Three (segment).
- Moderator should be similar to participants if discussing "personal" (e.g., health) issu[e]
- Hire a company to do the foc[us] group. If your team or your company runs the focus grou[p] it will be biased.
- Ask focus group facilitating company for both video files and transcripts.

The next question is, in effect, if you can't have all that, what are you willing to give up? Some customers will give up the scheduling regularity, and that tells us they don't value that feature that much. Some customers will say they're willing to pay more, and then we know that scheduling and delivery are priorities, and they're relatively less price sensitive. Thus, even going from the 1st to the 2nd preference, we already learn about what attributes are important to customers and what trade-offs they're willing to make.

In a conjoint, we run a regression on these data. The variables "schedule," "window," and "fee" are the predictors, and the consumer's judgments are the dependent variable, as in this model:

$$\text{Rating} = b_0 + b_1 \text{ Schedule} + b_2 \text{ Window} + b_3 \text{ Fee} + \text{Error}$$

Running the numbers in Figure 15.15, the regression yields the following (b) weights:

$$\text{Predicted rating} = 5 + 1 \text{ Schedule} + 2 \text{ Window} - 4 \text{ Fee}$$

Conjoint Analysis

Conjoint analysis uncovers the product attributes that consumers value most and allows marketers to determine what combination of attribute values to include for optimal pricing. This is accomplished through market research surveys in which consumers rate combinations of product attributes.

Here's an example on blue jeans. Marketers often want to understand the trade-off that consumers make between price and brand, both often being cues to quality. In the conjoint task, customers would be shown 3 brands of blue jeans (Walmart, Gap, Caché), each in every combination with low, medium, and high price points. It's simplest to imagine if the prices were constant, say $50, $100, and $150 for all 3 brands, but it's not very realistic that Walmart is going to carry a lot of jeans at $150 or that the high-end Caché brand would offer any cheap jeans. So, for Walmart, the low, medium, and high prices are $30, $50, and $95. For Gap, the prices are: $50, $100, $150. For Caché, the prices are: $100, $150, $250.

We create 9 descriptions, perhaps with pictures, 1 for each brand at its low, medium, and high price points. We ask consumers to simply say, "Which of these do you think you'd like the most?" (rate it 9). Then we ask, "Ok, next most?" (rate it 8), etc.

We create a spreadsheet for each respondent. Pricem is a dummy variable for medium prices, and priceh is a dummy variable for high prices. Brandg is a dummy variable for the Gap, and brandc is a dummy variable for Caché. The customer's preferences are reflected in the last column.

Price	pricem	priceh	Brand	brandg	brandc	Rating
Low	0	0	Walmart	0	0	1
Low	0	0	Gap	1	0	6
Low	0	0	Cache	0	1	3
Medium	1	0	Walmart	0	0	4
Medium	1	0	Gap	1	0	9
Medium	1	0	Cache	0	1	8
High	0	1	Walmart	0	0	2
High	0	1	Gap	1	0	7
High	0	1	Cache	0	1	5

Pop that data set into a regression, use rating as the dependent variable, and pricem, priceh, brandg, and brandc as predictors. You'll get this model:

$$\text{Predicted rank} = 0.67 + 3.67\text{pricem} + 1.33\text{priceh} + 5\text{brandgap} + 3\text{brandcache}$$

We'd conclude that, on price, the difference between low price (0) and medium price (3.67) is rather large and that medium price is preferred. High price is preferred less (1.33) than medium but more than jeans at low prices. Regarding brands, with Walmart at the base (0), Gap is greatly preferred (5), and Cache is somewhere in the middle (perhaps because of the overall higher prices, but the data do not say that explicitly).

The interpretation is this: We start in the middle of the scale (i.e., the 5). Then, as the schedule variable goes from code of 0 (monthly) to 1 (scheduled), preference ratings go up (by 1 unit). As the delivery window variable goes from code of 0 (1 day) to 1 (2 hours), ratings go up by 2 units. Finally, as the fee variable goes from code of 0 ($30) to 1 ($60), ratings go down (free is preferred to fee) by 4 units. The sizes of the weights are interpretable (as are the signs). Thus, we've learned that fees are the most important feature of this service offering, and scheduling regularity the least. (In standardized regression [β] weights, the model is: Preference = 0.22 Club + 0.44 Upgrade − 0.87 Fee.)

It should be pretty clear how helpful this information would be in designing a new product or brand extension. What's also great, as you've seen, is that a basic conjoint is quite simple—both the data collection and the data analyses.

15-6 SCANNER DATA FOR PRICING AND COUPON EXPERIMENTS AND BRAND SWITCHING

Scanner data have reshaped marketing and business. Scanners began in grocery stores to help inventory management, but it quickly became obvious that the information obtained was far more valuable. Whenever you go to a grocery store, your purchases are scanned, and in that simple gesture, the company knows what you bought, how much of everything you bought, what brands you bought, how much you paid for everything. If you offer your loyalty card for discounts and coupons, the company uses your buyer identification number to tie your current purchases to your past buying history.

In addition, these companies hire store and area auditors to integrate into the database what the prices were for competing brands, whether any brands were on sale or specially featured (e.g., in end of aisle displays), which brands were advertised in local weekend newspaper inserts, etc. Finally, beyond your grocery scanner swipes and the auditors' supplementing the data, panels of consumers are hired by marketing research firms (e.g., Information Resources, Inc. or A. C. Nielsen) who agree to participate (usually for ridiculously nominal gain), to have their media tracked (e.g., electronic hookups to TVs and the Web), and to provide the companies with household information (income, zip code, number and ages of children, etc.). Companies can use these single-source data to tie purchase patterns to demographics and media.

These data can be used to forecast demand or to watch consumer responses as a function of all kinds marketing mix activities. For example, if you want to know the answer to the question, "If we raise our prices by X amount, what happens?" These questions are answered via causal or experimental methods. The idea is that if you manipulate something (like price) and all else remains constant (which can be a big assumption in the real world), then any change in sales for your brand would be attributable to your intervention.

Field Experiment

A brand manager was studying the effect on pharmaceutical sales of three classes of factors:

1. *Product Characteristics:* Some drugs may sell better due to qualities inherent in the drug and its intended actions. For example, drugs taken to address chronic conditions (e.g., statins to lower cholesterol) or lifestyle choices (e.g., birth control pills) may well sell more than periodic pills for acute attention.
2. *Competitive Strategies:* Some drugs may sell better because they come from certain firms, with a certain approach to business, as measured by its drug's FDA ratings, how long the drug has been in the market, the firm's order of entry (e.g., the so-called pioneer effect).
3. *Marketing and the Promotional Mix:* Some drugs may sell better because they have crack marketing teams on them (crack meaning good, not street cocaine). For example, budget afforded to a sales force for detailing—i.e., visiting hospitals and docs' offices to explain new drugs and build relationships—and for providing samples.

What worked? Product characteristics helped sales (i.e., whether the product itself was good or not), and marketing helped sales (we rock), and, not surprisingly, there was a synergistic boost between the two. Supporting good product with good marketing is the best of all worlds. Wondering about the company's business philosophy? It didn't make a dent.

(For more info, see Latta's "What's Having the Most Impact?" at quirks.com.)

Price or packaging can be tweaked in one market or in one store in one town, and subsequent sales can be compared to those in the other markets or stores that serve as the control group. This kind of study provides the cleanest test possible of the ROMI (return on marketing investment) of any marketing mix lever: Tweak the marketing, and watch the sales move.

Many things also happen in the marketplace that you can't control; e.g., if it's not you but your competitor that raises prices, what happens? This scenario is referred to as naturalistic observation; you're not tweaking the environment, but you're constantly monitoring it. You can still run regressions to try to forecast and understand what happens under different scenarios. It's just that it's likely that many factors are moving simultaneously, so it's more difficult to attribute sales differences to one localized action, such as competitors' raising prices.

Experiments have the advantage of internal validity. In other words, when we tweak something, if all else is held constant, we can be rather confident in our causal statements: "We did X, so the changes are attributable to X." Natural observation has the advantage of external validity, meaning it's a little easier to believe that our findings will generalize to the real world because indeed it was unfolding in the real-world setting. These strengths are somewhat at odds. For example, field studies are conducted in the real world, so they are strong in external validity, but they tend not to be as clean in terms of internal validity. Often numerous alternative explanations must be eliminated before we can be certain about the reasons for the results we've seen. We may wish to attribute our sales increase over recent weeks to, say, our added promotional efforts but we'd need to eliminate the possibility that sales were going to increase naturally due to reasons such as the seasonality of the product. The good news is that the strengths of these two kinds of studies are complementary, so smart companies engage in both.

15-7 SURVEYS FOR ASSESSING CUSTOMER SATISFACTION

Many companies are interested in getting feedback from their customers. As a result, a little industry within marketing research has sprung up to offer their services at creating and evaluating customer satisfaction surveys. While surveys involve a bit of an "art," and therefore, relying on someone with experience is a good idea, the basic idea is not complicated. You write survey questions, pre-test them, and then put the survey out to a sample of your customers.

Questions about customer satisfaction can be as straightforward as "How would you rate the service you just received at our car dealership? 0 = very dissatisfactory to 100 = very satisfactory." It's also common to ask customers how the purchase rates compared to their expectations, e.g., "How did your visit at our hotel seem to you? 1= fell short of my expectations, to 4 = met my expectations, to 7 = greatly exceeded my expectations."

Beyond customer satisfaction, lots of surveys ask about repurchase intentions and intentions to generate word of mouth, e.g., "How likely is it you would fly with our airline again for your next trip? 1 = very unlikely to 9 = very likely." Or, "I am going to tell my friends to come to this restaurant. 1 = strongly disagree to 5 = strongly agree."

It is important to include actionable survey questions. If customer satisfaction is high, that's great, but, if it's low, there need to be some diagnostic questions that point to the priorities a company should take to enhance customers' perception of quality (recall Chapter 14).

Surveys are supposed to be short so that the respondent doesn't have to endure much pain or boredom, and shorter surveys enhance response rates. Responses are kept confidential, for research purposes only, not for subsequent sales opportunities. Marketing researchers are expected to attend to strict ethics (for AMA's standards, go to marketingpower.com).

Big Data

Scanner data, CRM databases, or any huge data set requires "data mining."

- The databases contain millions of customers and SKUs.
- The analytical techniques aren't that different from those used on smaller data sets.
- The challenges of working with large data set include IT (memory for storage) and time (for the number crunching to be completed).
- The largest practical concern for businesses is simply the coordination of disparate data. Data come from many sources:
  - Customer behaviors (e.g., purchase transactions, customer service and call center transactions, website visitations, warranties registrations)
  - Attitudes (e.g., postpurchase satisfaction survey data, sales contacts follow-ups)
  - Demographic data (e.g., zip codes from purchase data yield geo and income estimates)

The sources must be organized to have any value, before the data miners begin their dig.

Respondents can be consumers or B2B customers. Surveys can be administered in person (e.g., the people who intercept you at shopping malls with clipboards), over the phone, via fax, and, of course, increasingly, on the Web.

What's cool about surveys is that you can ask customers about anything. Even more impressive is that they'll answer you on just about anything. Recall the NPO segmentation study earlier in this chapter. We had 11 survey items, rather a lot of variables. A first step to simplify the analysis would be to reduce that number. That reduction is done via factor analysis.

Factor analysis is a technique that begins with a correlation matrix, like that in Figure 15.17 (this set of variables is a subset of the NPO study, to keep things simple). Factor analysis examines the strong and weak correlations to identify underlying factors common to the responses. Some of these correlations are larger than others, indicating that perhaps they're measuring the same underlying concept or factor. If two items are highly correlated, then we could take advantage of the fact that they're somewhat redundant by maybe just taking an average of the two items as we proceed to other models, such as regressions and forecasting.

	Q5	Q11	Q9	Q10
Q5 = Higher education is very important	1.00			
Q11 = I would help sponsor a kid	0.93	1.00		
Q9 = Only the very privileged	0.48	0.52	1.00	
Q10 = Higher ed is too expensive.	0.25	0.25	0.91	1.00

Figure 15.17
Correlations Among Some NPO Survey Items

© Cengage Learning

Helpful Data

Here are some helpful data sources:

- Stats on people and economies:
  - *US:* census.gov, stat-usa.gov, ita.doc.gov
  - *Global:* worldbank.org, un.org, country-data.com, greenbook.org, euromonitor.com
- Big, full-service marketing research providers: nielsen.com, symphonyiri.com, quirks.com, bases.com, npd.com, synovate.com
- Special interests:
- *Small biz:* sba.gov
- *Europe:* esomar.com
- *Asia:* apec.org
- *Latin America:* latin-focus.com
- *Health care industry:* dssresearch.com
- *Media:* arbitron.com
- *Customer satisfaction:* jdpa.com

Figure 15.18 provides the factor analysis solution. Within each factor, we're looking at the large numbers because those items define the factor. Thus, these results indicate that a perception of education being important and a willingness to help out hang together; i.e., many of the customers who rated education as important (or unimportant) also rated a higher (lower) willingness to sponsor, which is all to say the items were correlated and perhaps form a single factor. The second factor reflects the apparently overlapping opinions that only privileged people can get to college and that college is too expensive.

Figure 15.18		Factor 1	Factor 2
Factor Analysis on NPO Data	Q5 = Education important	0.94	−0.01
	Q11 = Help sponsor	0.96	0.01
	Q9 = Only privileged	0.18	0.89
	Q10 = Too expensive	0.12	0.99

© Cengage Learning

The computer produces a matrix that looks just like this figure, and it is up to the marketer to interpret what each of the factors means. The meaning is driven by whatever the variables with high coefficients seem to have in common. For example, for factor 2, we have to decide what "privilege" and "too expensive" have in common—something about money, obviously.

Factor analysis and cluster analysis are nicely complementary techniques. A factor analysis can be used first, to group variables into factors, and a cluster analysis used next, using the smaller set of factors (rather than the larger set of raw variables) to group customers into segments.

Direct Mail Experiments

Direct mail campaigns provide a great context in which to run experiments—to see what qualities of an appeal attract some consumer response vs. those features that provide no apparent lift. Marketing researchers did just that, experimenting with all kinds of content and forms of direct mail appeals. They studied the responses of 3,000 households throughout 1 year to 677 different direct mail campaigns, 396 of which ran for nonprofit clients and 281 campaigns were run for financial service providers. Together, nonprofits and financial services comprise approximately a 3rd of the direct mailing industry volume.

The panel of 3,000 households was asked to continuously collect any unsolicited mail they received. At the end of the month, they forwarded to the marketing research firm all of that mail that they normally would have thrown away, whether immediately or upon opening. They were asked to describe on a standard form the direct mailing pieces that they retained. The marketing researchers focused on two kinds of consumer behaviors: What properties of the direct mail campaign affected whether someone opened the envelope, and what properties affected whether someone kept it?

While there were a few differences between the nonprofits and financial services campaigns, in general, opening rates were enhanced if there was a teaser question on the envelope (e.g., "Gift certificate enclosed," "Your personal free invitation is enclosed," "Please open immediately," that sort of thing). Opening rates were hurt if the envelope was any color other than white. The marketing researchers didn't mention why color hurt, but we might hypothesize that a basic white envelope was perceived as more business-like and therefore more legitimate.

Next, the marketing researchers turned their attention to keeping rates, which presumably are more proximate to taking action, such as giving money to the nonprofit or making an appointment with a financial advisor. While the identification of the sender on the envelope seemed to work contrary to the suspense created by a teaser, the presence of the sending company's logo on the letterhead was very important in helping the keep rate. Keep rates were also enhanced by personalization, which suggests that it is important to continue to pay for updated databases. Finally, keep rates were stronger for letters that were longer than a page; the marketing researchers posited that length and the additional details provided therein probably signaled the seriousness of the request.

(See Feld et al., "The Effects of Mailing Design Characteristics on Direct Mail Campaign Performance," *International Journal of Research in Marketing*, 30: 143–159.)

Managerial Recap

There are many marketing research techniques, and just about any can be used to address marketing questions related to the 5Cs, STP, and the 4Ps. In particular, some methods nicely match some marketing responsibilities:

- Cluster analysis identifies groups of similar customers and ideal for segmentation studies.

- Surveys and MDS are used to create perceptual maps, which are useful in assessing current competitive positions.

- Focus groups offer a natural vehicle for investigating customers' early reactions to corporate ideas, e.g., new product concepts, new advertising approaches.

- Conjoint methods ask respondents for preference trade-offs, which allows marketers to infer the attributes that customers value most.

- Scanner data allow the investigation of brand switching and loyalty and price sensitivity and the conducting of marketing experiments.

- Surveys are very flexible, and these days are common instruments for assessing customer satisfaction. Survey results can be cleaned up and simplified using factor analyses.

Chapter Outline in Key Terms and Concepts

1. Why is marketing research so important?
2. Cluster analysis for segmentation
3. Perceptual mapping for positioning
   a. Attribute-based
   b. Multidimensional scaling
4. Focus groups for concept testing
5. Conjoint for testing attributes
6. Scanner data for pricing and coupon experiments and brand switching
7. Surveys for assessing customer satisfaction

Chapter Discussion Questions

1. It's common for a top-level manager (i.e., your boss) to watch a single focus group, get excited about something a customer says, and prepare a marketing plan around it. Why do you know this is premature? How would you handle your boss?

2. Imagine designing a conjoint for your b-school's café. In particular, you're in charge of the daily pizza orders. Pizzas are tricky. While they're a simple foodstuff, they can be created in a zillion combinations. What factors should you test in terms of your fellow students' likely preferences? Wheat crust vs. white, thick vs. thin, plain cheese vs. sausage vs. sausage and green pepper vs. vegetarian (you get the picture). Design a conjoint that would result in identifying 2 or 3 popular slices that your café managers could order every morning. The student body knows you're responsible. How do you make the most of them happy?

Mini-Case

How to Issue an Attractive Credit Card Reduxe

Recall from Chapter 1, a national retail bank was contemplating what attributes would appeal to its customers if it were to issue a new credit card. The features that the bank focused on and the dummy variable codes were these:

APR:	14.9% (1)	16.8% (0)
Interest rate:	Fixed (1)	Variable (0)
Annual fee:	Waived (1)	$20 (0)
Brand:	Visa (1)	Mastercard (0)

They ran a conjoint study on every 10th customer who came into the main bank office until they had a sample of 100. These 4 factors result in $2 \times 2 \times 2 \times 2 = 16$ combinations. Each person rated the 16 possibilities from 1 (would not apply for such a card) to 100 (would definitely apply for such a card). The regression results follow:

$$\text{Card attractiveness} = 0.6\ \text{APR} + 0.2\ \text{Rate} + 0.9\ \text{Fee} + 0.1\ \text{Brand}$$

Mini-Case Discussion Questions

1. What features matter to customers, and which do not?

2. What would the optimal card look like? If you were to cluster the customers first, and then run a separate conjoint on each cluster, do you think the results would vary? Could the bank issue different credit cards to satisfy multiple segments?

3. Are you worried at all about the sample. Are customers who visit the main office representative of those who visit branches, or ATMs, or do all their banking online?

4. What features do you wish the bank had included that might appeal to customers more?

Video Exercise: *Research Design at LSPMA* (14:25)

Lake-Snell-Perry-Mermin Associates (LSPMA) is a decision research firm that works on behalf of clients to determine what different segments of the population believe and feel about issues of interest to the clients. A 3rd of LSPMA's work is for political candidates, another 3rd is work for progressive issues organizations, and the remaining 3rd is work for foundations and major institutions. LSPMA uses telephone polls, online polls, and in-person and online focus groups to collect data and to identify population (or audience) segments. Audience segmentation enables an LSPMA client to identify groups of people who are supportive of its issue(s) or cause(s), groups who can be converted to being supportive, and groups who will never be supportive. A client can then target its resources toward connecting with and persuading those segments that are likely to be the most receptive to the client's message. The research enables the dividing of the audience into segments; once segments are identified, they are tracked in future decision research. Although audience segmentation can be useful, it can make the population seem more divided than it actually is.

Video Discussion Questions

1. Why do political organizations need marketing research conducted by LSPMA?

2. What is the relationship between marketing research conducted by LSPMA and identifying the needs and wants of specific market segments?

3. Why would a business rely on a marketing research firm that is heavily into political polling?

Chapter 16
Marketing Strategy

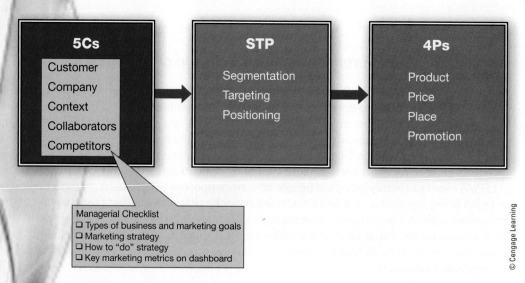

5Cs
- Customer
- Company
- Context
- Collaborators
- Competitors

STP
- Segmentation
- Targeting
- Positioning

4Ps
- Product
- Price
- Place
- Promotion

Managerial Checklist
☐ Types of business and marketing goals
☐ Marketing strategy
☐ How to "do" strategy
☐ Key marketing metrics on dashboard

© Cengage Learning

Marketing Management Framework

Strategy can mean a lot of things, so we'll begin by discussing business and marketing goals, and then we will look at several approaches to thinking about marketing strategy. We'll assess our company's current standing and what it will take to achieve our goals, and we'll consider measures to evaluate the extent to which we've been successful at doing so.

16-1 TYPES OF BUSINESS AND MARKETING GOALS

Let's begin by thinking about business very simply. Then we'll see more clearly what marketing goals should be set to achieve the broader business goals.

No company is in business to merely breakeven year after year. Even nonprofits want more money to be able to support their socially responsible missions. So let's agree that growing profit is the ultimate goal. Even that simple statement can be achieved via multiple paths. We know that:

(1) Profit = Sales revenue − Costs

Breaking the right-hand side down into its components,

(2) Sales revenue = Sales volume (in units) × Price

(3) Costs = Variable costs + Fixed costs

If we plug (2) and (3) into equation (1), we obtain

(4) Profit = (Sales volume × Price) − (Variable costs + Fixed costs)

Further:

(5) Variable costs = Variable unit costs × Sales volume (in units)

Thus, substituting equation (5) into (4), we see

(6) Profit = (Sales volume × Price) − [(Variable unit costs × Sales volume) + Fixed costs]

Every year, many business books are published, each promising the secret to great riches. Equation (6) shows there is no secret. The answer to riches is very simple (which is not to say it's easy). As Figure 16.1 also depicts, to increase profitability, we want to increase sales volume, change prices, or decrease variable or fixed costs. So, as marketers, let's see the myriad ways of achieving these goals.

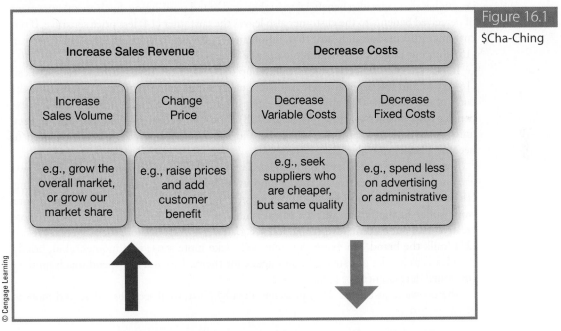

Figure 16.1
$Cha-Ching

© Cengage Learning

We can *grow sales volume* by (1) growing the market or the size of the overall pie or (2) growing our market share or our slice of the pie. Either of these can be achieved by (3) receiving more revenues from our current customers if we can up-sell our more expensive offerings to them, or (4) getting our current customers to buy more frequently, or (5) stealing customers from our competitors, or (6) finding another segment whose needs might not be far from those of our currently satisfied customer base. We can (7) create new products to satisfy our current customers or attract new ones; we can (8) reduce brand switching of our customers out to other competitors by enhancing our brand equity, (9) such as by raising

Definitions from dictionary.com

- *Goal:* The purpose toward which an endeavor is directed; an objective.
- *Objective:* Something that one's efforts or actions are intended to attain or accomplish; purpose; goal; target.
- *Strategy:* A plan, method, or series of maneuvers for obtaining a specific goal or result.

our customer satisfaction, (10) adding value through a loyalty program, or (11) otherwise raising switching costs so leaving our brand is not attractive. (Strategies 1 through 11 give us 11 means of increasing sales already!)

We can *change prices.* Unfortunately, most companies think about the option (12), cutting prices, which is deceptively easy to do. A drop in prices may bring additional volume in the short term by any economic prediction. But a marketer cares about the likely damage that will ensue to the long-term brand image and brand equity. Operationally, low prices and low margins also necessitate the hassle of having to deal in large volume. Furthermore, when we were looking at pricing, we saw that striving to be the low-price provider often initiates price wars and worse future margins. A far more profitable option is to (13) raise prices, which yields greater margins. A terrific side effect of this simple attempt to bring in more revenue is that customers usually believe that high prices are a cue to higher quality; i.e., higher prices are also beneficial to higher-end brand positioning. Such an enhancement of perceived benefits to the customer also leaves the customer (14) less price sensitive. If our customer information indicates that, unfortunately for us, they are price sensitive, we can (15) shift our target segment to more upscale buyers.

In our business delivery, we can tighten up our system to *decrease variable costs.* We can (16) try to find less expensive but requisite quality suppliers. We might (17) outsource the parts of our business that appear to be expensive for us but might be scalable and less expensive for a business partner. We might (18) choose to become a niche provider, to keep units down, and to keep price higher for our special customers. In general, we need to become a leaner provider.

The other cost-related lever is to *decrease fixed costs.* We can (19) spend less on R&D, unless our company prides itself on being innovative. We might (20) spend less on advertising. It's probably not a good idea to cut out advertising per se, so that our brand associations won't suffer in the future. But we can certainly cut advertising spending by being more creative with our current advertising dollar, e.g., fewer TV spots, more social media. We can (21) "milk the brand," an expression that will make more sense in a moment, but, briefly, the idea is to just let our strong brands speak for themselves and not spend much on their continued development or maintenance.

There—we've just listed 21 approaches already! Next, we'll see these ideas and more in other contexts.

16-2 MARKETING STRATEGY

There are numerous strategy gurus, each with a favorite approach to framing business and marketing situations. We'll look at the most popular frameworks. Marketers take more responsibility for increasing sales revenues and tend to pass much of the responsibility for decreasing costs to the operational side of the business. So it will come as no surprise that these strategic perspectives follow suit, emphasizing increased sales more than decreased costs.

16-2a Ansoff's Product-Market Growth Matrix

One very popular strategic tool makes no bones about it: It's all about sales growth. The question is what will be the source of that growth? Will we stick with our current product portfolio and simply try to get more purchases from our current customers or attract new customers? Can we create new products that might appeal to our current customers or use them to attract new customers? Thus, new stuff or new peeps?

Figure 16.2 shows all four possible product and market combinations. In the upper left of the matrix, we see the strategy of *market penetration*. In this scenario, we have no plans of expanding our product lines, nor do we seek new customers. We will simply encourage our current customers to purchase from us more frequently. This strategy is low risk, but obviously it also might max out quickly.

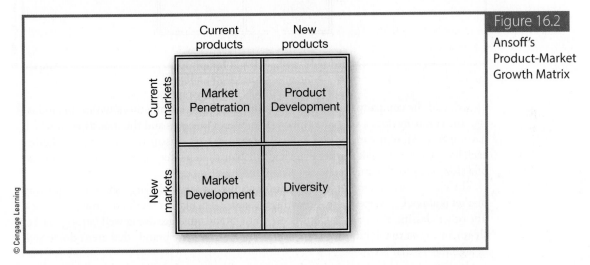

Figure 16.2

Ansoff's Product-Market Growth Matrix

In the lower left, we still have no new products, but we're reaching out to new customers. We're hoping to construct *market development*. Perhaps we have found a new use for our product that naturally suits a new customer segment, or perhaps we plan to advertise through new outlets (e.g., social media) to reach different demographics (e.g., younger customers).

In the upper right, we are introducing new products to our current customers. This *product development* strategy might fit well for a company that prides itself on being innovative, but it might be more of a stretch for more conservative companies. Entertainment and high-tech industries are masters of creating new products; they have the template (e.g., a DVD), and they just tweak the content. This approach is also thought to be a great way to really delight one's customers and strengthen their loyalty to us—by giving them even more value.

Finally, in the lower right, we have *diversification*, the most difficult and therefore riskiest strategy in this framework. We are trying to introduce new products to new customers, and obviously we're out of our depths in both. It is smarter to achieve diversification after first going through product development or market development. Get to know either a new product line or a new customer base before trying to do both simultaneously. Thus, to grow, we need to create new things or attract new people, or both.

16-2b The BCG Matrix

Figure 16.3 shows the BCG matrix, another strategic framework that has been useful to marketing managers for a portfolio analysis. It is also all about growth. The industry's

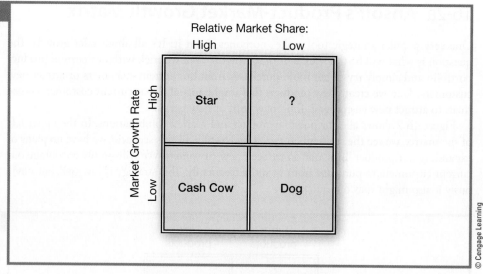

Figure 16.3

The BCG Matrix: Portfolio Analysis

© Cengage Learning

growth and the company's relative growth are compared to competitors' within the industry. The company does a self-assessment of its overall business and the industries in which it competes. All of a company's products (or brands) are classified according to whether each has a strong or weak market share and whether that market share occurs in the context of a slow or a growing market.

The classes have memorable labels. A brand with a relatively large share in a growing market is a *star*. Conversely, a brand with small share in a market that's not growing is a *dog*. The other classifications are *cash cows*, describing brands that are doing well (strong market share), in a nongrowth industry and *question marks*, which are brands that aren't doing well in an industry that is.

A company wants to optimize the number of its stars. It will also fiercely protect its stars. Thus, if company A's strategy is to enter into the market space near company B's star, company B will typically move swiftly to do whatever necessary to hold onto its star.

Cash cows are also desirable. These brands are literally milked; that is, usually advice is given that not much marketing attention (or budget) should be paid to these brands. It's not clear that that's great advice because in the spirit of a product's life cycle, withdrawing marketing support can propel a brand into faster decline. But the overall point is that the brand is very strong (awareness, trial, repeat purchasing, loyalty, etc.), and it is being leveraged, for the greater good of the company, by not devoting resources to it.

The future of question marks are somewhat unknown and also somewhat under control of the company. The industry shows potential, so the company might wish to support the brand with richer marketing (quality improvements, promotional campaigns, temporary price cuts to attract more trial), in an attempt to transform the question mark into a star with an enhanced market share. These question mark products may be in development via new technologies, entering different markets, etc., and they may need time and additional supporting resources to pay off for the company.

Finally, the dogs are brands that should be minimized. The company could just let them be, and reap whatever profits they bring in, however meager. Alternatively, if these brands have any residual value, they're also candidates for divestment. Note that moving a dog west to become a cash cow is not easy, and moving it north to be a question mark doesn't give us clear closure (what will that question mark become?). Thus, who let the dogs out? Probably the brand manager.

16-2c The General Electric Model

The General Electric model is a strategic tool that forces the marketing manager to make explicit some judgments about the brand's (or the company's) performance, as well as the assumptions that the company operates under with respect to expected performance.

As shown in Figure 16.4, two dimensions are measured: market attractiveness and business strength. These dimensions are analogous to the external and internal pieces of SWOT analyses. For the external element (the market attractiveness), the particular ratings might vary, but in this example, the strategist is asked to fill in 2 sets of numbers:

1. The figures in the Weights column concern how important are sales volume, market growth rate, and competitive intensity to the firm? Constrain these weights to sum to 1.0.

2. What are the perceptions about how well the brand (or company) is doing in each of those areas? The ratings are made on a 1–5 scale, where 1 = awful and 5 = outstanding.

		Weight	Rating (1–5)	Value
Market Attractiveness	Sales volume	0.2	4	0.8
	Market growth rate 0.4	3	1.2	
	Competitive intensity	0.3	4	1.2
				3.2

		Weight	Rating (1–5)	Value
Business Strength	Market share	0.2	3	0.6
	Brand strength	0.2	3	0.6
	Unit costs	0.6	2	1.2
				2.4

Figure 16.4

The General Electric Model

© Cengage Learning

For the internal element called business strength, a number of subdimensions are also rated, both for importance (the weights) and for the achievement level (the performance ratings).

Next, we multiply the weights and ratings to obtain the numbers in the Value column. Those values and summed, and the sums are plotted in Figure 16.5.

This brand or this line of business is in a moderately attractive market, but the brand or firm is not doing as well as it might. Obviously, it is difficult to control the attractiveness of the market, but we need to find a way to get our business strength score up. Ideally, we'd be in one of the green (go-go-go) cells. We want to avoid the red disaster cells.

When we look at our business strength scores (back in Figure 16.1), we can diagnose that we are apparently an expensive shop—we need to control our costs better. Costs are important (the largest weight by far), and we get our lowest performance scores here. We're not doing remarkably well on market share or brand strength either, but neither are those facets are important (at least according to our own previously stated judgment).

16-2d Porter and Strategies

Porter offers another approach to classifying strategies. He says that generally a company can dominate its market in one of three ways. First, it can strive for *cost leadership*, producing goods and services more efficiently than the competition. To deliver such, the company might have resources such as easy access to plentiful, good raw materials, cheaper labor

Figure 16.5

The General
Electric
Model

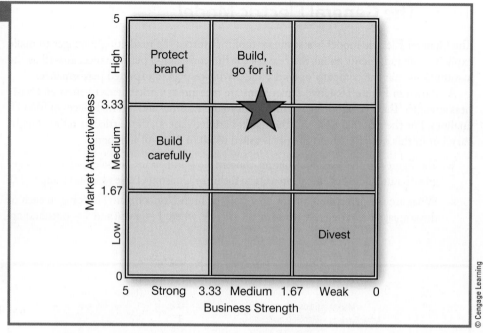

© Cengage Learning

sources, better information or other technologies, etc. The cost savings might be passed along to customers in the form of low prices, or they may be retained as higher margins than those of the competition, thereby fueling other actions, e.g., R&D, more advertising, etc.

Second, a company might take the approach of *differentiation*. This strategy is an attempt to distinguish one's products as unique in the industry. Differentiation may be fostered through excellent quality in products and customer service, distinctive design, exclusivity, value-addeds bundled into the core purchase, etc.

Porter calls the final approach *focused*. Whereas the cost leadership and differentiation approaches are said to be broad, the focused strategy is narrower. The mantra of these companies is typically "We do one thing very well." Such players often serve niche markets, and customers in that segment can be very satisfied, very loyal, and rather price insensitive.

Here are examples of companies implementing Porter's classes of strategies:

- Costco and Priceline show cost leadership and tell customers, "We're efficient!"

- Giggle stores sell baby stuff, and Buddhaful sells clothing online, and each positions itself via differentiation, telling customers, "We're unique!"

- EB Games (formerly Electronics Boutique) and Nunu Chocolates pursue the focused strategy, and the message to customers is "We do one thing very well!"

16-2e **Treacy and Wiersema Strategies**

Another major approach to classifying business strategies offers a slightly different set of three philosophies. Companies can seek to achieve and maintain *operational excellence, product leadership, or customer intimacy.*

Operational excellence is the ability to deliver products or services smoothly, reliably. In some industries, it is a necessity; e.g., a package delivery company or a cell phone company wouldn't go far if they could not provide excellent operations.

Product leadership is achieved by providing predictably excellent quality in products and services or by being a market leader in terms of innovations in those products and services. The churn of new products in high tech and electronics is a show of competing for product leadership. Just watch who is producing the newest, coolest toy.

Customer intimacy involves the knowledge of a customer's fuller set of needs and trying to offer customers a full package of benefits, highly tailored to their unique desires. While there are nontech versions of intimacy (e.g., a customer's relationship with a good hairstylist, realtor, banker, etc.), it's no surprise that this approach is huge, and hugely effective, online. There, customer relationship management hits new highs because of the data storage and access capabilities. Hence, all of the recommendation engines for books, music, movies, and such demonstrate a strong advance toward customer intimacy.

Here are examples of companies implementing Treacy's and Wiersema's classes of strategies:

- Fandango and TurboTax pursue operational excellence, telling customers, "We're smooth and reliable!"

- Apple, BMW, and Mont Blanc demonstrate product leadership, and the message to customers is "We're excellent and special!"

- Amazon, Facebook, Netflix, Pandora, and Xmarks demonstrate customer intimacy, with a positioning that says, "We know our customers very well!"

There are probably as many ways to think about strategy as there are strategy theorists. We will describe a few more as the chapter unfolds, but these—Ansoff, BCG, GE, Porter, and Treacey and Wiersema—are the big ones.

16-3 HOW TO "DO" STRATEGY

While the word "*strategy*" sounds abstract, in truth, it is usually grounded in practicality. A company must know itself, its environmental context, its competitors, its collaborators, and, of course, its customers (yes, the 5Cs) before knowing where it wants to go next or deciding there is a problem to solve or opportunity to exploit.

Strategic planning involves a reflection of our corporate identity. We pose the questions, "Who are we?" and "Who do we want to become?" Stated differently, recall the $2 \times 2 \times 2 \times 2$ positioning matrix in Chapter 5. The question is, "Are we positioned where we want to be?" Do we wish to be high quality, high price, selective promotion, and exclusive distribution? Or do we wish to be basic quality, lower price, broader band promotion, and mass distribution? If we wish to vary from either of these extremes, why do we think that makes sense for us, and how do we proceed?

Strategic planning questions may be revisited for a number of reasons: (1) A company may simply be a thoughtful, reflective one that revisits its assumptions from time to time. (2) The company may be considering launching a new product, or a line extension, or a new partnership, or something new, and it wants to be smart about it, either by being consistent with its current business or in using the new action to move purposely through the positioning matrix. (3) Contextual issues may arise, such as the economy tightening up, a competitor gets acquired by an international company, etc. (4) A company or industry might be experiencing changes in profitability or its component drivers (equation 6). Note that these scenarios are easily discoverable via periodic SWOT analyses. That's terrific because SWOTs are so easy to do and communicate. Let's see how an internal examination of the company's strengths and weaknesses lend clarity to the strategic exercise.

Corporate Ethics

- If a company screws up, how should it be punished? A firm can't go to jail. Picking some executives as scapegoats doesn't capture the complexities of decision making in large organizations. So a company pays fines. But who really pays the fines? The company can increase their prices to recapture its finances! Plus, the fines are tax-deductible!

- Is it okay when consumers don't know certain facts? For example, Miller markets "Plank Road" beer as if it's from a small brewery, and Disney produces R-rated films under name Miramax. Some might argue that it's impossible to tell customers everything about their products and how they're made.

- What about pricing? What constitutes a fair price? Economics tells us that the right price is where the supply and demand curves cross, but does that means the price is fair? When buyers and sellers agree on price in their negotiations, does that mean the price is fair? Customers often complain about prices being too high, but they rarely understand the complexities of a company's costs (e.g., for wireless phone service, health care provision, etc.). If we also believe in the economic premise of utility maximization, and so believe that buyers and sellers are both looking out for their own interests, how often or how easily could they arrive at a price they both consider fair? As a final twist, consider that economists might say that the market determines the price, but marketers want more than a single transaction with their customers.

- PricewaterhouseCoopers, in their Sustainability Survey, reported the top reasons that companies try to be socially responsible. The reasons aren't exactly altruistic. Companies hope their social responsible actions will provide them an enhanced reputation, a competitive advantage, cost savings, and a way to meet industry trends. When MBA students were surveyed, they thought that the benefits to companies would be a better public image or reputation, greater customer loyalty, a more satisfied and productive workforce, and fewer regulatory or legal problems.

- Some nice corporate practices:
  - Xerox employees who are selected for its Social Service Leave Program can take a year off with full pay to work for a community nonprofit of their choice.
  - Green Mountain Coffee Roasters pioneered in helping struggling coffee growers by paying fair trade prices (which exceed regular market prices) and offering microloans to coffee-growing families.
  - Chick-fil-A operates foster homes, summer camps, and sponsors major charity golf tournaments.
  - BP spends money on energy-efficient product development.
  - GE's Ecoimagination conducts research on minimizing pollution.
  - Starbucks donates money from its sale of Ethos bottled water to places that need clean drinking water.
  - Home Depot no longer stocks lumber or wood products from endangered forests.

For more, see Davidson's *Moral Dimension of Marketing* and the *Sage Brief Guide to Marketing Ethics* (Sage).

16-3a SWOT's S&W

An important assessment in strategic thinking is corporate identity with regard to the company's typical philosophy toward the marketplace. For example, some companies pride themselves on being innovative and want to invest in R&D so that they can enter the marketplace with cool new things, frequently and regularly. Other companies have a more conservative, careful culture, so they will rarely lead temporally (although they may lead in market share). Similarly, some companies are more inclined to take offensive initiatives (initiating price wars or launching competitive advertising claims), while others are more likely to respond defensively.

Whether a company shows tendencies toward offensive or defensive actions isn't correlated with size; a company with a large market share may have the resources to take the initiative and lead the other players in a new direction, but small entrepreneurial companies frequently create something new in the marketplace that may elicit responses from other (bigger, older) competitors. In addition, the role that a firm plays in the marketplace can change over time; it is not unusual for a company to be more aggressive (risk seeking) in its youth and to age toward conservatism (risk averse), when it has market share, sales, and customers to protect.

Companies can be referred to as leaders for various reasons. They may have the largest market share; they may have been first to market; they may be known for being innovative, quick to improve another company's ideas, a company known to please its customers, etc., showing leadership in any of a number of ways. And, of course, life is rarely black and white, so there aren't just leader and follower companies. There are leaders, quick followers, followers, also-rans, barely-in-the-games, etc.

Furthermore, while many companies think of themselves as innovative, it's not clear that being first to market is always a good thing. For example, launching really new products can be risky, adoption can be slow, and the pioneering company can take quite a hit. In comparison, the so-called quick-follower companies can learn from the leader's mistakes and benefit from customers learning how the new offering might be valuable in their lives. Yet few companies want to think of themselves as quick followers.

Finally, it's completely rational to have a slightly split personality in that a company can be a leader for some of its brands in their respective industries and more of a follower for its other brands. For example, the company's orientation to offense or defense may vary across its brand portfolio; mature, cash cow brands are treated carefully, whereas more risk is taken with newer ventures. This distinction depends on the products' life cycles and the maturation of their respective industries more broadly. Lastly, natural dynamics coincide with the 5Cs, such as the economic context. If innovativeness is central to a company's identity and economic times are good, then venturing into a large-scale offensive action can be sensible. If the corporate culture is more conservative or if the economic context is weaker, then more moderate actions make better sense, such as mere line or brand extensions in the case of new product launches.

16-3b SWOT's O&T

A reexamination of strategic goals can also be brought on by changes in the external elements of SWOT, or when observing the effects of the 5Cs on perceived opportunities and threats. If market shares are being eaten away by new competitors, or if our prices are no longer attractive to our customers, how shall we respond? These motivating questions would bring us to the strategy table.

When considering any variation of goals, it is helpful to keep in mind that when all is said and done, there are really three strategies. The first two are a little lame, but they're done all the time. The 3rd is more exciting, but naturally it's more complicated.

The 1st strategy is to *do nothing*. We'd let a brand sink or swim on its own with no infusion of marketing budget (and we'll probably watch the brand decline). This passive strategy might be used on a cash cow brand to funnel funds to another brand that needs resource support.

The 2nd strategy is to *do nothing differently* from status quo. We may have a mature brand in a stable market, so we maintain business as usual, same price, same marketing support, etc. This strategy is somewhat nonthinking. If business is good, keeping on track seems sensible enough (i.e., "Don't fix what's not broken"), but when business drops or competitors step up, a status quo strategy won't yield good results.

The 3rd strategy is to *do something different*. Then the question is what do we wish to change? Very common, very popular, and very timely goals follow.

Let's make more money! Most organizations have monetary goals: A company can set sales objectives in terms of some currency or relative to other providers (i.e., market share goals). We can aim for profitability objectives, such as routing some cash cow monies toward some question mark brands. Sales goals can be stated in terms of units or in terms of change from last year or quarter. Goals can be stated per region, e.g., minimal or typical growth in the company's standard markets but more aggressive growth in the company's newer markets. Sales goals can be formulated against investments made toward the current sales, per the philosophy underlying the ROI or ROE or ROM (return on marketing) or ROQ (return on quality initiatives), etc.

There are many profitability goals: Show cost leadership, or grow share or volume. But goals must be simplified into component strategies to be achieved. For example, to grow the market, a company typically needs to spend a lot on advertising in order to convince nonusers to become purchasers in this product category and, in particular, to choose the company's brands. Thus, the goal of growing the market is really convince nonusers? → need to increase the advertising budget → that should help grow the market.

Similarly, the goal of increased market share may be described as a string of minigoals. One company may say, "We will grow our piece of the pie by persuading our current customers to buy more or to upgrade to our more expensive (and profitable) brands." Another company might say, "We will increase our market share by siphoning off our competitors' customers—we'll steal share!" These companies have different philosophies, and their messages to their customer bases will differ accordingly.

Let's delight our customers! A company can try to enhance customer satisfaction, create an attractive loyalty program to lock in customers, reward customers for being influential and spreading good word of mouth, etc. If marketing research indicates that customization is valued, the firm might investigate whether it can offer such personalization profitably. Perhaps CRM systems could be used to tailor messages to the target segment better, in turn reducing acquisition costs and enriching customer lifetime value.

Let's reposition our brand! Strategic goals must integrate all 4Ps, but sometimes it seems like the focus is more on one P than the others. For example, goals regarding better promotional communications can include spending our advertising dollars more wisely, figuring out which media make most sense to our segments and for which part of the message. Place or distribution goals involve identifying what channels the target customers find most desirable. Perhaps multichannel touch points are no longer needed; e.g., some industries are successfully moving their value-sensitive segments to self-service or to lower-cost channel interactions.

Goals about broader social concerns. Different goals arise when a company broadens its scope and sets goals beyond marketing and sales per se. The goals may reflect the health of the broader organization, such as human resource and internal marketing (e.g., employee wages and benefits, career development, reduction of turnover, etc.) or societal concerns—giving back to context C (e.g., charitable or community contributions, boosting stability of local employment, demonstrating leadership in environmentally friendly business practices, etc.).

The core of marketing is 5Cs, STP, and 4Ps. Typically we don't have control over all the 5Cs, but the other elements have some malleability. So, shall we seek a new target segment(s)? Change one of the 4Ps? If we change 1 P and we're truly practicing integrated marketing and wish to build consistency for brand equity, we need to be sure to examine how the other Ps are affected as well. For example, if the boss says, "We should raise prices," think through what the other Ps should look like to ensure that a consistent message is sent to the customer.

Strategy Snippets

- P&G wants to sell more razors. India's a large population. P&G has launched a campaign to get Indian men to shave more often. Tagline says, "W.A.L.S. Women against lazy stubble." P.S. P&G by-passed China for now (less facial hair).
- China may still seem new and unfamiliar to some companies, but it is a highly developed market for many products. Globally, China is the largest consumer of bicycles and motorcycles (7%), shoes (12%), cars (22%), cell phones (22%), and luxury goods (19%). They're number two in consuming home appliances (12%), consumer electronics (15%), jewelry (13%), and Internet usage (63%).
- When you think of Talbots, you think of a place where your mother would shop. Talbots launched younger, fresher lines of women's clothing. The young women aren't convinced yet, and the older women—the traditional target—are a little annoyed.
- What is RIM to do? As the BlackBerry declines in the States in favor of iPhone-like machines, it is still doing great globally (43% market share), especially in Indonesia. That's not a bad gig, given that that the market is 242 million people, the world's 4th largest population.
- Ugg needs to change plans too. Sales have been slipping, not even responding to offerings of animal prints or sparkly patterns or to Tom Brady as a spokesman. The novelty of the Ugg boots has worn off, and interested consumers have already made their purchase. For more customers or more of the wallets of current customers, it has been recommended that Ugg's branch out: Broaden the product line beyond boots into more outerwear, or create lighter-weight sheepskin products for warmer weather climates, or appeal to another segment, like men.
- Viva manufacturing!
  - A recent report by McKinsey's Global Institute describes how manufacturing is important for developing and advanced countries. In developing countries, it is commonly acknowledged that manufacturing helps take a country's citizens from an agricultural subsistence to circumstances with greater incomes and living standards. By comparison, in already developed countries, manufacturing is still where a great deal of innovation and competitiveness occurs, R&D grows and contributes, exports are created, and indices of productivity grow.
  - Globally, manufacturing typically creates some 16% GDP and 14% of employment. As manufacturing grows toward 20–35% of GDP, its relative contribution declines, not because manufacturing itself is in decline but because as wages have risen and consumers have money to spend, they begin to spend more money on services, so it appears that service sectors grow and accelerate. Governments and educational systems are considered important conduits to the growth of either manufacturing or services and to the transition from the one to an emphasis on the other. The results of manufacturing continue to dominate international trade—70% compared to 30% services, which are more likely to be created and consumed locally.

Corporate vision goals, not unlike personal goals, can be complex, numerous, interconnected, and at times overwhelming. And, like individuals making progress by focusing, companies too usually make faster progress by choosing the goals that, at the moment and for the times (see the 5Cs) and for the company's philosophy, seem the most important. After these goals are achieved or modified, the company can stake out more territory and achieve more goals.

16-4 KEY MARKETING METRICS TO FACILITATE MARKETING STRATEGY

How do we know how our customers see our strengths and weaknesses? How do we know what our competitors are doing? We monitor marketing metrics.

There's an old management adage that goes "You can't manage what you don't measure." More recently, it's morphed into "You measure what matters." The clear implication is that, if something is important to a company or its CEO, they're going to want to know how the company is doing. So it needs to be measured.

Measures are important both in the assessment phase (how are we doing) and in the strategic planning phase (what measures do we want to raise or lower). So let's consider some of the measures on goals that a company might pursue.

First, we'll surely keep an eye on a company's profitability. It was the beginning of this chapter, and it is the motivating basis of a company's actions.

But let's look beyond just finance. We can also measure indicators such as customer or employee satisfaction, a company's stewardship of the environment, etc. In terms of marketing, we can look at sales, share, average prices, levels of awareness, and penetration in trial. Some of these measures should be correlated with a company's financial health. Some indeed will be leading indicators.

Much has been made lately of a company's dashboard—the idea being that there are many indicators of a company's success, like the indicators on your car's dash representing fuel, speed, engine temp, and so forth. Finance looks at sales and profits, marketing looks at share, customer satisfaction, average prices charged, etc. HR looks at employee satisfaction and turnover rates. Operations track indices of a lean, mean, green, customer-pleasing machine.

Some proponents of company dashboards refer to a balanced dashboard. But balance is not a great goal. It suggests that being good at something implies that you would or even should be bad at something else.

Alternatively, take the sporting analogy of a scorecard: How are we doing on RBIs, errors, runs scored, etc. Choose your analogy, but the point is that companies also have multiple dimensions on which they can be measured. Some measures will confirm the ways the company is great and has advantages over competitors. Other measures can serve as a diagnostic in identifying problems that the company can strive to perfect. Anyway, whether we're keeping score or monitoring the dash, what are we looking for?

Figure 16.6 shows what a simple dashboard might look like for a company (or brand) whose sales are good, market share is good, profit margins are so-so, and employee and customer satisfaction aren't so great. What story does this profile of indicators tell? This particular brand operates in monopoly-like conditions; thus, sales and share are indeed strong because the customers don't have many alternatives. The lack of options might contribute to the relative poor status of customer satisfaction. The company's weak profit margins suggest that it's not operating cost efficiently, which does not portend well for the poor employee satisfaction. Why are they dissatisfied? Are employees not paid well? Are they working with old equipment? The solutions to either of these problems would cause the profit margins gauge to tilt farther to the left.

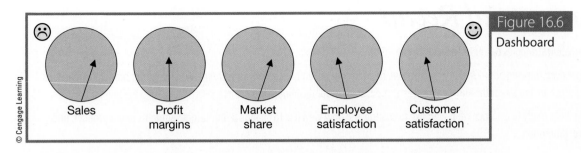

Figure 16.6

Dashboard

© Cengage Learning

Dashboard indicators represent information analogous to what our car is trying to convey: Are we driving on empty? Are we going too fast? Is our engine overheating? What's the temperature in the car? And so on. When the gauges head to the center or to the left, there's not necessarily reason for panic, but the levers give us a heads-up: Is it time to ease off the pedal (stop pushing our employees)? Go get fuel (invest in new plant equipment)? Turn the A/C down (conduct some marketing research to find out what bells and whistles would make our customers happier), etc.

Dashboards can take any shape. Figure 16.7 collects a number of diagrams in different formats that, together, express the attributes that this company cares about: revenue per customer over time and loyalty per segment, market share against the two primary competitors, quarterly customer satisfaction confidence intervals, and employee turnover per department.

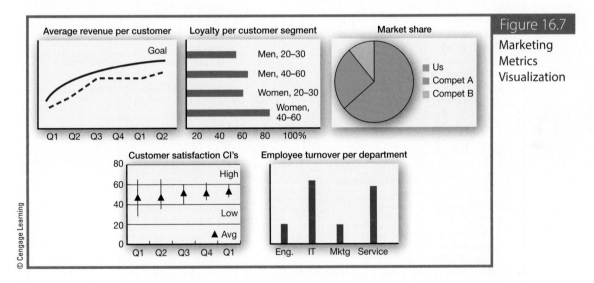

Figure 16.7

Marketing Metrics Visualization

© Cengage Learning

Use whatever format works for you. What's important is that you're overseeing multiple measures to optimally manage the company.

Some parts of marketing strategy may sound overwhelming, but you can do it, and you can do it well! Remember: If you *think about* your customers, and try to *think like* your customers, and simply *try to please* your customers, you will beat the competition. It is that easy. Really!

Managerial Recap

Many marketing strategies can be successful (Figure 16.8):

- Before even thinking about making changes, we need to conduct an honest self-assessment. What does our brand portfolio look like? What are our strengths and weaknesses as measured by our dashboard indicators?

- Then we're ready to consider what we'd like to change and how we'd like to change it: our target segments or our product, price, place, promotion.

- There are many ways to increase profitability, and some may fit our corporate culture and strengths better than other ways. There are also goals beyond profitability.

Figure 16.8

Strategies, Strategies, and More Strategies to Increase Profits

I.   Growing sales volume
  A. Grow the market, size of overall pie
  B. Grow our market share, our slice of pie
  C. More revenues from current customers
    1. Up sell them our expensive offerings
    2. Get them to buy more frequently
  D. Steal customers from competitors
  E. Find new customer segment(s)
  F. Create new products for current/new customers
  G. Reduce our customers' brand switching
    1. Raise customer satisfaction & brand equity
    2. Add value through loyalty program
    3. Raise switching costs
II. Changing price
  A. Cut price, but worse margins and rely on volume
  B. Raise prices
    1. Cue to quality, customers price insensitive
    2. Seek upscale buyers
III. Decrease costs
  A. Decrease variable costs
    1. Find less expensive suppliers
    2. Outsource
    3. Be niche provider
  B. Decrease fixed costs
    1. Cut back R&D (if we're not "innovative")
    2. Spend less (or smarter) on advertising
    3. Milk cash cow brands
IV. Ansoff Product-Market Growth Matrix
  A. Market penetration
  B. Market development
  C. Product development
  D. Diversification
V.   BCG
  A. Star (large share, growing industry)
  B. Cash cow (large share, non-growth industry)
  C. Dog (small share, slow market)
  D. Question mark (small share, growing market)
VI. The GE model
  A. Market attractive, business strength
  B. Weight, combine, matrix insertion
VII. Porter
  A. Cost leadership
  B. Differentiation
  C. Focused strategy
VIII. Treacy and Wiersema
  A. Operational excellence
  B. Product leadership
  C. Customer intimacy
IX. Positioning matrix
  A. High quality, high price, selective promotion, exclusive distribution
  B. Basic quality, low price, broad promotion, mass distribution
  C. If veer from either, have a good reason
X.   Company & Portfolio Strengths
  A. Offense or defense?
  B. Aggressive (risk seeking), conservative (risk averse)
  C. Leader or (quick) follower?
XI. Currently popular goals
  A. Make more money
  B. Delight our customers
  C. Reposition our brand
  D. Broader societal concern
XII. Ultimate strategy choices
  A. Do nothing
  B. Do nothing different
  C. Do something: What? See above.

© Cengage Learning

Chapter Outline in Key Terms and Concepts

1. Types of business and marketing goals
2. Marketing strategy
   a. Ansoff's product-market growth matrix
   b. The BCG matrix
   c. The General Electric model
   d. Porter and strategies
   e. Treacy and Wiersema strategies
3. How to "do" strategy
   a. SWOT's S&W
   b. SWOT's O&T
4. Key marketing metrics to facilitate marketing strategy

Chapter Discussion Questions

1. Consider the Treacy and Wiersema strategies for market dominance. Which of them (operational excellence, product leadership, customer intimacy) do you think guides these companies: Calvin Klein, Harley, Hermes, Lego, Microsoft, Nokia, Starbucks, Virgin?

2. If countries were brands, what metrics do you think these brands monitor: the U.S., China, Japan, Germany, Brazil? Are these brand managers watching the right indicators?

Mini-Case

How to Watch Movies

Consumers looking for entertainment have many options. Each content provider has business strengths and weaknesses. For example, Netflix has a recommendation engine, relatively quick delivery of DVDs and instant downloads for an increasing library. Hulu is all about instant downloading, is free because of advertising sponsorship, but has limited selections in particular movies and in availability durations. Cable services' on-demand features are not free, but some customers like the convenience of one-stop shop for cable and phone, etc., and selections are limited (in numbers and duration). Redbox has altogether different model, with vending located in popular places (e.g., near McDonald's, in airports), interchangeable pickup and returns locations, and, of course, limited selections.

Mini-Case Discussion Questions

1. How would you advise any of these companies with regard to their strategy, positioning, and tactical execution? Take one (Netflix, Hulu, Cable, or Redbox), and draw a scenario in which strengths might be retained, weaknesses strengthened or eliminated, and future directions pursued to make the business model more solid, more profitable, and less prone to competitive matching or attack.

2. Could Blockbuster reenter this arena? What would you recommend they do? If not, imagine you were to design an entertainment provider from scratch (movies and video games, mostly). What would it look like—STP and 4Ps? What elements in the 5Cs are likely to be most relevant to address in the near future?

3. If these companies start looking even more similar and commodity-like in the next 3–5 years, how would you advise one of them to break out of the pack and distinguish itself by offering … what?

4. How can any of these providers take greater advantage of a CRM philosophy? Most of them have little by way of retention programs; e.g., customers can cancel or rejoin anytime. Are there any benefits for staying?

Video Exercise: *Blue Dot* (6:00)

Blue Dot cofounders Maurice and John discovered they did not like the furniture they could afford after graduating college and wanted the furniture they could not afford. Blue Dot was conceived as a business venture to address what was perceived as a void in the U.S. furniture market. The furniture market can be segmented into several levels, ranging from the promotional level of inexpensive furniture on up to expensive, high-end furniture that is custom designed and accessible only through interior designers. The challenge for Blue Dot was to merge the affordability of the low-end furniture market with the craftsmanship and quality of the high end. Each Blue Dot product is expected to rely on a smart design composed of two components: (1) Be simple to put together, use straightforward materials and manufacturing processes, pack flat, ship efficiently, and (2) be attractive and interesting. Blue Dot's pricing is determined on the basis of cost plus the specified profit margin needed.

Video Discussion Questions

1. What would a SWOT analysis of Blue Dot reveal to a marketing professional?

2. What are Blue Dot's strategic goals?

3. Is Blue Dot's strategy one of cost leadership, differentiation, or focus? Explain your answer.

Marketing Plans

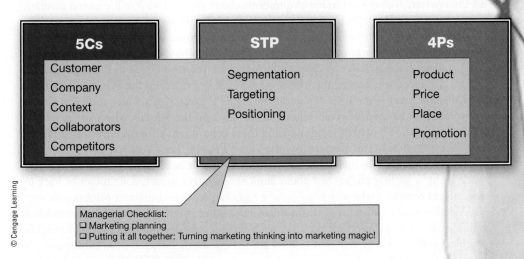

Managerial Checklist:
- ☐ Marketing planning
- ☐ Putting it all together: Turning marketing thinking into marketing magic!

Marketing Management Framework

17-1 HOW DO WE PUT IT ALL TOGETHER?

You've been reading and reading about marketing. Now, let's do it.

As Figure 17.1 indicates, the marketing plan begins with an executive summary. It provides a brief overview of the content of the larger planning document that follows. The marketing place retraces the marketing framework. Figures 17.2 through 17.5 collect the main themes and call-out questions from each of the previous chapters. Compiling these provides a good review, and seeing all the questions posed together gives a perspective on how the pieces fit together: The marketing framework pulls it all together.

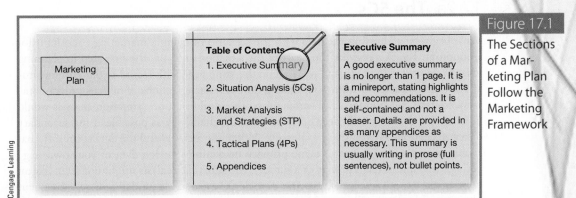

Figure 17.1

The Sections of a Marketing Plan Follow the Marketing Framework

Table of Contents
1. Executive Summary
2. Situation Analysis (5Cs)
3. Market Analysis and Strategies (STP)
4. Tactical Plans (4Ps)
5. Appendices

Executive Summary

A good executive summary is no longer than 1 page. It is a minireport, stating highlights and recommendations. It is self-contained and not a teaser. Details are provided in as many appendices as necessary. This summary is usually writing in prose (full sentences), not bullet points.

Marketing Plan

© Cengage Learning

A marketing plan begins with an assessment of where things currently stand. This situation analysis is documented by the 5Cs. We draw on those Cs to develop segments and choose segment(s) to target, per STP strategizing. The STP section usually involves summaries of marketing research, e.g., a segmentation study. Marketing and financial goals follow that stipulate the objectives the company wishes to achieve and how success and ROI will be measured. The next big section is an action plan for positioning by implementing the marketing mix 4Ps. Typically, this section is long and detailed because it contains both the big picture on strategy and the details on tactics.

Many workbooks are designed to assist in writing a marketing plan. They function like an interviewer, asking multitudes of questions about your brand. We'll proceed similarly. The questions and logic in Figures 17.2 through 17.4 offer a static approach, but we have also created an interactive module, available online to guide you in creating a marketing plan. Thus, the easiest way to develop a marketing plan is to go online (www.cengagebrain .com) and use the interactive spreadsheet built for you. There, you'll see an Excel spreadsheet. On the 1st sheet, you'll enter the information you have regarding the 5Cs, and, when you click on tabs 2 and 3, you'll see the questions for STP and the 4Ps. Once you enter all that information to the best of your ability, you can click on the 4th tab, where you'll see that all the information has been integrated and there is produced a (rough) marketing plan. If you can't get online at the moment, use the 5Cs-STP-4Ps framework to guide you to be as systematic as possible to include all the factors that might be relevant. For example, if your work group is getting all psyched about launching a new product, don't forget to back up and look at context, make sure you have the right target, have consistent price points, etc.

Whether you're gathering your information to enter it into the interactive spreadsheet online or to create a thumbnail sketch of what further considerations must be addressed for a project you're working on, what follows are the questions gathered from throughout the book. The information you'll need are categorized into the 5Cs, STP, 4Ps buckets, but don't forget that the creation of marketing plans isn't perfectly linear. When you find the answers to 1 of the Cs, you might need to adjust, say, your proposed T.

In this chapter, we illustrate all three parts of a marketing plan, applying it to one of three different marketing scenarios: marketing a nonprofit, getting into social media, and launching a new service. Alternatively, we could look at the plan for a single product, but it is better pedagogically for newbie marketers to see a breadth of examples to enhance the likelihood that they can apply the tools beyond the single exemplar.

17-2 SITUATION ANALYSIS

17-2a The 5Cs

We'll begin by addressing the 5Cs with the scenario of being a marketing consultant for a nonprofit. The 5Cs provide the heart of the situation analysis. The first step in planning what to do next is to make sure we're all on the same page with regard to our current situation. That assessment requires our nailing down characterizations of our customers, company, context, collaborators, and competitors. The ideal result of a situation analysis would be to answer every part of every question as comprehensively as possible, using secondary data and citations as extensively as possible. When the answers and the data seem soft, that should motivate you to gather some primary marketing research data of your own (e.g., perhaps a couple of focus groups or a survey). The situation analysis might not seem like an exciting place to spend a lot of time, but if we don't have a solid foundation here, subsequent planning and actions will be problematic.

Interactive 5Cs

To help you, we've provided online interactive tools to help you build a marketing plan.

- Go to www.cengagebrain.com, and download a spreadsheet that contains these questions. Fill them in, and they'll create a marketing plan for you. The online exercise is interactive, so it's easy to do what-if scenarios and tweak the input data and assumptions to see varying results.
- In the first 3 tabs, input your answers to the questions about the 5Cs, STP, and 4Ps.
- If we fill in all the answers on the 5Cs, STP, and 4Ps forms, then those answers will populate their respective boxes on the final spreadsheet, so that the end result is a draft of a marketing plan. Thus, click on the 4th tab to reveal the prize of your marketing plan.
- Let's begin with the 5Cs:

Spreadsheet Tab on 5 Cs

Customer	Fill in descriptions here:
Demographics (e.g., age, income, household composition, zip code):	Customer1
Psychographics (e.g., attitude to product, to competition, to ads):	Customer2
Buying behavior (e.g., frequency, only on sale, etc.):	Customer3
Current levels/measures of customer satisfaction:	Customer4
Do we have a loyalty program, efforts at CRM?	Customer5
Why don't nonbuyers buy?	Customer6
When our buyers buy, what channel do they prefer?	Customer7
When our buyers buy, do they seem to be price sensitive?	Customer8
What changes have we seen over buyers, expect any in future?	Customer9
Company	
What are we good at? Known for? Do a SWOT!	Company1
What do we want to become? Future strategy.	Company2
Context	
Is the economy a factor? Is it stable? Growing? What's the consumer mood?	Context1
Are politics a factor? Are our partners stable?	Context2
Is legal a factor? Any consumer laws looming?	Context3
Is technology a threat/opportunity? Machines? IT?	Context4
Any societal concerns? Demographic shifts? Attitude shifts?	Context5
Collaborators	
Good relations with supply chain providers?	Collaborators1
Good relations with distribution channel members?	Collaborators2
Want any modifications?	Collaborators3
Competitors	
Who are our major competitors (define this broadly)?	Competitor1
What are our competitors' strengths?	Competitor2

The 5Cs of the marketing framework are blown up in Figure 17.2, with the managerial checklist questions posed from their respective chapters to remind us of the basic issues. These figures provide the marketing questions in the interactive marketing plan builder that we emulate.

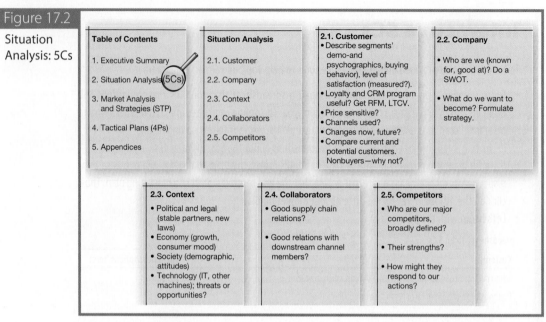

Figure 17.2

Situation
Analysis: 5Cs

© Cengage Learning

5Cs Example

As an example, let's cover the 5Cs for a nonprofit. A new nonprofit organization, Brain Trust, was registered last year, and its aim is to offer scholarships to offset university students' expenses. The NPO wants to achieve strong brand recognition, like many successful medical or children's charities. Some progress has begun, thus far only locally, but several good lessons have been learned that will facilitate rolling out nationally next year. So far, the answers to the company C questions on the marketing plan would be as follows:

Company questions and proposed answers:

- What are we known for? As a central point to coordinate the receipt and dispersal of scholarships, to enhance college attendance and graduation rates.
- Who do we want to become? A brand as well-known as Unicef or World Wildlife Fund so that we would be the 1st NPO a donor would think of when wishing to spend their largesse.

For the customer C, many NPOs have reasonably good data on their donors. Last year, Brain Trust began by renting lists of 50 universities' alumni and 10 cities' voter registration lists. Each person on the lists was sent two solicitations: One was a hard-copy mailing in mid-December (to cash in on the holiday spirit or in anticipation of annual taxes). The other was via e-mail for some people (and hard-copy for others), and the months were varied (in an experiment to see when and how responses might be most favorable).

Donors were allowed to specify how their dollars are to be spent in terms of (1) the kind of students to support, (2) the universities they'd attend. What was obviously the most appealing, however, was the choice to support students by the topics they were interested in studying. For example, some employees from DuPont and 3M (at least according to their addresses) sponsored chemical engineering students, whereas several alumni of a liberal arts college near LA earmarked their provisions for drama students, etc.

The target of donors from the alumni lists were between 30 and 60 years old. The voting lists ran a little older, 45 to 65. Most donors enclosed checks of $20 or $50. Brain Trust doesn't yet have a loyalty program, but it is being scrupulous about putting any new information into its CRM database (which was first populated by the alumni and voting lists). For donations of $100 or more, the CRM database triggers the NPO to send out a nice calendar (each month has a picture of some well-known brainiac).

Brain Trust ran a couple of focus groups to explore various elements of their programs, and one of the themes they heard was that people thought they had to donate large amounts of money, and they'd be embarrassed to give $5 or $10. In truth, obviously the NPO could use even those small donations. With that description of the NPO's donors, we fill in their customer answers:

Customer questions and proposed answers:

- Demographics are about 30–45 to 60–65 years.
- Psychographics: The donors care about higher education.
- Buying behavior: They tend to give $20–50 once a year.
- Customer satisfaction? It's never been measured, and it's assumed OK, given the repeat donations. There isn't a loyalty program as such, but those who donate $100 or more receive a calendar in thanks. Nondonors don't donate because they think they have to give large amounts.
- Channel for donors? Most send checks by mail.
- Are our "buyers" price sensitive? We could do a better job of letting our donors know that giving only a little is OK, and we could try to encourage them to give more frequently.
- Changes to expect? The NPO should grow as awareness grows.

In terms of the context, the NPO hopes giving will increase as the economy recovers; people probably don't want to give away money that they think they might need. The examination of the context factors pointed the Brain Trust people to something they hadn't considered before: the possibility that the Democratic and Republican donors might seek different things (e.g., education vs. fiduciary responsibility). So now they're thinking about how to explore that idea. No real legal issues have popped, so they count themselves lucky (and we'll leave it alone). In terms of technology, it obviously would be easier for the NPO and more cost-effective if more of donors would give directly online. In terms of broader societal concerns, it would seem that the NPO mission is already fairly enlightened.

Context questions and proposed answers:

- Economy: People are concerned with their economic security right now.
- Politics : This factor is somewhat unknown; they've never tried a different appeal to Democrats and Republicans.
- Legal seems not applicable as yet.
- Technology: Perhaps we can move more donors to give online, and perhaps we can post videos of students' testimonials.
- Societal: We can easily emphasize the many benefits of an educated populace.

The NPO admits that they hadn't thought about collaborators per se, before trying to do this marketing plan exercise. But doing so prompted them to consider who its suppliers and distribution partners were. One sense of a supplier is the route through which the NPO obtained its list of potential donors. While that seemed to work, it also seems limiting going forward. In terms of the downstream channel, the NPO began to think about where they might place ads to reach a broader base. In particular, their basic thoughts seem to be

Collaborator questions and proposed answers:

- Good relations with the supply chain? Fine so far—perhaps try to partner with some professional associations?
- Good relations with distribution channel members? Perhaps post ads on professional sites, LinkedIn, etc., to broaden appeal.

The discussion at the NPO was grim when the marketing plan turned to the question of competitors. While there may be few or no direct competitors (focused on higher ed), there are many competitors in the sense of an NPO to whom a person or household might give their donor dollars. Furthermore, many competitors dominated due to their very strong brand names. (It had to be pointed out to the NPO that, in fact, there are even zillions more NPOs, albeit relatively less known.) Thus, for competitors, the questions and proposed answers were

- Who are the main competitors? Any donation behavior: medical and health, museums and the arts, etc.
- Competitors' strengths? Some have very good brand names.

At this point, we compile our NPO answers and have the basis for part one of the marketing plan, the situation analysis:

Situation analysis for the NPO:

- Our current customers are 30–65 years old and care about higher education; their satisfaction is assumed to be OK if they donate repeatedly. We're beginning a CRM program and issue a calendar if they give $100 or more. This is what our customers do: They give $20–50 once a year, they send a check by mail, and they are price sensitive. We need to tell them that giving only a little is OK and get them to give more frequently. Here are possible customer issues to consider: Giving is not strong yet, perhaps due to the economy or lack of awareness, so could we develop a loyalty program, and could we assure them that giving only small amounts is still helpful?
- Currently, as a company, our position is our uniqueness in the NPO world to support higher ed. This marketing plan is to further strengthen brand recognition.
- Our current business environment reflects people's concerns with the economy. The NPO has never tried different appeals to Democratic and Republican donors; it is possible they seek different things. No legal issues are looming. We would like to move more of our donors' giving online, and perhaps we could post small video clips of our students.
- We might be able to leverage more donations if we partnered with some professional societies. We might consider a greater ad presence online, e.g., via LinkedIn.
- Our competitors are many—whoever receives donations. In particular, certain competitors may be a threat, given their strengths of big brand names.

Company. In a marketing plan, we'll start with a corporate self-examination. Much of the company C is knowing our own strengths, such as in a SWOT analysis, and knowing our goals, which we've delineated in Chapter 16. A SWOT is a strong tool that helps us understand who we are in the marketplace. At that point, we might begin to imagine what our desired position is so that we can begin to formulate a strategy to move us there. The primary company questions we need to analyze are these:

- What are we known for?
- What do we want to become?

Customer. We also require a good understanding of our customers. The only way to do so is to get data on them. We can begin by studying secondary data to know the background trends, but, at some point, we're going to have to roll up our sleeves and get in touch with our customers—get fresh data on our current customers, past customers, potential customers, our competitors' customers, everyone. To be systematic, we can lay out classes of customer questions and try to answer each as thoroughly as possible, at least the ones that seem most relevant. Specifically, we seek to describe our customers in terms of their

- Demographics.

- Psychographics.

- Buying behavior.

- Customer satisfaction and loyalty.

- Preferred channels.

- Levels of price sensitivity.

- Whether any of these descriptors are likely to change soon.

Context. Regarding context, assess the macroenvironmental issues you must attend to, e.g., legal, technological, social changes and trends. If you're working in the industry, you'll be familiar with these factors. If you're new to the industry or job, start reading in-house white papers and go online and study up. The PEST acronym covers the basic questions to pose for an understanding of the business context:

- Politics/legal

- Economy

- Societal

- Technology

Sometimes marketers gloss over these contextual factors, and sometimes that's okay because many of these factors are relatively stable. We revisit the questions only as we see changes in the environments or as we change; e.g., we choose to change our brand or target different segments. In addition, early in one's career, strategic decisions like "Should we go into Indonesia or Brazil next year?" are few and far between. But as you advance up the corporate ladder, increasingly your job responsibilities will become more global (literally), and you need to do a quick check to convince yourself that the factors aren't relevant in the new (to you) marketplace or that, when they are, how they affect your goals and plans.

Collaborators. Networks of support functions can be complex. Even good relationships between providers in the supply chain and the firm or the channel members downstream from the firm can be in flux, such as when new products are offered, with implications of shared shelf space, shared ad space, etc. If modification seems desirable, begin to sketch its nature (profit sharing, vertical integration, etc.) to try to maintain good relations. We'll begin by documenting the nature of those network ties upstream and downstream:

- Do we have good relations with supply chain?

- Do we have good relations with distribution channel members?

Competitors. For competitors, we'll have considered them implicitly in the SWOT, but we need to be sure to define our competition as broadly as possible, in order to identify true threats and opportunities, and from the customers' point of view. Next, we'll analyze our competitors' strengths and weaknesses relative to our own, once again doing so through the eyes of customers (i.e., with data), not just our own managerial assessment:

- Who are our competitors?

- What are their competitive strengths?

17-2b **STP**

STP is the essence of marketing strategy: What kinds of customers are out there (segments)? Which targets do we wish to serve? Then we'll begin to formulate our brand position.

With the 5Cs nailed down, we should have a good background for understanding and interpreting our customer segments, which in turn offers a clearer basis for choosing the segments to target. Figure 17.3 expands the STP portion of the marketing management framework for our planning purposes, and Table 17.2 emulates the interactive module on the STP strategic questions and choices.

Figure 17.3				
Market Analysis and Strategies (STP)	**Table of Contents** 1. Executive Summary 2. Situation Analysis (5Cs) 3. Market Analysis and Strategies (STP) 4. Tactical Plans (4Ps) 5. Appendices	**3.1. Segmentation** • What kinds of customer knowledge do we need to form segments? (Do we have demographic, geo, psych data? Shall we run surveys?) • Use cluster analysis to identify segments, and descriptive data to validate the "marketing segmentation" scheme.	**3.2. Targeting** • Choose segments to target: • "Size" the market, estimate its profitability (lifetime customer value) • Consider fit with corporate goals, and actionability (can we find target)	**3.3. Positioning** • Positioning via perceptual maps • Where are we in the positioning matrix? • Write position statement

© Cengage Learning

Interactive STP

Spreadsheet Tab on STP

Segmentation:	Fill in descriptions here:
Base segments on data; gather marketing research to conduct cluster analyses;	
describe marketplace in terms of demographics, psychographics, buyer behaviors;	
First, identify describe current customers:	Segment1
Next, describe nonusers:	Segment2
Finally, describe ideal customers:	Segment3
Targeting:	
Estimate size and profitability (lifetime customer value) of segments:	Target1
Characterize fit with corporate and marketing strategy of each segment:	Target2
Using financial and strategic info jointly, rank desirability of segments:	Target3
Positioning:	
Strategically choose high-quality/high-price or basic-product/low-price position:	Position1
Show how strategic position compares to competitors' positions:	Position2
Sketch distribution (wide or exclusive) and promotion plans (mass, light):	Position3

STP Example

To execute the STP of a marketing plan, let's visit a social media host company. The purpose of the site is to host friendship communications like any other social network service, but, in particular, they want to sell travel vacation packages through testimonials and word of mouth.

Naturally, to date, the site isn't the size of FaceBook, but there are about 800,000 users who sign on at least once a month. When people sign up (for free), they are asked some basic demographic questions, which, of course, can be tied to their online behavior. Most of the frequent users are young (low 20s), most of whom are online to stay connected to friends. A very small proportion (<10%) click through and actually buy trips. There are almost no users 40 years old or older. The younger profile is fine for now, as long as they have some money to spend, but they realize that, down the road, attracting people in their 30s and even 40s is likely to bring in more people with greater discretionary income. Compiling that description, we can characterize the current users, nonusers, and aspirant users:

The segmentation questions and proposed answers would be

- *Current Customers:* Young 20s. Some stay connected to friends; some click through and buy trips.
- *Nonusers:* 40s and older
- *Ideal Customers:* Mid-20s with good disposable incomes

The network managers hadn't previously considered the notion of acquisition costs. In particular, many site visitors were not only not bringing in money, but they were also costing real money. Of the people who did purchase a travel vacation, they took approximately one trip every other year. (The site is only about 5 years old, so these data, while better than nothing, are probably a little soft.) The typical trip purchased was $1,350, so, on average, this segment brought in about $625 a year. The stark monetary picture startled the network managers who had tried for a young, hip website. We might need to encouraging them to think more about money and less about being hip, and therefore we probably the need to bring in a slightly older, richer crowd. Thus, to prioritize the segments for potential outreach,

Targeting questions and proposed answers:

- *Estimate Size and Profitability:* The friendship connectors bring in no direct revenue and only minimal from word of mouth, whereas buyers are worth $625 a year (they take one trip every other year, approximately $1,350).
- *Corporate Fit:* Perhaps the network needs to aim for a little older customer, and in fact, trying so hard to be hip may be turning off an older crowd.
- *Rank the Desirability of the Segments:* Perhaps the best target may be the 25- to 35-year-olds; they have greater disposable income than younger people and probably more time than the slightly older, 35- to 50-year-old crowd.

The social media network site is obviously not the only game in town. There are also plenty of travel channels. From the beginning, this network's managers wanted to offer high-end travel, and the notion of the referrals was originally to help ensure that only similarly high-end others would be traveling companions on the trip. They were even thinking about instituting an invitation-only threshold to sign on and become members—that such exclusivity would be a good signal and would distinguish the site from many others (in social networks or travel). The problem then becomes how to seed the invites. As with any service that is fundamentally network based, this service would succeed better with some scale, but the numbers seemed acceptable already in this regard.

The positioning questions and proposed answers:

- High quality and high price or low quality and low price? The site wants to offer high quality, with prices that are high but an ability to claim that they're good value.
- Compare to competitors? No other provider is exclusive,
- Should distribution be mass or exclusive, and promotion heavy or light? To succeed, the site needs some scale, which suggests wide availability and presence and mass promotion if it is affordable (e.g., via an e-referral program).

Now we compile our social media answers and have the basis for part two of the marketing plan: STP, that is, strategic development.

Strategic development for social media network host:

- Based on our marketing research, customer segments may be described by age, online activity, and purchase activity of the trips. We currently serve the segment of young 20s. Some stay connected to friends; some click through and buy trips. We are considering moving toward (or also) serving mid 20+ with good disposable income. And, for now, we are not interested in serving customers in their 40s or older.
- To serve a customer base of sufficient size and profitability, we should pursue: Friendship connectors bring in no direct dollars and only minimal from WOM; buyers are worth $625 a year (they take one trip every other year, approximately $1,350). We believe that a focus on this customer base fits with our strategic corporate goals: Maybe aim a little older; maybe we should stop trying so hard to be hip (we may be turning off older crowd). We considered other segments, and their relative attractiveness is as follows: The 25- to 35-year-olds have better disposable income than younger visitors and more time than the 35- to 50-year-old crowd.
- In terms of positioning, overall, we will seek a strategically market position of high quality. Prices are high, but we say they're good value. This market space should compare favorably to our competitors' positions: No one else is exclusive. The marketing mix variables are described shortly. As an overview: To succeed, we need some scale, which suggests wide availability/presence and mass promo if very cheap (e.g., an e-referral program).

We'll start with segmentation, and recall that numerous variables could be relevant: (1) demographic, (2) geographic, (3) psychological, (4) behavioral, and more. We'll want to be able to describe groups of customers using hard data that may be satisfied with online secondary sources or industry-level trade publications. This assessment will draw a lot from the customer section in the 5Cs. In forming segments, we aim to formulate an understanding of

- Current customers.

- Competitors' customers.

- Nonusers.

- Ideal customers.

In *targeting*, we'll iterate between a managerial assessment of the fit of the segments' needs with our corporate and brand strengths and data-based estimates of market size and profitability. Even if the sizing exercise of chain estimates and lifetime customer value are based on making some assumptions, they're worthwhile. The assumptions themselves often bring issues to life, and if not, a high and low estimate can be inserted (where numbers are softer) to see the plausible range in estimates. We need to choose segments that are big enough to pursue. Specifically, we'll consider whether the segment(s) (1) has potential to be profitable enough, (2) has enough growth potential to pursue, (3) will fit with our corporate goals, and (4) are actionable, which often means finding an easily identifiable characteristic to serve as a proxy for the more central quality we're seeking. The act of targeting requires that we

- Estimate the size and likely profitability of the segments from which we might choose.

- Characterize the likely fit of each segment with our corporate goals and brand image.

- Conclude with a ranking of the desirability of the segments.

Finally, STP closes with *positioning*, which is executed by means of the 4Ps, and we'll turn to them shortly. Recall that part of positioning includes perceptual mapping and writing a positioning statement. In addition, we can consider where, in the positioning matrix, we desire our brand's presence. Do we want to be known for

- High quality and high price or low quality and low price?

- Do we plan on mass or exclusive distribution? Heavy or light promotional plans?

17-2c The 4Ps

The 5Cs tells us where we are, STP tells us that we have big-picture goals of becoming something else, and the 4Ps tell us how to achieve those goals. Thus, after segmentation and targeting, we will begin to craft the tactical decisions to achieve our desired product positioning, using all 4Ps: the product, price, promotion, and place. In Figure 17.4, we see the key questions for each P as elaborated on in each of their respective chapters. The biggest concerns among the 4Ps are (1) making sure they're consistent from P to P and (2) considering scenarios about competitors' likely responses to try to begin to anticipate possible risks.

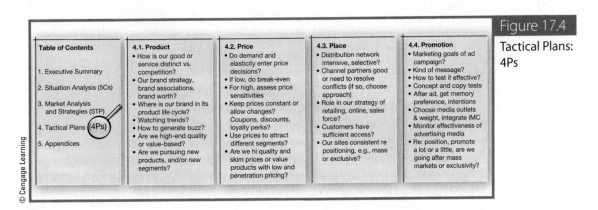

Figure 17.4

Tactical Plans: 4Ps

Regarding the *product* P, let's begin in the positioning matrix and consider whether we wish to occupy the high-quality or basic-quality ends of the spectrum. We can use conjoint tests to determine primary attributes and features, and we can use surveys to understand customers' perceptions of our brand associations. The positioning will be key to shaping those associations such that positive ones are retained and negative ones are replaced. The product life cycle will also affect how we and customers think about our brand; we can move more freely for newer brands. Thus, there are numerous questions to address in marketing planning: (1) Do we seek a high-end-quality position in the market place or one of offering value to our customers? (2) What is the assortment of product features we wish to offer to satisfy our customers and attract new customers, and what customer service plans supplement our core business? (3) Is this a new product? Are we taking our product to a new segment? To map the product basics, we'll examine

- Whether we are we high-end or basic.

- Our primary features.

- Our brand associations.

- Where we are in product life cycle.

Decisions about *pricing* should be tied to the product quality choice. Thus, (1) do we want a high price to be consistent with high-quality positioning or for skimming purposes early in a product's life cycle or low price to be consistent with a value offering or for penetration early in the life cycle? We need also to consider how frequently we're likely to create price variations, from prices at the product's introduction (skim or penetrate the market), to discounting for yield management unless our equity perceptions will be affected. And we need a basic understanding of whether our customers are price sensitive or willing to pay for better product, service, loyalty engagements, etc. Thus, (2) what supplement pricing components will we entertain: couponing, occasional discounting or consistent pricing

Interactive 4Ps

Spreadsheet Tab on 4Ps

Product:	Fill in descriptions here:
Choose high-end-quality or basic-quality level:	Product1
Use conjoint on target segments to determine primary attributes/features:	Product2
What are our brand associations, and what do want to trade in/out:	Product3
Where are we in the product life cycle; is it time to jump-start:	Product4
Price:	
Given strategic positioning, shall we price high (skim) or low (penetrate); if price low, conduct internal audit to assure exceed breakeven, if price high, conduct marketing research to assess:	
Customers' price sensitivities:	Price1
Shall we consider occasional price discounts:	Price2
How might we benefit from pricing differentially to our segments:	Price3
Place/Distribution:	
Design distribution system to be extensive or selective:	Place1
Integrate with promotions as push or pull:	Place2
Any conflicts needed to be resolve? Communication, contract, profit-share:	Place3
Promotion:	
What are our marketing communications (advertising) goals?	Promo1
How to measure the effectiveness of the ads, whether goals were achieved:	Promo2
How to apportion advertising budget across media for true IMC:	Promo3

(e.g., EDLP), warranties, loyalty programs and rewards in some currency (price rewards or points)? A good marketing plan identifies

- Our customers' price sensitivities.

- Whether we should we offer occasional price discounts.

- Whether it would be beneficial to price differently from competitors.

For *promotional* campaigns, (1) Do we want to promote a lot for mass exposure or, minimally, for a more exclusive appeal? (2) What is the goal of the integrated marketing campaign? (3) What is the message of the advertising communications? (4) What media fit our position, and have we attained true integration in the IMC? Promotion is the P that naïve people think is the totality of marketing, and we know better. It is indeed a fun P, and the media choices are more exciting and confusing than ever. To keep an eye on the goal, focus on the goals of, in order, the business and brand, marketing, and then marketing communications or advertising. Try to set up a measurable promo launch to help defend budget allocations in order to support the different selected media. Thus, we explicate our goals and our budget intended to reach them and propose some means of measuring our success:

- What are our marketing communications (advertising) goals?

- How shall we budget across IMC?

- How might we measure the ads' effectiveness?

4Ps Example

To illustrate the 4Ps, we're going to focus on an innovation whose skunkworks codeword is DigiMe. If launched, DigiMe would be a service that coordinates households' digital libraries. People would drop off all their movie DVDs, old VHS tapes, music collections, photographs in frames and in scrapbooks, etc., whatever they want. The first part of the service is to digitize everything. The second part of the service is to organize the files into a user-friendly (as defined in consultation with each customer).

For the product, the questions and proposed answers are

- Are we high-end or basic? The plans are for DigiMe to be high-end and innovative.
- What are our primary features? DigiMe wants to position a service as convenient, trusted, and offering a good product.
- What are our brand associations? N/A yet, due to minimal awareness.
- Where are we in product life cycle? New product.

Price questions and proposed answers:

- What are our customers' price sensitivities? Minimal, given that what is being digitized is prized, and the time savings for the typical household would be great.
- Offer occasional price discounts? No reason to do so yet, and benefits outweigh the high price point.
- Beneficial to price differently from competitors? No competitors yet, but keep price high to gain margin and spend on R&D.

Promotional questions and proposed answers:

- Our marketing communications (advertising) goals? The substantive goals are awareness and beginning to develop brand associations of convenience, quality, etc. Given the typical entrepreneurial budgets, we might begin simply with advertising via search engines.
- How to measure ad effectiveness? Click-throughs.
- How to budget across IMC? Spending on search engines and across photo and A/V hobbyist sites and blogs.

Place or distribution questions and proposed answers:

- Will we be extensive or selective? Currently, we are selective, working out of only one office.
- Use more pull or push? Pull.
- Any conflicts to resolve? No, we're still forging relationships.

We now compile our final data to create part three of the marketing plan—the 4Ps section.

Market Positioning via 4Ps

- Our service is in the initial phase of the product life cycle. The quality should be considered by customers to be high end and innovative. Our customers primarily seek these benefits: quality, convenient, time savings. When they think of our brand, they have minimal awareness or associations yet because we're so new.
- Regarding price, our customer price sensitivity seems to be minimal. This is seen as a valuable service that will simplify their lives. Price discounts are probably not necessary; the convenience and lightness are likely to outweigh any perception of high price. We are not worried about segmentation pricing per se yet. We have no competitors, though some are likely to follow. We'll keep prices high to enjoy high margins and subsequent R&D.
- Our marketing communications (advertising) goals are search engines and perhaps getting into some nice catalogs and stores. We will measure the effectiveness of our online promotions by click-throughs.
- Our ideal distribution system may be more extensive, but currently it is very selective. We expect to see consumer involvement and pull. We don't have partner conflicts yet because we're still developing retail relationships.
- In sum, this marketing plan offers a strategic vision to attain long-term customer satisfaction, their loyalty, and our firm's profitability.

For *place* or distribution, the concerns are mostly about breadth—whether the system should be extensive or selective. However, directional concerns also arise regarding promotions encouraging push or pull and marginal gains for channel members. Thus, (1) do customers have sufficient access, or will the very customers we wish to attract not tend to be online? For those who do go to the website, does it look consistent with the positioning (e.g., exclusive vs. mass)? (2) Is our online arm of the business truly integrated, or are we running an incidental website? In terms of distribution, will we

- Be extensive or selective?
- Use more pull or push?
- Have any conflicts to resolve?

Next, we need to check to see whether our plans for the 4Ps are internally consistent, or are we sending confusing messages, say, signaling exclusivity (via channel choices), at the same time screaming "mass" (via low price points or poor quality). Furthermore, if we're not confident that our proposed Ps are those that our targeted segment desires, we'd need to go out and retest. Doing so might mean a delay and spending more research money, but it is better than proceeding and failing and comforting ourselves that "At least we saved that research money!"

17-3 SPENDING TIME AND MONEY

Finally, to make sure that the marketing plan isn't pie-in-the-sky, we'll include estimates on scheduling and expenditures (see Figure 17.5). These logistics and monetary details help keep the marketers, and extended team, on track, and it's the language of the C-suite.

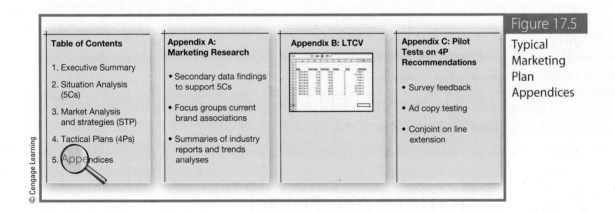

© Cengage Learning

Figure 17.5

Typical Marketing Plan Appendices

A timeline and budget estimate can build from a basic structure like this:

Time Line	Marketing Activities	Budget
September	Create direct mail materials	$15,000
September–October	Create marketing literature for reach beyond lists	$17,000
November	Refresh video and other content online	$3,000
December	Sending out the direct mailing	$15,000
January–March	Measure response of December push	$2,000
April	e-mailing follow-up appeal	$3,000
8-month program		Total = $55,000

Obviously, these time and monetary elements are sketches. When the elements are elaborated in greater detail, then the estimates of durations and expenses can also be made more precise. Doing both—more refined detail and more precise estimates—would make the marketing plan much improved. The better the marketing plan, the closer it is to being actionable, and the more accurate the implementation can be forecast. When the components of the timeline and budget are more detailed, it enables even better planning, audits of costs, tighter ops delivery, etc. Finally, more precision can shed light on weaknesses in the plan, presumably before executing the plan.

Managerial Recap

We've pored over these questions about the 5Cs, STP, and 4Ps throughout the book. Few of the questions are trivial to answer, but in answering the prompted questions, you'll have compiled the heart of the marketing plan. You've now got the data of the document, and the rest is just elaborating and editing. The marketing plan comes together as a document to remind you and your colleagues of the goals and to serve as a guide in achieving those goals.

It's important to know that all of marketing (strategy and planning) is iterative. In particular, something to look for is internal consistency throughout the plan; it's critical for good branding and good marketing that the whole of the plan be synchronous. For example, after working through the 5Cs and STP, you might be well into the 4Ps when you realize, "This plan makes no sense, considering what we said about our target" (or whatever). Thus, return to targeting, tweak, and move forward again.

In a sense, marketing plans are always works in progress. While they're intended to keep everyone on track, they're also not carved in stone. Thus, as situations change, so must we modify the marketing plan. For example, we occasionally encounter challenges that bounce us back up to earlier considerations that we thought we had nailed down. Perhaps we had ignored economic factors in the context because in our country, it's stable. Yet if one of our strategic goals is to go into underserved markets in places with poor infrastructures, then our working assumptions have changed because now we must address new questions, i.e., how to set up shop locally with issues we hadn't encountered before. Thus, we have to go back and elaborate on the economic conditions under context in the 5Cs. That's ok—that's why we have cut-and-paste.

Admittedly, our marketing planning exercise is just the beginning. When creating marketing plans, be detailed, listing absolutely every factor even remotely relevant, to cover various contingencies.

Lastly, massage the document to be readable. Use the 5Cs, STP, and 4Ps as headers throughout the document. Writing is a lot like marketing; be sure your document speaks to its intended audience. Writing a plan for your boss will look different from the version you'd show investors, for example. That is, market your marketing plan!

17-4 THAT'S ALL, FOLKS!

You've seen a remarkable number of marketing issues throughout this book. It's time to put the concepts into practice. Marketing planning is the roadmap or blueprint for the implementation of all the collective marketing decisions.

Having a good understanding of marketing will be extremely useful in your career, whether you're going to be a marketer or not. Don't forget: Put the customer above all else. If you do, you'll conquer the competition. Yes, it's that easy. ☺

Chapter Outline in Key Terms and Concepts

1. How do we put it all together?
2. Situation analysis
    a. The 5Cs
    b. STP
    c. The 4Ps
3. Spending time and money
4. That's all, folks!

Chapter Discussion Questions

1. Pick your favorite brand, and look at the 5Cs for that company. What is the brand's situation analysis? Based on that assessment and what you know of the brand, what recommendations would you make to the company regarding that brand or its business?

2. With talk of elections all over the place, look at voters through an STP lens. How should a politician of your favorite party proceed?

3. Imagine a young person, recently graduated from college, who is trying to launch a career as a (pick one: comedian, singer, sports agent). Sketch out the best set of 4Ps you could suggest to help him or her get an ideal job and make career progress toward his or her goal.

Mini-Case

Jeeves

When people feel as though they have more money than time, certain services flourish. Imagine setting up a butler service called Jeeves. Jeeves would see to all the logistical details in your life that consume more time than you wish to grant them. Jeeves will take care of your information needs, from making doctors' appointments or play dates for the kids, to stylist appointments for you, to helping you do your banking, paying bills, and even coordinating and evaluating your investments, if you wish. If you were stinkin' rich, you'd also have a chef and a driver. While strictly speaking, these domains fall outside the usual butler responsibilities, in the Jeeves service, the butlers fill in with whatever household and related duties the customer wishes to be done, and a payment package is chosen accordingly. Thus, your Jeeves can drive your kids to school and pick up groceries to have a 7 p.m. dinner ready for the family, if those are add-ons you desire (and for which you're willing to pay).

Mini-Case Discussion Questions

1. Create a marketing plan to introduce Jeeves to your local community. Gather the secondary data to help substantiate the business case. Make clear notes throughout the plan where you would seek additional primary marketing research to provide guidance about those components of the plan. Etch the market and its segments, and characterize the segment(s) you would target.

2. Create a storyboard for an external website and an internal one. The external website would be the positioning you want customers to see; thus, create pages for that website, which is a composition of the 4Ps for Jeeves. The internal website is for your sales force to give them parameters about different price packages and the like.

Video Exercise: *White Rock* (5:02)

White Rock Beverage, a producer of soft drinks and sparkling waters, was founded in 1871. In 1900, White Rock was the upscale beverage of choice, ranked number one in the market; a century later, White Rock ranked number 100. When the company's current president, Larry, who is the great-great-grandson of the founder, took over the business, it was struggling mightily. Half of White Rock's distribution was controlled by one customer, and that customer dropped the White Rock brand. To keep the business afloat, White Rock adopted a hybrid distribution system and acquired a new brand. Growth has been fueled by the acquisition of the Old Brooklyn brand of beverages. White Rock revamped Old Brooklyn's production process to make it a tastier, healthier product—a move that is consistent with White Rock's positioning as a brand that is healthy and unique. The Old Brooklyn brand gives White Rock the opportunity to gain entry into premium outlets like Trader Joe's and Whole Foods, as well as into supermarkets with premium beverage sections. After getting the White Rock brand back on track, the company has enjoyed continued growth, but it is nonetheless a mature brand. The more substantial growth opportunity is in the Old Brooklyn brand.

Video Discussion Questions

1. What does a SWOT analysis reveal about White Rock?

2. How has White Rock used market segmentation, targeting, and positioning in developing and executing a plan to ensure the survival and success of the company?

3. How has White Rock used the 4Ps of marketing—product, price, place, and promotion—to develop and execute a plan for ensuring the survival and success of the company?

Endnotes

Chapter 1

- American Marketing Association's website: www.marketingpower.com
- Books on ethics: *SAGE Brief Guide to Marketing Ethics*, Brenkert's *Marketing Ethics*, and Davison's *The Moral Dimension of Marketing*.

Chapter 2

- Consumer behavior:
  - Professors Wayne Hoyer, Deborah MacInnis, and Rik Pieters, *Consumer Behavior* (6th ed.) (South-Western, 2012).
  - Professors Frank Kardes, Maria Cronley, and Thomas Cline, *Consumer Behavior* (1st ed.) (South-Western, 2010).
  - Professor Michael Solomon, *Consumer Behavior* (9th ed.) (Prentice Hall, 2010).
- Consumer choice processes in the *Journal of Consumer Research*:
  - Professor Ravi Dhar, "Consumer Preferences for a No-Choice Option,"
  - Professors James R. Bettman, Mary Frances Luce, and John W. Payne, "Constructive Consumer Choice Processes,"
  - Professors Stephen M. Nowlis, Naomi Mandel, and Deborah Brown McCabe, "Consumption on Consumption Enjoyment,"
- Brand names:
  - Professor Eric Yorkston and Geeta Menon, "A Sound Idea: Phonetic Effects of Brand Names on Consumer Judgments" (*Journal of Consumer Research*).
  - Professors Jennifer J. Argo, Monica Popa, and Malcolm C. Smith, "The Sound of Brands" (*Journal of Marketing*).

Chapter 3

- Eugene W. Anderson, Claes Fornell, and Donald R. Lehmann, "Customer Satisfaction, Market Share, and Profitability," *Journal of Marketing*, 58: 53–66, The authors suggest that success can bring its own problems. Success usually means more sales from more customers, yet, as a segment size grows, the group becomes more heterogeneous (by definition, given human nature). It then becomes increasingly difficult to serve such a large diverse segment well, bringing a need to refine the segmentation.
- To find the Prizm information, go to Nielsen.com. At the bottom, under Solutions, click on Segmentation. Near the bottom (under "How we do it"), click on "Segmentation & Market Solutions." Look for the Prizm link.

Chapter 5

- For a terrific example of the low-price and modest-quality positioning, read Fishman's book, *The Wal-Mart Effect*.
- For a great example of the higher-price and better-quality positioning, read Michelli's, *The Starbucks Experience*.

Chapter 6

- Bendapudi and Leone, "Psychological Implications of Customer Participation in Co-Production," *Journal of Marketing*, 67 (January): 14–28.
- Lovelock and Wirtz, *Services Marketing: People, Technology, Strategy* (7th ed.) (Prentice Hall).
- Marzocchi and Zammit, "Self-Scanning Technology in Retail," *The Service Industries Journal*, 26 (6): 651–669.
- Meuter, Ostrom, Roundtree, and Bitner, "Self-Service Technologies," *Journal of Marketing*, 64 (July): 50–64.
- Rust, Zahorik, and Keiningham, "Return on Quality: Making Service Quality Financially Accountable," *Journal of Marketing*, 59 (April): 58–70.
- Rust, Lemon, and Zeithaml, "Return on Marketing: Using Customer Equity to Focus Marketing Strategy," *Journal of Marketing*, 68 (January): 109–127.
- Zeithaml, Parasuraman, and Berry, *Delivering Quality Service* (Simon & Schuster)

Chapter 7

- Brand communities research:
  - Muniz and O'Guinn, "Brand Community," *Journal of Consumer Research*, 27 (4), 412–432.
  - Schau, Muniz, and Arnould, "How Brand Community Practices Create Value," *Journal of Marketing*, 73 (5), 30–51.
- Research on self-brand connections:
  - De Ruyter and Andreassen, "Image Congruence and the Adoption of Service Innovations," *Journal of Service Research*, 7 (4), 343–359.
  - Escalas and Bettman, "Self-Construal, Reference Groups, and Brand Meaning," *Journal of Consumer Research*, 32 (3), 378–389.
  - Fournier, "Consumers and Their Brands," *Journal of Consumer Research*, 24 (4), 343–353.
  - Swaminathan, Page, and Gurham-Canli, "My Brand or Our Brand," *Journal of Consumer Research*, 34 (2), 248–259.

- Research on brand personality:
  - Aaker, "Dimensions of Brand Personality," *Journal of Marketing Research*, 34 (3), 347–356.
  - Brakus, Schmitt, and Zarantonello, "Brand Experience," *Journal of Marketing*, 73 (2), 52–68.
- Store brand research: Hansen, Singh, and Chintagunta, "Understanding Store-Brand Purchase Behavior Across Categories, *Marketing Science*, 25 (1), 75–90.
- Brand equity research:
  - Keller, "Conceptualizing, Measuring, and Managing Customer-Based Brand Equity," *Journal of Marketing*, 57 (1), 1–22.
  - Berger, Bolton, Bowman, Briggs, Kumar, Parasuraman, and Terry, "Marketing Actions and the Value of Customer Assets," *Journal of Service Research*, 5 (1), 39–53.
  - Kamakura and Russell, "Measuring Brand Value with Scanner Data," *International Journal of Research in Marketing*, 10 (1), 9–22.

Chapter 8

- Mahajan, Muller, and Bass, "Diffusion of New Products: Empirical Generalizations and Managerial Uses," *Marketing Science*, 14 (3), 79–88.
- Sultanm, Farley, and Lehmann ["A Meta-Analysis of Applications of Diffusion Models," *Journal of Marketing Research*, 27 (1), 70–77] found that *p*s tend to range from 0.02 to 0.06 and *q*s from 0.3 to 0.6 and that, for whatever product category and for whatever market (e.g., U.S. vs. Europe), *p:q* was on the order of just about 1:10.
- Urban, Hauser, and Dholakia, *Essentials of New Product Management*, NY: Prentice Hall).

Chapter 9

- Hamilton and Urminsky, "Inference, Not Reference: The Price Image Heuristic as an Alternative to Reference Price Theories," a working paper that says the brand image of the retail outlet affects the price expected to pay on their items, and vice versa.
- Auctions:
  - Greenleaf, "English Auctions," *Journal of Consumer Research*, 31 (2): 264–273.
  - Jap and Haruvy, "Inter-organizational Relationships and Bidding Behavior in Industrial Online Reverse Auctions," *Journal of Marketing Research*, 45 (5): 550–561.
  - Reddy and Dass, "Modeling On-Line Art Auction Dynamics Using Functional Data Analysis," *Statistical Science*, 21 (2): 179–193.
- Compromise effect:
  - Chernev, "Extremeness Aversion and Attribute-Balance Effects in Choice," *Journal of Consumer Research*, 31 (2): 249–263.
  - Kivetz, Netzer, and Srinivasan, "Alternative Models for Capturing the Compromise Effect," *Journal of Marketing Research*, 41 (3): 237–257.
  - Fischer, Carmon, Ariely, and Zauberman, "Goal-Based Construction of Preferences," *Management Science*, 45 (8): 1057–1075.

Chapter 10

- Anderson and Narus, *Business Market Management: Understanding, Creating, and Delivering Value* (Prentice Hall).
- Research on channels:
  - Anderson and Narus, "A Model of Distributor Firm and Manufacturer Firm Working Partnerships," *Journal of Marketing*, 54 (1): 42–58.
  - Bradford, Stringfellow, and Weitz, "Managing Conflict to Improve the Effectiveness of Retail Networks," *Journal of Retailing*, 80 (3): 181–195.
  - Grayson, "Friendship versus Business in Marketing Relationships," *Journal of Marketing*, 71 (4): 121–139.
  - Heide and John, "Do Norms Matter in Marketing Relationships?" *Journal of Marketing*, 56 (2): 32–44.
  - Onyemah, Rouzies, and Panagopoulos, "How HRM Control Affects Boundary-Spanning Employees' Behavioral Strategies and Satisfaction," *The International Journal of Human Resource Management*, 21 (11): 1951–1975.
  - Palmatier, Dant, Grewal, and Evans, "Factors Influencing the Effectiveness of Relationship Marketing: A Meta-Analysis," *Journal of Marketing*, 70 (3): 136–153.
  - Sa Vinhas and Anderson, "How Potential Conflict Drives Channel Structure," *Journal of Marketing Research*, 42 (4): 507–515.
  - Szymanski, Bharadwaj, and Varadarajan, "An Analysis of the Market Share-Profitability Relationship," *Journal of Marketing*, 57 (3): 1–18.
- Research on online channels:
  - Bodapati, "Recommendation Systems with Purchase Data," *Journal of Marketing Research*, 45 (1): 77–93.
  - Lattin and Bucklin, "Reference Effects of Price and Promotion on Brand Choice Behavior," *Journal of Marketing Research*, 26 (3): 299–310.
  - Lichtenthal and Eliaz, "Internet Integration in Business Marketing Tactics," *Industrial Marketing Management*, 32 (1): 3–13.
  - Moe, "Buying, Searching, or Browsing," *Journal of Consumer Psychology*, 13 (1/2): 29–39.

Chapter 11

- Priester, Wegener, Petty, and Fabrigar, "Examining the Psychological Process Underlying the Sleeper Effect: The Elaboration Likelihood Model Explanation," *Media Psychology*, 1 (1): 27–48.

Chapter 12

- Bishop and Peterson, "The Impact of Medium Context on Bilingual Consumers' Responses to Code-Switched Advertising," *Journal of Advertising*, 39 (3): 55–67.
- Fisher and Dube, "Advertising: A Social Desirability Perspective," *Journal of Consumer Research*, 31 (4): 850–858.

Chapter 13

- Micek and Whitlock, *Twitter Revolution.*
- Miller's book, *YouTube for* Business, says customers simply love videos. Videos can be used to: inform, educate, entertain (and sell!).

Chapter 14

- Anderson and Mittal, "Strengthening the Satisfaction-Profit Chain," *Journal of Service Research*, 3 (2): 107–120.
- Bijmolt, Leeflang, Block, Eisenbeiss, Hardie, Lemmens, and Saffert, "Analytics for Customer Engagement," *Journal of Service Research*, 13 (3): 341–356.
- Bolton and Lemon, "A Dynamic Model of Customers' Usage of Services: Usage as an Antecedent and Consequence of Satisfaction," *Journal of Marketing Research*, 36 (2): 171–186.
- Bowman and Narayandas, "Linking Customer Management Effort to Customer Profitability in Business Markets," *Journal of Marketing Research*, 41 (4): 433–447.
- Brady, Voorhees, Cronin, and Bourdeau, "The Good Guys Don't Always Win: The Effect of Valence on Service Perceptions and Consequences," *Journal of Services Marketing*, 20 (2): 83–91.
- Burton, Sheather, and Roberts, "Reality or Perception? The Effect of Actual and Perceived Performance on Satisfaction and Behavioral Intention," *Journal of Service Research*, 5 (4): 292–302.
- Davidson, *Moral Dimension of Marketing.*
- Fornell, Johnson, Anderson, Cha, and Bryant, "The American Customer Satisfaction Index," *Journal of Marketing*, 60 (4): 7–18.
- Kumar, Jones, Venkatesan, and Leone, "Is Market Orientation a Source of Sustainable Competitive Advantage or Simply the Cost of Competing?" *Journal of Marketing*, 75 (1): 16–30.
- Parasuraman, Berry, and Zeithaml, "Refinement and Reassessment of the Servqual Scale," *Journal of Retailing*, 67 (4): 420–450.
- Zeithaml, Berry, and Parasuraman, "The Nature and Determinants of Customer Expectations of Service," *Journal of the Academy of Marketing Science*, 21 (1): 1–12.

Chapter 15

- Baumgartner and Steenkamp, "Response Styles in Marketing Research: A Cross-National Investigation," *Journal of Marketing Research*, 38 (2): 143–156.
- Chandon, Morwitz, and Reinartz, "Do Intentions Really Predict Behavior?" *Journal of Marketing*, 69 (2): 1–14.
- Iacobucci and Churchill, *Marketing Research: Methodological Foundations* (10th ed.) (Thomson).
- Menon, "Are the Parts Better than the Whole? The Effects of Decompositional Questions on Judgments of Frequent Behaviors," *Journal of Marketing Research*, 32 (3): 335–346.
- Neslin, Gupta, Kamakura, Lu, and Mason, "Defection Detection," *Journal of Marketing Research*, 43 (2): 204–211.

Chapter 16

- Gruca and Sudharshan, "A Framework for Entry Deterrence Strategy: The Competitive Environment, Choices, and Consequences," *Journal of Marketing*, 59 (3): 44–55.
- Mizik and Jacobson, "Trading Off Between Value Creation and Value Appropriation: The Financial Implications of Shifts in Strategic Emphasis," *Journal of Marketing*, 67 (1): 63–76.
- Porter, *Competitive Strategy: Techniques for Analyzing Industries and Competitors.*
- Quelch and Desphande, *The Global Market: Developing a Strategy to Manage Across Borders* (Wiley).
- Tracey and Wiersema, *The Discipline of Market Leaders: Choose Your Customers, Narrow Your Focus, Dominate Your Market.*

Index

barter, 150
BCG matrix, 291–292
BE (breakeven) analysis, 151–156
behavior advertising goals, 200
beliefs, defined, 26
belonging, 25
beta testing, 127–129
biases about pricing, 160–163
big-screen televisions, 211–212
billboards, 210. *See also* integrated marketing
    communication (IMC)
BlackBerry, 299
blind taste tests, 20
bottom-up product development, 123–124
brand associations, 21, 107–110
brand awareness, 228
brand communities, 107, 109–110
brand equity, 115–117
brand experience, four dimensions for, 118
brand switching, scanner data for, 280–281
brand zealots, 24
branding
    overview, 119
    association networks, 107–108
    brand personalities, 108–109
    conjoint studies for, 277–280
    defined, 103–104
    equity determinations, 115–117
    extensions for, 111–112
    globally, 114–115
    logos and colors as, 104–105
    names as, 104
    reasons for, 105–106
    sounds of brand names, 20
    store brands, 115
    strategies for, 110–115
    umbrella vs. house brands, 110–111
breadth strategy for segmentation, 48
breakeven (BE) analysis, 151–156
breaking bulk, 175
budgets, 217–219, 229–231, 319
business format franchising, 190–191
business strength, 293
buyers, 16
buzz marketing, 237–238

C

case analysis, 31
cash cows, 292
catalog sales, 191–192, 222–223

celebrity endorsements, 207, 232
Census data, use of, 63, 66
centrality, 239–240
channel members, 177–178. *See also* distribution
    channels
channels of distribution. *See* distribution channels
Chicago White Sox logo, perception of, 21
China
    branding from, 73
    branding to, 72
    as consumer, 299
    luxury goods, demand in, 29
    millionaires in, 139
    outsourcing to, 190
choices, too many as difficult, 27
classical conditioning, 21–24, 104
click-thru rates, 233
cliques, 240
cluster analysis
    B2B vs. B2C, 43–44
    factor analysis with, 283–284
    for segmentation, 270–271
CLV (Customer Lifetime Value), 260–263
co-branding, 112
co-creation, 124
coefficient of imitation, 135–136
coefficient of innovation, 135–136
coercive power, 182
cognition advertising goals, 200
cognitive ads, 202–204
collaborators, 5–7, 311. *See also* 5Cs of marketing
collectivism, 28
colors, use of, 19, 104–105
communication. *See* advertising; integrated marketing
    communication (IMC)
companies, 5–7, 310. *See also* 5Cs of marketing
comparative advertisements, 202–203
comparative evaluation process, 251–252
compensatory models, 27
competition, defining broadly, 97
competitive comparison analysis, 59–61
Competitive Strategy (Porter), 83
competitors. *See also* 5Cs of marketing; strategy
    overview, 5–7
    defined, 5
    in marketing plans, 311–312
    perceptual maps to depict, 59–61, 71–74
compromise effect, 161–162
concept testing, 210, 276, 278
conformity vs. individuality needs, 26

gross rating points (GRP), 219
growth matrix, 291
growth predictions, 66
growth strategies, 137–138, 189
GRP (gross rating points), 219

H

hearing, sense of, 20
Hierarchy of Needs, 25–26
higher-involvement purchase evaluation, 251–252
Hispanic Americans, 39, 139
Hofstede, Geert, 28
honesty, 199
horizontal competition, 187
houses of brands, 110–111
humorous advertisements, 204
hygiene attributes, 253

I

ideals motivation, 40
IKEA, 72
image advertisements, 205–206
IMC. *See* integrated marketing communication (IMC)
imperfect competition, 35–36
importance weights, defined, 27
impulse purchases, defined, 16
India, outsourcing to, 189–190
individuality vs. conformity needs, 26
inelastic demand, 146–148
influencers, 16
influentials, identification of, 239–240
information power, 182
ingredient branding, 112
initiators, 16
innovators, 133–134
inside-out product development, 124
intangibility of products, 91–92
integrated marketing communication (IMC)
    overview, 222–223, 233
    budget for, 217–219, 229–231
    consistency across departments, 225–226
    decisions to be made in, 217–222
    effectiveness, evaluation of, 231–233
    goals and, 229–231
    media comparisons, 223–225
    message and media, integration of, 231–233
    push and pull strategies and, 226
    sales force compared, 225–229
    scheduling for, 220–222

integration of distribution channels, 186–188, 193
intensive distribution channels, 178–181
Interbrand method for brand equity determinations, 116–117
international expansion, 189–190
Internet, 191, 222–223, 224–225, 236. *See also* integrated marketing communication (IMC); social media

J

jingles, 22–24

K

keeping rates for direct mail, 284
key performance indicators (KPIs), 241–242
KFC, 72

L

laggards, 134
large-screen televisions, 211–212
late majority, 134
launch of new products, 129–130
leaders, 297
learning, defined, 21
learning and memory, role in customer behavior, 21–24
legitimate power, 182
lexographic, 27
life cycles of products, 130–136, 166–167, 200
line extensions, 111–112
linguistics, 20
logistics of distribution, 175. *See also* distribution channels
logos. *See* branding
long-term advertising effects, 198
loss leaders, 150, 162
low-involvement purchase evaluation, 251
loyalty, 106, 148, 257–263. *See also* customer evaluations; customer satisfaction
loyalty programs, 17, 24

M

magazines, 223–225, 236. *See also* integrated marketing communication (IMC)
make-or-buy decisions, 176
manufacturer-suggested retail price (MSRP), 162
manufacturing, 299
marginal costs (MC), 158–159
marginal revenues (MR), 158–159
margins, defined, 184
margins versus markups, 169–170
market attractiveness, 293

operant conditioning, 24
operational excellence, 83, 294
opinion leaders, 239
outsourcing, 189–190

P

P&G, 299
Parker, Robert, 239
Pavlov, Ivan, 21
perception and sensation, role in customer behavior, 19–21
perceptual fluency, 21
perceptual maps, 59–61, 71–74, 272–276
peripheral cues, 207
perishability, of goods and services, 93–94
personal selling, 225
pharmaceutical companies, advertising by, 130
philosophy of glocalization, 114–115
PI (purchase intention), 129–130
places, 5–7, 318. *See also* distribution channels; 4Ps of marketing
P_{max} (profit maximization), 158–159
point-of-purchase coupon pop-outs, 229
Porter, Michael, 83
Porter strategy, 293–294
positioning. *See also* advertising; STP of marketing
    overview, 5–7, 86
    defined, 70
    distribution channels and, 179–180
    elements of, 70
    in marketing plans, 315
    matrices for, 74–83
    perceptual maps for, 71–74, 272–276
    statements for, writing, 83–86
postpurchase phase, 15, 244
power, types of, 182
power distance, 28
PR (public relations), 227–228
predatory pricing, 162
prepurchase phase, 15, 242–243
press kits, 227
prestige pricing, 150
price bundling, 166
Price Discrimination, 163
price discrimination, 150, 163
price fixing, 162
price sensitivity (PS)
    conjoint studies to infer, 158–159
    elastic demand as, 146–148
    loyalty and, 258
    stability in, 156–158

price wars, 168
pricing. *See also* 4Ps of marketing
    overview, 5–7, 170
    auctions and, 168–169
    branding and, 106
    changes in, factors for, 166–170
    as communication tool, 145
    conjoint studies for, 157–158, 277–280
    demand management, 164
    ethics and, 258
    forecasting model and, 129–130
    game theory, 167–168
    high prices, effects of, 156–158
    low prices, effects of, 149–156
    in marketing plans, 316–317
    nonlinear pricing, 165–166
    psychology of customers and, 159–164
    quantity discounts, 164
    scanner data for, 156–157, 280–281
    segmentation pricing, 163
    strategy issues, 288–290
    supply and demand, effect on, 145–149
    volume or profits decisions about, 158–159
private labels, 115, 187
Prizm, 39
product category extensions, 111–112
product demonstrations, 203
product development, 291
product development growth strategy, 137–138
product distribution franchising, 190–191
product leadership, 83, 294–295
product placements, 205, 228, 232
products. *See also* branding; 4Ps of marketing; goods; new products; services
    overview, 5–7, 100
    breadth and depth of product lines, 97–99
    breakeven pricing analysis, 151–154
    core offerings, identification of, 95–99
    defined, 5, 89–90
    life cycles of, 130–136, 166–167
    in marketing exchange, 90–91
    in marketing plans, 315–316
    services compared, 91–95
professional service providers, 92
profit, defined, 146
profit maximization (P_{max}), 158–159
profitability
    discounts, effects on, 167
    pricing and, 146
    segmentation and, 46

setting goals and, 288–290
strategies for, 302
targeting and, 56–59
promotions. *See also* advertising; customer satisfaction; 4Ps of marketing; integrated marketing communication (IMC); social media
overview, 5–7
customer engagement levels and, 17
defined, 5
IMC and, 228–229
in marketing plans, 317
pricing and, 167
PS (price sensitivity)
conjoint studies to infer, 158–159
elastic demand as, 146–148
loyalty and, 258
stability in, 156–158
psychology of customers
overview, 29. *see also* customer evaluations; customer satisfaction
attitudes and decision making, 26–27
emotions, 24
learning and memory, 21–24
motivation, 25–26
pricing and, 159–164
segmentation and, 40–41
sensation and perception, 19–21
public relations (PR), 227–228
publicity, 228
pulsing, 221
purchase intention (PI), 129–130
purchase phase, 15, 243–244
purchases, 16–17
push and pull strategies, 180–181, 226

Q

quality
branding and, 105–106
customer satisfaction and, 256–257
defined, 59
levels of, expectations and, 253–254
pricing as cue to, 160
question marks, 292
quick followers, 297

R

radio, 222–225, 236. *See also* integrated marketing communication (IMC)
rates for social media, 243
ratings, 221

rational appeal advertising approach, 202–204
reach of advertising, 219–220, 242
rebuys, defined, 16
recency, frequency, and monetary value (RFM), 259–260
receptionists, 257
recognition tests for advertising, 209
recommendation agents, 241
recommendation systems, 240–241
referent power, 182
referent pricing, 162
register marks, 114
reinforcement schedules, 24
relational ties, 238
reliability, 105–106
research
overview, 285
cluster analysis, 270–271
conjoint studies, 277–280
focus groups, 276, 278
importance of, 268–269
perceptual maps, 272–276
process of, 268–269
scanner data, 280–281
survey data, 282–285
results, quantification of, 4–5
retailing, 188–190
return on investment (ROI), 241–247
returns, 258
revenue sharing, 184–187
reward power, 182
RFM (recency, frequency, and monetary value), 259–260
risk, defined, 106
risk seeking or adverse motivations, 26
ROI (return on investment), 241–247

S

sales, advertising effects on, 231–233
sales dynamics, product distinctions instead of, 2–4
sales force role in advertising, 225–226
sales force role in distribution, 192–193
sales potential ($SP), 129–130
satisfaction. *See* customer satisfaction
scanner data, 156–157, 280–281
search engine optimization (SEO), 242–243
search goods, 252
search qualities, 92
seasonal advertisements, 221